THE BOOK

THE BOOK: 5 DAYS TO CHANGE YOUR LIFE

forever

AUTHOR: - Keki C. Darbary, DME, DEE, PGDPE

Certified Master Practitioner & Certified Master Trainer of NLP, Neuro Linguistic Programming

Made with ❤ on the Notion Press Platform

www.notionpress.com

CONTENTS

PREFACE

Apples fell from the trees straight down to the ground. One particular day it ignited a spark in Isaac Newton. That changed the course of Physics to a new level. All of us have this ability to think a little differently from the masses. If not for anything else, just for fun, open up Newton's 3 laws of motion in front of you. In school you studied this with the help of billiard balls and solid objects. Now see how you can apply the same to our thoughts and beliefs. Do not worry; the apples will still continue to fall straight down to the ground as they used to.

Even today you can see the sun turning around the earth during the day time and the entire firmament turning around the earth at night time. Therefor just simple so called 'common sense' of the people considered the earth to be the center of the universe. This continued vehemently until Galileo and Copernicus came into the scene. You know what The Scholars and the very learned authority figures did to them. It has become history or his story. These Scholars and learned authority figures tried hard to pass on their beliefs to the following generations; anything else was blasphemy.

Is this good? Is that bad? It is neither. It just is. Is It desirable? Perhaps Newton's third law of motion may have an answer.

Every coin has two sides to it. The best of people; the best of communities; the best of nations has something that we may call 'good' as well as something that we may consider as 'not good'. Then how shall we proceed?

I have lived for over a decade in five different cities and small towns. Therefore, I have a fair idea of their comparative worth. In one particular capital city there were a class of people who considered themselves superior to anybody anywhere else in the country and thought the same about their city. They would vehemently defend if anybody tried to show them the other side of the coin. One thing that was common amongst these people was that they had never lived for any extended period anywhere else except for some cursory visits.

Moving from the external world of the objects to the internal World of The Mind the founding fathers of NLP and the science of NLP (Neuro Linguistic Programming) is also undergoing the same process.

A word of caution at this point is I think, appropriate. Do not believe anything and everything that you read in this book or anywhere else as the final truth just because it is put in black and white. Mull over it, apply it practically and leave it to your intelligence to come to any conclusion. I have often found the comments that may fall in the category of the previous paragraphs. On the other hand, NLP is an evolving science. Concepts can undergo evolution for genuine reasons and even sometimes for commercial reasons. Whatever is put in this book is what I have personally experienced in myself and my participants for the past over two decades. Participants in our program are generally 18 years and above. Same protocol should be followed for reading this book also.

The narration in 'The Book' is not about showing the destination on a map from your starting position. It is about step by step walking the path to your chosen destination from the starting point of wherever you are. Your hand will be held but your legs will have to do the walking.

Have you ever been to your favorite restaurant, read the menu and come away without eating? Maybe your mouth salivated; maybe you got some good Aroma but you left the place hungry and unsatiated. Certainly, read the book as you would read the menu. But savor it with a few friends or at least one, to experience the exercises. Only then you will you get the true taste of it.

The book: 5 days to change your life forever, will take you closer and closer each day to the destination you wish and will continue even beyond. Each minute of the day will also take you towards the same. And what if you need more clarity? No issue at all. It is all integrated into the program.

The book is in a conversational style. Each participant brings their own characteristics and the background into the program as we have found over a period of more than two decades. You will find the

INTRODUCTION OF PARTICIPANTS; CHARACTERS IN THE BOOK soon after the Tributes pages.

Each participant or character in the book brings a bundle of characteristics of similar nature from others. The names have been changed and instead of representing a single person it represents multiple people of similar characteristics. Just by chance in case you were in one such program of ours and you find some character that may remind you of someone then only the extent that the person has shared in your program belongs to that person, everything else would be from anyone else.

TRIBUTES / ACKNOWLEDGEMENTS

First and foremost, I take this opportunity to pay my tributes to the founding fathers of neuro-linguistic programming who by their lateral thinking created this whole new science for creating excellence.

Next, I pay my tributes and express my gratitude to all the Master-Trainers at whose feet I learnt this science.

The major contributor for the outcome of this book are of course the participants who attended my programs and thereby enriched me.

The book in its present format is absolutely due to the grace and selfless permission from my affiliate NFNLP, The National Federation of Neuro Linguistic Programming, for using their manual freely. Any thanks that I offer to its founder Dr. William Horton and his charming wife Christina is totally inadequate.

I am grateful to those who I shared the manuscript with for their encouragement and suggestions. These include both, my non-NLP friends and my past participants. One name that stands out is that of my participant Varun Chhibber who has now settled in Canada after completing my programs up to the Trainer's level.

Nature provides opportunities. Quite often they are disguised in/ as Problems. One such thing happened in 2020. The Pandemic; the lockdown. I too was locked in. And The Book unfolded.

I had prepared the cover page which captured the essence and purpose of the entire book in just one page. I was struggling to find a proper agency who could homogenize the various parts together. It was not working out. Niloofer, one of my 4 daughters, who is settled in the USA suggested a name. Vivian Gomes. He is a local guy from my city of Pune, India, settled in the USA since many years and he is into AI, Artificial Intelligence. He designed an AI generated Cover Page which

I felt captures even a higher level of the essence and purpose of me bringing out this book for you. I am eternally grateful to him.

One person that I just cannot leave out over here is my wife, Aban. She has stood by me in times that were pleasant and not so pleasant. She has been by my side at almost each and every pre program meeting as well as during the Programs. Just her presence and occasional quips and sharing has had a Suttle and major effect on all present. I am sure she will continue till I continue.

INTRODUCTION OF PARTICIPANTS; CHARACTERS IN THE BOOK

1. **ANKUR: - Male, Age around 21; Representing** all those confident, curious and adventurous youth of both sexes. about to complete their professional studies and embark on their independent life's journey. **Here** Ankur is in his final year of studying Computer Engineering.
2. **SHANKAR: - Male, Age around 38; Representing** all those approaching their Middle Ages of both sexes, having established themselves in their own profession and somehow getting a feeling of stagnation. **Here Shankar** is a college professor married but without a child.
3. **Nirav: - Male, Age around 50; Representing** all those successful professionals of both sexes who have seen the shortcomings of the system in which they work and want to change it but either hesitate or do not know the way out. **Here Nirav** is a highly respected Surgeon often at loggerheads with the authorities.
4. **Lily: - Female, Age around 27; Representing** all those, of both sexes, prejudiced against an idea or a person propounding it, that does not fit with their own existing beliefs. Often believing in their own superiority out of their learning, qualifications, religion or just about anything else. Could also be a rebel towards all authority figures. **Here Lily** is qualified in Clinical Psychology, is working in a government hospital, has come to the program only to get a certificate (particularly a foreign one) which gets her small benefits in her career and salary. She is also at loggerheads with her own Father.

5. **Padma: - Female, Age around 43; Representing** mainly women, of conservative nature of middle class with high sense of Morals and Ethics. A housewife, a home maker; raising an otherwise happy family. **Here Padma** is living happily with her husband and raising 2 sons, both in college.
6. **Saira: - Female, Age around 37; Representing** mainly women, having been divorced some 6/8 years back but have managed to get back on track without remarrying. **Here Saira** is living with her one teenage daughter and her dogs and is an upcoming soft-skills professional.
7. **Jaya: - Female, Age around 27; Representing** both sexes, in an unhealthy marital situation, seriously contemplating Divorce. **Here Jaya** is a working woman living at her in-law's place. Somewhat Opinionated.
8. **Anwar: - Male, Age around 32; Representing** both sexes, in an unhealthy professional situation, in a large organization mainly relations with his Boss and at the corporate level.
9. **Manju: - Male, Age around 43; Representing** mainly male Entrepreneurs struggling for survival of the Enterprise and in some cases even the self. Highly Opinionated. **Here Manju** has an Engineering manufacturing unit (An SSI -Small scale Industry) and has relationship issues even at home within family and mainly with the spouse.
10. **Guneet Singh: - Male, Age around 40; Representing** mainly male Entrepreneurs managing their Enterprise extremely well and expanding. **Here Guneet** also has an Engineering manufacturing unit (An SSI -Small scale Industry); is fully in control and has even other interests in life.
11. **Vipul: - Male, Age around 46; Representing** mainly male Businessman whose motto is money and profit at any cost. Often cunning and unethical. **Here Vipul** is running a highly profitable cloth and garments shop and dreams of making his son a textile engineer running a mill so that he does not have to pay 'exorbitant' prices for his purchases.
12. **Gautam: - Male, Age generally over 30; Representing** both sexes of Businessmen or professionals or just about anybody, whose

purpose is to uplift the society. **Here Gautam** has branched out from HR (Human Resource Development) department on his own to take Training programs to empower people in need. He is 29 and yet to be married.

13. **Anusuya:** -Female**,** A victim of child abuse and a major contributor to this book.

CHAPTER 1

PRE-PROGRAM MEET

My name is Anusuya. Friends call me Anu. You can call me Anu too.

This is not the story of my life. This is a narration for the multitudes who, like me, might have soared on the wings of success and perhaps even plummeted into the abyss only to rise again with the help of something like this.

It was 7 years ago that I was totally down in the dumps. Somehow, I managed to have a 2-year-old son. My husband had two choices, actually only one. To give me a divorce, and take custody of the Son. The second choice was actually mine. To leave this world permanently.

My husband Suresh is in a multinational company. He was attending a seminar on management, organized in his company. During the seminar, the speaker somehow mentioned something like NLP and what it can do and that he had himself undergone the training. After the seminar my husband approached him and talked to him about the situation, we were in. My husband requested him if he could pick up the case. The gentleman said that he was into quite a few other things and the best person to help would be his trainer in NLP one Mr. Keki Darbary. He gave my husband the phone number and address. When my husband came home, he pleaded and persuaded me to give the family one last chance. I don't know why but I accepted.

At the appointed day and time, we reached Keki's house. I was quiet most of the meeting.

Keki: (as he opened the door) Hello you must be Suresh.

Suresh: Yes

Keki: Welcome, did you find the place easily

Suresh: Thank you, your instructions were very clear and precise, including for the parking.

Keki: Please make yourself comfortable, this must be Anusuya.

Suresh: Yeah, my wife

Keki: That's my wife. Aban, she is a doctor and assists me in the programs and meetings.

Aban: Hello Suresh, how are you Anusuya.

Anusuya: (raising her eyes from the ground and a slight nod)

Suresh: One of your students recommended me to meet you.

Keki: So, tell me what can I do for you?

Suresh: Situation is not simple; in fact, it is pretty complicated. I would like to know what this NLP is and whether it can help

Keki: Oh, good that's the best way to start. Hope, both of you have enough time, about an hour?

Suresh: Oh yes, that's why we are here.

Keki: NLP or Neuro Linguistic Programming is a behavioral science. However, unlike some other behavioral sciences like psychotherapy, psychoanalysis, which focuses on what is wrong with a person, here in 1972 one named Richard Bandler, a mathematician and a computer scientist, both, hardware and software, was studying psychology at Santa Cruz, California. He didn't like what he was studying. He said we are studying the sick and we want to apply it to the well; to hell with it. So, he got along with his professor of linguistics one John Grinder and together they said 'let us start from the other end, not what is wrong with a person but what is right with a person. Why is it that some people are successful and some are not? Why is it that some people are happy and some are not?' So, they studied 3 world famous people. One was Dr. Milton Ericson, a world-famous Hypnotherapist; another Dr. Virginia Satir, a world-famous Family Therapist; and third was Fritz Pearls who started the Gestalt method of Psychology. They studied these three in a particular manner and they found a lot of commonalities between them. Surprisingly when they started using some of these commonalities, they started getting fantastic results themselves. That was role modeling.

Now role modeling is nothing new to us in India. You might have heard the name of Eklavya. What do you know about Eklavya? Good. When I wave my thumb, most people talk about the Guru Dakshina, of cutting and presenting of his right-hand thumb to his Guru: because this is very dramatic. But tell me; thousands of years this story is going around in India has anybody applied their minds as to how Eklavya learnt archery from the mud statue of his guru Dronacharya? None. Richard Bandler has converted this into an exercise whereby you can role model a person living or dead, known or unknown. In fact, this exercise proved to be so powerful that they had to down play it. What happened was that one of Bandler's students had role modeled one of these three people that they had studied; Dr. Milton Ericsson.

Ericsson is a very unusual guy. When he was 17 years of age, he was totally paralyzed. His mother had shifted him to the hospital. In the evening all the specialist doctors came and examined him and they all shook their heads saying this guy is not going to live till morning. Milton heard this, his mother heard this and they both **chose** not to believe the experts. At this time Milton only had his eyeball movements available and nothing else. With his eyeball movements he created a communication with his mother and he said 'lineup my bed in line with that window I want to see the sun rise'. His mother did it. Not only did he see the sun rise next morning but he went on recovering. He went on to become a medical doctor. He specialized in psychiatry and he became the world's best Hypnotherapist. However, throughout his life he was in a wheelchair and his voice was affected. What happened was that the student of Bandler who had role modeled Milton, in two years' time started developing the health symptoms of Milton. This was a big warning bell and since that time we do not role model a whole person we role model only those qualities and behavior patterns that we want for ourselves.

Realize one thing. Mind and body are one. What happens in the mind affects the body. What happens to the body affects the mind. They say we choose our sicknesses based on the unknown unconscious benefits that it is giving us**.** Realize also that sickness is the only socially acceptable way of getting out of what we do not want to do. When your son does not want to go to school, he wakes up from the bed and tells you "Mama, I don't want to go to school today, I have a headache". What does mama say? She says "it's ok Beta (son), you can sleep, no need to go to school". Now, that son could be a student of class 5, he could be the teacher of 5th class, mama will tell the same, even if he is the principal of the school his mama would also say the same.

When Advaniji did not want to go to Goa, what did Rajnathji say on the National TV? 'No no, Advaniji is unwell, I myself have told him to stay back, no need to come to Goa. **Sickness is the only socially acceptable way of getting out of what we do not want to do**. Even today in many organizations there is a rule that I do not subscribe to, which says that if you are absent for three days or more you are to get a doctor's certificate. So, what does the person do? He goes to his ESI doctor, puts the appropriate denomination note on his table and tells the doctor 'please give me a sick certificate'. Doctor asks 'what shall I write down?' 'Write anything, loose motions, motion stopped, whatever, but give me the certificate'. The doctor obliges. Many doctors have confirmed to me that often in 15 days' time the same patient comes back with actual symptoms of what was written down. **Sickness is also a behavior pattern**.

So, what is this animal called NLP. N refers to the neurons. Between your two ears, in that 1.4 cubic liter space is the most complicated arrangement of atoms that you will find anywhere in this universe; as we know the universe today. Nowhere else in the universe in such a small space there is such a complicated arrangement of atoms as you have it between your two ears. Does that not put some responsibility on you? There are 10 raised to the power of 11, neurons in your brain. And each neuron can connect to 1000 other neurons, that means you have 10 ^ 14 connections available. I do not know how much the super supercomputer has but I think it has a few zeros less.

The second word linguistics refers to languages. But not languages as in Hindi, English, French etc. **Research shows that we are communicating only 7% by words, 38% is how you say those words and 55% is your body language.** Most of the communication seminars that I have been to and maybe, what you have been to, focus on the words, the 7%. If you are lucky and in school or college you joined debating or dramatics then maybe you learnt how to say those words. Otherwise by the process of growing up, as it is, when you are talking to an elderly person your voice is little different and when you are talking to a child your voice is little different. But talking and listening with your body; nobody even knows that such a thing exists.

In our 5 days program, on the first day itself you will learn how to talk and listen with your body.

Ours is not, and I repeat, it is not an information-based program. It is all doing, doing and doing. I show the exercise either to the group or to an individual volunteer depending upon the nature of the exercise. Then you will do it to your partner and your partner will do it to you. Tell me, did you ever cycle in your life? Yes. For how many years you have not cycled. 15 years, friend? But if I take you down and give you a bicycle you will be able to cycle it, right? That is because cycling has become your unconscious competence and you can never forget it. Likewise, the exercises which you do will always remain with you. If I give you a book on swimming, you read it and you understand it, does that mean that you know swimming? Likewise, if I give you a book on cycling, you read it and you understand it, does that mean that you can cycle? Life is about doing. Our education system has put the three-dimensional world on a two-dimensional blackboard. You read it, you understand it, and you mistake it as if you know it.

Tell me 'Who is the most important person in your life?' Somebody says my wife, somebody says my mother and if husband and wife come here together then they look at each other. I ask them, if you are miserable, is your spouse, your mother, your daughter, are they going to be happy? No. Therefore the most important person in your life is you yourself. Therefore, what you are saying to yourself, either loudly or within your mind, is very, very important. If somebody says "I can't do this." Do not expect anything from him. If somebody says "this is not for me" that's it, do not expect anything from him or her either. On the other hand, if somebody says "hey, I have never done this before, but I wonder how it would be like". That's a totally different story. Therefore, what you are saying to yourself loudly or within your mind about yourself is very, very important. **Because you are programming yourself at every moment**.

The third word Programming. You already saw how you are programming yourself each moment. Before we move further tell me: at the most fundamental level how do we interact with this world? Hahaha, WhatsApp? Email? I am asking you 'at the most fundamental level' this is something which you learnt in the kindergarten. This morning as I got up, I was looking at the sun rising. Neither the sun was talking nor was I saying anything. Was I not interacting with this world? You 'See'? Yes. You hear? That's right, the five senses. Seeing-Visual; Hearing- speaking-Auditory; Touching-Feeling-Kinesthetic; Smelling-Olfactory and Tasting-Gustatory. Is there anything else at all besides these five senses? All the inputs that you get from the world around you, you are picking up through your five senses and five senses alone. Those are the only five Windows to the world; you have nothing else besides.

Under deep hypnosis you could be taken down to the time when you were one and half years of age, two and half years old, 3 and half years old and on that particular day, what happened, who did what, what was your reaction, each and every minor detail comes out. **Whether you believe it or not we are all biologically programmed robots.** Tell me; you like somebody very much; now think about that person. Your face glows. Now think of someone that you do not like. See how your face changed. Your entire physiology changed.

Programming helps us. If you happen to go to your friend's empty house in total darkness, you turn the key, open the door and even in total darkness your hand will go to the adjoining wall looking for the switch and you will find it. Why? Why, because you have programmed your mind for it. Programs are useful. However, many programs pull you down, they may not allow you to reach your full potential. Imagine somebody who has grown up with the staple diet of "do not talk to strangers", "do not talk to strangers". Do you think this person can become a good door to door salesman if he continues with that programming? Obviously not.

NLP is the art and science of altering the programs in your mind. The costliest hardware sitting on your table or on your lap is only as good as the software you put into it. If you want to prepare a document and you find 'word' is not adequate you may go to 'excel'. If you want some more facilities which are not available in your version of the program you may go for higher version. You may delete some programs, you may upgrade some programs, and you may install some new programs. It is the same with your brain. NLP allows you to modify some programs in the brain, delete certain programs, and install some new programs very, very easily and naturally. Anyway, your existing programs got installed at some time somehow.

Talking about hardware and software reminds me of something. During my corporate life when I wanted to go for behavioral type of trainings my Director would say "Keki you are going for 'fill' programs, you should go for 'core' programs". And what were the core programs for Engineers like me, those days? They were for example 'Finance for non-finance executives', 'Inventory management', 'ABC analysis', 'Pert CPM' and so on. Realize one thing. In any organization, the highest qualified person does not necessarily reach the top. Less qualified person but with better Man- management skills may reach the top. **Soft skills enable us to utilize our hard skills far more efficiently.**

Suresh: Your explanation is quite interesting but at the same time also intriguing. I have quite a few questions in my mind.

Keki: Go ahead and shoot

Suresh: Somewhere you mentioned hypnosis. If Anusuya comes for your program are you going to hypnotize her?

Keki: Good question and a very common one. A friend of mine, also a trainer answers this saying,' No, you are already hypnotized; I am going to De-Hypnotize you'. What is hypnosis? Most people's idea of hypnosis comes from the stage shows which they have seen where a person is made a monkey out of, for entertaining others. Hypnosis is much more than that. Hypnosis has been used for childbirth during delivery, for tooth extraction without any injection, even for amputation. I learnt some hypnosis from late Rishi Kumar Pandya. He was then a Canadian citizen. He was coaching the Canadian Olympic diving team for the Montreal Olympics. I do not know whether he was able to dive himself or not. He says **all hypnosis is only Self-hypnosis**. When somebody gives a suggestion and your subconscious accepts it; that is Self-hypnosis. When mommy says 'do not talk to strangers' and you accept it that is Self-hypnosis. When mama said vegetables are good for your health and you did not have them, you chose not to accept the suggestion. From morning to night, we are bombarded by suggestions. Some of them, our logical mind accepts, some get rejected. You will get more clarity about this during the program. So, what is your next question?

Suresh: I am curious to know exactly how this works.

Keki: Here is the hard copy of the brochure that I send to prospective participants. Both of you please go through this first page loudly. Please start.

EMPOWER 360°

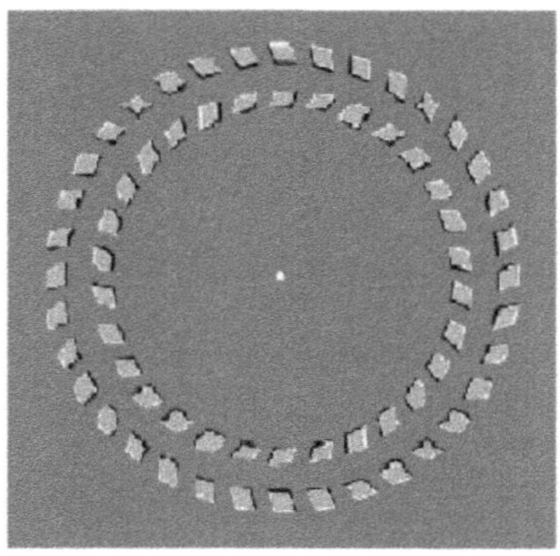

Focus your eyes on the dot in the center and move your head forward and backwards.
Did you see the circles turning?

What is it? An illusion; a delusion; a fragmented reality?
I can't do that; this is not for me; I am stressed;I can never get along with her/him;
things will never change around here; I am perfectly OK with everything.

Is that also not an illusion,a delusion due to our fragmented perception of reality.

Figure 1

Suresh: 'Empower 360 degrees. Do you want me to read through?

Keki: I said please go through it loudly.

Suresh: 'Focus your eyes on the dot in the center and move your head forward and backward. Did you see the circles turning? What.... '

Keki: Stop. I did not see either of you doing what it says. That's right. You can either move your head forward and backward or you can even take the hard copy and move it forward and backward. So, what's your answer? Are the circles turning?

Suresh: Yes, I see the inner one turning faster.

(Almost for half of the session, Anusuya was sitting on the edge of the sofa with her handbag tightly pressed against her lower abdomen, legs tightly together and as the session progressed, I could see minor changes happening. First the hands relaxed, and then slowly her legs relaxed, then the moroseness on the face was reducing. And I took this opportunity)

Keki: Anusuya, can you also take the brochure in your hand and move it forward and backward to see if you can find the circles turning.

(Anusuya moves the purse from her lap to hold the brochure. She moves the brochure forward and backward and has a slight smile on her face)

Anusuya: (very softly) yes.

Keki: Very good Anusuya. Do you see them turning? By the way can I call you Anu? Quite nice, short and sweet.

Anusuya: (little happier) Yes.

Keki: Yes what? That I can call you Anu or that the circles are turning?

Anusuya: Call me Anu (smiling). Yes, the Circles are turning also.

Keki: Excellent now go ahead Anu, read further.

Anu: (Softly) 'what is it? '

Keki; Sorry I can't hear what you are saying, can you read it a little louder?

Anu: 'What is it, an illusion, a delusion, a fragmented reality'

Keki: I want your answer: both of you.

Suresh: It's an illusion.

Keki: Do you know the difference between Illusion and delusion?

Suresh: Not really.

Keki: Do you go hiking or trekking?

Suresh: I have been once or twice.

Anu: I went while I was at college.

Keki: You people should go more often. OK. Imagine you are in the Rajasthan desert. Early morning the guide takes you out of the tent and points out at a hill far away and says "see that yonder hill; can you see the palm tree-top there? Before Sun down you have to reach there". So, you start off with your ration and two big bottles of water. But the sun is coming down fiercely by 10 in the morning itself. By noon your second bottle of water is also getting over. Soon both the bottles are over and now it is a question of your survival. You have to go ahead straight but on the left what do you see? WOW! Water! It is a question of life and death now. You are desperate for water. Your goal lies straight ahead but you are desperate for water. Yes, you did learn about Mirage in the school. But that definitely looks like water. So, you move to the left and start going for that water. The water was an illusion, **when you start believing your illusion, you get deluded.** Getting back to the circles; the circles are printed on paper; how can they turn? Ok one of you read further.

Suresh: 'I can't do that; this is not for me; I am stressed; I can never get along with her or him; things will never change around here; I am perfectly Ok with everything'. 'Is that also not an illusion a delusion due to our fragmented perception of reality?'

Keki: Your answer has to be for that entire paragraph not individual statements there.

Suresh: Delusion?

Keki: Yes, each and every statement in that paragraph. But tell me, if the circles were not fragmented and if they were complete would you be able to see any movement.

Suresh: No. I don't think so.

Keki: That's right, because movement is relative; there are black and white gaps in the circles. If the circles were complete, you would have no reference point for comparison. Look here (I take out my left hand with fingers outstretched and slap my right hand on the palm, and ask 'when 5 people are looking at the same event what do you think happens?

Suresh: I suppose five different perceptions.

Keki: That's right. Each one thinks that what she or he is thinking is the correct thing. It doesn't stop there; each one thinks that what she or he is thinking is how others should be thinking. And we get into fights, misunderstandings, relationship issues, rape, murder, divorce, all sorts of things.

The question is why does this happen. It happens because each one is picking up only fragments of the information. So, the next question is; on what basis are they picking up these fragments? Whenever something happens our brain is searching for something similar that has happened in the past, some reference experience or in other words our past programming. This is the story of your life; it is the story of my life and everybody else's life. Is this clear now? Suresh? Anu? Do you understand?

(Suresh and Anu discuss something within themselves and then Suresh turn to me)

Suresh: What are the program dates? Anusuya will attend the program. But will it not be better if she has session 1on1 with you instead of the program.

Keki: Individual sessions may be alright at times when something is event based, for example grief at somebody passing away, failure in examination, something like that. Even then our behavior is based mostly on multiplicity of programs in our mind. At the program we take care of so many different aspects of life which becomes necessary for changing our behavior patterns, our attitudes and thereby our life. As for the program dates, Aban will give you the details.

Suresh: I have one more question. After the program how many times will she have to repeat the exercises?

Keki: None. These are fit and forget type of exercises. We do it just once at the program and then she will do it to her partner and the partner will do it to her. The same exercise can be repeated for a different event or issue. When somebody asks, how many times he or she will have to repeat the exercise, the message they are giving to their own subconscious mind is that the first time may not be enough. Our subconscious mind pictures everything literally and it will make that happen. People get surprised. Regular psychiatry will tell you that if somebody is suffering from something for 20 years it will take 20 months to get out of it; if somebody is suffering from something for 6 years it will take 6 months to get out of it. None of that. The reasoning is very simple. Imagine a young boy going up in a lift alone and suddenly the power fails; he gets a shock of his life and personally I know some people even in Mumbai, at Nariman Point, if they have to go up 10th floor, they do not enter a closed lift; they walk up. This is what we call as a **'one shot learning.'** It is not necessary that the mind learns only negative things like this. Under capable hands, positive things can also be installed which are instantaneous and permanent. And that is what we do.

Suresh: One last question. How much do I owe you for this session?

Keki: Nothing. I never charge anything for the first session. This session is basically to understand what the participant is looking for, expecting and to get to know what NLP is. But this session is not over yet. What we have done is hardly one third of what we have to do. Each one of us, no matter what our station in life, is carrying some baggage from the past which is preventing us to reach our full potential, which is preventing us from being happy. We will continue this session some other day when you Anu, will have to come alone. Two of us will be here. Most people feel that what they are going through is something very unique. It is not necessarily so. Lots of people in lots of different circumstances are going through the same or similar situations, as nothing is really so private and personal. Everything that happened to somebody has also happened to a few others. NLP is content free. At the program it is not necessary to share all our gory details. **Who did what to who is not important. How your mind processes it; that is important.** So, the next session is to understand what baggage we are carrying from the past and how it has affected us. So that during the program, in a very subtle manner, I can deal with it. So Anu will you please ring up Aban to fix your next appointment. Thank you.

Anusuya shares her history

Exactly seven days prior to the program I get a call from Suresh. He said Anusuya would like to come and share her issues. I asked if Anusuya had asked for the meeting. He said yes but after some persuasion from his side. I asked him as to how he persuaded her. He said, she was reluctant as to how a stranger who does not know her would be able to help her. So, I said when we go to a specialist doctor, he or she looks at the case in its new and entirety with the facts in hand. If the specialist wants to check the patient, he may have to ask the patient to remove some clothing; likewise, she should also open up and not hold back anything that you two may ask. I reminded her that madam Aban is a qualified MBBS doctor and Keki sir comes highly recommended with many years of experience. With this we fixed an appointment for the next day morning 9 am.

Exactly as the clock was to strike 9, I hear the doorbell. I welcome them in and Suresh walked in first with Anusuya in tow; as if there was a cowherd towing a cow in on a rope.

Suresh: Now I will leave Anusuya here because I have to proceed to my office. (Suresh left leaving Anusuya sitting exactly where she had sat on the earlier occasion and in the same manner and looking even more morose. Aban sat diagonally opposite her on the right and I sat towards her left).

Keki: Did you have your breakfast before coming here? Anu.

Anu: Yes

Aban: What did you have for breakfast?

Anu: Aloo paratha and curds.

Aban: Do you have a maid coming for helping you or you made it yourself?

Anu: The maid kneaded the flour, put the potatoes to boil and then I made the rest.

Aban: So, who is looking after your son when both of you are away from home?

Anu: My mother has come home today so that I can come and meet you all.

Aban: And what would you like to tell us today?

Anu: What do you want me to tell?

Keki: Anything that comes to your mind.

Aban: Tell us about your childhood. Some happy memories. Who did you grow up with? Your brothers or sisters?

Anu: I am the only child. I have no brother, no sister. Childhood was good, although I wish I had a sister or even a brother.

Aban: What can you tell us about your parents and grandparents? How did your mom and dad meet and what is their relationship?

Anu: That's a long story and I'll be taking up your time.

Keki: We like long stories and our time is all reserved for you.

Anu: You want to hear everything?

Keki: Absolutely.

Anu: My mom and dad relationship are very good. Theirs was a love marriage. My mom's dad was running a very successful business. He had employed my dad to assist him in his business and day to day work. I believe grandpa used to rely on my dad quite a lot and trusted him fully. My dad has a very Helping Nature. Grandpa used to be very conservative and very protective of his three girls. My mom was the youngest. The elder 2 sisters were already married and gone to their in-law's place. My dad used to drive my mom to her college. Gradually they fell in love. It was my mom's examination day when she turned 18. Next day was the final day of her examination. After the exam they eloped, got married, took their proof of age, went to the police station and declared what they had done. Grandparents were totally broken. Grandpa was raving mad and tried whatever he could with the influence in the police but to no avail. Grandma would have nothing else but driving her daughter out of the house and the family, for bringing disrepute to the family.

I was born in my father's parental home. A small little thing overcrowded with his parents and brothers and their kids. I believe my mom was treated like a princess but soon she took part in all the household chores and won over everybody's heart. I was 4 years of age and dotted by my cousins, uncles and even my dad's parents. My mom's household had boycotted us and they had never seen me or exchanged a word with my mom. My dad used to keep on getting information regarding his earlier boss's business and knew that, because of the shock it was not doing well at all, in addition both, his father-in- law's and mother-in- law's health was deteriorating. Some five years earlier to my dad marrying my mom his boss had received a gift of a son from his wife. A son that they were waiting for all their life. My dad came to know that his mother-in-law was seriously ill and had to be moved to the hospital and that his father-in-law needed help. He was insisting on going and helping them but my mother was not in favor of that. Finally, my father said 'I have eaten their salt and I must help'.

I believe he went to their house, did not say a word about the past. If anybody opened their mouth about it, he would say 'right now we have to move aunty to the hospital as fast as possible'. Picked up my grandma on his back, carried her down to the car, got her admitted to the hospital, completed all the formalities and settled my grandpa.

Grandpa was left aghast with mixed feelings of resentment as well as happiness and satisfaction of seeing things getting done. My dad went to the hospital every day and helped grandpa like in the old days. This went on almost for a month and then it was time to bring grandma back home. It seems that grandpa had forgiven my dad and had started taking dad's help regarding his business also. With grandma almost bedridden it was difficult for him to manage the household. During the early days of hospitalization my dad had taken me and my mom also to the hospital, with instructions not to talk anything about the past. One day grandpa proposed that he has a big house, with 4 big bedrooms and if three of us can return to the house then my mom can help her mother and dad can help him with the business. With hesitation my mother accepted this and three of us moved to my mother's original house. Maybe this was a mistake.

Keki: Very interesting story and very well said. Why do you call it a mistake when everything seems to have worked out well?

Anu: No. Because of what happened afterwards.

Aban: What happened afterwards? Please continue.

Anu: After 3 failed attempts of getting daughters, he finally got a son. Everybody was dotting over him. He became a thoroughly spoilt brat. He would throw tantrums and always get what he wanted. And from his mother's comments after my mom eloped, he always considered me as their servant's daughter.

Aban: Did he ever play with you? After all you were both kids when you entered that house.

Anu: I was like a new toy for him. His play was also funny. He would lift me up, put me down and try to tickle me by digging his nose into my belly button. I really did not want to play with him.

Aban: Then what happened?

Anu: Then I started going to school, He went to college. He had his way and got a powerful Motor cycle. Within 6 months he had a bad accident and was in comma for 10 days and the left leg broken at two, three places.

Aban: Did he survive?

Anu: He came home after about 2 months and a physiotherapist used to come home 3 times a week. It was expensive and my grandpa's business was also going down so they asked me to be present and learn the massage therapy.

Aban: Good; you learnt something new.

Anu: No. Not good.

Aban: Why? What happened?

(The little liveliness that had come earlier disappeared and the moroseness came back.)

Keki: Go ahead Anu; whatever we discuss over here stays here and between the 3 of us.

Anu: Yes, but.... (She was avoiding looking at me and looked up at Aban. I excused myself telling Aban that I will be back soon and the 2 of them can continue. I went out of their sight and hearing, on to my balcony for a smoke. After 10-12 minutes when there was no sound from inside, I went back in)

Keki: Well?

Aban: Seems like a case of Child abuse. But from the age of 10 to the age of 13; 3 years.

Keki: Another one?

Anu: How, another one?

Keki: It keeps coming.

Anu: So, you cure them?

Keki: No. I do not.

Anu: No? (Puzzled). Then...?

Keki: They cure themselves. I only show the way. They walk the path. I may smoothen the path; I may remove some hurdles.

Anu: How?

Keki: You have the 5 days of program for that. But I need information on where it needs smoothening and where the hurdles are. Then you can walk the path. But before we get there, I would like to know what were the best years of your life and what were you doing then.

Anu: When I was 13, I was very close to my cousin. My mom's sister's daughter. I used to spend a lot of time with them. My cousin used to go to an all-girls school and was one year elder to me. I persuaded my mom-and-dad to send me to that same school because I did not like the rowdy behavior of the boys in my school. Somehow it all worked out and I started living with my cousin. It was fun. My cousin finished School and joined a fashion design program. So, one year later I also joined the same and even topped it.

Aban: Keki; I did not tell you she is also very creative. She told me that when she was 10, she was making miniature paintings of Lord Ganesha in various different attires. She even made stamp size miniatures for her friends.

Keki: What is this? Anu; can you explain it to me.

Anu: In the arts class of my school, I had learnt to cut a Potato into half and carve some designs of a star or a cross mark on it so that it would stand out by removing 2-3 mm material around it then take an ink stamp pad and put the Impressions on the book just the way you have the company stamp or a date stamp. So, at home I would do that with the image of Lord Ganesha and take multiple Impressions on paper and give it to my friends.

Keki: Great; creativity and ingenuity are already within you. That should help you a lot in walking your path. What else did you achieve in life?

Anu: After the fashion design program I joined a department store and worked as a salesgirl. I was not interested in just selling. So, I would make friends with the customers, study their body structure and either recommend ready garments or suggest some alterations which we would carry out in the store. The customers were very happy. Every year I was declared as the best salesgirl and by the third year I was in charge of the lady's garment department.

Keki: And after that?

Anu: I was happy. I was earning well. I thought I was at the top of my life. My mom and dad wanted to get me married. They found me a boy from my father's side relatives who was going to the US and wanted to take a wife from here. I did not want to leave this country so I refused. After sometime I got settled with Suresh and I married.

Keki: So how is it being married to Suresh?

Anu: Terrible. He is very good all through the day but Nights are terrible.

Aban: Keki, I think you should now listen to her story when she was between 10 and 13.

Keki: So Anu; what terrible things happened between the age of 10 and 13.

Aban: Anu, you can tell him very openly, he has heard many incidents of this type.

Anu: After the physio stopped coming, I had to give massage and exercise to my uncle 3 times a week. Initially for few weeks it was ok but then my uncle turned obnoxious. So often he would taunt me that I am the daughter of his servant and I must obey him and do whatever he asked me to do. I did try to tell my mom about it but every time she would say that we are living in their house for which we should be thankful and do whatever we can for them.

At one time uncle suddenly became very nice to me. He got interested in my Lord Ganesha stamps. He asked me to bring my potato stamp along with the carving tool that I used. My father had brought me a tool from his barber that the barber used to use for cutting the hard nails of fingers and toes. It is a hard-twisted band of steel for grip, pointed at one end and transversely cut chisel point at the other end. This is perfectly suited for my carving work. I was happy that uncle was taking interest in my work and I brought this tool as well as my potato carving to show him. He looked at it. Admired it and asked me to get the red ink stamp pad from his drawer. He opened the stamp pad and asked me to put the Lord Ganesha stamp on his forearm. I got a perfect impression and we are both very happy but what happened next took my breath away.

He suddenly took his shorts down and exposed himself. I was horrified. I had never seen a grown-up man's thing in my whole life. What he did next was most unforgettable. With his left hand he grabbed my wrist and in his right hand he held the carving tool pointed threateningly at my stomach and ordered me to put a stamp on his thing. I refused. I was feeling repulsed and nauseated. He tightened the grip on my wrist and pointing the pointed end of my carving tool at my belly button, using all the bad words that I can't repeat, calling me a servant's s*** girl, threatened to poke the carving tool into my belly button saying it will hurt you so bad you will die with your screams only. I was terrified knowing that he was capable of doing anything. I said I cannot put a stamp on a soft and wrinkled surface, plus you are also holding my hand. He put the carving tool down away from me, grabbed his thing in his fist and started shaking it violently. It grew bigger and fatter. I was seeing something like this for the first time. He again picked up the carving tool and threatened me to do it. I said I cannot do it with one hand. So, he let go of my hand and grabbed my hair. Now I had to do it. I was crying and begged him to let me go. Instead of letting me go he said now kiss it because Ganesha is revered and prayed for giving success before taking up any new project or work. I loudly said 'never' and ran out of the room leaving all my things there. As I was leaving the room, I heard him shout 'you will'.

Next day morning at the breakfast table when everybody was present, he was showing off his forearm to everybody like a Trophy. Everybody was so happy including my mom, dad, Grandma and Grandpa, that we two were bonding well. I had to keep a straight face. But then he went a step further and that made me feel like running away from home. He told everybody that Anshu had given him one more trophy at a different place. Everybody wanted to see that also. He rolled up his left-hand half sleeve and showed another impression near his shoulder. I was taken by surprise but also relieved.

The worst phase of my life had already begun.

The next time when I visited his room for his Physio, he immediately lowered his shorts and started doing what he had done last time. He pulled my head down tugging at my hair and said 'kiss it you s***'. When I refused, he threatened me that he would show it to everybody and tell them that, from the day the Physio left, you have been playing with it, and you know what can happen then. I knew that he was blackmailing me. Things started getting more and more worst as days and weeks and months passed by.

Keki: (She had started sobbing now. We had the general idea of what happened; so, we gave her time to recover. Aban brought some paper napkins. I still needed to know the extent. After a few minutes when she was sober, I continued) Anusuya, we can see that it was a terrible experience for you. And you said it went on for three years?

Anusuya: Yes, at least two and a half years from the time it started.

Anusuya, during those two and a half years, was there any penetration?

Anusuya: (hesitantly) yes.

Keki: Yes?

Aban: He means intercourse. Did uncle use his penis?

Anusuya: No. Fingers. There was blood even.

Keki: Did he force you to use your mouth?

Anusuya: Yes. He used his also. So many times, I had to run to my room to spit it out. When I could not, then I would vomit in his room itself. But then I had to clean it up myself. It was all very nauseating.

Aban: You told me you had started using the fourth bedroom which was lying vacant. Did he ever try to get into your room?

Anusuya: Yes once. I got very angry. I slapped him; picked up my pillow and covers, went and slept in my mom and dad's room and warned him that if he ever repeated it, I will expose everything to everybody. He never came into my room again. Even today I do not allow Suresh in my room at night.

Keki: Thank you for sharing all this with us. You are a very bold girl. I think you should be proud of yourself. Did your uncle have any other addiction?

Anusuya: Addiction? No, I don't think he ever touched alcohol or tobacco or drugs.

Keki: (with a smile) addicted to torturing you only? (Anusuya showed agreement with just a shrug of her shoulders) and now he is indirectly torturing your husband Suresh. **Personally, I believe that thought addiction is worse than product addiction.** Can you complete this sentence for me? Sex is......

Anusuya: Torture?

Keki: Are you asking me or telling me. Please complete the whole sentence.

Anusuya: Sex is torture.

Keki: (Once again with a smile) How would it be for someone who says 'sex is adventure' or she says 'sex is nurture'

Anusuya: Should be good for that person.

Keki: It is almost getting to be 10:30 now. Your son must be missing you and probably your mom is waiting for you. So, madam, fabulous Department Head of a store, also with a pretty face, (she smiles a little) but only when you smile, now run along to your happy home and make it happier. (At last, we see a smile on her face)

Anusuya: Things will be ok, no?

Keki: No. It can be ok only for those who want to make it ok. Now Run. Get lost. (Three of us have a big grin on our faces).

CHAPTER 2

DAY 1

As the participants start coming to the seminar hall, I greet them and give them the Sachet containing the manual and let them know that there is a single page hand out in it which they should go through while awaiting others. I also give them the register to fill in the details and their ID card with a Marker Pen to put their first name on their ID card.

The seminar hall is arranged with straight back cushioned chairs placed in a U formation or rather a parabolic formation with my standing position more or less at the focal point of the parabola; my work table & chair behind me, followed by the White board.

Once all the participants are in and have gone through the handout, I take the stand to start the program.

Keki: Friends; Good morning; to each and every one of you, a hearty welcome for this 5 days Certified NLP Practitioner Program. We will begin this program with an exercise. But before we start the exercise let us see if anybody has any comments on the SMS hand out.

An SMS chat that changed my life
By I, Me, Myself

God: Hello. You called me.

I, Me, Myself: Called you? No, who is this?

G: This is God. I heard your prayers. So, I thought I will chat with you.

IMM: Sure, I pray. Just makes me feel good. Actually, am busy now. In the midst of something, you know.

G: What are you busy with? Ants are busy, too.

IMM: Don't know. But I can't find free time. Life has become hectic. It's rush hour all the time.

G: Sure. Activity gets you busy. But productivity gets you results. Activity consumes time. Productivity frees it.

IMM: But I still can't figure it out. By the way, I was not expecting YOU to buzz me on instant messaging chat.

G: Well, I wanted to help you resolve your fight for time by giving you some clarity. I wanted to reach you through the medium you are comfortable with.

IMM: Tell me, why has life become so complicated?

G: Stop ana-lysing life. Just live it. Analysis is what makes it complicated.

IMM: Why are we then constantly unhappy?

G: Your today is the tomorrow that you worried about yesterday. You are worrying because the act of worrying has become a habit. That's why you are not happy.

IMM: But how can we not worry when there is so much uncertainty?

G: Uncertainty is inevitable, but worrying is optional.

IMM: But then, there is so much pain due to uncertainty.

G: Pain is inevitable, but suffering is optional.

IMM: If suffering is optional, why do good people always suffer?

G: Diamonds cannot be polished without friction. Gold cannot be purified without fire. Good people go through trials. With that experience their life becomes better, not bitter.

IMM: You mean to say such experience is useful?

G: Yes. Experience is a hard teacher, though. She gives the test first and the lessons afterwards

IMM: But still, why should we go through such tests? Why can't we be free from problems?

G: Problems are Purposeful Roadblocks Offering Beneficial Lessons to Enhance Mental Strength. Inner strength comes from struggle and endurance, not when you are free from problems

IMM: Frankly in the midst of so many problems, we don't know where we are heading

G: If you look outside you will not know where you are heading. Look inside. Looking outside, you dream. Looking inside, you awaken. Eyes provide sight. Heart provides insight.

IMM: Sometimes not succeeding fast seems to hurt more than moving in the right direction.

G: Success is relative, quantified by others. Satisfaction is absolute, quantified by you. Knowing the road ahead is more satisfying than knowing you rode ahead.

IMM: Sometimes I ask, who am I, why am I here? I don't know the answers.

G: Seek not to find who you are, but to determine who you want to be. Stop looking for a purpose as to why you are here. Create it. Life is not a process of discovery but a process of creation. IMM: How can I get the best out of life? G: Face your past without regret. Handle your present with confidence. Prepare for the future without fear. IMM: Sometimes my prayers are not answered. G: There are no unanswered prayers. At times the answer is NO. IMM: Thank you for this wonderful chat. I'll try to be less fearful. G: Keep the faith and drop the fear. Life is a mystery to solve, not a problem to resolve. Life is wonderful if you know how to live.
LEFT BRAIN SHOPPING LIST FOR THIS WHOLE BRAIN PROGRAM

Manju: (Who struggles to run a small manufacturing unit) I find it very appropriate when it says 'life has become hectic. It's Rush hour all the time.'

Keki: Who is saying it God or I, me and myself

Manju: IMM is saying it

Keki: So, what is the reply by God?

Manju: God replies 'Sure. Activity gets you busy. But productivity gets you results. Activity consumes time. Productivity frees it.' But times have changed now. Nobody prefers any activity today. Today, the type of employees that we get would rather have minimum activity and demand maximum wages. Nobody wants to do any actual work.

Guneet Singh: I also run an industry. And I tend to somewhat agree with his observations. Where I differ is his conclusions.

Manju: Your case is different. You are already having a turnover almost 20 times bigger than mine.

Guneet Singh: Yes, but I Started 4 and half years after you. What impressed me most in this SMS is When God says 'If you look outside, you will not know where you are heading. Look inside. Looking outside you dream. Looking inside you awaken. Eyes provide sight. Heart provides Insight.'

Gautam: (Successful self-employed, Training business in Singapore) I cannot agree more with him.

Saira: I also just love that statement. After my divorce I was totally broken. But I am on the path of recovery since I started looking within myself. What attracted my attention the most in the SMS is when God says 'pain is inevitable but suffering is optional'

Keki: Yes Jaya; you want to say something?

Jaya: At your home I shared with you the relationship issues I am having with him.

Keki: Him?

Jaya: My husband. When I came to your home, I almost asked a question similar to what IMM is saying here, 'Sometimes I ask who I am. Why am I here? I don't know the answers.' And God replies 'Seek not to find who you are, but to determine who you want to be. Stop looking for a purpose as to why you are here. Create it. Life is not a process of Discovery but a process of creation.' And I am wondering if this program will help me to that purpose. After all they say 'you can't clap with one hand'; and he is not here.

Keki: Very true. Isn't it? And I am also wondering if we would find the purpose for that clap, and if that purpose can be met single handed. (Turning towards Shankar). Yes professor

Shankar: (professor). I am wondering when God says 'Yes. Experience is a hard teacher, though, she gives the test first and the lessons afterwards.'

Ankur: (University Student-final year computers) 'Problems are purposeful roadblocks offering beneficial lessons to enhance mental strength'.

Padma: (An ordinary middle-class housewife with 2 college going kids) I agree with Ankur but I think the second part of the statement saying 'inner strength comes from struggle and endurance, not when you are free from problems' is far more important.

Vipul: (Businessman –own profit first) Sometimes not succeeding fast seems to hurt more than moving in the right direction

Keki: Doctor? (Surgeon) Nirav

Nirav: IMM says 'sometimes my prayers are not answered'

Keki: And what is God's answer

Nirav: 'There are no unanswered prayers. At times the answer is NO.'

Keki: So, do you pray every time you perform a surgery or treat a patient?

Nirav: Don't you wish for the best? Any time you are wishing for something: what are prayers anyway?

Keki: Good. So, Madam Psychologist Doctor? (Lily) you have not said anything so far!

Lily: I am listening.

Keki: Ah ha; Oh Yes Anwar (work place employee) you are still remaining

Anwar: I like it when God says 'Keep the faith and drop the fear. Life is a mystery to solve not a problem to resolve. Life is wonderful if you know how to live.' But I have no idea how I can deal with my boss. Yes. (Laughter all around)

Keki: Anu, you want to say something.

She just lifts up her hand from the wrist and nods, No.

Keki: Can somebody please read the handwritten comments below the SMS

Ankur: Left brain shopping list for this whole Brain program

Keki: What is a shopping list? Is a shopping list enough? What do we have to do? We have to go to the market, select the items as per the list, pay the amount and bring home the items. What you all have just done is like making the shopping list of what you know, you want. The shopping list is not shopping itself. Like the menu is not the meal. Likewise, we have to convert what we want into action. To make it happen we have to program it. Your shopping list is only a Left-Brain logical statement. We have to program it into action all throughout the brain and that is what we will be doing.

Program opening Exercise

So, let us begin this program now with the exercise which I mentioned earlier. The exercise is in four parts. In the first part you will use both your arms fully extended sideways and then I'll tell you what to do. In the next step you bring your arms a little closer. In the 3rd stage we will bring them closer still and on the 4th Stage you'll actually put them on your heart and integrate whatever happens in the previous three stages. Now early morning on the first day we do not want to slap our neighbors, do we? So, I request you that alternate person please pull your chair out about two feet so that you can stretch your arms sideways fully. That's fine.

Now put your feet flat on the ground; sit up straight; backbone straight; push your tailbone into the chair; take a deep breath and as you exhale close your eyes and relax. Let go of any tension or stress of the morning so far. Take another deep breath and as you exhale relax the top of your head your crown. Relax your forehead, your cheeks, your shoulders, your arms, your chest, and your stomach; feel your weight on your buttocks. Relax your thighs, calves, heels, and your feet. Let all the tension and stress of the day just shoot out of your toes 6 feet away in two Jets of streams. Good; now once again take a deep breath and as you exhale let all the residual stress and tension of the day just sink down and out of your toes.

Ok, now take position 1, stretch out your arms, stretch; what I want you to do now is, think of a time when you had lots of fun. It could be a party or a picnic, wedding, birthday party, office party, anything. Important thing is that you are having lots of fun. I want you to have it now, re-live it, now. Good. When you are actually having fun, it shows on your face. I can see it on some faces. No, no, when you are having fun you do not look like meditating Buddha. That's better. Increase that fun. Be into it. Double it. Good. I can see some hands are becoming heavier. I will not torture you more so have as much fun as you can, relax your arms and take position 2. Bring your arms little closer.

Now what I want you to do is, think of a time when you learnt something new and it was so easy. Maybe you learnt a new game. Maybe you cooked a new dish. Whatever it was you found it very, very easy. It is something new that you are doing for the first time. But you feel as if you already knew it. And you said to yourself, 'oh so easy'. Get that feeling. Good, double that Feeling. Make it 10 times stronger. Good. Now bring your arms closer and take position 3.

Now what I want you to do is, think of a time when you did something new and it has been so very useful to you. You might have taken it over a period of time. May be even a few years. But it has proved to be so very useful. Maybe it is providing you your bread and butter. Maybe you spent years. Maybe you spent a lot of time and energy and effort, maybe it has changed your life. Get that feeling. 'Yes, I did it. Yes, I can do it again'. Enhance that feeling. Make it 10 times stronger.

Now take all these three feelings and integrate it into your body somehow, maybe by putting both your hands on your heart. Position 4. The feeling of having some fun; the feeling that it is so easy; the feeling that it is so useful. Integrate all these three feelings into your body, into your heart. Take a deep breath and fill it within you.

Good, we will go through this exercise couple of times faster and faster. Take position 1, stretch out your arms, have fun. Position 2, you learnt something new and it was so easy, position 3, you spent a lot of energy and time on it and it has been so useful to you, and position 4, integrating all that within you. Now on your own, 2, 3, 4 times repeat the exercise. But now you will take it from position 1 to position 4 in one clean sweep. Do it now. No, no. No hesitation in between, just one clean sweep. That's better. Absolutely no stoppage on the way. Just 1 clean sweep from position 1 to position 4. Let me see yours once again. That's better, one clean sweep. Good. Get those integrated feelings within you. Now gently rub your hands together, rub them on your face, open your eyes and come on back.

How did you all feel?

Ankur: Shankar: Energized; Jaya: Anwar: Expectant; Guneet Singh: Rejuvenated, Good.

Keki: Hello, who likes to hear a story? (Some raise their hand, some say 'me', some say 'I').

Come on now. Put some energy into it. After all each one of you is at least looking younger than me. Those who like to hear a story will say 'I', loudly. So, who wants to hear a story?

All: I

Keki: That's better.

The Archer Story

There is this story of a young American guy who was good in Archery. He was good. So, he wanted to join the Olympics. Now

for Olympics good is not good enough. You got to be what? Yes, the best. So, he went around asking people as to where he can learn the art and science of archery. Quite a few people told him the same thing. They said 'Go to Japan. There is a monastery there, where there is a Great Master; the best, go learn archery from him.'

So, he packs up his bags and baggage and goes to that monastery in Japan. He greets the Great Master and says 'Great Master I have heard so much about you. I want to learn archery from you'. The Great Master says 'OK you can stay here. Every morning I go to the range, come and learn archery there'. So, he stays. Next morning with the first light he goes to the range. The Great Master is already there. The Great Master picks up the bow, puts the Arrow in it and releases the arrow. Bingo bull's eye. Now the young boy picks up the bow, he puts the Arrow in it, and releases it. Sometimes he gets it. Sometimes he does not.

This goes on day after day. Every time the Great Master picks up the bow, puts the Arrow in it and releases it, he gets it. Bingo bull's-eye. This young guy sometimes gets it sometimes does not. He is getting frustrated. One fine day he is asking the Great Master, 'Great Master, teach me'. The Great Master says 'Watch Me'. Whenever the young guy says 'Great Master, teach me' all that the Great Master does is, he says 'Watch Me'. This guy now thinks; these Eastern masters are a funny lot. Whenever I ask him to teach me all he says is watch me. Almost a month has passed and he is getting nowhere. Olympics are coming closer and he has got nothing so far. Finally, he decides enough is enough. So next morning he packs up his bags and baggage, goes to the range. Greets the Great Master and says 'Great Master, I am learning nothing'. The Great Master says" I know.' The boy says 'I am going'. The Great Masters says 'go' and points in the direction of the gate.

The boy picks up his bags, baggage and starts walking towards the gate. But as he is walking towards the gate something within him is not OK. So, he stops, looks back at the Great Master, approaches him and says Great Master,' just once, let me watch you'. The Great Master picks up the bow, puts the arrow in it and releases it. Bingo bull's-eye. Now this guy picks up the bow, puts the arrow in it, and before he can even release the arrow the great Master says 'fantastic, you got it'. The boy says 'what? I haven't even released the arrow'. The great Master says 'release it'. So, he releases it. Bingo bull's-eye. Once again, he picks up the bow, puts the arrow in it and releases. Bingo, bull's-eye. One more time he picks up the bow, puts the arrow in it and releases it. Again, Bingo Bull's-eye.

Now the question for us is; how did the Great Master know that the student has got it. What the master was using is what we call in NLP parlance as his **Sensory Acuity; or the acuteness of his senses.** And what he was watching in the student is what we call as the **Submodalities; or the minute differences in his behavior patterns.** For example, right now as I was saying it; Padma's left foot big toe just went up a little and Jaya's head got slightly tilted towards the right.

Now, this may seem a little farfetched for us. However, it is happening all around us. I am an Engineer so I will give you an example from engineering. When an engineer wants to interview a job inspector, after talking to him he places a Vernier caliper in front of him and maybe a small cylinder. The way the new job inspector picks up the vernier, the engineer knows whether that guy knows his job or not. He may put a Micrometer in front of the job Inspector. The way that person handles the micrometer; the engineer knows whether that guy knows his job or not. Consider a new lawyer handling his first case. The way the opposition lawyer carries himself the young lawyer knows who he is up against. These are the skills we pick up unconsciously. But what they say about this type of skill, which we pick up unconsciously, is that when we try to use it consciously, we may falter. Take the case of a ticket checker at a large railway station. He cannot check each and every one that is passing by. So, he watches the crowd, picks somebody from it and demands the ticket. He caught the right guy. However, they say the same guy when he reaches home, he cannot make out whether his daughter is telling the truth or a lie, as to where she had been in the evening and with whom. What skills we develop unconsciously we are able to use unconsciously.

This lady sitting over here my wife, Aban, she is a MBBS doctor. Her mother was a Principal of a Montessori School. With the Montessori apparatus she had helped many boys to understand and clear their High School exams. Aban feels that prevention is better than cure. She feels that the time to start is when the child is small. She also feels that if a drop of water can cure then there is no need for any medicine. Therefore, we don't make much money.

She has a whole set of Montessori apparatus. There's a whole lot of Apparatus which are called 'Sensory apparatus". These are for developing the child's five senses. So, there is a box of eight tiles, all red, but of various hues. In Montessori we do not teach the child. We allow the child to learn. Like Vivekananda says **'Education is not about pushing in but about pulling out'**. The child picks up whatever catches his or her attention and starts playing with it. Accept that we do not call it playing we call it working. The child realizes at some stage that these colors are little different. One fine day he or she organizes them in ascending or descending order. That's the Eureka moment for the child. The child may repeat that process several times. Like that, there are Boxes for green color, blue color, yellow and so on. There are taste bottles. There are smell bottles. There are tiles and different items for texture. Thereby the child develops his or her sensory acuity. This means developing acuteness of his or her senses. Now all of us may not have had a chance to be in a Montessori School. But like they say it's never too late. So, what we're going to do now is do some exercises for improving our own sensory acuity.

Are you all ready? Who is ready?

All: I

Keki; Good!

SENSORY ACUITY - K

We will work in groups of three. This exercise is to enhance our kinesthetic sense. One person will be sitting on the chair with eyes closed and hands on his lap, facing downwards; for example, Shankar. The other two will be standing side by side. Say, Me and Ankur. I will spread out my index finger and the middle finger a little and touch Shankar on the back of his palm and say my name, 'Keki', and then Ankur will do the same and give his name as Ankur. Shankar is calibrating these touches, in the sense that he is making out the minor differences in the touch. Now if I am touching Shankar lightly and Ankur who goes to the gym every morning and is feeling more energetic; if he touches with force then it does not need great intelligence on the part of Shankar to find out who is who. Or if I am separating my fingers about one and half inches and Ankur is separating them three inches, once again it does not take great intelligence on the part of Shankar to find out the difference. Therefore, what we are supposed to do is to match each other perfectly. We will do this 4-5 times matching each other as well as we can. And Shankar is calibrating. He will say ready and then two of us will touch at random without telling our names. Two of us will give the feedback to Shankar's response. However, **during no time in the program, we use the words 'you are wrong'**. If Shankar has guessed my touch as Ankur's, then Ankur will just say who was that correct person as 'no that was Keki'. Like that out of say 5 occasions if Shankar has got it three or four times correct then the next person will sit down and the other two will do the touching. Suppose if Shankar has guessed all five correctly, then we can assume that the matching has not been of good quality and there are lots of differences in the match. Then you can extend the exercise further. Are there any questions? None. Good. Get into groups of 3 and complete the exercise for each one of the three.

Please have no discussions during the exercise or even after you finish the exercise and are waiting for others to finish. We will have a discussion after everybody has finished the exercise.

Aban says to me, "but there are 13 of them" (I respond) "so there will be one group of 4, no issue."

Keki: Ok, so did everybody get a chance to be on the seat? Yes; Good. Did everybody get at least 3 times correct out of 5?

Ankur: Padma could get it right only twice.

Shankar: Nirav got it correct all the times.

Keki: Ok, Padma who were your partners? And Nirav who were your partners?

Padma: Ankur and Manju

Nirav: Shankar and Lily

Keki: So Nirav was it very easy for you?

Nirav: Yes, there were major differences between their touches

Keki: And Padma what made it so difficult for you?

Padma: While I was calibrating it was easy, but when they started touching randomly it was all very different particularly what Ankur was doing

Keki: **Each one of you please remember that you are here to train your partner**. Therefore, once you have matched Each Other properly you have to be Consistent with that.

Ankur: But that is why I was making it more difficult for her by doing something differently.

Keki: Also remember that Chalaki or being over-smart has no place in this program, in fact it has no place in life. Chalaki may give you some temporary thrills but it does not get you ahead in life. Sincerity will. I suggest that the two partners of Padma and Nirav will repeat this exercise with them, before we go further. (After they complete the exercises)

Let us now find out how you made out the differences. Manju; how did you make out the differences.

Manju: Padma's touch was quite delicate so it has to be a lady's touch.

Keki: Delicate? I ask all of you, is that a fact or an opinion**. Remember one thing; all opinions are based on facts. In the position that you are enjoying in life it is very, very important for each and every one of you to know as to when somebody is stating a fact and when somebody is making an opinion.** So, when he says 'delicate ', is that a fact or an opinion?

Almost all: Opinion

Keki**: Generally, facts will be sensory based; I saw this; I heard him or her saying such and such**; etc. etc. Who were your partners, Manju?

Manju: Padma and Ankur.

Keki: Ok, sit the way you were sitting during the exercise, with your eyes closed and palms facing downwards.

(I go around first to Anwar to inspect his fingertips and as expected I find them quite soft. Then I go around to Saira, knowing that she does lot of gardening and housework and inspect her fingertips which are quite rough and used. I signal both of them to come to Manju)

Ok Manju here is one lady and one man who are going to touch your hand just like they did during the exercise; you have to guess who is who.

Anwar touches very lightly for a moment only, and then Saira touches with just a little extra pressure and rub. Manju responds 'the first one was a lady and this one is a man'. I ask him to open his eyes while Saira was still touching. Manju has a confused expression as he moves his eyes from these two to me and then the crowd.

Keki: Do you also see how our prejudices come in our way? OK so Jaya, how did you make out the differences?

Jaya: By the way they were touching.

Keki: Yes, I am talking about the touch, the differences in the touch, what differences did you find in the touch of Gautam and Guneet? They were your partners, right?

Jaya: Guneet felt warm whereas Gautam's was cool.

Keki: I hope you are stating it as a statement of fact regarding temperature, and not as an opinion. Or did Guneet really warm up to you?

Jaya: Dhut; No way; I am talking temperature.

Keki: What other differences did you make out?

Jaya: Just the temperature was enough; I did not need anything else.

Keki: That may be so; but your subconscious has picked up a lot more information than what was just obvious. I want you to focus on that touch and give me three more differences.

Jaya: Three more! But I told you Sir, I could make out the difference just by the temperature.

Keki: Yes, temperature was the most prominent but I want you to find four more differences.

Jaya: I don't have even one more, Sir, when you are increasing it from three more to four more. Now, this is unfair.

Keki: Oh, please Jaya, and everybody else. Please stop Siring me. My name is Keki and that's how you will address me always. I may be 3 times more in chronological age from say Ankur over here; but he is several times ahead of me in computer science. Each one of you is way ahead of me in your own chosen field. Padma as a housewife is way ahead of each one of us in managing a family. She does a marvelous job of nurturing and developing so many lives in the family. We can all learn something from each other. Not just each other. When I see a 10-year-old son of a cobbler at a street corner mending some shoe or expertly cutting leather in beautifully curved shapes; I want to learn that from him. Many of us do not even consider others as humans. They are cobblers, drivers, rickshaw pullers etc. to the extent that at times even our own family members cease to being human for us.

The point is Jaya, that your subconscious mind has already recorded more than 4 other differences, we are only going to dig them out one by one. So, relax, take a deep breath, and sit the way you were sitting during the exercise and feel those touches once again and see what other differences you find. Jaya, you continue to dwell on what you need to do while I talk some more to your friends here.

Turning towards the group I ask 'am I working only with Jaya right now? Most respond with a no and Ankur says 'you are working with all of us'

I think I got the sacrificial goat correct. I am here up to 6 o'clock evening and nobody ever gives up during my program, we will wait till you get the next difference, Jaya. You can take your time.

Jaya is now getting a little emotional as well as angry. I think Shankar who was sitting by her side is murmuring 'pressure'.

Immediately I stand up and shout 'STOP, is she your enemy?'

Shankar: I was only trying to help her a little

Keki: This is not help. This is the worst thing that you could do; by not allowing her to develop herself. You can only do that to your enemy. Understand? (I sit quiet in one of the participant chairs. All are waiting in quiet patience)

Jaya: The pressure was different.

Keki: So, whose was what? Just keep your eyes closed and feel as if your partners are touching you one by one now and make out the differences.

Jaya: Guneet's pressure is heavier and Gautam's is lighter.

Keki: Good, take one more deep breath, keep your eyes closed and just notice that along with the heavier pressure there might have been some more changes. Relax yourself. You work best when you are relaxed.

Jaya: Guneet's finger is rough and his touch is for a longer duration. Gautam's touch is light and lifts up immediately.

Keki: So now Jaya you have the temperature, the texture of Guneet being rougher, and the duration of touch being shorter for Gautam. You got two new ones out of the four, I want two more.

Jaya: And pressure.

Keki: That was an accident. It should not have happened.

Jaya: Can I go to the Washroom and come?

Keki: Absolutely not. **Mind and Body is one. Control your mind, you control your Body. Control your Body and you control your Mind**. So, give me 2 more differences. You said Guneet was pressing harder and longer with his rougher finger tips; focus on that touch and compare with Gautam's.

Jaya: It is bigger.

Keki: What is bigger? (She traces a circle or oval on the back of her palm) you mean where the finger touches? (She nods). OK so you mean the area of contact is bigger. Whose is bigger?

Jaya: Guneet's is bigger and the gap (she separates the index finger and her middle finger of the other hand).

Keki: You mean the gap between two fingers, so whose is wider (she points at Guneet) OK, everybody give her a big hand.

All: Clapping together and congratulating in their own way.

Keki: Remember one thing. **We always know much more than we think we know**. You can play a game with children or at a party. Ask the group to write down on a piece of paper how many types of birds (or flowers), whatever you like, do you recognize. They will put down some number. Now ask them to silently write down the names of the birds that they know. You will find that most of them will write at least 50% more than the figure which they mentioned earlier. Now ask one by one, each one, to read the names they have written. Many will say I also know it; I also know it. Ultimately the total number of birds (or flowers) that they recognize is at least three times more than the figure that they estimated in the beginning. Try it yourself.

So. madam Jaya. What happens is that **we hook up to the most prominent characteristic that we find in anybody and then we assume that person to be just that and hardly anything more**. But there are so many facets which we are neglecting to look at. Would you agree with that now? In the beginning you were saying that temperature is the only difference that you found; then slowly you came out with 3, 4, 5 additional qualities. (It was nice to see a smile spreading across her face) I am throwing this question open now to the rest, anybody who found some differences beyond what we covered so far, please mention them now.

SENSORY ACUITY - A

Keki: We will do the same exercise now but with sound. Let us say I am working with Gautam. We can either click or clap. I find clicking is more difficult to match, so I prefer clapping. Of course, Gautam will be sitting with his eyes closed. I will clap about two feet away from his ear and tell my name. Then let's say Jaya is my partner and she will clap. I will vacate the spot from where I clapped, so that she can take that exact same spot. Like in the previous exercise Gautam will calibrate our claps while we match each other as much as possible and then when he says 'ready', we clap at random and Gautam will guess whose it is. Is that clear? Good. Form groups of three and finish this exercise as quickly as you can.

Keki: (Once they were finished with the exercise) Is everybody done with the exercise.

Jaya: I found this more difficult than the first one.

Manju: Even I found the first one easier.

Keki: Ok, so how did you make out the difference Manju?

Manju: From Ankur the sound was heavy but Jaya it was lighter.

Keki: Lightness and heaviness are characteristics of weight, how does the sound become light or heavy?

Manju: Ankur was making bigger sound compared to Jaya.

Keki: Bigger means?

Manju: I think I should say 'louder'.

Keki: That's correct, what other difference did you find? Yes Jaya?

Jaya: Actually, when I was in the chair, I found Manju clapping even louder than Guneet Singh.

Keki: And what other difference did you find?

Jaya: (with a smile) I don't want to be grilled by you again.

Keki: Do you have a music system at home. Yes. What are the controls on it?

Jaya: There is volume control. (After some hesitation) yes, there is another for bass and treble. I think it is called, tone control.

Keki: Out of a metal flute and bongos which one would be bass and which one would be treble?

Jaya: Bongos would be bass and metal flute would be treble.

Keki: So which sound is vibrating at higher frequencies, Manju?

Manju: Metal flute is producing sound at higher frequencies.

Keki: We will see the other auditory submodalities a little later.

Keki: I get the Aroma of some hot snacks outside.

Ankur: I smell Idli.

Keki: hm, Idli (Rice cakes) with yummy chutney (spicy syrupy). Jaya must be waiting to visit the washroom. But before we break for snacks let me make a few rules clear. For you all to take the maximum out of this program It is necessary that we follow **a few simple rules.** Rule No. 1. All musical instruments and personal vibrators to be 'off'. Rule No.2, First go to the washroom and then have your snacks and tea coffee so that at the end of the break when I say 'come on in' you come into the seminar hall and not rush to the washroom.

Rule No. 3, We have five occasions for going to the restroom; 1st, before you come to the seminar hall in the morning; 2nd, at this snack time; 3rd at lunch; 4th, evening tea and 5th when we break in the evening; this should be sufficient. There should be no need for anybody to go in in-between. In case of an emergency if somebody just has to go or else wet the carpet here, the rule is to take everybody else with you. (Laughter) No; this is not a laughing matter. What happens is that we all have what we call as **'mirror neurons'** in our brain. If one person goes and comes back somebody else also wants to get up and go. You know how a yawn can be catching at times. We do not want this to happen; we will save time going parallel rather than serially. Rule No. 4. When you take your seat after any break, make sure you are sitting somewhere else in a different place and with different neighbors. Rule No. 5, says **"If you can't, you must".** Do not expect it to be easy always. Ask Jaya about it. After all that is the reason why you are here.

Ok, we can take the break now.

Keki: Ok, come on back, change places, change neighbors, So, we did 1 exercise for K; 1 exercise for A; Now let us see what we can do with V.

SENSORY ACUITY - V

I take my chair and put it a few feet in front of let's say, Anwar, in such a way that I can see him totally from head to toes. Now I take a mental picture of Anwar, and I close my eyes. Now Anwar will make a major change in the way he is sitting and say ready. I will open my eyes compare the way Anwar is sitting now, with how he was sitting earlier. I will mention the differences. Anwar makes the change and says 'Ready'.

Keki: For example, he was sitting with his legs flat on the ground and now he has taken his right leg over the left leg, the left foot has gone a little inside, his right palm is on top of his left hand and his left shoulder has gone down just a little bit. Are there any other changes you have made Anwar?

Anwar: No that's about it. Yes.

Keki: I again close my eyes; can you make some changes which are not so drastic and when you have done it, say ready. (Anwar makes the change and says 'Ready').

Keki: (I open my eyes) I think he has turned his back from the waist, slightly towards the right, so now the right foot is pointing more towards the front, his right shoulder has gone a little backwards and is more or less in level with the left shoulder; also, whether he is aware of it or not, but his left foot has come a little forward. Is that correct?

Anwar: Yes, that's it. But I am not aware of having taken the left foot forward, it might have happened as I was relaxing and straightening myself, yes.

Keki: I again close my eyes. Now Anwar will make a very small change and tell me when he is ready.

Anwar: Ready

Keki: (I open my eyes) I do not think you made any changes in your feet and legs, your head seems very slightly tilted towards the left, but the little finger of your right hand is now gripped between the little finger and the ring finger of your left hand. Is that correct?

Anwar: That is perfect. The head tilt might have happened as I was changing the position. Yes. I am not aware of it.

Keki: So, I close my eyes again now and this time you make the most subtle change that you can make and then say ready.

Anwar: Ready

Keki: (With eyes open and scanning Anwar). Everything seems exactly as it was. Your ID! You have turned it over.

Anwar: (with a big smile on his face) that's it.

Keki: So, you all will pair up now. Make sure your chair is not too close so as to block any view, neither too far. Start from a major change and come down to a very subtle change in your 4th round and then change over and do it to your partner. Have fun.

(As usual after demonstrating the exercise and giving precise instructions I walk down a winding flight of stairs to the ground floor open area where there are Palm trees and by the side is a swimming pool, to sit there and be within myself. Generally, I climb back that flight of stairs to reach the hall just in time when they are finishing the exercise. Today Aban has paired up with Anu since there are total 13 participants. I enter the hall and find the group in an animated state looking quite pleased with themselves. One pair is still working. I wait for them to complete).

Keki: Was it fun? The group responds, 'yes'. I raise my voice and ask who had fun? The group responds 'I'. Raising both my hands upwards I ask who wants to have more fun and the group responds with a louder 'I'.

OUR SENSES

Keki: Before we have more fun let us clear something else. We said that we interact with this world through our five senses and five senses alone. That is V- visual; A- auditory; K-kinesthetic; O-olfactory & G-gustatory. So far, we did 1 exercise each for K, A & V. We will do something about O & G just before lunch. But tell me one thing; Is there anything at all besides these 5 senses?

Saira: What about the 6th sense?

Keki: As expected. Tell me Saira, have you or anyone else over here, ever experienced this 6th sense.

Saira: Oh yes (and a few other hands went up)

Keki: All those who feel you have experienced the 6th sense, please sit up straight; close your eyes and go back into that experience as if it is happening now. (After a while) Yes Saira, what is happening? How do you know that you are experiencing this 6th sense? Are you seeing something within your mental screen? Are you hearing something within you? Or are you feeling something within yourself?

Saira: I am seeing something and then getting a feeling

(Next one says 'I just feel it'. The other says 'I hear an internal voice'.

Keki: OK you all can open your eyes. You see **the so-called 6th sense is only an unknown trigger. You do not know from where it comes. But it Has to manifest itself in one or more of our 5 senses. THOSE ARE THE ONLY 5 WINDOWS TO THE WORLD THAT WE HAVE.**

LEAD SYSTEM & PREFERRED REPRESENTATIONAL SYSTEM

To proceed further; you will find some people to be more visual, some more auditory while others may be more kinesthetic. This is how they take in the world. We call this as **the lead system**. Then they represent the world to others in their communication. Once again while doing so somebody maybe more visual, somebody maybe more auditory, somebody may be more kinesthetic. This we call as the **preferred representational system**. Very often the lead system and the preferred representational system may be the same however that is not the rule. For communication to be good it is necessary that we talk in the other person's language. For example, if you are in Maharashtra and even if you do not know Marathi, if you meet someone and say 'kasa kai, bara ahet' (meaning 'how are you? all well?) then you have a better chance of being accepted. Likewise, if you are in Bengal if you say 'bhalo achi?' once again you have better chances of being accepted. When John Kennedy, before the Fall of the Berlin Wall was addressing the crowd there and said back in 1963, 'Im itch a Berliner' he got a thunderous applause around the world.

Who wants to hear another case-story?

The group: Loudly. 'I'

In one of the programs, a mother was attending the program. During the previous week her daughter had gone on a school trip to a bird sanctuary. She came back highly excited and started telling her mother all the different types of birds she had seen, and their colors, and sizes and plumage that she had seen. She talked about the 'whistling school boy' which is a type of a bird. You see, the girl was highly visual. But her mother was more auditory. The mother kept on asking the girl 'did you hear this bird; did you hear the whistling school boy'. Did you hear that bird singing? The girl found her mother is not interested in what she saw and left the room. She was so disappointed that for two days she did not talk to her mother.

So is there a way to find out whether a person is coming from V, A or K mode. Please open page 11 of your manual. Somebody, please start reading from the top.

Ankur: Representation systems. Seeing- VISUAL. Eyes: This people look up to the right or left or their eyes may appear unfocused.

Keki: When people are in a visual mode their eyes are moving above the Horizon.

Ankur: Gestures: Their gestures are quick and angular and include pointing.

Keki: What do you think they are Pointing at? As they are narrating, they are seeing in pictures and unawares they are pointing to various things. Now, they say that 'a picture is like a Thousand Words' so what do you think that will do to their breathing and speech?

Ankur: Breathing and speech: high, shallow and quick.

Words: The words that capture their attention include see, look, imagine, reveal, perspective.

Presentations: pictures, diagrams, movies.

Keki: Next person.

Shankar: Hearing- AUDITORY

Eyes: This people look down to the left and may appear shifty eyed.

Keki: Actually, their eyes go in level with their ears, either to the left or right. In many books you may find some variations, because people like you would have attended the programs and not everybody would have taken down the notes in the same way and they might have continued with it even when they wrote the books. Please proceed. Shankar: Gestures: their gestures are rhythmic, touching one's face, rubbing the chin. Breathing and speech: from mid chest, rhythmic.

Keki: In visual mode, since the picture is like a Thousand Words a person is in a hurry to pack as many words as possible and therefore the speech is fast; breathing is almost from the upper chest and therefore shallow, whereas when somebody is in auditory mode the breathing goes down to the mid chest and it is moderate. Continue.

Shankar: Words: The words that captures their attention include hear, listen, ask, tell, clicks, in-tune. Presentations: they prefer list, summarize, quote, read.

Keki: Next person.

Nirav: Feeling- KINESTHETIC: Eyes: these people look down to the right. Gestures: their gestures are rhythmic, touching chest, Breathing and speech: deep slow with pauses.

Keki: When a person is in Kinesthetic mode the breathing is all the way down to the diaphragm and the speech is also slow with pauses. Please continue.

Nirav: Words: The words that capture their attention include feel, touch, grasp, catch on, contact. Presentations: they prefer hands on do-it demonstrations, test drive. Motivation direction: Toward (goals) achieve, attain, gain. Away from (problems) avoid, out, relieve.

Keki: So now it is the time to have some fun. Go back to your school days. Think of your favorite subject. Now think of the teacher who was teaching that subject. Was he or she making it fun? Yes. **Realize that we only learn when we have fun**. Open the next page; Page number 12. Somebody please read from the top.

Nirav: Can I continue with it? I find this very important for my medical profession.

Keki: Yes, it is. Not just in your profession but any profession and even in regular life. It reminds me of an actual case. Some years back a well-known hospital psychiatric ward had called me for their monthly lecture address for the existing and new psychiatrists, so that I may make them familiar with NLP. I thought since I am an engineer, they may find it difficult to gel with me. A year before that, we had a Surgeon who attended our program. He was well read in NLP, and particularly by the language patterns; and was so taken up by it that he went ahead and did MA in English literature. He further did MBA and along with his surgery practice he is also teaching the MBA classes. So, I requested him to accompany me. At the appropriate time I gave him the stage. He started out by saying, how proud he was to be at his alma mater and to address the colleagues. His words; **'medicines do not cure. It is who gives the medicine and how it is given that cures.'** Regarding NLP he mentioned that he had trained his anesthetist in using language patterns before the operation with the patient. And because of that he could use almost half the dosage of anesthesia and the recovery of the patients had also much improved.

Nirav: Who is this doctor? I want to meet him.

Keki: Sure, later, if you don't mind. Can you please continue with the reading now.

PREDICATES

Nirav: Predicates. The following lists are predicates in language (verbs, adverbs and adjectives) that are associated with specific representational systems. A way of detecting the primary (most commonly used) representational system a person has in consciousness is by listening to the language, the sentences generated and noticing the predicates used.

Keki: I have been promising some fun to everybody for quite some time now. So, it is time to have it. Shall we from groups of four; one group will have five. One person will sit in the chair and 3 others will be standing around this person. One of these three people will take up Visual words, the next will take up Auditory and 3rd will take up Kinesthetic; in the group of 5 the 4th person standing will take up the 'unspecified' list. Using these words under that category, you are going to make sentences to praise the person sitting in the chair. Can somebody pull out a chair in the front? Thank you, Jaya. Why don't you sit down on it? Any three of you now stand around her the first one will take up Visual words 2nd Auditory and 3rd Kinesthetic. In the list of words, you will find both types of words; positive as well as negative. So, if you come across a word on the visual list as "ugly" please do not say by way of praise "Jaya, you are not absolutely ugly, ok". That is not a 'praise'. Just look at her. How pretty she is.

And she looks so nice when she Smiles. (Her smile broadens) Is that clear? Yes. Avoid such negative words and use only positive words. The important thing is that you will all praise simultaneously and continuously without stopping and while you are making the sentences you do not have to go into her ears to say so, you will be walking around her slowly, talk loudly and continuously, Create such a cacophony that the manager comes running over here to find out what's happening. Get into groups and start. Any questions?

Jaya: Till when will they continue praising me?

Keki: Good question. After about 10 or 12 sentences Aban will ask you all to switch, at that time the person sitting in the chair will stand up and stand between the Visual and Kinesthetic partners, that person will now take up Visual words the person who was doing Visual words will take up Auditory words, person doing Auditory words will take up Kinesthetic, and the person doing the K words will take the chair. This way each one will get all the four positions. And very importantly, change the direction in which you are taking rounds around the chair. Good? Continue. Create a cacophony. Have fun. Praise.

I come back into the hall midway to check how things are going. I make them to talk louder and walk slower. I come back again when the third group is just about to finish. I wait and then;

Keki: Please put back the chairs in their positions and sit down. So how was it?

'Super great, fantastic, energizing, awesome, never been praised so much, giddy'.

Keki: Who said 'super great'? Gautam, very good; who said 'Fantastic'? Guneet Singh, Anwar, also Padma, that's good; who said 'energizing'? Ah ha Ankur; and who said 'Awesome' Nirav you. And what about 'Never been praised so much'? Jaya, Saira, Manju you too? And Vipul; somebody said 'Giddy'. Lily just raised her hand. Shankar, you felt giddy? He replied, 'somewhat'.

Keki: So, was it fun? The group responds 'yes'. I raise my voice and ask who had fun? The group responds 'I' raising both my hands upwards and I ask who wants to have more fun and the group responds loudly 'I'.

Lily: Like they say 'you scratch my back I scratch yours' and everybody is happy.

Keki: We will have to consider that aspect also; isn't it? Gautam. Fine those who said fantastic; what made you say that?

Guneet Singh: We had a chance to pay compliments.

Anwar: Receiving so many praises yes and that too from so many ladies.

Padma: Fantastic because it makes you feel nice and also act nice.

Keki: Ankur, energizing, how so?

Ankur: After hearing so many praises, I got energized and praised some more as I was going around.

Keki: Nirav, you said awesome, in which way?

Nirav: I was watching the transformation taking place in the people sitting on the chair, and getting praised, and that was awesome.

Keki: But did you all have fun? (Amongst the group the most audible was 'great fun'). Now on a more serious note, do you think the praises that you received while you were sitting, were genuine? (the group was divided on this while most said 'yes' a few, not difficult to guess who, said 'no') My next question is that those who feel that the people praising them may not have been genuine; my question is, while you were going around and praising, did you mean what you said? (Most with one or two exceptions said 'yes'). So, you see, most of you felt that while you meant what you said, you are ready to doubt the others. Are we even able to accept the praises that we receive? It needs a certain level of trust. Trust of others; trust of the world; and most importantly trusting your own self. **Generally, many people are too free with their criticisms and very stingy with their praises**. What we give out returns to us. Do not believe me, Try it out yourself. (I scan each participant not just to give them time for it to sink in but also to see their internal response).

Guneet Singh: I feel this could be the recipe for Manju's organization to grow well.

Keki: Thank you Guneet. We will leave that to Manju. I notice a few question marks on some of the faces. Lily, are you still feeling giddy?

Lily: A little.

Keki: Vipul, what's happening to you?

Vipul: I am feeling a little Giddy now.

Keki: And Ankur what's up?

Ankur: Two things; how can I Praise someone I just meet and what is the logic in praising without reason? Also, I want to feel Giddy. I didn't feel anything while I was going around praising,. (Laughter in the group).

Keki: Three things actually, but let's take up your questions first then we will deal with the giddiness. There must be some pretty girls in your college? Yes? Did you ever give an interesting smile to a new entrant that you found very pretty, but never met before?

Ankur: (beaming) I must have.

Keki: Must have? Or you did.

Ankur: Yes, I did.

Keki: Now professor Shankar; you are into TA (Transaction Analysis). Aren't you? Would you call this action as praise?

Shankar: It is a positive Stroke, Yes, we can call it praise.

Keki: Thank you. Now, about Giddiness. Will 3 of you please stand up? Lily and Vipul; can you check the direction in which you think the giddy feeling is turning? (Lily shows clockwise and Vipul, anti-clockwise). I want both of you to take 3 rounds slowly in the opposite direction with eyes open or closed as you like. But do it after I explain to Ankur what he has to do. Ankur, take out your right-hand palm with fingers spread out. Now place the tip of your small finger into your umbilicus, that is, your belly button and bend down to touch the tip of your thumb to your nose. With your eyes open take 7 full turns as fast as you can and then walk straight in the direction you are facing. All can start now.

(Lily and Vipul complete their 3 rounds and I signal them to sit down) (Ankur finishes the last 3 rounds somewhat gyrating away from his original spot; stops, still somewhat bent, starts to walk and in 3 or 4 steps turns around and falls barely missing the lap of Padma, to the uproar of the group.)

Did you feel giddy, Ankur?

Ankur: Phew.

Keki: When in school, we used to play this because some kid said; this is the first test they will take if you want to be a Fighter Pilot.

I want each one of you to answer 2 questions. One is; when you were sitting in the chair, try and remember just one statement that somebody might have said to you. 2nd question is; when you were going around making sentences, did you find that in a particular representational system the sentences came to you very easily whereas in some other you had to struggle.

Shall we start from the left here, Ankur?

Ankur: V was easier. A was a little difficult. Sentence I remember was somebody said I am looking handsome.

Shankar: Actually, K was easier for me and I had some difficulty with V. Somebody said I have a well sculpted body.

Nirav: I was fine making sentences. Gautam said 'You are quite focused'.

Lily: The sentence I remember is somebody saying 'you have an authoritative voice' and I was ok making sentences but yes auditory came easier.

Padma: I had some difficulty in all three. The sentence I remember is 'you appear to be quite cool.

Saira: I have no problem making sentences. The sentence that I remember is somebody saying 'you look beautiful'.

Jaya: K was easier than A and V. I am trying to really remember the sentence but it was something about me knowing what I want.

Anwar: Somebody said I am a warm person yes. And I was ok making sentences yes.

Manju: K was easier than V and K. Somebody said you are quite outspoken.

Guneet: Making sentences in V were easier than the other two; Sentence I Remember is Jaya saying 'you are quite organized'.

Vipul: Sentence I remember is that I tell the truth. 'A' sentences were easier than V and K.

Gautam: Guneet said 'You are quite euphoric'. Making sentences were very easy in all three.

Anu: Somebody said I am a warm person. 'A' sentences were more difficult than V or K.

Keki: How many of you noticed that very often the sentence you remember and the ease of making sentences is from the same representation system (Most hands went up)

Let us proceed further now. Predicates were single words. Here is a list of Rep System Phrases. (See Appendix 1) You can see it at your leisure. I will tell you how to use it sometime little later.

VAK TEST & SCORES

Who wants to know their own personal score of V, A and K as to which mode you are in. (The group says 'I') OK, before we start on it let me tell you one thing. I am against all so called psychological testing; because I have seen even the Nation's premier institution giving psychological tests like Fero-B etc. and branding the people and sending them home without doing anything about it. This is one test which I give because it gives you your present comparative status and that status can and does change. There are 30 statements. You will mark out only those statements which you think applies to you. Complete it and then I will say what to do.

(After each one of them have completed marking out the statements which they think apply to them).

So once again starting from the left each one of you will read out one statement and indicate whether you think it comes from V A or K; Ankur. Will you start?

Ankur: 'I prefer to have communication in written form'. A?

Keki: Are you telling me or are you asking me? No, it is not A. Once again, I repeat that only the person I am addressing has to answer.

Ankur: Maybe it is V.

Keki: Not maybe. I want you to tell me what you think it is.

Ankur: Yes, it is V.

Keki: Why do you think it is V?

Ankur: Because I read it. The communication.

Keki: Very good. That's right. Next person.

Shankar: 'I often hum to myself'. A.

Nirav: 'I have High Telephone bills. A.

Lily: 'I can tell a lot about a person by the sound of his or her voice' A.

Padma:' I spend a lot of time on looking good'. V

Saira: 'I really enjoy getting massages'. K.

Jaya: 'People watching is one of my favorite pastimes'. V.

Keki: Yes, bird watching while at college. And crow watching for the girls. (laughter)

Anwar: 'I like to get up and stretch frequently'. K.

Manju: 'When I've had a bad day, my body tenses up'. K.

Guneet Singh: 'I often read while I am eating.' V.

Vipul: 'I think fresh flowers are worth the expenses to brighten up a home or office'. V.

Gautam: 'I like taking a hot bath at the end of the day'. K.

Anu: 'I would rather hear poetry than read it'. Is it A?

Keki: I want your answer not a question.

Anu: A.

Ankur: 'I have a tendency to gain weight'. K.

Shankar: I write down my goals. V.

Nirav: I talk to myself a lot. A.

Lily: I judge a person by the way he or she dresses. V.

Padma: I have lot of Record albums and tapes. A.

Saira: I often admire the artwork used in advertisements. That's a V.

Jaya: I have a hard time falling asleep at night if I hear a clock ticking. It's an A.

Anwar; 'In my family there is a lot of hugging and touching'. K

Manju: 'I am a good listener'. A.

Guneet: 'When I have spare time I like to dance or exercise'. K

Vipul: 'I enjoy good conversations'. A

Gautam; 'I go to art museums and exhibits pretty often'. V

Anu: 'When there is music playing, I can't help but tap my feet'. K?

Keki: That's right. It is giving you a condition and what you do within that condition. That's why it is K.

Ankur: 'I like to keep my house looking good. V.

Shankar: 'I talk to my dog or cat'. A

Nirav: 'I tend to touch people when I am talking to them'. K

Lily: 'I can tell a lot about a person by the way he or she shakes hands'. K

Keki: Now everybody: Considering only those statements that you had marked as applicable to you, just check out how many 'V' you got, how many 'A' you got and how many 'K' you got.

(Once everybody is finished) OK now please read out your scores in the order of V, A and K. But before you read out your scores, just look around in the group and watching them guess who may be scoring more on V

Gautam: I think Saira is, and perhaps Guneet.

Keki: And what makes you say that?

Gautam: Their colorful dresses and also some makeup in case of Saira.

Nirav: Even in that case, Gautam himself.

Keki: Let's find out. Start reading your scores please.

Ankur	:	5,	4,	8
Shankar	:	4,	6,	7
Nirav	:	5,	4,	4
Lily	:	0,	7,	4
Padma	:	5,	4,	4
Saira	:	7,	7,	5
Jaya	:	2,	3,	4
Anwar	:	3,	3,	4
Manju	:	3,	6,	3
Guneet	:	6,	4,	4
Vipul	:	3,	5,	2
Gautam	:	7.	8,	10
Anu	:	3,	2,	3

Keki: First of all, let me tell you that this is not about whose score is high and whose score is low. This is not your school or college test or exam results. It just gives you your present preferred representational system preference. Tell me who amongst you is regular at doing exercises.

(Ankur raises his hand).

Shankar: I used to but I am not regular now.

Nirav: Gautam has scored 10 out of 10 but he is not raising his hand.

Gautam: I can't do exercises. I am getting some Physio from time to time.

Keki: As far as V and A are concerned it is easy to understand what they are. When it comes to K let me give you an example. Suppose Jaya comes to me and touches me that is K. But instead of just touching me she pinches me. And it hurts even after she has stopped touching me. That is also K. Now the pain is gone but I am wondering and feeling bad as to why the hell did, she pinch me? That feeling is also K. This may appear as three distinct and different things but they are all K, Kinesthetic.

Jaya: Must be because you made me a sacrificial goat in the morning session (laughter).

Keki: Guneet, when you put on your TV, what channel do you generally like to see?

Guneet: I see news channels generally but I like to see the travel channel also. I like to see different places. (I point out to Guneet's relative score of V and A).

Keki: Vipul, what about you?

Vipul: I also see news channels but I prefer serials with interesting conversations. (I point out at Vipul's score).

Nirav: Lily could make sentences in V; she is also dressed rather colorfully yet she scores zero on V. How is this possible?

Keki: Anything and everything is possible. Whatever is happening has significance. We have to accept it and move forward. It is possible that somebody for certain reasons may consciously block out certain things. But the subconscious knows and has almost all the answers. If you can help the person to bring out the answer from the subconscious it can be very useful.

Anwar: So how do we use this, yes for our day-to-day life?

Keki: Imagine there are two partners running a company or a business. The senior partner scores high on visual. He likes to plan out things put it on paper and monitor the progress. He calls for a meeting. The other partner who does not score high on V, after a few reminders comes for the meeting. During the meeting somebody's name props up. This other partner scores high on A. During the meeting he picks up the phone and starts talking to that person. Along with being high on A, he is also high on K. He tells the other partner to wait and he goes out to meet that person. As he is walking out of the door, he says to himself 'you can't get anything done sitting on your big fat ass, you got to move and act'. The senior partner is getting exasperated and says to himself about his partner 'he is very impulsive, cannot plan or work in an organized manner'. And they have friction which goes on increasing. Actually, it is a symbiotic relation. In any organization you need planners, talkers, and action people. I have seen this happening in one of the businesses that I go for counselling..

Anwar: So yes, what happened there?

Keki: It's work in progress.

Padma: What about home?

Keki: Suppose there are two housewives, one is scoring high on V and the other is not. Whose house do you think will be well organized, spick and span.

Padma: The one who is scoring high on V.

Keki: Good. Now imagine that her husband is scoring low on V and maybe high on K or A. What do you think will happen?

Jaya: Boxing bout. Things flying around in the house; at each other.

Keki: Yes. The housewife soaring high on V is keeping her house spick and span, who has just cleaned out the hall, comes inside and finds her husband's Pajama lying around on the sofa and screams 'Who put this on the sofa, I just cleaned the hall?' Or a husband who scores high on V. but the wife does not; enters the bathroom in the morning and suddenly shouts 'where is my razor? Who has any business to take my razor? Don't you know everything in its place and a place for everything. Why can't you just leave things in its place?'

Padma: Actually, this happens in my house but not with my husband, my younger son who is mostly busy with his music, goes around throwing everything everywhere and I have to clean it up.

Shankar: Is it useful in education?

Keki: Very good question. Have you heard of a school boy who was doing well in his studies of say, science? He might have been more visual. Suddenly one year the teacher changed and he started going downhill in that subject. The new teacher was perhaps low on V and high on A, so maybe the new teacher went on talking more and using less of demonstrations, diagrams and drawings.

Shankar: I hear of it very often. Does that mean I will have to raise my score of 'V's? I think I'll have to visit places like the zoo pretty often.

Keki: Please make sure you come back from there. (Laughter).

Ankur: I know some professors do belong to the zoo. (Shankar gives a stare)

Ankur: No, No, No, not you. My professor. (More laughter).

Gautam: You said you will show us how we can change these scores.

Keki: Yes, I will; but before that let me ask you, if there was an artist or a painter in this group, which rep system do you think he will score high in? V, that's right. And if there was a singer or a professor, what then? A, that's right. And a personal trainer? A body sculptor? K, correct again. So, you see your natural tendencies may develop you into certain fields or the other way around. There once was electronics engineer in our group and she had given up her job. In the same program there was a director who was running a computer training center, so she tied up with him for taking computer programming classes. Two years later, when she was refreshing this program, we noticed that her A had gone up by 2 points. This happened due to the change in her profession, she was talking far more now. I consider a change of 2 points and more, as significant.

It helps us to be flexible and be able to communicate and respond to the other person in that person's preferred representational system. You already have the list of predicates as well as list of rep. system phrases. Imagine you are visiting a Marketplace, a railway station or even a zoo. Describe this visit in one page using only V words and phrases. Rewrite the same visit using only 'A' words and phrases. And write a third using only K words and phrases. This way you will be adapt at switching your rep system. Naturally the More you practice it the More you will gain.

Gautam: That means, comparisons can be made between scores.

Keki: Yes, but not between your score and someone else's. That will lead you nowhere. It is between your own scores at different time periods. As your sensory acuity increases your score will increase, and as you deal more with a particular system you will use more sensory acuity in that area.

Everybody can take a 3-minute bio-break. If you don't need to go inside the restroom you can just walk up to there and come back. Shake your legs. Move and come back. (Once everybody is in).

EYE ACCESSING CUES

They say your face is the mirror of your mind. Important organs on your face are your eyes. We saw earlier as to how the eyes take different positions while the mind is in different representational mode. Here is a handout for your eye accessing cues. First put your name on it. You will work in groups of three. One will be an observer. He will sit opposite his subject. The subject will hand over his or her handout to the observer. The third person will sit on the left of the subject little behind and out of the subject's visual range. This third person will be reading out the questions given. The subject does not respond auditorily but is thinking about the question and the answer. Subject's eyes will move in certain direction. The observer will observe this movement and put an arrow in that direction. One Arrow is enough since normally both eyes go in the same direction; unless one has a squint. Nobody has a squint here, right? (Smiles on the faces). The subject will keep looking slightly above the observer's head with, what we call as Soft-Eyes that means somewhat unfocused.

Eye accessing questions

1. What does it feel like to be wet?
2. Can you see yourself the last time you got caught in the rain?
3. What did it sound like?
4. What color shirt would you buy the next time you went shopping?
5. What would you look like with purple hair?
6. How do you sound when you are angry?
7. Do you remember how your laugh sounds?
8. When was the last time you had a debate with yourself?
9. What did you have for lunch yesterday?
10. Describe a cross breed between a giraffe and a cat.
11. When you are walking, which foot makes the most noise?
12. What would a crew rowing, a cat meowing and a horn blowing sound like?

13. Can you feel your toes now?
14. Which way do you turn a key to open a lock?
15. Describe the contents of a room you would like to create.
16. Mentally rehearse brushing your teeth.
17. When was the last time you received an order?
18. What was the most exciting thing that happened to you lately?
19. How do you look dressed up formally?
20. Whose voice is the most pleasing?

For the sake of uniformity, we will mark the arrows, in response for each question, from left to right in a row and continue in the next row. When you finish with one person, rotate so that each one gets all three positions. Any questions? None. Good, Go ahead. Have fun. (And I leave the Hall).

Figure 2: Eye accessing

(I return to the hall when the last group is just about to finish. I draw a circle on the whiteboard to represent a face and put two eyes into it. I draw 3 arrows going outwards from both eyes. One upward, one horizontal and one downward as in the diagram).

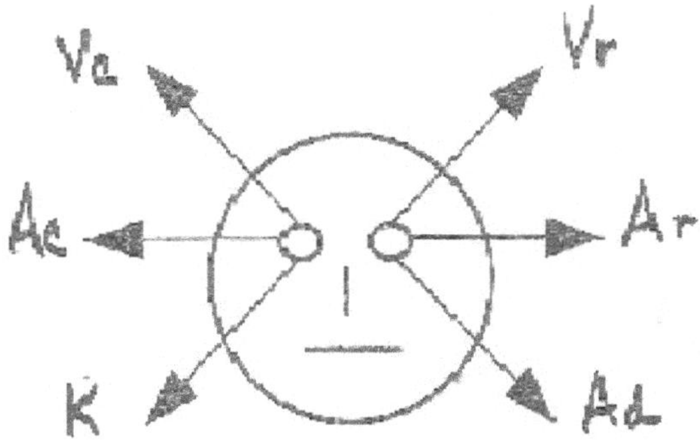

Figure 3: Eye Accessing Movements

The figure in front of you represents the face of the person you are in front of. Therefore, your right side is that person's left side and your left side is that person's right side. As you learnt earlier the arrows going upward show that the person is in the visual mode. When the eyes are going upwards towards the right, the person is creating something new we call it Visual Construct; (Vc). When it is going upwards towards the left then the person is Visually Remembering something (Vr), seeing a scene which the person has seen earlier. Likewise, when the arrows are going in the horizontal direction towards the right the person is Auditorily Constructing something (Ac), or may be creating a new song or speech. And when it goes towards the left the person is remembering some words or something he or she might have heard earlier (Ar). When the eyes go downwards towards the right that person is in a feeling mode, Kinesthetic (K) mode. Going download towards the left means the person is in Internal Dialogue or self-talk (Ad, or id). In some cases, the whole thing could be reversed, that means what we expect on the right side may be on the left side and what we expect on the left could be on the right.

One of you please come and sit in front of me. The rest of you go behind me but leave the corridor in front of the subject free behind me, which means, do not occupy space in front of the subject. (Shankar comes and sits down as a subject). Shankar, you look above my head and beyond without focusing on anything in particular, what we called as, with Soft Eyes. I and some others will ask you a question; you do not have to answer anything. Whatever goes on in your mind, we will be observing. Now here we are going to observe the sequence of eye movements, not just the most prominent one. So, watch carefully everyone.

Shankar when you had bath this morning, you had bath, right? (Shankar smiles along with others and says yes by a nod. I continue) the hot water adjustment is towards your left, or right?

What did you all observe?

Ankur: The eyes went all over.

Keki: Yes, it went 4 to 5 locations, but what was the sequence?

Gautam: It first went upwards right, Vc and then upwards left Vr.

Nirav: I think it went downward toward the right in the beginning.

Keki: Very good observation Doctor.

I think he first felt the water on him and then he was visually constructing as to where the hot water arrangement is; then it went towards left to remember it visually. Maybe he does not use hot water. Tell me Shankar, is that how it went?

Shankar: Yes, I always take cold water bath and I was a little confused because I haven't used the hot water adjustment for a long long time, so I was searching and I did feel the water on me to begin with.

Gautam, Ankur, Nirav and some others: WOW.

Keki: Shankar, I think you bathe under a shower and do not use bucket and mug.

Shankar: Always under a shower.

Keki; I hope you are not saying all this just to please me because then we won't learn anything.

Shankar: No, why should I? I also want to learn.

Ankur: How did you guess about the shower?

Keki: Did anybody notice a slight eye movement straight up just for a moment towards the end?

Anwar, Guneet: This is superb.

Keki: Shankar, who is the last person you saw just before leaving the home this morning?

(To the group). Which way did the eyes go?

Saira: They went upwards towards the left and then came back to the center.

Keki: And what does that tell you.

Saira: The first movement shows that he remembered somebody but what about the second movement?

Keki: He got his answer. Decision was made. And then came back to normal. Shankar, what is the last thing you said to somebody before leaving your house this morning?

What did you all observe?

Saira: His eyes moved leftwards but then it went downwards towards the right.

Keki: And what does that tell you?

Sarah: That he remembered what he said and then there were some internal dialogues?

Keki: Shankar, would you like to answer that?

Shankar: Yes, I said something to my wife. She answered me and I left the house thinking about it.

Keki: Anybody would like to ask anything?

Saira: Who is your favorite actor?

Keki: What did you observe?

Jaya: I think he was confused because his eyes went up towards the right then left, right again and then left.

(Shankar nods in agreement)

Jaya: Who is your favorite actress?

Keki: What did you observe?

Jaya: Definitely has a favorite. Initially his eyes went to the right and then more or less settled upwards to the left visually remembering his favorite actress. (Shankar gives a broad smile in agreement) (Turning to Saira) you must know what to ask, to catch them. (Then to Shankar) you did not tell me who that actress is.

Shankar: Catherine Zeta Jones.

Guneet: My my, do leave something for us also. (Laughter all around)

Keki: Fine, everybody back to their seats please.

SUBMODALITIES

It is getting to be 1.30 now and we have one more exercise to complete before we go for lunch. In the morning while doing the sensory acuity exercises, we did K, A and V and we said we will do Olfactory-O and Gustatory-G, smell and taste before lunch time to get the juices running into the stomach. We will start with the sweet dish. Before we start the exercise, tell me who likes to have laddu? (Laddu is two or three fingers wide round balls and can be made out of quite a few different base materials or flours) most give enthusiastic 'I', so I ask ok is there somebody who does not like Laddu. (Lily raises her hand)

Do you like Swiss chocolates Lily?

Lily: I love them.

Keki: So, when I say laddu, it is chocolate for you, OK.

Let us start the exercise now.

Everybody, empty your Laps. Put your feet flat on the ground, sit up straight, backbone straight, push your tailbone into the chair, take a deep breath and as you exhale close your eyes and relax.

Imagine there is a plate in front of you, with laddu in it, next to the plate is a spoon. I want you to physically move one hand and pick up that spoon now. Now bang the spoon on the plate and listen. Put away the spoon. Once again physically move your hand to pick up a Laddu. Slowly bring the Laddu closer and closer to your mouth but keep your mouth shut, do not open your mouth. Get the Aroma of the Laddu. Let the juices flow in your mouth. OK I will not torture you more; you can open your mouth and take a small bite. Listen to the sound of that crunch. Chew it well. Finish eating that laddu, wipe your hands in your hanky, open your eyes and come back.

So how was the experience?

Saira: Very nice.

Keki: Did you all see the plate. Good. Please describe the plate that you saw.

Gautam: White porcelain plate, size of a side plate.

Shankar: Same as his.

Keki: It is never the same. You did not see what he saw. Did anyone of you have a border on the plate? Was there any embedded design on the border?

Gautam: Mine had a blue border and embossed relief pattern at the rim.

Keki: So, you had that too, Shankar?

Shankar: No, mine was plain with......

Keki: Stop. We will come to that in a moment.

So how many Laddu in your plate? That's what you are about to tell right? Shankar.

Shankar: One.

Keki: How many of you saw only one laddu in your plate? Raise your hand.

(Shankar along with Lily, Jaya, Manju and Anu raise their hands)

Five of you! What a sorry state. Tell me you five; who is putting this restriction on you? Who?

Lily, just one Swiss chocolate?

Lily: Yes, I am dieting

Shankar: You said **a** laddu.

Jaya: One is enough for me; I am not greedy.

Manju: I am suffering from diabetes I cannot have more.

Anu: There was only one in my Plate

Keki: So, everybody, who is putting this restriction on them?

Anwar: You said Laddu, yes you did not say laddus.

Keki: And I did not say 'a' laddu any time, did I? No. You see I purposely choose the word Laddu because when you go to buy them and if you want 1 kilo of laddu you still say give me one kilo laddu, you do not say give me one kilo laddus. Do you? Anwar?

Anwar: No, I don't; yes, not for Jalebi also, I suppose.

Keki: So once again my question to everybody is, who is putting this restriction on these 5 people?

Most in the group say 'they themselves'.

Keki: How many people at your home Manju? 3 you said? All are having diabetes? Or are they dieting? And Shankar?

Shankar: I know, I know, I am putting this restriction on myself. Maybe that is why I am not getting promoted, (with a very slight nod to the left).

Keki: Are you the only one putting this restriction on yourself?

Shankar: I prefer to speak only for myself.

Keki: So here is an opportunity to turn off all those restrictions and enhance our fun for those who want it. Fine. Who wants to enjoy it even more? (Almost all say 'I'). We will go through this experience once again with a major difference this time. So once again close your eyes. This time visualize things without any restriction at all and go beyond the limits. Visualizing costs you nothing. It only needs your intention. Intention to be restriction free for you to enjoy life.

Once again imagine a plate in front of you. It could be a half inch thick plate made of solid gold. **If you can't even imagine something, how the hell will it ever come into your life?** This plate contains the world's best Laddu that you can think of. Extend both your arms and hold that plate. Move the plate a little closer to you, away from you, little up, little down, until you get the best position. Leave it there, it will stay there. Next to the plate is a very ornate spoon. You may like to make the spoon out of solid silver, well decorated. Your world's best laddu can be of whatever type you want. You can load it full of dry fruits and goodies that you love. Next to you, is a variable knob. This knob controls the brightness of the light above the plate. Extend one arm to that knob and adjust the brightness. Take a look at your Laddu. Do you want to enhance the colors? Do it. You can see the contrast between the Laddu and the goodies you have put into it, the dry fruits and whatever else. Now pick up the spoon and hold it in your hand. Would you like to make it little heavier, little lighter, change the size and shape of it, the decorations of it? Do it. Now bang that spoon on the plate and listen to the difference in the sound this time. Put away the spoon. Extend one arm once again and just touch one of the Laddu. In the morning exercise of kinesthetic sensory acuity, you learnt so many submodalities of the touch. Feel the temperature, the pressure, the contact area, the texture and all the rest that you can, of this Laddu. Now lift it up just about half an inch and feel the weight of it. Would you like to make it little smaller, little bigger, little heavier or lighter? Make it. Now very very slowly bring this Laddu closer and closer to your mouth, keeping your mouth shut. As the Laddu comes closer and closer to your mouth you are able to see the details in fine focus, see the changing texture, see the grains becoming bigger and clearer, see the contrast improving between the Laddu material and the goodies it is carrying. Aha, get the Aroma of this world's best Laddu, and your mouth waters. You are already tasting the Laddu. Now open your mouth and take a bite. Feel the crunch. Chew on it. Let the juices flow. Keep the Juices in your mouth only. Do not gulp it down. As you chew further you will feel the fine particles in your bite. You will feel the difference in texture as you bite on the dry fruits. Move these sweet juices of this world's best laddu, from one side of your mouth to the other. Ok gulp it down. Finish eating this Laddu and open your eyes and come back.

Now everybody, tell me if this experience was more enjoyable or the first one. (Everybody without exception says the second one)

The Handout for sub modality comparison is already with you. Let us take up one by one. 'Number of images' we saw one plate, one spoon, many Laddu; 'Motion or still' when you are moving it there was motion otherwise it was still. 'Color or black & white' did everybody see it in color? Yes ok. Bright/Dim' what happened when you had the brightness control in your hand? Did you all increase or decrease? Most of you increased it and it became better.

'Focused/Unfocused' it was focused and it was more focused as you brought it closer to you and may be when the brightness increased. 'Bordered/Borderless' It was with borders. 'Associated/Dissociated' is a very important concept we will see it soon. 'Centre weighted/Wide-Angle' mostly Centre weighted.

"Size Relative to life' so you did play around with the size of the laddu 'shape' '3 dimensional or flat' everybody saw it three-dimensional, correct? 'Close/distant' so when you moved the plate around, ultimately it became closer to you or farther away from you? Closer. That is as was expected. Location in space/panoramic'

In Auditory; to understand all the things one will have to be a Sound Engineer. But we do have details of it from the perfect source

I'll talk about it later on, but number of sounds, the volume; we played around with in the morning exercise. Also tone, high pitch low pitch etc.

Kinesthetic submodalities are easy to understand.

Location in the body, skin temperature, pressure, intensity. We experienced most of it in our morning exercise.

The second experience was more enjoyable than the first one because we enhanced the submodalities. **Submodalities affect the finer aspects of the behavior pattern**. Now let us look at the last one, 'associated versus dissociated'.

This time there will be a major difference from how we did the previous two exercises. In the previous two exercises we are holding the plate, we were moving it, we were picking up the Laddu, and we were eating it ourselves. We were personally associated with the whole event. In this third exercise I will ask you to move out of your body and imagine that you are standing by your side. Of course, you will physically continue sitting in your chair. Your standing self will be watching your sitting self, going through the second exercise. So, there will be no movements in either of you. Once your sitting self has finished with the exercise, you will get back once again into your sitting self, rub your hands together rub it on your face and, come on back. Are you ready?

Close your eyes once again and relax. Gently pull yourself out of your sitting self and imagine you are standing by your side and watching your sitting self, going through that second exercise. I will give you 30 seconds. (Pause . . .) As your sitting self, completes that exercise number 2 now; I want you to gently merge back with your sitting self. Now rub your hands together, rub it on your face, open your eyes and come on back.

Which exercise was more enjoyable this one or the previous one?

(Everybody says the previous one except Jaya)

Jaya you found this 3rd exercise more enjoyable than the previous? (Jaya says yes) No problem, we will see about it later.

Almost all of you found this exercise to be less enjoyable than the previous one. In the previous exercise you were associated, you were doing the things yourself, and you are experiencing the enjoyment yourself. In this 3rd exercise you are doing it with dissociation. You were only an observer and watching yourself having the fun of having the Laddu. Like I said before, everything that happens is of significance. Sometimes it may so happen that the idea of enjoying ourselves is far better than the actual enjoyment. And there will be reasons for the same.

OK, everybody's stomach juices must be running now, so let us go and Associate ourselves with lunch. We will be back here in 1 hours' time.

At lunch

After taking a small breather at my favorite place near the swimming pool, giving time to the group to go to the restroom and proceed to the restaurant; I myself start for the restaurant. Halfway I find Anu slowly walking towards the restaurant, hands folded and the purse under her arm. I catch up with her and ask her if she knows the way to the restaurant. She says no but she will find out. I extend my arm to take her's. She holds my hand and we proceed towards the restaurant hand in hand. A table for 15 of us is already reserved. There are few vacant seats. I select two seats closer to the center, pull the chair out for Anu and make her sit. I take the adjacent seat and sit down. Pretty soon all the seats are taken, and the bearers start serving soup and starters. I asked Anu if she is a vegetarian or a non-vegetarian. See answers in one word 'vegetarian'. This is the total communication she had all through the lunch on that first day. I tell her that there will be only two non-vegetarian dishes and the bearers will ask each person before serving; all the rest of the dishes will be vegetarian.

I asked the group as to how did they find the morning session, was it too fast, too slow, were they able to understand my talking easily? Most of them said it was easy for them to catch what I was saying and did not find it either too fast or too slow.

Shankar: But I could not keep up with taking notes of what remarks you were making in between.

Keki: Shankar, when you are focusing on taking down notes you are operating at the conscious level; it is always better to allow your subconscious to take down the notes in your mind, then it will stay there. One thing I would advise everyone is that whenever you find a program interesting you should go home and the first thing you do is tape edit.

Ankur: How do you do that?

Keki: Tape edit is when you rerun the entire program in your mind sequentially and take notes of whatever you might have missed writing.

Vipul: Actually, I found it a bit slow particularly when you were with Jaya and she was not giving you the answers you wanted.

Keki: Yes, that is possible. Very often when that happens there is a background program running which may be saying 'what is there in it for me?'

Lily: (overheard while talking to her neighbor) I have done 4 years of Clinical Psychology. I am here only for the Foreign Certificate; it will enhance my career.

Gautam: I found the whole morning packed with possibilities that I can use in my training programs.

Saira: I am taking a program from this Monday and I have already decided where I would use what.

Vipul: You people are teachers. In business it is very different. My main intention in business always is 'how to transfer what is in somebody else's pocket into my pocket'

Many ears in the group perked up. They looked at Vipul and then at me. I let it pass.

Saira: There is a difference between being a teacher and being a trainer. (With annoyance) but you may not understand it.

Keki: Here comes lunch. Let's enjoy the lunch now.

When the group was almost finishing their sweet dish, I excused myself telling them that we will start the afternoon session after 13 minutes and meanwhile they can come near the swimming pool to talk to the trees.

Keki: Come on back, (as I enter the seminar hall from the lobby) please take your seats, sit somewhere else, change your partners, good.

So how was the food? (Almost all say good, very good.)

Better than the program, isn't it? (Most say 'no', some say, 'both are good')

Ankur: If you remind us of it now, I may feel like going for a second round of hot Gulab jamun with cold vanilla ice cream.

Shankar: Ate too much. May go off to sleep now.

Keki: Don't worry, I will organize that also. Tell me who amongst you is not confused with our morning session.

Saira, Gautam: (surprised) Not confused?

Keki: Yes. Not confused. Remember that confusion is good. Confusion always precedes clarity. In the morning session we were building seemingly unconnected different types of bricks, jumping from one to the other. Now let us see what happens when we put these bricks together.

So put your feet flat on the ground, sit up straight, backbone straight, push your tailbone into the chair, take a deep breath and as you exhale close your eyes and relax. Now think of a time when things did not go the way you wanted it to. Something that makes you feel bad even now, when you think of it. Do not take up any major issue right now. Take up something where either due to your act of omission or commission somebody might have taken you to task. You might have been blamed rightly or wrongly and you are feeling bad about it even now. And that is crucial; you should be feeling bad about it even now.

Imagine that event is happening right now in front of you on a stage. You are able to see yourself on that stage undergoing the treatment from somebody who might have blamed you rightly or wrongly. Watch yourself, watch that other person, listen to the words, feel the feeling that you might have felt at that time. Even if you felt angry, anger is a disempowering state. Somehow you feel that the lighting on the stage is becoming dimmer, the sound and the words are getting muffled, and the stage is receding further away from you becoming smaller. In fact, now the stage is almost turning upside down and you are not able to hear anything.

Now all of us have some favorite piece of music or a song that we love to hear from time to time, and whenever we hear it, it makes us feel just great. Imagine you have a music system next to you and you are putting this, your favorite piece of music or song into it and starting the music system. Adjust the volume to slightly louder than the usual. Whenever you listen to this piece of music or song you feel just great. Feel great. Soon you will come to the end of this piece feeling great. Come to the end now and switch off your music system. Rub your hands together rub it on your face and eyes, open your eyes and come on back.

I want all of you to go back to that same event one more time. Consider that the bad feeling you had before this exercise was at 10; now after having done the exercise, tell me at what intensity it is.

Let us start from the left here, yes Gautam.

Gautam: Around 4. Anwar: 6. Lily: maybe 9 or 8. Shankar: I would say 5. Nirav: Almost gone maybe at 1. Padma: 2 or 3. Guneet Singh: at 4. Manju: 7. Saira: Almost gone; I would say 1. Jaya: At 6. Vipul: May be 6. Ankur: at 4. Anu: six.

Keki: How much time did we spend on this exercise; about two and half minutes? In two and half minutes we have reduced our pain level from 10 to almost zero in couple of cases and 40 to 60% in most others.

Let me ask you Saira, when did that event occur?

Saira: 7 years back.

Keki: And you Gautam?

Gautam: 12 years ago.

Keki: So, we have been carrying that pain for so many years and in two and half minutes we can reduce it so drastically. This was just a Jhalak, (a glimpse) to make you aware of the potential and power of NLP. We still have four and half days. Aage Aage Dekho hota hai kya. (Wait and watch as to what can happen) Today as we put together some of those bricks, we built a sort of a Room; tomorrow will be a mansion; on the 3rd day your city; on 4th the country and on the final 5th day the World. Lily, I would like to know when the event occurred for you.

Lily: It is ongoing.

Keki: NLP has specific exercises for specific purposes. This exercise was event based. For ongoing issues, we will have some different exercise later.

LANGUAGE OF VISUALIZATION

During the second half of the last century many self-help books appeared. They all asked you to visualize. However, none of them taught you how to visualize. Whether you are aware of it or not, there is a language of visualization within each one of us. Shall we examine it? Yes? Then empty your Laps, put your feet flat on the ground, close your eyes and relax. Think of a person that you like very much. Open your eyes. Shut your eyes. Now think of a person that perhaps you hate, or even if you do not hate anybody, you like this person much less than the earlier one. Ok, open your eyes and come back. Tell me which image was closer to you, distance wise. (Almost all said, the first one).

Lily: No, actually the second image was closer.

Gautam: I think I also found the second image closer.

Keki: Once again, all of you close your eyes. All of you bring that second image back and let it come closer and closer to you and check what happens to your feelings; then moving it away from you till you become comfortable with it. Fine. Open your eyes and come back. Tell me what happened when you brought the second image closer to you?

Nirav: It made no difference to me.

Ankur: I said 'get lost'.

Keki: Ankur, 'get lost' is a thought. I am asking you, what were your feelings? The test to find out if it is a feeling is when you can say I felt 'x y z'. To say I felt 'get lost' does not make sense

Ankur: The feelings were 'why are you bothering me?' ok, I get it; that could also be a thought. The feelings were 'I was bothered', some irritation and anger.

Saira: Past unpleasant memories cropped up in me. So, a bit of sadness; but I moved the image away, not very far and I was comfortable.

Vipul: When the image came closer, I said 'I will show you' ' I will take my revenge'.

Keki: But that is also not a feeling.

Vipul: I can tell you what happened, and then you will understand.

Keki: That will not be necessary. Remember when you came home, I had told you that NLP is free of content. **Who did what to whom is not important. How our mind is processing it. That is important.** So once again when the image was brought closer what were your feelings?

Vipul: My feeling was to take revenge. Anger.

Keki: And wanting to take revenge came out of what? What were your feelings when that person performed the act which makes you feel that you need to take revenge?

Saira: Jealousy perhaps?

Vipul: Of course, I feel jealous.

Keki: Saira, I would have preferred if that word would have come from his mouth. But I also know that it would have taken us quite some time. Anu, do you want to share something?

Anu: I could not bring the image closer. I had mixed feelings of anger, resentment, and irritation. So, I moved the image far out where I can't even see it.

Keki: Lily and Gautam, this second person is important in your life and you cannot shake him or her off. Is that so?

Gautam: Yes, the person is important in my life.

Lily: I do not know if he is important but I just cannot shake him off. I live with him.

Keki: Nirav, Ankur, Saira and Gautam; please close your eyes and bring that second image in the place where the first image of the person you like was. And check your feelings now. You may open your eyes and tell me what happened.

Nirav: The feelings are positive and I think ok, I had not understood the person properly.

Ankur: It's ok.

Saira: I could think of the good times we had together.

Gautam: I am feeling good.

Keki: My suggestion is that you 4 meet this person and who knows, you may find out something which you are not aware of so far. Guneet, you are looking pretty cool. What's your story? Do you want to share anything?

Guneet Singh: Yes, for the first image I saw my wife. She was smiling and waving at me. For the second image I was struggling and could not find anybody that I actually hate; then since you had said that if you do not hate anybody think of someone that you like less than the first person. So, I thought of my two Female friends that I had, prior to my marriage, whom you might say, I was dating. Their images were right behind where the first one was. It was fine and even welcome when I brought those images a little closer. I and my wife still meet them occasionally and when we visit our hometown my wife even goes out shopping with them and their friends.

Keki: Excellent Guneet. (To the group) That's the way to live. That should be the destination for each and every one of us. Thank you, Guneet.

Manju: But in business you are bound to find some people whom you hate.

Guneet Singh: I may not like their behavior or their decisions but then that is what business is, Manju.

Keki: Let me share something with you. Who likes to hear a story?

Group: 'I'

Keki: I couldn't hear you.

Group: (louder) 'I'

Keki: That's better. When I was in college there used to be a lot of (I bring my hands in front, open out two fingers and twist and turn them clockwise and anticlockwise against each other) what?

Shankar: Love affairs.

Keki: Yes, the professor knows. But very often that used to be one sided. The guy would go on while awake or in dreams; today she wore a yellow dress, today she did a ponytail, today she kept her hair open, so on and so forth. The girl may not even know that such a person exists.

Very often as we grow up, we get into one sided hate affairs also. Even if it is two sided, my question is who is collecting the toxins? That person or you? Who is likely to get acidity? That person or you? Who is likely to get ulcers? That person? And if this just continues who is likely to get even cancer. That person? Please awaken yourself and live healthy. Do I make sense Doctor?

Nirav: Totally.

Keki: Totally

Keki: Realize one thing. **Everybody is just a mirror. The qualities which you dislike in the others are your own qualities that you dislike in yourself. And the qualities that you like in somebody else are again your own qualities that you wish to enhance. If you keep this in mind, your life is bound to change**. You will reach a stage where you will be thankful that the five fingers are different and yet it helps to form a fist.

EXPERIMENT IN BREATHING

For the next exercise I need two volunteers. Thank you, Anwar. Thank you Ankur. Please stay seated. This exercise is just an experiment. What is an experiment?

Ankur: Trying to prove something?

Keki: No. An experiment is the process or procedure that you setup to find the result. Whatever result you get is the result. Leaving aside the fundamental scientific research experiments; I am told that most of the other research going on is all sponsored result research.

For our experiment one of you two will come and sit down on the chair, the other person will go out of the hall away from the hearing distance of the hall. One of you please come and occupy this chair. (Ankur comes and occupies the chair; Anwar goes out of the hall)

Ankur, when Anwar comes in, I will ask him to sit in the chair opposite to yours, you have to observe his breathing pattern and match it. I will also be observing the same and when Anwar is breathing in, I will move my hand upwards, when he is breathing out, I will move my hand downwards; once I find that the rhythm is setup and you are both breathing inwards together and exhaling outwards together, I will raise my hand upwards fast and from that moment onwards you will start taking deep breaths. You will continue to take deep slow breath from then onwards and we will see what happens. Now Anwar who will be sitting with his eyes closed should have no indication from you that you have made some change. So, for practice follow my hand movements and when I raise my hand up fast start taking deeper breaths. Start. No, no I could hear your breath changing. There should be no indication at all from your side. So, once again. Good; that should do.

Will somebody call Anwar in now? (Aban goes out and brings him in.)

Anwar, you sit in this chair opposite to Ankur. The group is sitting on one side, only so that they can observe you much better. Remember this is only an experiment, we are not playing any games, and there is no chalaky, (=over smartness). So now close your eyes and just relax.

I watch the breathing of Anwar and Ankur both. I point out to Ankur as well as the group, Anwar's shirt moving up and down close to his stomach as he would breathe in and out. As I find both of them breathing in and out synchronously, I signal to Ankur to raise his breathing deeper. Ankur starts taking deep breaths and within two or three breaths Anwar is also breathing Deeper. The movement on his shirt also indicates longer duration. I point that out to Ankur and the group. Many, nod in agreement. I bring the experiment to a close by asking Anwar to open his eyes and come out.

Keki: How are you feeling, Anwar?

Anwar: Fine, relaxed.

Keki: Did you feel anything different?

Anwar: Not really. Yes. Why, what happened?

Keki: Ankur, would you like to tell him what happened?

Ankur: When you went out Keki instructed me to watch your breathing as you sit there with your eyes closed and relaxed, and to match your breathing. He said when he finds my breathing synchronous to yours, he will raise his hand up and from that moment I have to take deep and long breath (kinesthetic), and watch if there is any change in your breathing. He also made me practice so that when I change my breath no sound of my breathing comes out. Then he asked the group to move on the side opposite to you so that they can also observe your breathing. When you came in, sat down and started relaxing I followed those instructions. Surprisingly when I increased my breathing rate, within two breaths, your breathing also changed accordingly.

Anwar: Really?

Ankur: You can ask the group.

Most of the group: We saw it happen.

Anwar: Wow

Ankur: But Keki, how did it happen?

Keki: I have no idea.

Saira: So why does it happen?

Keki: I have no idea.

Gautam: Will it happen always?

Keki: I have no idea.

Jaya: Then why do we do it?

Keki: (with a broad smile) I have absolutely no idea: May be just because it happens.

Lily, Vipul and Manju look at me quizzically and some others have a mischievous smile on their face.

Keki: Ok everybody please go back to your seats and let's do something else. Once again, I need two volunteers. (Guneet Singh and Padma raise their hands first).

RAPPORT DEMO

I arrange two chairs facing towards the group at an angle such that as if they are on two sides of an equal sided Triangle spreading out towards the group. They are kept at a distance of 3 to 4 feet so that both occupants can see each other from the top of the head to their toes. I stand near one chair and ask one of them to come and occupy the other. They both start for it and I ask Guneet to come first. Both of us occupy respective chairs.

Keki: Are you comfortable, Guneet?

Guneet: Yes, very.

Keki: (To the group) what are the two words that the Great Master would say to his student?

Manju: 'Now you do it'.

Keki: Those are not two words. What were the two words?

Group: 'Watch me'.

Keki: That's right. Only in this case it will be 'watch us'. Now tell me what organ do you use for watching?

Group: Eyes.

Keki: That's right. Just remember it.

Keki: So Guneet, tell me all that you did yesterday from the time you got up from bed to the time you went back to bed at night.

Guneet: I got up at 5:45 in the morning as usual.

Keki: The alarm rang?

Guneet: No, no I do not use any alarm. On my weekly holiday I get up two to two and half hours later. My wife had brought my hot bed tea; I had that and did some 15 minutes of stretching exercises. Then I went to the bathroom for my morning duty, brushing teeth, and so on. Do you want details of that also?

Keki: No, that will do.

Guneet: By 7, I was ready for breakfast. While my wife was setting up the breakfast, I went to the kid's room to wake them up for their school. Had a little fun time with them. Went back for my breakfast. Had breakfast and said bye to my wife and kids and left for my factory by 7:30. My factory is about 20 minutes away and when I reached there at 10 minutes to 8. I had a round of the machine shop where the shift starts by 7:00 a.m. Then I went to our first-floor office and entered my cabin. I started my computer and was checking the previous day's production report as well as the quality check report. Just then our works manager entered, we greeted each other with 'Good morning'. We discussed the previous day's production results and quality reports and compared the same with our plans. Before leaving my cabin, the works manager mentioned that Surendra, our CNC machine operator wanted to meet me urgently today for some private issue and added 'I believe it is something about his father's operation'. I asked him to check with Surendra if it would be ok to come to my office at 9:30 during the tea break where we can have tea and snacks together in my cabin and in the meanwhile, I could catch up with my mail. At 9:30 Surendra came to my office with a file in his hand. He greeted me. I got up from my chair and led him to the sofa chairs with coffee table and made him sit there. I asked him what the issue was. He handed over the file to me and started narrating regarding his father's health and immediate operation that was needed. Meanwhile tea and snacks had come for both of us and I asked him to start at it while I flipped through the file. I told him that it looks serious and he should immediately start for his hometown. He first expressed concern regarding the urgent work that was going on, on his machine. I asked him who he thought would be the best person to take care of the same. He mentioned the name of Sunil. I told him that we will arrange to put him on the train by the evening and in the meantime, he should have Sunil with him for 1 hour as he works and then supervise Sunil's work for another one hour.

Keki: That was a fine job, what about his father's operation?

(Manju raised his finger to ask something. I signaled him to be quiet and use his eyes instead.)

Guneet: I already made two things clear to him that his job will be taken care of and also his father's operation. So now I called Lakshmi, our Accounts Officer, who I am training to do the HR function also. I enquired with her about the employee's Group Insurance and the status of emergency funds in Surendra's account. She already had both the figures ready with her. Three of us discussed this together and I asked Lakshmi to call up our travel agent and book a ticket for Surendra for the evening train. After they left, at about 10:05 a.m., I took up the new enquiry we had, for doing the estimation. While I was still at it, maybe at about 12 noon the works manager called up to say that there was a breakdown at a machine and he would like me to come down. I went down and it took us about 2 hours to set the machine right.

Keki: Quite a busy day, wasn't it?

Guneet: Yes, quite. And while I was having my lunch at about 2.15, I received the call from my old college friend who had come down from Canada and wanted to meet me. We fixed up to meet at 3:30 in my cabin. Our chatting of the old times and new developments went on till evening. Then I took him home to meet my wife and kids and have dinner with us. He left home at about 9:30 and we all retired to bed by 10.

Keki: Very interesting; tell me, what do you consider as the highlight of yesterday?

Guneet: The highlight of course was meeting my friend. He was interested in going to Hem Kund Sahib and he knew that last year, I had been there.

Keki: Oh, I have also been to Hem Kund and Valley of Flowers. Did you also trek upwards from Govindghat?

Guneet: You have also been? Fantastic. The trek from Govindghat to Ghangaria is the most memorable one.

Guneet was quite animated as he started describing how it is 6 hours estimated trekking took him almost 9 hours because as he started from Govindghat and reached at a tiny village, it started raining and the rains became heavier and there was a small room made with bare bricks and no plaster, with just one door and a small window and there a yogi, a swami, who was quite elderly but youthful; who had done his M Phil. and then roamed the Himalayas, was living alone since so many years and how he explained about the science of unseasonal rains and what that meant for the rainy season and he had nothing else in his room except a small packet of Parle glucose biscuits which somebody had left in the morning and he opened it out for us and how after the rain stopped he had to leave that yogi and proceed almost in the setting sun to go towards Gangaria and how that area is infested with wild bears and even the local dogs have been fitted with spiked collars to save them from wild Bear attacks and here he was without his Kirpan or even a pen knife or a stick and how he reached the Gurudwara at Gangaria almost in total darkness at about 10:00 p.m. and had dhal roti and couple of blankets at the Gurudwara and so on and so on.

Keki: (He could have gone on but I had things to do so I had to cut him short). Very impressive and very interesting and I would like to spend more time on this with you some other time however right now let's get on with the program so please go back and take your seat.

Guneet: Thank you very much. I also enjoyed it a lot and I would like to hear your experience of the same also.

DEMO- 2

As Guneet Singh took his seat I called out loudly 'who's next? Come'. Padma stood up slowly from her seat and walked towards me. I motioned her towards her seat and with hand signals reminded the group to use their eyes. I sat up straight to be about 2 inches taller.

Keki: (in stern voice) So Padma, tell me all that you did yesterday from the time you got up from bed to the time you went back to bed at night.

Padma: Yesterday?

Keki: That's what I said (continuing with the same earlier tone of voice)

Padma: Yesterday was a bit of an unusual day.

Keki: I am waiting.

Padma: The alarm went off at 5:30 in the morning and I got up.

Keki: And that was unusual? What time do you get up every day?

Padma: No. That is my usual time. Some of the events that happened yesterday were unusual. (She looks at me).

Keki: Continue.

Padma: I went to the washroom for my morning duties, brushing teeth etc. Then I went to the hall- dining to sweep, swab, dust and generally tidying it up.

Keki: I thought you would go to the kitchen to prepare tea and breakfast for your family.

Padma: Yes. I did go to the kitchen after tidying up the Hall Diner, because I feel sending out the family members from a tidy home is auspicious for them. My elder son likes kanda-pohe (flattened rice with onion and other things) so I prepared that along with tea. My husband wakes up by about 6 o'clock and the eldest son soon thereafter. The younger one gets up around 7:30 to 9 anytime depending upon what time he went to sleep. It's about 7:30 and my husband comes for breakfast. While he is having his tea and breakfast the elder son comes down for his tea and breakfast, ready for going to his college. As they are having breakfast, I pack up their Tiffin which they carry with them. My younger son sometimes carries his Tiffin sometimes he doesn't and sometimes he brings the Tiffin back as it is unused.

Keki: My question was about what you did yesterday and you are giving me the narration of all your family members?

Padma: Sorry.

Keki: (I take audible deep breath, which makes her even more uncomfortable and then say) continue.

Padma: My husband and son left home little after 8 o'clock and I gave them their Tiffin. I picked up everything from the dining table, took them to the kitchen, came back and cleaned the dining table. Went to the kitchen and washed off the vessels I had used in the morning. I heard some sounds from the children's room and knew that my younger son was up. I called out for him but there was no answer. After completing the vessels, I went to his room and called out again, again there was no answer. I went behind him and pulled out the big earphones that he had around his ears and again called out his name. My son protested and said 'Mom. Don't do that. You are disturbing me.' I told him 'God should have sent you down with two big earphones around your ears instead of the ears. Aren't you going to the college today? What time are you going? I said, the college is at 10:00 and it is already past nine o'clock. Finally, he came to the Diner and I had tea and breakfast along with him. He gulped down his breakfast and was hurrying to leave when I asked him about his Tiffin, and he said he didn't want it because he was having something with his friends. So, by 9:45 I was all alone by myself. As usual, I cleaned up the kitchen; then cleaned up our bedroom and went to the children's room to clean it up. My elder son likes everything neat and tidy and things in its own place, so I had to be very careful to leave things arranged as they were. Cleaning of his side did not take much time. Whereas the younger son's area was fully messy. I was making his bed when I got my first major surprise. As I was tucking the cover under his bolster, I felt something. It was an envelope. I opened it and found ₹.1450/- inside it. I was shocked. Where did he get so much money from? What is he up to? Did he steal it from his dad? Or somebody else? What is he going to do with it? My God, I hope he is not into drugs. Who will cure him of drugs, Sir?

Keki: Yes. Parents can get devastated if such a thing happens. And particularly when imagination runs wild and takes over. So, what are you going to do about it?

Padma: I immediately wanted to call his papa and tell him everything. Somehow, I stopped myself, saying that my son, even the younger one cannot do all this and first I must find out. Not only that, I should make him say if he has any difficulty or problem. Initially I did not feel like having lunch also but then I had something and it was past

1 p.m. After that there are some yoga programs coming on the TV so I switched on the TV to learn yoga.

Keki: I have also done yoga. You cannot and should not learn yoga like that. After college when I went to Bombay for a job the yogashram was 10 -12 minutes' walk from my house.

A medical doctor, who is also adapt at Yoga, first examined me and then wrote out the Asana that I should be doing. After that, the yoga teacher taught me the asana. I attended yogashram for six months and felt the effect of it lasting for almost 10 years. Any good yogashram will follow that practice. You cannot and should not do Asana just because somebody knows some of them.

Padma: Something like that must have been going on in my mind because after that TV program I went to my younger son's laptop to do some research myself. I went to the videos section to see if I would find something on the YouTube. There was a file labeled 'private'. Out of curiosity I opened it. And there was the second Shock of the day. I came across some dirty pictures and videos. Is my son not only into drugs but also this type of a thing? What is happening to him? Have we as parents failed him completely? This is what was bothering me all through the evening and I was waiting for him to come home.

Keki: Wait a minute. You said the videos were dirty. I do not understand. Are you saying they were faded or something was sticking on them, like dirty dishes to be cleaned?

Padma: No, they were dirty. You know, no?

Keki: No, I don't. What was dirty about them?

Shankar: May be sex.

Keki: Was it? Padma?

Padma: Yes, dirty.

Keki: Are you telling me that I was born from dirt and dirty things that my father and mother did? All these people sitting here also are born out of dirty things. I thought what my parents did was something auspicious. Otherwise, I would not be here.

Padma: No, no. I will never say that, but the videos were dirty.

Keki: So, what you are saying is that what you do in the bedroom is ok, but if there is a picture or video of it then it becomes dirty. Tell me my friend, did your son have any sex education classes when he was in school?

Padma: No never. We sent him to a good School where our Samskara (=culture + ethics + values) was more important than sex education.

Keki: Good School, is it? I wonder. Did you give any sex education at home yourself?

Padma: We do not talk about such things at home; it is against our culture.

Keki: Culture changes with time. Sometimes for the better, sometimes for the worse. Centuries back, in this country sex was not a Taboo; it was a celebration; until Invaders from Central Asia came repeatedly via land, followed by some Europeans who came via sea. They both were able to loot and plunder this country and ultimately rule. Our present culture is a result of all the deletions and distortions that they made to promote their own interest. This has left a mark on the present-day culture. Centuries back we had hundreds or thousands of temples with erotic statues on it. Many of them can be seen even today. By the way how many sex videos did you see on your son's laptop?

Padma: There were three of them.

Keki: That's all? Only 3? So, what did you do after that, until your son returned?

Padma: I was broken. I was sulking. All sorts of Ideas were going around in my head as to who would be able to help my son.

Keki: And what happened when he came home?

Padma: He came home around 6:45 with those big earphones around his head. Unlike me he looked very happy. He went to his room. I was wondering how I would start the conversation. He was all ready and dressed up when he came out after half an hour. By that time my husband and elder son also came home. He said 'bye Mom I will not be home for dinner'. I told him 'You cannot go out I have to talk to you'. He said he had to go out because he has promised and he is part of a music and dance concert. He complained that he does not even have a proper guitar and he has to borrow it from his friends. That he can't wait as he is getting late and he walked out of the door.

Keki: Did you talk to your husband?

Padma: No, I was mostly quiet. I did not know how to start. And I went to bed by 9:30.

Keki: OK. Good, you can go now.

DISCUSSION ON DEMO

Padma got up to go towards her chair. I stood up and stopped her by holding onto her arm.

Keki: (To Padma) Wait, where are you going? Are you running away from me? (To all) What you just saw are two demonstrations of rapport making and rapport breaking. **Rapport is defined as, creating conditions of Trust, Harmony and Cooperation**. My question to all of you is- with whom was there a greater rapport, with Padma or with Guneet.

Those who spoke, said 'Guneet'

Keki: Guneet, did you enjoy talking to me?

Guneet: Yes of course, very much.

Keki: And Padma did you enjoy talking to me?

Padma: Yes, I did. I feel lighter now having talked to somebody at least.

Keki: Having spent so many years with NLP it is now easier for me to get into rapport rather than breaking rapport. In any case Padma has spent time with me at my home prior to the program and also full morning over here. The demo with her about breaking rapport was not perfect. Instead of breaking rapport, very often it went towards a directive therapy. You will learn more about directive and non-directive therapy on the fourth day morning.

We spent just a few minutes with each one of them. If in a few minutes we can create rapport or break rapport then isn't it useful to know how it was done? Yes? So first tell me which chair was responsible for what we did. Was it mine or the volunteer's?

In the group some say it was my chair, and some say both. So, I asked the volunteers as to what they were doing to me. They both said 'nothing'.

Guneet: I think whatever difference was there was made by you.

Jaya: You were rude to Padma; (with a smile) just like you were to me in the morning.

Keki: Yes, maybe. Whatever I do; whatever I say; whatever you expect me to do and I do not do; whatever you expect me to say and I do not say; everything is deliberate and with a purpose. And the purpose is to help the participant. My loyalty is always to the participant. Making a difference is more important to me than just being Goody Goody. So, what were the two operative words of the Great Master that we adopted over here? Yes 'Watch Us'. And remember as to which organ we use for watching. The eyes; right? Ok Jaya, tell me what did you watch to reach the opinion that I was rude?

Jaya: Your voice was loud and harsh.

Keki: Oh, so your eyes can hear also?

Jaya: No, but there was nothing to watch so I was listening to you both.

Keki: Nothing to watch? Maybe both of us were invisible. The rest of you, what did you see? I want only the facts not opinions, and not what you heard.

Saira: You are more attentive to Guneet and not so much to Padma.

Keki: More attentive. Is that an opinion Saira or a fact?

Saira: Sorry, yes that is an opinion.

Keki: Thanks. So, what is it that you observed which brings you to this opinion?

Saira: With Guneet, you were slightly leaning towards him, whereas with Padma you were sort of laid back, excuse me, that becomes an opinion again, you were leaning backwards.

Keki: Did anyone else observe anything else.

Nirav: You were sitting almost the same way as Guneet was sitting, whereas with Padma you were sitting in a very different style.

Keki: So, tell me how were Guneet's legs and feet placed and how were mine.

Gautam: Guneet had his feet flat on the ground and so were yours.

Keki: Were Guneet's two feet placed the same way?

Gautam: I am not sure. I did not notice it so well.

Keki: Guneet was sitting on my right and his left foot was slightly inside and the right foot a little more forward. And how were my feet? Did anybody observe?

Ankur: At one time I thought I saw Guneet's right foot turning a little more towards you and soon after your left foot turning a little towards him.

Keki: Good. Now we are talking. Once again remember that **we communicate only 7% by our choice of words. 38% of the communication is the way we speak those words and 55% of our communication is through body language.**

So, my legs and feet were listening to Guneet's legs and feet and answering back in the same language. My body posture was listening to Guneet's body posture and answering back in the same language. Whereas with Padma I was purposely mismatching whatever she was doing and that is what made all the difference. Yet you are all hooked up on the 7%, the choice of words.

Shankar: But why is that so?

Keki: Because of our education system and the ignorance of our educators.

10 POINTS OF RAPPORT MAKING

Here is the handout regarding rapport making. Start reading from the top. Let us start from the left hand over here. Gautam, please start.

Gautam: 'Rapport. The structure of matching. The basic rapport building pattern is matching. Matching is the process whereby you adjust the same aspects of your external behavior to approximate those same aspects of the other person's external behavior. For example, when the other person tilts his or her head to his or her left you adjust the tilt of your head in a corresponding fashion to match his or her particular movement '

Keki: Stop. Gautam, just raise your right hand up. Now when I raise my right hand up, I am matching you. However, I can also raise my left hand up and then I am mirroring you. Both will have the same effect. Next person; Anwar, please read it further.

Anwar: 'The ongoing process of matching is referred to as pacing: that is, you move as the other person moves, matching his or her sequence of movements.'

Keki: So, if we both raise our one hand up and then if he moves his hand down on his head to stroke his hair and I do the same and then he moves his hand towards his cheek I will do the same. I will be pacing him. Next.

Lily: 'The chart below offers a variety of behavior outputs to match that can lead to creating very powerful states of rapport, both consciously and unconsciously.'

Keki: Both consciously and unconsciously. My question to all of you is which one do you think will be more powerful? (More than half the group said 'unconsciously' some with certainty and a few in a questioning manner) Yes. Remember our breathing experiment? Anwar's response even with closed eyes occurred unconsciously. Lily, please continue with the next line.

Lily: 'Mastering the art of matching will develop your ability and give you choices to establish rapport with anybody you choose.'

Keki: Anybody you choose. Any age, any sex, any skin color, any known person, any stranger, any friend, any 'difficult' person. Understand? Just about anybody. Next person. One by one.

Shankar: 'Whole body matching. Adjust your body to approximate the other person's postural shifts.'

Nirav: 'Body part matching. Pacing any consistent or stylistic use of body movements; i.e., eye blinks.'

Padma: 'Half body matching. Match the upper or lower portion of the other person's body.'

Keki: Suppose you are sitting across the table or standing at the counter and you are not able to see the lower half of the person. You will match the portion that you can see but go beyond that. Imagine how that person's hidden body parts maybe placed and you take that stance; when the other person makes some movement in the hidden part you will be able to make out and you make some corresponding move. Please continue.

Guneet: 'Head shoulders angle patterns predicates. Match characteristic poses that the other person offers with his or her head shoulders and predicates.'

Manju: 'Vocal (analogue) qualities. Match shifts in tonality, tempo, volume, timber, intonation patterns.'

Keki: If you noticed, I was maintaining the same volume, tone, speed and other qualities of tonality with Guneet. Whereas with Padma, even before she sat down in the chair, I had raised my volume and tone. Next person.

Saira: 'Verbal. Hear and utilize sensory system predicates and match and pace the sequence of representational system predicates used by the other person.'

Manju: Can you please explain this, Keki.

Keki: It means Manju, that if the other person is using words like ' I see', or 'the picture is clear to me now', and so on, then you also respond using Visual types of words like 'so shall we focus on the further path now' or something like that. Similarly, if you find the other person using more Auditory words or Kinesthetic words you will respond back in the same representational system. Next please.

Saira: 'Facial expressions. See the ways in which the other person uses their face; i.e. wrinkles his or her nose, puckers his or her lips, raises his or her eyebrows'.

Jaya: 'Gestures. Matching the other person's gestures in ways that are elegant and respectful.'

Keki: Everybody pay attention over here. Gestures are hand movements. This is the only place where they are asking us to be elegant and respectful. This will determine whether you are making rapport or copying and aping the other person. If you had noticed me with Guneet, I was repeating Guneet's hand movements but not immediately; I was doing it while responding to what he was saying. Understood? Any questions? None? Good. Next person.

Vipul: 'Repetitive phrasing. Hear and utilize the repeated phrases of the other person.'

Ankur: 'Breathing. Adjust your breathing patterns to match the other person's breathing patterns.'

Keki: This is a very powerful rapport making tool. Next.

Anu: 'Indirect matching (cross over mirroring) using one aspect of your behavior to match a different aspect of the other person's behavior; i.e. adjusting the tempo of voice to match the other persons rate of breathing; pacing the other person's eye blinks with your finger or head nods.

Keki: Thank you. Imagine Anwar is going to his boss's cabin and as he enters, he finds his boss is digging his nose. What will he do? Will he also start digging his nose? (Laughter) Of course not. But if he has a ball pen in his hand with a clicker at the top for getting the refill in and out, he can start clicking it as his boss is digging his nose. Can't he? Or he can tell his boss 'Sir, have you seen what they are doing at the entrance of a building? They are digging it up and it looks so dirty. You cannot even enter the building easily. Such things can be done after office hours when everybody is done with their work.

RAPPORT EXCERSIZE

Now; what we have done so far is totally useless. You can all bring your handouts here so we can burn them. (The group looks at me quizzically and says no, no). It is useless. Can somebody tell me why it is useless?

Gautam: Because this is only theory until we put it into practice, is that so?

Keki: Precisely. They say 'an ounce of practice is worth a ton of theory'. So, shall we practice it? Who wants to learn how to create rapport?

The group: (loudly) 'I'.

Keki: Who wants to have fun? Unlimited fun.

The group: (once again louder this time) 'I'.

Keki: So please get up; arrange two chairs facing each other and the third one in between at a little distance for the observer. One group will have four members, so two of them will be observers. Occupy these chairs. Out of the two facing each other, one is rapport maker and the other is a client. Right now, you are not going to be elegant and respectful. The rapport maker has to copy everything that the client does. It is the client's job to make the Rapport maker cry. The client can climb up on the chair and do some dance; he or she can go under the chair and come out from the other side; whatever weird things the client does, the rapport maker has to copy. It is all monkey see; monkey do. Forget about what you talk. You can make some monkey sounds and The Rapport maker will have to copy that. Remember you are here to train your partner. The more difficult the client makes, more the rapport maker will learn. After about two minutes Aban will ask you all to stop and change places. At that time, you change places in rotation either clockwise or anticlockwise. Before you change places, the observer will give some observation of what you did, out of the 10 points and what result he or she observed. Some people have a habit of focusing on what is not done. May be, they enjoy finding other's faults. Please do not do that. Just give a feedback on what 2 or 3 things they did and what you think was the result of it.

But before you start let me loosen you all up a little bit. Come on, copy me. Do all that I do. Say all that I say. (I stretch my arms, take certain body postures, and the group follows me.) Am I doing all this sitting down? Come on; copy everything that I do and what I say. (The group gets up, follows all my stupid moves, makes the senseless sounds that I make. I sit in the chair with a sigh. They do the same. I turn around in the chair and take my legs up on the back rest. I check if everybody is doing it. A few are not. Gautam has talked about his back pain. Padma is feeling shy because of her saree. Lily is in her own world. I goad some of them successfully to do it. Then I get off the chair on the ground on all four and start barking like a dog; OAF, OAF, OAF. The group is doing the same to each other and having fun out of it.)

Keki: Good. Go ahead. Do your exercise now. Make a Hungama (Cacophony). Have lots of fun.

(And I left the hall to go down near the swimming pool to my private place. After giving them adequate time, I came up again to a noisy boisterous group having hell of a lot of fun. I give them time to finish the pending matters.)

Keki: So, was it fun? Who had fun? (The group shouted 'We') It is almost 4.20 now. Let us break now for some tea, coffee and cookies and come back in 15 minutes to understand a little bit about how our brain functions.

OUR BRAIN

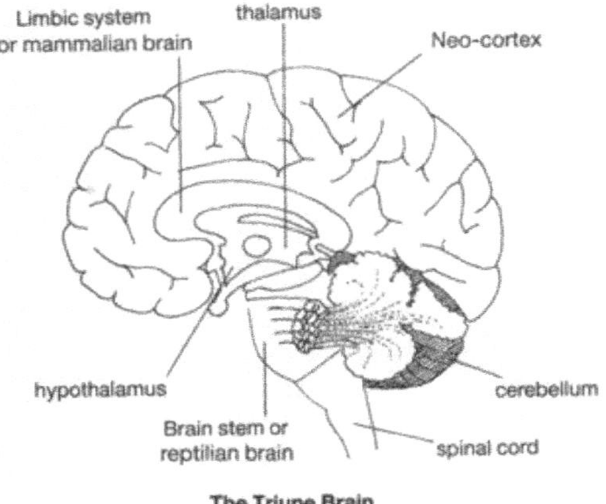

Figure 4

Keki: Our brain is called a triune brain. Why? Because it is in three layers. When the sperm of a male penetrates the ova of a female and becomes a single cell; our journey as a human begins. In the mother's stomach, it undergoes the journey that took place on this planet from the time life began. So that single cell breaks up into two, like in an Amoeba. Then 2 into 4 and 4 into 8 and so on until it starts to look like a tiny fish. Then it develops two appendages which become our arms. Even a little tail is formed. Now it looks like a tadpole, an amphibian. Then onwards it starts taking the form of a human. Doctor Nirav, I would appreciate if you stop me and correct me whenever you think I am erring He nods). The most basic level of our brain is the reptilian brain. Our spinal cord is connected to it. As shown in the accompanying Figure 5.

Everything that is needed to keep this finely tuned Electrochemical Machine in a perfect running order is programmed into our reptilian brain, including all our autonomous working systems. Reptiles would lay their eggs and move away. They have a sense of territory; and therefore, protection of that territory. Therefore, aggression is in the most basic part of our brain. Then came the mammals. The mammalian brain is over the reptilian brain. Mammals give birth to a fully formed baby and then nurture it for some time. Therefore, love is in this part of the brain. Of our interest is the third layer, the neocortex; which makes us who and what we are as humans.

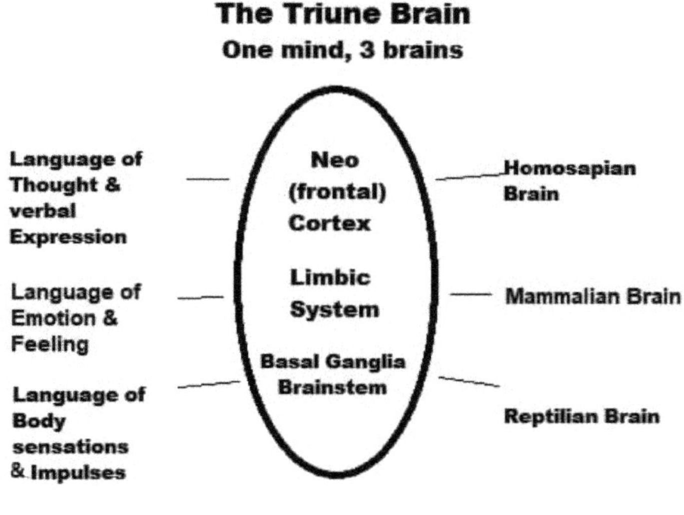

Figure 5

Figure 5 also shows these three layers and their functions.

Has anybody seen the actual brain? Dr Nirav raises his hand. Of course, doctor, you would have.

Anwar: I have seen a goat's brain.

Guneet Singh: I have seen the human brain being sliced. My friend was doing her medical studies and she was in the mortuary dissecting a brain.

Keki: Very good. How about a model of a brain or a picture of a brain for the rest of you?

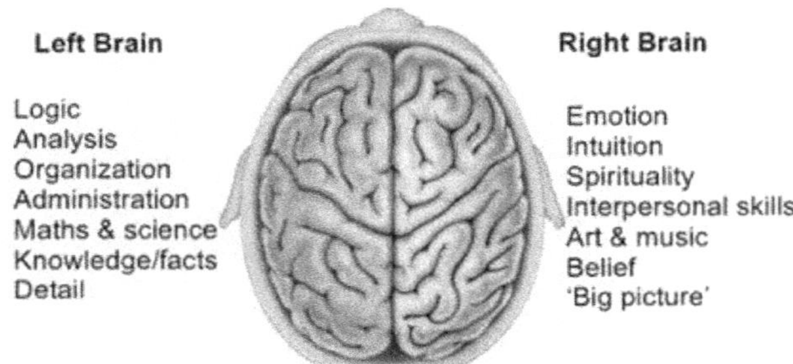

Figure 6

The group: Few say 'a model' the rest say 'a picture'.

Keki: If you look at the brain top down you will see that it is in two halves connected together by what we call as the Corpus Callosum. The left side of your brain is logical, sequential, and analytical. It is like a serial processor. Reading, writing, arithmetic, solving Sudoku puzzles is all done by the left brain. Whereas the right side of your brain is like a parallel processor. It takes things holistically. Remembering faces, your emotions and so many other things, are all functions of the right side of your brain. Now we can demonstrate this. I need one volunteer. (Ankur raises his hand. I take out my left hand as if holding a brain in it and chop it into two with my right hand. Ankur tries to get up with a smile.)

Keki: Stay seated. Ankur, tell me your father's name.

Ankur: Mohandas.

Keki: Please spell it. (Ankur spells it and I purposely miss spell it and write on the board MOHANSAD)

Ankur: That's not correct.

Keki: Oh sorry. Please spell it again. (Ankur spells it and I purposely miss spell it again and write on the board MOHANSAD)

Ankur: (puzzled) That's not correct again.

Jaya, Manju and Vipul: The spelling is wrong again.

(I repeat the same thing one more time. Now people smell a rat and are quiet)

Keki: Ok, forget the spelling part and just describe his face to me I will draw it. (Ankur describes his father's face as somewhat oval with big eyes, thick eyebrows, a mouth. 2 ears, a nose, bald at the top with a little hair on the sides and the figure comes out something like in figure 7,) what is your mother's name Ankur?

Figure 7

Ankur: Mohini.

Keki: So, if I show this picture to Mohini and ask who this is? She is going to say ' Oh, that's my darling Mohandas, isn't it?

Ankur: (with disgust) Of course not.

Keki: Oh, I know I am not so good at drawing faces. Who scored high on V in the morning test? Was it you Lily?

Lily: No, I scored a zero, remember?

Keki: Oh yes, a zero.

Now, what shall we do? Shall we call M F Hussain? Do you think if he was still alive, he would have been able to draw Ankur's father's face as per his description?

Ankur: He should have seen my father or my father's photograph.

Keki: Correct. He had to experience your father's face. Figure 6 showed the comparison between the left brain and right brain. What we call mind can be compared to an iceberg as shown in figure 8. Can somebody tell me what the line A B is?

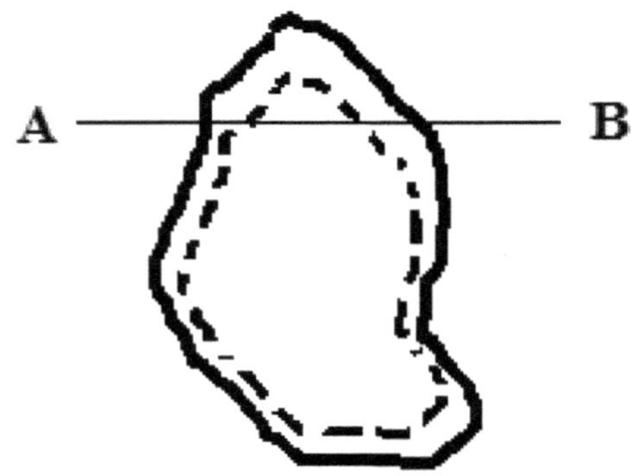

Figure 8

Ankur: That is the water level.

Keki: Correct. Only about 10% of the Iceberg can be seen above the water line. 90% is submerged. That 10% is like our conscious part of the mind. And the 90% is like the subconscious mind; hidden from our consciousness. **What we are going to do during the program is going to affect our entire mind. However even at the end of the program we will be aware of the changes that happen consciously and in the 10% of our brain. 9 times more change will happen as we live out our life.** My daughters and some friends have suggested to me as to why I do not take feedback at the end of the program. The reason is that it would be injustice to my participants. That type of a feedback will only give a message to the participant's subconscious that this is it and nothing more. It can therefore stop further progress. **There is no logic in the right brain. The right brain takes things literally. That is why we make our affirmations as if the thing has already happened and in the present tense.** When somebody does not use logic or is illogical, we tend to brand that person as an idiot. Just in that sense you may apply it to the right brain where most of our past experiences, long term memories and programs may be stored.

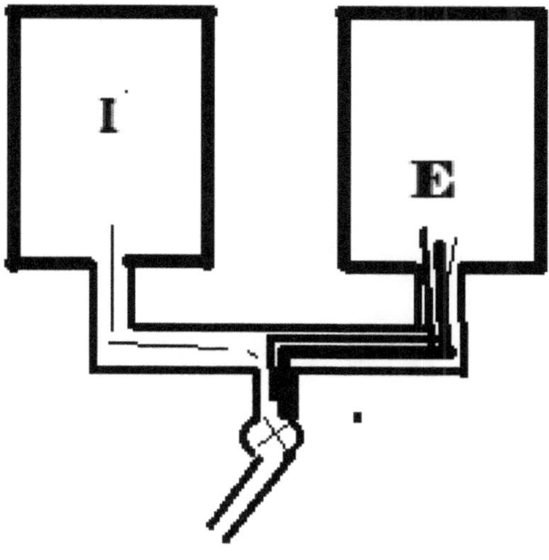

Figure 9

Let us look at our brain slightly differently now. Figure 9 shows two water tanks. From the left tank, intelligence comes down and from the right one, emotions. These two then combine and lead to our action. Have you seen someone raving mad, angry? Have you seen any family where there might have been a sudden death of a young person? The family is so devastated and highly emotional that, even the funeral details are left to a close relative. So much of emotion is coming down under pressure from the right brain that no intelligence from the left brain can have any effect. When a person is very angry or highly emotional otherwise, she or he is not able to make any rational useful decisions. Let us now look at the brain functioning one more way. As we already know we have just 5 windows to the world V, A, K, O, & G. I look at you, I am aware of it. You say something, I can hear it. Likewise, if somebody touches me, I feel something within me, taste something, and smell something. I am aware of all this. I am taking it in through my conscious part of the brain. It stays in my short-term memory. Then it gets processed. At the time of processing, our past programming, our values, our beliefs, play a part. And that Wall of our values and beliefs is indicated in figure 10. Once it passes through that Wall, either as it is, or modified in whichever way, then it enters our long-term memory in the subconscious brain and stays there.

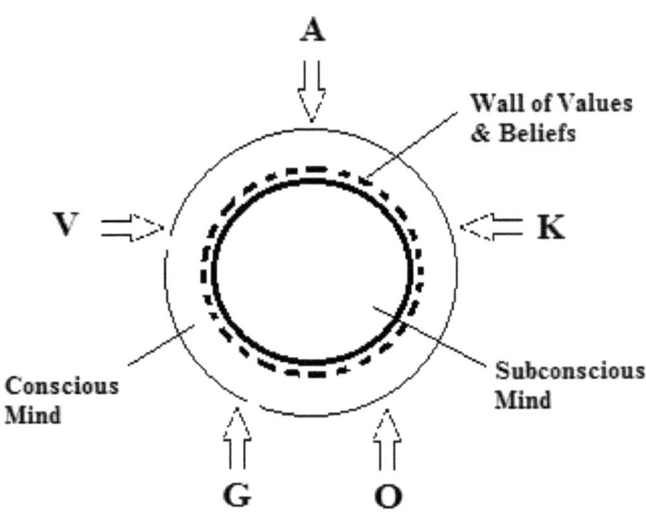

Figure 10

The conscious part contains your short-term memory, will power, rationality and logic, analytical ability and sequence, the concept of time, what comes first and what comes next. You are generally aware of all these. Willpower, I say, is what you do on the 31st of December and if you are lucky it may last till 2nd or 3rd of January. Your New Year resolutions. Why? Because Will Power itself is located in your short-term memory.

Subconscious part of your mind contains your long-term memory, emotions, habits, values and beliefs, as well as your identity.

Ankur: Keki, what is the difference between the subconscious and the unconscious.

Keki: Here I am using it interchangeably; however, I would like to believe that if the program already exists in your mind but you are not aware (conscious) of it and you are bringing it to awareness then it is coming from your subconscious. However, if something is not there in your subconscious also and you are somehow, sort of downloading it, making brand new connections, may be from the universe, then I say it comes from the unconscious.

Just as we have electrocardiogram ECG for our heart; we have an EEG electroencephalogram for our brain. It measures our brain waves frequency.

For a child of about four years of age the brain is beating at four cycles per second. Then every year it increases by one cycle.

During normal working day life your brain is beating between 14 and 21 cycles per second. The Beta frequency.

When you are about to wake up or just about falling off to sleep, your brain is beating between 7 and 14 cycles per second; called, the Alpha frequency.

When you are sleeping including the dreaming state, your brain is beating between 4 and 7 cycles per second. Called, the Theta frequency.

Something to 4 cycles is your deep sleep. Called, The Delta frequency.

When that becomes zero, you are on your way up; brain dead.

For our interest it is the Alpha frequency; because that is when you are able to communicate with your subconscious. Realize one thing. In any major religion the deep religious initiation ceremonies are held between the ages of 7 and 11. Why? Because that is when the brain is beating between 7 and 11 cycles per second, or the Alpha frequency, and whatever is given goes straight into the subconscious, the long-term memory.

Now my question to all of you is. Is anybody interested in learning how to get into Alpha? (Almost all say 'yes'. I raise my voice and ask) ok, who is interested to learn how to get into Alpha? (Now everybody says loudly 'I').

Good. I suggest you all take a small bio break and come back. However, before you go let us do a little something.

HOME PLAY

Tell me how many of you are parents? (About eight of them raise their hands). I know that the parents just love to do the homework. Whose homework? Yes, their child's homework. Therefore, I do not give any homework to parents. I give Home Play. And the home play for all of you is this.

From the time you go out this evening till the time you come back tomorrow morning, you are going to do rapport with whoever you meet. You will be elegant and respectful while doing rapport. How will you know that you are in rapport? One of these two things will happen or even both can happen. a) The person may voluntarily give much more information than you have asked and b) If you make a certain body movement the other person follows you unconsciously. When either of these two happens, you know that you are in rapport. It may take you 2 minutes to get into Rapport, or it may take you 20. Tomorrow morning the program will start only after each and every one of you have shared at least two of your success stories. Out of these, one should be with a stranger and one with a known person. Are we clear? Good. Now take your Bio break.

CLOSING EXERCISE, GETTING INTO ALPHA

Keki: Ok come on back. Pack up everything before we start the closing exercise.

Please empty your laps now. Good. Put your feet flat on the ground, sit up straight, backbone straight, push your tailbone into the chair, take a deep breath, close your eyes, and while exhaling mentally repeat and visualize Number 3, three times.

Take another deep breath and while exhaling mentally repeat and visualize number 2 three times.

Take another deep breath and while exhaling, mentally repeat and visualize number 1 three times.

You are now at level 1. This is a basic plain level that you can use for a purpose, any purpose you desire.

To help you enter a deeper, healthier level of mind, I am going to count from 10 to 1. On every descending number you will feel yourself going deeper and you will enter a deeper healthier level of mind.

10, 9, feel going deeper; 8, 7, 6 deeper and deeper; 5, 4, 3 deeper and deeper, 2, 1.

You are now at a deeper healthier level of Mind deeper than before. To help you enter a deeper healthier level of mind I am going to direct your attention to different parts of your body.

Concentrate your sense of awareness on your scalp, the skin that covers your head. You will detect a fine vibration a tingling sensation that is there a feeling of warmth caused by circulation. Now release and relax all tensions and ligament pressures from this part of your head completely and place it in a deep state of relaxation that will continue to get deeper and deeper as we continue.

Concentrate your sense of awareness on your forehead, the skin that covers your forehead, you will detect a fine vibration, a tingling sensation that is there, a feeling of warmth caused by circulation. Now release and relax all tension and ligament pressures from this part of your head completely and place it in a deep state of relaxation that will continue to get deeper and deeper as we continue.

Concentrate your sense of awareness on the eyelids and the tissues surrounding your eyes. You will detect a fine vibration, a tingling sensation that is there, a feeling of warmth caused by circulation. Now release and relax all tensions and ligament pressures from this part of your head completely and place it in a deep state of relaxation that will continue to get deeper and deeper as we continue.

Concentrate your sense of awareness on your face, the skin covering your cheeks. You will detect a fine vibration, a tingling sensation that is there, a feeling of warmth caused by circulation. Now release and relax all tensions and ligament pressures from this part of your head completely and place it in a deep state of relaxation that will continue to get deeper and deeper as we continue.

Concentrate on the outer portion of your throat, the skin covering your throat area. You will detect a find vibration, a tingling sensation that is there, a feeling of warmth, caused by circulation. Now release and relax all tensions and ligament pressure from this part of your body completely and place it in a deep state of relaxation that will continue to get deeper and deeper as we continue.

Concentrate within the throat area and relax all tensions and ligament pressures from this part of your body and place this part of your body in a deep state of relaxation going deeper and deeper every time.

Concentrate on your shoulders. Feel your clothing in contact with your body, feel the skin and the vibration of the skin covering this part of your body. Relax all tensions and ligament pressures and place this part of your body in a deep state of relaxation going deeper and deeper every time.

Concentrate on your chest. Feel your clothing in contact with this part of your body. Feel the skin and the vibration of your skin covering this part of your body. Relax all tensions and ligament pressures and place this part of your body in a deep state of relaxation that is going deeper and deeper every time.

Concentrate within the chest area. Relax all organs, relax all glands, relax all tissues, including the cells themselves and cause them to function in a rhythmic healthy manner.

Concentrate on your abdomen. Feel the clothing in contact with this part of your body. Feel the skin and the vibration of your skin covering this part of your body. Relax all tensions and ligament pressures and place this part of your body in a deep state of relaxation that is going deeper and deeper every time.

Concentrate within the abdominal area. Relax all organs, relax all glands, relax all tissues including the cells themselves and cause them to function in a rhythmic, healthy manner.

Concentrate on your thighs. Feel your clothing in contact with this part of your body. Feel the skin and the vibration of your skin covering this part of your body. Relax all tensions and ligament pressures and place this part of your body in a deep state of relaxation that is going deeper and deeper every time.

Sense the vibration at the bones within the thighs, by now this should be easily detectable.

Concentrate on your knees. Feel the skin and the vibration of your skin covering the knees. Relax all tensions and ligament pressures and place this part of your body in a deep state of relaxation that is going deeper and deeper every time.

Concentrate on your calves. Feel the skin and the vibration of your skin covering the calves. Relax all tensions and ligament pressures and place this part of your body in a deep state of relaxation that is going deeper and deeper every time.

To enter a deeper, healthier level of Mind, concentrate on your toes. Enter a deeper healthier level of mind.

To enter a deeper healthier level of Mind, concentrate on the soles of your feet. Enter a deeper, healthier level of mind.

To enter a deeper healthier level of Mind, concentrate on the Heels of your feet. Enter a deeper healthier level of Mind.

Now cause your feet to feel as though they do not belong to your body. Feel your feet as though they do not belong to your body.

Your feet feel as they do not belong to your body.

Your feet ankles calves and knees feel as though they do not belong to your body.

Your feet, ankles, calves, knees, thighs, waist, shoulders arms and hands feel as though they do not belong to your body.

You are now at a deeper healthier level of Mind, deeper than before.

Establish this as your frame of reference. Any time you take a deep breath and while exhaling visualize Number 3 three times, you will automatically and at once reach this level of physical relaxation, and more so every time you practice.

To help you enter a deep and healthy level of mind I am going to count from 1 to 3. At that moment you will project yourself mentally to your ideal place of relaxation. Your ideal place of relaxation maybe a place where you have already been, or a place that you would like to be in. Your ideal place of relaxation maybe on the mountain top, seaside, a lake, river, forest, garden, anywhere. I will then stop talking to you and when you hear my voice again, one hour of time will have elapsed at this level of mind. My voice will not startle you. You may take a deep breath and as you exhale you will relax and go deeper.

1 (pause) 2 (pause) 3. Project yourself mentally to your ideal place of relaxation until you hear my voice again for now. Relax (snap fingers. Remain silent for about 30 seconds).

Take a deep breath and as you exhale, relax and go deeper.

Establish this as your frame of reference. Any time you take a deep breath and while exhaling, visualize number 2-three times, you will automatically and at once reach this level of mental relaxation. And more so every time you practice.

You will continue to listen to my voice. You will continue to follow the instructions at this level or any other level, including the outer conscious level. This is for your benefit; you desire it and it is so. Whenever you hear me mention the word relax all unnecessary movements and activities of your body, brain and mind will immediately cease and you will become completely passive and relaxed physically and mentally. I may bring you out of this level or a deeper level by counting to you from 1 to 5. At the count of 5 your eyes will open you will be wide awake feeling fine and in perfect health.

I may bring you out of this level by touching your left shoulder three times. When you feel my hand touch your left shoulder for the third time, your eyes will open you will be Wide Awake feeling fine and in perfect health. And this is so

The difference between genius mentality and Lay mentality is that geniuses use more of their mind and use it in a special manner. You are now able to use more of your mind and use it in a special manner.

Repeat mentally after me.

My increasing mental faculties are for serving humanity better.

Every day, in every way I am getting better, better and better.

Positive thoughts bring me benefits and advantages I Desire.

Negative thoughts have no influence over me at any level of the mind. Negative thoughts will never have an influence over me at any level of the mind.

I will always maintain a perfectly healthy body and mind.

I have full control and complete Dominion over my faculties and senses at this level of the mind or any other level including the outer conscious level. And this is so.

Affirmations: At this point you can repeat the affirmations that you might have made for yourself.

Recap of the day: Let us recap what we did all day today. Start from how you woke up this morning and all that you did till you entered this seminar hall. (Pause 10 seconds) You were perhaps greeted by Aban or me and then I handed you over your manual and I asked you to go through the single page handout within it. You registered your name in the register and put your first name on your ID. Maybe you had your cup of tea or coffee and went through the SMS handout while you were waiting for others to come. When everybody was in and had gone through the SMS, I started the program by welcoming you all to it. We discussed the parts of the SMS that affected you. Then we started the program with an exercise. The exercise was in four parts mainly you having fun, you learning something new that was so easy, you learning something new putting a lot of energy and time and money, and integrating all this within you. Then you heard the story of the Archer and the Great Master whose key words were 'watch me'. You got some idea about Sensory Acuity and Submodalities. We did 3 exercises on sensory acuity starting with K, followed by A, followed by V. We learnt something about the Lead System and Preferred Representational System. After tea break, we praised the partner sitting in the chair using V, A and K words, or predicates. You received the handout for rep. system phrases. We elicited ourselves on V, A and K scores. Then we worked on the Eye Accessing Cues. Followed it up by learning about submodalities including Associated and Dissociated states. After lunch we put together whatever we learnt in the morning to see what effect it could have on our past experiences. We saw that the language of visualization is within us. We did an experiment on

Breathing Induction. You experienced two different situations of rapport making and rapport breaking. You learnt what influences rapport making. And then you practiced aping and mimicking and to loosen out, you copied me including getting onto the floor and barking OAF.OAF. OAF like a dog. After tea break, we learnt about our Triune Brain and various models regarding the same. Right now, you have learnt how to get into Alpha Frequencies.

Fast time slow time:

Think of a time when time flew. Maybe you are reading a very absorbing book. You felt you were reading it for 40 minutes when actually it was 3 hours. Or you are seeing a very entertaining movie. Maybe you are having sex and time just flew, when you felt, oh my God, so much time already gone? Make a picture of something like this. Frame it and leave it there.

Now think of a time when time dragged. Maybe you're waiting for a loved one to come back home late in the evening and the person is not yet back and you are fretting. Few minutes seem like half an hour. Time drags. Or maybe you are waiting at the street corner where you have arranged to meet someone important. And you are waiting and waiting and the person does not come. Time drags. Make a picture of something like this and frame it. Now mentally take frame number 2 and snap it on top of frame number 1. For the duration of this program until the 5th day evening you will be 'fast time' inside 'slow time' outside. Once again take frame number 2 of time drags and snap on top of frame Number 1, Time Flies. For the duration of this program till the 5th day evening you will be fast time inside slow time outside.

Every time you function at these levels of the mind you will receive beneficial effects physically and mentally.

You may use these levels of the mind to help yourself physically and mentally.

You may use these levels of the mind to help your loved ones physically and mentally.

You may use these levels of the mind to help any human being who needs help physically and mentally.

You will always use these levels of the mind in a constructive creative manner for all that is good, honest, pure, clean and positive.

You will never use these levels of the mind to hurt any human being. If this be your intention, you will not be able to function within these levels of the mind. And this is so.

You will continue to strive to take part in constructive and creative activities to make this a better world to live in, so that when we move on to have left behind a better world for those who follow. You will consider the whole of humanity depending on their ages as fathers or mothers, brothers or sisters, sons or daughters. You are a superior human being; you have greater understanding, compassion and patience with your fellowmen.

Bring out: In a moment I am going to count from 1 to 5. At that moment you will open your eyes, be Wide Awake, feeling fine and in perfect health, feeling better than before. You will have no ill effects whatsoever in your head, no headache, no ill effects whatsoever in your hearing, no buzzing in the ears, no ill effect whatsoever in your vision and eye sight. Vision, eye sight and hearing improve every time you function at these levels of the mind. 1, (pause) 2, coming out slowly now. 3, become aware of your body. At the count of 5 you will open your eyes be Wide Awake, feeling fine and in perfect health, feeling better than before. 4, become aware of your environment and 5, eyes open, wide awake, feeling fine, in perfect health feeling better than before, feeling healthier than before, feeling happier than before. Smile at the world and smile at your neighbors.

CHAPTER 3

DAY 2

Once all the 13 participants were in the seminar hall, I took my Central position.

Keki: So, how are we all today? (From the group some said fine, some said good and a few said excellent)

Once again, I welcome each and every one of you for this second day of our program.

All Rise please. (All 15 of us were standing now)

Good morning.

Group: Good morning.

Keki: Every morning is a good morning.

Group: Every morning is a good morning.

Keki: Because I make it a good morning.

Group: Because I make it a good morning.

Keki: Today is a good day.

Group: Today is a good day.

Keki: Because I am going to Make it a good day.

Group: Because I am going to Make it a good day.

Keki: Thank you. Please sit down. Who wants to come first? Please come.

RAPPORT SHARING

Lily: Homework?

Keki: Home play. You want to start? (I move towards the right vacating the central space and indicating it I said 'come'. Lily rushes to the spot with somewhat a glee on her face.

Lily: (Facing the group) It does not work.

Keki: What? (I was already finding her behavior a little queer) You are here to share your success story?

Lily: Yes.

Keki: Yes what? Did you do anything?

Lily: Yes, I tried and it does not work.

Keki: Good Discovery. (In my over a decade of experience-till then- I was facing this situation for the third time and I was wondering about some similarities. I recalled that in yesterday's closing exercise of getting into Alpha, there was a conscious body movement with a slight shrug of her shoulders, when the word 'father' had come up.) So, Lily can you move slightly to the left so that we can hear what some others have to say. (She moves towards the left making the center portion available).

Whoever has a successful success story, please come.

Gautam came up and took position in the center facing the group with Lily on his left and me on his right.

Gautam: Yesterday during lunch break I got a call from my friend saying that my distant cousin and a good friend is in the hospital with an accident and he gave me the name of the hospital. So yesterday evening straight from here I went to the hospital. I quietly entered his private Room Number 21 and was taken aback. My cousin's bed headrest was against the left wall, his face was bruised and swollen, he was bandaged at several places. He had a saline bottle injection needle in his right hand. I was more taken aback to find my aunt (my father's sister) sitting on a chair next to him instead of his mother. His mother has always been good to me and happens to be the sister-in-law of my aunt. This aunt of mine has refused to even look at me since past few years and we have not even had eye contact during all those years. As I approached my cousin to greet him, I noticed my aunt moving her chair little away from me even though there was enough space. My cousin enquired mainly with hand signals as to when did I come here from Singapore. He had difficulty in speaking so I just answered 'a week back'. I pulled another chair out to sit behind my aunt at an angle and even out of her peripheral vision. I was at a loss as to what to do. So, I said 'Rapport' to myself. The saline was reaching the bottom of the bag. My aunt picked up the buzzer button and pressed for the nurse. I matched her movement. I sat exactly the way she was sitting.

All three of us were quiet, but whatever small movement she made I was matching those. I searched for her breathing patterns but was not successful. Now this saline was getting almost empty and she buzzed for the nurse once again. I matched this time once again. It must have been about 10 minutes since I entered and I had not spoken a word except what I did with my cousin. Suddenly I find my aunt turning towards me and asking as to how I am. I said 'fine aunty, but just a minute, please'. The Saline would have been empty from the pipe also, so I got up to close the valve at the needle and went out saying 'I will get the nurse'.

I went and stood at the nursing station. The nurse was taking out something from the cabinet drawer and putting it in a tray. Her actions were quick. The call indicator showed our room number 21 plus two more. She quickly switched off one of the other two and quick-stepped out of the cabin to that room. I waited for her and sat down in one of the chairs close by. A few minutes later she quick-stepped back into the station and I matched her walk up to the counter and stood there quietly. The phone rang and she was attending to the phone. I took out my cell phone and did something. As she finished her call, I also stopped the phone and put it in my pocket. I said to her 'quite a busy day for you, isn't it'? She responded 'yes, are you waiting for me?' I said 'yes, the saline bottle is totally empty'. She asked 'Room 21?' I nodded. She stopped what she was doing picked up another saline bottle with some medicines, switched off number 21 and quick-stepped to our room. As I was matching my steps with her, she said 'you should have told me earlier when you saw me'

Saying this she entered the room and I followed behind her. She went straight to the saline stand and asked who shut the cock here. I said 'I'. She quickly finished replacing the bottle injecting the medicines into it and while on the way out she told my aunt 'Madam, you have a very smart son. I wish other patients had attendants like you all' and walked out of the room.

Once again, the room was quiet for a while and my cousin seemed to be resting peacefully. My aunt stood up from the chair and said with a slight smile ' I am going for some coffee, why don't you join me'. Actually, this made me feel good and I readily accepted. On the way out I stopped at the nursing station and told the nurse that 'we are going down for some coffee and this is actually my aunt; we are meeting after a very long time'. The nurse smiled back and said 'Oh, I am sorry. I will keep an eye on room 21'.

At the Coffee shop we ordered our coffee. My aunt was enquiring about my visit and what I was doing and when I said that I was attending a program and coming straight from there, she said 'then you must be hungry' and ordered some eats for us.

Gautam looks towards me and asks ' Keki, should I tell everything that we discussed because our conversation went on for over an hour?'

Keki: Absolutely not. Just the outcome and as to why you consider this as your success story.

Gautam: Totally unexpected and absolute reversal in her behavior towards me. Unbelievable. As for the outcome she wants me to go and meet my dad when she would also be present.

Keki: So, what are you going to do?

Gautam: We have tentatively decided to meet on Monday evening itself. I have never met him or had any contact since I walked out of my Kolkata house in a huff, 12 years back.

Keki: Close your eyes Gautam, and mentally just go through the 10 points of rapport making that you learnt yesterday. See how easy or difficult it was for you and the results that you got.

Gautam: But I have one more success story with a stranger.

Keki: Let's give chance to others also. You have already narrated what happened with the nurse. Just close your eyes and recall what all you did. (As Gautam goes through his experience, I pass on the handout on Hypnotic Language Patterns of Milton Erickson to the first participant sitting close to where I was standing and signaled her to read the last paragraph. I cup Gautam's right shoulder with the five fingers of my left hand as she reads out aloud.

"You can talk to someone about a client of Milton Ericsson's who wanted to really learn about hypnosis. He listened to Ericsson talk about hypnosis and thought that he understood. Then Erickson turned to him and said emphatically "you don't really know something until you've practiced every piece of it thoroughly!"

Keki: (After allowing time for Gautam to seep it in I remove my hand from his shoulder) OK Gautam, you can take your seat now.

Gautam: (looking at Keki) Thank you. Unbelievable. (Walks back to his seat)

Keki: Give him a big hand. (Everyone claps)

Before I could say 'next', Ankur raises his hand, gets up and walks up to the central point facing the group, smiling all The Way. He seemed to be in a hurry.

Ankur: (looking towards me) I can start? (I nod, 'yes') I was returning home on my motorcycle last evening from here when at one point I saw a young shapely thing on the scooter.

Saira: A 'thing?'

Ankur: Ok, sorry, I young girl.

Keki: Nobody will interrupt anybody while they are sharing. Understood. OK Ankur. Please continue.

Ankur: She was riding her scooter in the middle of the road, so I went on the left of her trying to see her face from her visor. Suddenly there was someone crossing her path and she braked. I also braked automatically although there was nobody in front of me. She glanced sideways at me and I returned the glance. I said to myself, this is almost like rapport making: let me see if I can continue. So, I slowed down every time she slowed down and I accelerated every time she accelerated. I swerved when she swerved.

(I could see that Saira wanted to say something again but I stopped her with my subtle hand signal.)

Ankur: There was someone in my way so I braked and to my surprise I found that she also braked. She took out her left hand and I was wondering if she wanted to hold my hand. I lifted up my visor. She withdrew her hand, switched on the left turn signal and lifted her visor. I gave her way to cross over to the left and once she crossed me, I caught up with her. As she was taking the left turn, she turned her face to look at me and smiled. I smiled back. (Looking towards me) did I make rapport?

Keki: I guess you did. What about your second story?

Ankur: That is also with the stranger; but a very important one, can I share it?

Keki: Go ahead.

Ankur: On the way was a computer shop and I wanted to buy some two gadgets. As I parked my bike a light drizzle started. I went inside the shop looking for the gadgets I wanted. I found one but could not find the other. So, I took the one and went to the cash counter and asked the counter guy regarding the second item. He said it was out of stock and that I can collect it tomorrow evening.

Keki: I will have to stop you here, Ankur. As you all know **NLP is content free. Who did what to who is not important. How our mind is processing it is important.** Words convey only 7% of communication. 93% is how we are saying those words and our body language. Throughout our life we have been brought up on words, words, words; 'I said this' and 'he said that', 'I said this' and 'he said that'. While sharing your experiences we do not want that. Keep that to the minimum necessary and focus on what you did out of those 10 points; what makes you think that you created rapport and what was the end result. That's all we are interested in. Normally the first one who comes up for sharing is at a disadvantage because I have to interrupt that person for this. This group is really fabulous because you all are learning fast. So Ankur, please continue.

Ankur: I am sorry. I will try. As I came out of the shop, I saw that the drizzle had now turned into a shower. I went towards my bike and over there I saw the most amazing thing of my life. There was this Perfect Girl of my dreams in a yellow dress standing on one leg and with the other leg resting flat against the wall, under the shadow of the first-floor balcony; her shoulder-length open hair was jet black and shining. She was fair with a perfectly trim and shapely body. Just the girl of my dreams.

Keki: Ankur, can you leave out her geography and anatomy for the present.

(We all have a smile on our faces)

Ankur: I have to give you the background. It is very important. As I was waiting for the rains to stop, I also reached under that balcony stood exactly the way she was standing with one leg resting on the wall. I also took out my cell phone and did something there. She looked towards me as if I was an intrusion in her privacy. I pointed with two hands towards the sky and said ‘sudden rains, I have my bike over here’ and pointed towards my bike. She took her leg down from the wall and I did the same. She had some computer item in a plastic bag hanging from her left-hand wrist. I transferred my plastic bag from my right hand and hung it on my left-hand wrist just like her. Pointing at her transparent plastic bag and forwarding my left hand towards her I asked ‘are you also in computers?’ My heart was racing and I realized that I was speaking fast, whereas she was speaking in monosyllables in a soft voice and said ‘yes’. We exchanged notes as to where she was working where I was working, what she was doing, what I was doing. (Ankur turns towards me and says I am cutting out all the important content but I was matching her speed of talk, repetitive phrasing, volume and whatever else I could). By that time, we were freely talking, laughing and she was even giggling, her phone buzzed with a message. She read it and put it away. I asked her ‘expecting somebody? She said ‘yes’. I asked ‘is he very handsome?’ she replied with a broad smile ‘very handsome’. By that time a car arrived with a middle-aged man inside. She laughed pointing at that person and said ‘my very handsome dad’. Before she could go to the car I asked ‘when do we meet again? I have to come here tomorrow to pick up one item which they did not have today’. She replied ‘ me too, same time tomorrow evening’. I was so very relieved; I have found my dream girl. (Ankur again turned to me with a big grin; the group had a big smile on their faces)

Saira: Congrats, Ankur.

Keki: Ok Ankur close your eyes and relax and instead of focusing on the girl focus on her as a person with whom you created a rapport and what exactly did you do in both cases to get the result that you think you got. And also think of where all you can apply it. (I cup my five fingers on Ankur’s right shoulder and asked the participant sitting close to me to pass on the Milton Ericsson model to the next person to read out the same paragraph aloud. Once that was over, I asked the group to give him a big hand and saw that Padma was ready to come and I told her to take the stage)

Ankur: Can I ask you something before Padma comes? Does it really happen or am I dreaming? Because I want it to happen.

Keki: If you do not get your answer by lunch break then you can ask me again. But there is a case-story I want to share with you all. Can you please wait for some time, Padma?

Many years back there was one participant girl. She must have been about 26-year-old. In her community if the girl does not get married by that time, people start worrying. Parents were not finding a proper match. If they did then the boy's side would call it off. In those days the program used to be of four days. Almost exactly a month after completion of the program we received a wedding invitation. She was getting married to a boy from the same community but settled in Australia. **NLP does not take credit for this. It calls it a phenomenon**. There are other cases of phenomenon which I may narrate at appropriate time later.

Padma takes the stage.

Padma: Yesterday evening I took an auto from outside the hotel to go back home.

(Auto rickshaws, in short Autos, some places they are also called tuk-tuks and are commonly seen in most cities and small towns. These are three-wheeler, motorized and can find their way zigzagging through the traffic. Auto drivers do not enjoy the best of a reputation. In many areas, and many of them, haggle with the customer for the fare instead of using the meter. They are often considered rude; although you will find a lot of them to be decent)

(Padma continues) I was sitting behind the auto driver and could not even see his face so even though I wanted to make rapport with him I did not know how to, so most of the way I was almost quiet. On the way I suddenly saw a shop which said 'Ayurvedic Medicines and Supplies'. We normally use ayurvedic medicines and breakfast supplements. My husband has been taking some Ayurvedic medicines and we do not get them easily in our area. So, I asked the auto driver to stop at that shop. He seemed a little annoyed and told me to hurry up because he cannot wait for long. I entered the shop and was impressed by the variety of supplies and medicines that they had. A middle-aged man, who could be the owner, was sitting on a chair with rollers at a side table doing some calculations with his calculator on the table. He was punching the calculator keys and I caught myself tapping my fingers on the counter glass since I was in a hurry. He looked up at me, said 'yes' and rolled his chair towards the counter. I asked him regarding some medicines. He again rolled his chair from one shelf to the other to collect the medicines. I was wondering what to do so I just moved in the direction that he was moving by sliding my feet as if I was floating and every time, he was picking up the medicine and putting it on the tray in his lap I would put my hand on the counter as if I was putting it on the counter. I inquired about some breakfast supplements whereby he again rolled his chair to pick up two or three different ones, rolled back to the counter and placed them before me. I matched his actions like before and asked him to make the bill for the medicines. As he was picking up each item to check its price for the billing, I was picking up the items that he had brought to check its contents and more so as an exercise for rapport making. I got interested in couple of items which he had brought and asked him to add that also in the bill. He was happy. He smiled and asked me if I was living close by somewhere, because he had not seen me before in his shop. I said no I was living around 3 kilometers away from here. By the time the bill was getting done the auto rickshaw driver was getting impatient and was honking for me. I asked for the bill, opened my purse and to my horror I found that I did not even have half the amount of the bill with me. I was in a fix. One side the auto rickshaw driver was in a hurry, on the other side I had mounted up my bill and did not have enough cash. The man in the chair saw my predicament and asked me if I was returning back from work. I said, no I am returning from a program, and was not expecting to be at your shop so I don't have enough money, I will pick up everything tomorrow. I was surprised when he said, 'no madam you should not delay with the medicines, please take everything with you and you can pay me tomorrow. I said you don't even know me, you do not know where I live, you do not have even my telephone number, and how can you do this? I offered to pay him whatever I had and the balance I can bring tomorrow but he insisted that the auto driver is honking again and I will need to pay him also, so it is perfectly alright. Anyway, I gave him my phone number and hurried out with the parcel. As I was entering the auto, the driver was annoyed and said all you lady customers are the same, they do not understand the problems we face from the customer as well as from the police. Anyway, I reached home. That was my story with the stranger.

Keki: So how was it any different from any other time? After all, the shopkeeper was trying to attract customer. Why do you consider this as your success story, if you do?

Padma: Because I just told him my telephone number. I don't think he even noted it down and he trusts me with such a big bill amount without knowing my whereabouts. I have not experienced such a thing before.

Keki: Have you brought the money today? Are you going to stop by?

Padma: Yes, yes to both. (With a smile) Can I start, what happened after I went home?

Keki: Go ahead.

Padma: I reached home and there was loud music coming out of the house as I was buzzing the doorbell. Since there was no response, I took out my key and opened the house and entered. The music was pretty loud and it was coming from my younger son's room. My son with his eyes closed was singing and dancing to the rhythm of the music and playing the drums in the air. I was already happy with my experience at the shop and I did not want to disturb my son so I also started swaying and dancing to the music and the song was also familiar to me. I was standing opposite my son and was matching and mirroring him. I must have made some noise with my feet because suddenly he opened his eyes, switch off the music system and said 'Mom, when did you come? What are you doing in my room? Why are you dancing? What happened on the first day of your program?' I said I will tell you all that but first tell me where is your father and your brother? He said they had gone to the market to buy the week's vegetables and grocery so that I could use the scooter for my program on Saturday and Sunday. He said 'but why are you dancing with me and singing? You have never done that before'. I said 'You are always with those big earphones around your head.'

Keki: Sorry to interrupt, Padma, but less of 'I said this and he said that' and get on with what else you did for rapport making and what was the result.

Padma: Ok, he asked me about my favorite song from the past, put that on, we danced, and I matched and mirrored all his movements. After that I inquired with him about the money and where he got it from. I learnt that he is part of a group of four boys and one girl and they perform at private functions and concerts. He took part in three such functions and was paid rupees 500 for each program. The guitar he has is pretty old and out of tune. He wants to buy a new one, a costlier one from his own earnings. Rupees 50 out of his earning, he had paid to the helper boy when that boy did not have money to go back home late. Then I asked him about those videos in his laptop. He said 'come on mom, my friends are already calling me naive, including the girl in our group, when will you let me grow up. I promise I will not rob a bank or do anything else that puts you to shame. You have to promise that you will let me pursue my interest. Now the doorbell is ringing, let me go and open it'.

Keki: Are you at peace now? Do you think you can trust your son?

Padma: Totally and totally at peace. Thanks to you.

Keki: It is you who did everything. I am only showing you all the possibilities. Now close your eyes and go through whatever you did at the shop and at home to get you the success which you desired and deserved. (I cup my five fingers on her right shoulder and ask the next person to read from Milton Ericsson's. When that was over, she opened her eyes and everybody gave her a big applause)

Next to come was Saira.

Saira: I was keen to hear Padma's story before I would come.

Saira: Good morning everybody. As per Keki's instructions I will cut out as much of content as possible and stay with the rapport making process and the results I got. Yesterday evening I also took an auto back home. He was a middle-aged man with a stocky figure. After we exchanged some words regarding where I wanted to go, he started the auto. His voice volume was low and a bit rustic in a sing song way. I am familiar with this dialect which comes from about 100 - 150 kilometers south. I could only see his broad back and the way he was holding the handle bar with elbows slightly spread outside. I held the bar behind his seat in the same fashion and matching his voice I asked him his name. He said it was Maruti. As he was negotiating through the traffic his body would slightly move this way and that. I matched those movements. Taking his name, I asked him about his family, his children, their education and whether the family was with him. Using either the last words from a sentence or the keywords I would probe little further about his village. He got quite animated and started narrating about his village, about the school over there, about the people, about the poverty with happiness verses the city life and the hassles of it. He was talking most of the time till I reached home. The 40-minute journey seemed like 15-20 minutes. The bill was rupees hundred and sixteen but I could find only hundred and bigger notes with me. I gave him two hundred-rupee notes but he did not have adequate change for the second hundred rupee note. He returned the other note and said it was ok and it was a pleasure to serve a passenger like me. He gave me his phone number and said that he was living in the vicinity and I could call anytime when I wanted. He was delighted when I gave my small chocolate that I had in my purse as a compensation for the rupees 16 he had foregone.

(Saira looks at me and says) The second story is a bit unusual (I gave her a go-ahead signal)

As some of you already know I have four dogs at home along with my teenage daughter. The youngest dog is about 7 months old, very frisky and playful, the other two are about 3 to 4 years of age and the eldest is almost 12 years old Golden Retriever that I had named as Sonu. Sonu is now pretty old and has become grumpy and irritable. As I enter the house the younger 3 were all around me jumping and playing and wanting my attention, Sonu was sleeping prone with hind legs stretched behind and the front left paw over the right with her head resting on it. She wagged her tail just once and looked at me with a soulful eye. After I played with the other three and shooed them off, I went to Sonu. She did not even move. So just for fun I also slept prone on my stomach in front of her. Mirroring her, I put my right hand over my left and rested my head on it, looking straight into Sonu's eyes. The youngster must have thought I am playing with Sonu so he also came over and was all over my head. Then he suddenly jumped off and started nuzzling Sonu's head. Sonu lifted up her head and growled at him. I took my opportunity. I also raised my head and shooed off the youngster saying 'go sit in your den', with a stern voice and pointing towards the den. Poor thing went with his tail between his legs. As I turned my head towards Sonu, her head was still up so very lovingly I took my face forward to give a slight kiss on her nose. She responded by licking my face, continued for quite some time till I took her head in my lap and patted her with love.

(Facing me Saira asked) is that a success story?

Keki: It certainly is, although a bit unusual. Or not even so.

Now close your eyes and replay whatever rapport making you did out of the 10 points and how easy it was. But before you do that, I want to ask you some questions. These are about the rickshaw driver. Tell me, whatever the rickshaw driver was telling you for almost over half an hour did you find it interesting?

Saira: Of course. Very interesting. It was almost like learning something new.

Keki: My next question is; what was the state, the feelings with which you left the rickshaw driver?

Saira: As I mentioned earlier, he was very happy.

Keki: So, what do you think will happen when he meets his next passenger?

Saira: Oh, I get the point. I am sure he will be in a happy mood, friendlier, maybe even more courteous and make the next passenger feel good.

Keki: So now tell me when that next passenger reaches home happier, what may happen at his home?

Saira: Happiness will spread. His or her world will be a better place to live in.

Keki: Ok, now you can close your eyes and replay what you did. (Once again, I cupped her right shoulder with my five fingers and asked the next person to read out Milton Ericson's)

(Before Saira could say something Ankur was already ready with the question.)

Ankur: Does that mean we can do rapport which animals also?

Keki: Let me share something with you all. Years back I used to take a few of our practitioners and go to various schools, institutions for physically or mentally challenged people, old age homes, etc. Those days there were hardly any books on NLP in the market and there was no computer with net with me. I had heard that British Council

Library had some books on NLP. So, I became a member there and went in search of some books. I found one book with the title 'NLP for Schooling'. I said this is the book for me and I brought it home. On the cover page was a picture of a girl in riding dress sitting on a horse. It appears that in Britain training a horse and rider for riding was termed as schooling. The entire book was about training the horse and rider through NLP. Today we have one of our trainers who not only conducts programs in animal communication but she has some fantastic results herself regarding communication with and through animals. I am told there was an article in the Time Magazine on her with a photograph of herself sitting next to a tiger.

Ankur: Great

Next to come is Shankar.

Shankar: As I reached home last evening, I entered my society gate and drove towards my building to park the car in the underground, I saw our security guard having an argument with somebody whom I did not recognize and who was obviously a visitor. Both where arguing loudly and animatedly. I got out from my car and reached them. I waited a minute to listen to them and understood that as usual the security guard (SG) wanted him to park in a different place from where he had done so. I was pondering as to whom to start with. I took the stance of the security guard (SG), pushed my hands down signaling him to slow down and told him that the gentleman is a guest in our society and he looks like an educated person. Then I took the stance of the visitor and told him I am sorry on the behalf of the society and the SG should not have been so rude with you. Then I looked towards his car and ask him 'is that your car?' When he said yes, I started walking towards the car and simultaneously started admiring the car. I told him that I always wanted this model and particularly this color of the car. He seemed happy and started telling me about the salient features of this model. I told him that I would not like such a beauty to be bashed up by some immature kid coming from the side lane and taking a sharp turn because he is sure to hit the car in that case. I asked if I could take a small ride to test out the car. He said he would drive it himself and I can sit by his side. We did that and I negotiated him to the place where the SG wanted him to park. Even while doing so, I was matching and mirroring his gestures, his whole-body posture and his vocal qualities. I told him that his car is now in a safe place and I was very happy to have met him and feel the ride. We shook hands, exchanged our names and parted with a big smile. As I crossed our SG, he too had a big smile and he said to me 'sir, you handled this chap very well; some of these visitors behave as if they own the society'. I put my hand on his shoulder matching his stance and told the SG that sometimes the visitors also feel as if some SGs believe that they own the society, particularly when they tend to become a little rude. I think he got the message because he said 'sorry sir I will be more careful'. I patted his back and gave him a big smile.

The second story is about what happened with my wife. I was already feeling happy with my success at Rapport making and that too in my first attempt. My wife was in the kitchen preparing dinner for us. I have no issues with my wife.

Jaya: No issues as in issues or that you have no kids?

Keki: No interruptions please. Just listen. Continue Shankar.

Shankar: Both, Jaya. So, I entered the kitchen, hugged my wife from behind, praised her looks, praised the way she was dressed, taking a deep breath taking in the Aroma of the cooking – and my wife (with a wicked smile)- I praised her cooking. She said ' You seem very happy, what happened? How was your first day of the program?' I said I will tell you everything, let me go and wash first, gave a peck on her neck and went. When I returned, I started Matching and Mirroring in bits and pieces. Like while chopping some vegetables she had to attend to the stove so I took up the knife and started chopping the way she was standing and chopping or when she washed some vessel, I did the same soon after her. This continued till we finished our dinner. The main rapport making started after dinner. It was quite an extended event but I will narrate it in brief. After dinner and clean up we generally sit opposite our TV for her regular serial. As usual she sat on the single sofa with her legs folded up and her hand over her head and the headrest of the sofa. Generally, I sit on the big sofa with my legs down. But yesterday I matched her sitting posture absolutely. I continued with all the matching and mirroring including her voice. I could see that she was getting a little restless. In the last com. break, she got up from her chair came next to me and snuggled up. We had some lovey-dovey and she asked me if I was getting old. She said in the earlier days I would pick her up and carry her. I needed no further hint. What happened after that for the next couple of hours was like our honeymoon or even better because she was taking a lot of initiatives and I loved it.

Keki: (as I was about to cup my five fingers on his right shoulder, I noticed some movement in Aban's chair) Aban, you want to say something?

Aban: Can I?

Keki: Of course. Go ahead.

Aban: This happens quite often in our programs, but what I want to share with you all is something little different. After the first day of one of the programs, when we reached home, I had a little argument with Keki. He was not willing to look at my point of view. Often at such times, I would just leave him alone to go do my work, thinking that he is a man; he will not understand a woman's point of view. That day I decided to create rapport. **As I matched and mirrored all his behavior patterns, I started feeling the feelings that he was feeling.** We had a much better understanding of each other's point of view and I no longer considered him as Adamant. It was a perfect understanding. So, **Motions create Emotions and Emotions create Motions**. (The group applauds)

Keki: While on this subject let me tell you something. You will learn more about mental strategies on the 4th day afternoon; but strategies are sequence of mental events that often happen very quickly and unawares to you. Somebody once said that **How you do something is How you do Everything.** Your strategies from Bedroom to Boardroom are the same. I have devised a set of 20 questions which can be applied either to the bedroom or the boardroom. You answer for either situation, make necessary changes and it will equally apply to either situation. Trouble is that the corporate world is not ready for it and shies off.

Guneet: I am ready for it.

Keki: Good. I am sure your wife has no complaints against you. But is your staff ready to be open about it. (I cup my 5 fingers on Shankar's right shoulder and complete the Milton Ericson process) Thank you, Shankar. Give him a big hand. (That was the loudest applause so far)

(Vipul comes up next)

Vipul: Last evening straight from here, I went to my shop. As I was checking the day's billing and cash receipts a young lady entered and asked me about some sarees. I pointed in the direction of the saree section. I noticed that she was wearing a colorful dress with big designs in various colors. She had marks of a newly married bride. She was not satisfied by what the sales girl was showing her and started looking at the shelves to choose one herself. She looked at the bunch of 4 sarees kept on the top shelf and asked the sales girl to show them to her. The sales girl instead of showing her the sarees told her in a soft voice,' 'Madam these are not appropriate for you, I will not recommend them to you.' I was annoyed at hearing this. I left my cash counter and went to the saree section. I sent the sales girl from there and started showing different colorful sarees to this lady. Her eyes again went up to the 4 sarees and she requested me if she could take a look at them. I said 'sure madam but they are a little more expensive', maybe that is why the sales girl possibly thought that you could not afford it. She picked one out of those 4 and I could see that she was really interested in it. I told her 'Excellent choice madam, this will make you look even more beautiful. Let me put the Pallu over your shoulder and you can see for yourself in the mirror. I did that and knew that she was sold on it. When she asked for the price, I increased the price by 50% and told her that since she likes it so much, I will give her at 20% discount. She was happy to hear it and I had a sale.

Saira: But why did the sales girl not want to sell that to her?

Vipul: That is our business secret.

Saira: No but still.

Vipul: Ok the designs are good but it's the fabric, which has come new in the market and they say it catches fire easily.

Saira: My God! Your sales girl deserves to be complemented.

Vipul: Madam; I am into business. Who gets burnt and who survives is not my concern. God decides that. And as for the sales girl I fired her that same evening.

Keki: OK so how about the second story?

Vipul: I do not have one. This was like a test dose. I wanted to know if it works and whether I can do it.

Keki: So, does it work?

Vipul: It seems to work and now I can use it whenever I need it.

Keki: Vipul, just close your eyes and think only about the points that you picked to use out of the 10 points of rapport making and the result that you got. That's all. (And I completed the Milton Ericson process. This time hardly 2 or 3 people clapped)

Saira: But......!

Keki: I know. I will be taking it up after tea/coffee snacks break.

(I was pleasantly surprised to find Anu coming up next and taking her stand. But before she could start saying anything.)

Lily: Can I go and sit down now, sir?

Keki: Again, sir? Just Keki is enough my dear, I am not your father, you know.

Lily: I know it very well Keki; you won't find me sitting in this classroom if you were my father.

Keki: Classroom? Where? I am teaching you all, just about nothing, neither am I lecturing.

Lily: My legs have started aching.

Keki: Oh, I am also aching, particularly after listening to Vipul. Professor Shankar can give you a chair over here (pointing where she was standing) when you just can't stand anymore, won't you professor?

Shankar: (Nods with a smile) and one for you also, Keki,

Keki: Oh no. I can tell myself that I can stand and then I can. Ok Anu, please proceed.

Anu: I went home last evening. I was very uncomfortable. I was confused. I did not know where to start. I did not know what to start. How to start. As usual Suresh, my husband, was taking care of everything. He changed my 2-year-old son into night clothes. He sat with my son to feed him dinner and had dinner with him. He washed him. He played with him. Finally put him to bed and covered him. All the time I felt as if I was under his inspection. That he was scrutinizing me. After he had dinner, I told him to leave everything and I will clear the table after I finished my dinner. He went to his room to sleep. After I finished everything, I went to bed to sleep next to my son. I love my son. I know I had neglected him for over a year. I had neglected everything. Nothing made sense. Before switching off the light I wanted to make sure that his clothing was covering him well. I opened the bed cover. His chest was moving up and down with his breathing. I remembered the breathing experiment of the afternoon. I started breathing in and out along with him. I continued with that for quite some time. I started feeling more love toward him. I continued breathing along with him and suddenly I became emotional. I automatically took a sudden deep breath in. I was so surprised that my child did the same almost instantaneously. I kissed him on the forehead. I wanted to take him in my arms. His breathing had become deeper. I realized that I was breathing deeper. I started normalizing my breathing pattern. He started breathing calmly. He was sleeping on my right. I had already turned towards him. With my left hand I patted his right cheek and softly spoke in his ear 'mummy loves you, my baby. I always loved you'. I was surprised as he took a turn towards me to face me. I put my left hand across him and moved closer to him to reduce the weight of my arm on his body. I switched off the light and soon I was asleep. I got up in the middle of the night with a nightmare of wanting to punish myself. I became aware that he was still facing me and his right hand was resting on my right hand. It melted me completely. It was not a peaceful sleep. I got up several times. I alternated between several emotions, remorse, punishment, guilt and love.

In the morning I got up late. My son was still sleeping. Suresh was in his room. He must have opened the door for the maid because she was working in the kitchen. I hurriedly finished my bath and other morning duties and changed into the clothes for coming here.

As would happen so often, even today, the maid was babbling loudly in the kitchen which could be heard in all the rooms. Mostly it would be complaining about me but it could be anything and everything that came in her way. Suresh had tried to stop her but to no avail. He was tolerating her only because she would be good to the kid. Just on impulse I went to the Puja (Altar) place. I picked up the tiny Bells and started ringing the bells in unison with her babbling. I also started reciting some slokas in tune with her babbling. When her sound level increased, I picked up the bigger Bell to ring, in accompaniment to her. Surprisingly her babbling reduced. I went into the kitchen to get my breakfast. I tried to match and mirror as much as I could. If she started babbling even softly then I would start singing with my slokas at the same level. She would look at me quizzically. She generally refuses to clean my vessels used by me. I started washing them and suddenly my right leg was grasped tightly. I looked down and it was my son hugging my leg and wanting me to pick him up. As I continued washing and my son continued cajoling me to pick him up, the most surprising and unexpected thing happened. She said 'madam, please pickup your son and play with him I will do all your vessels.' 'you sit down at the table I will bring your breakfast because you have to go out for your class today.' I was dumbfounded. My son was all over me and wanted me not to go for the class today. I somehow persuaded him and promised that when I come back in the evening, I will spend all the time with him. (Looking at me) I can't believe it all**. It was like magic**.

Keki: (I put my hand around her shoulder and repeat) I can believe it all. It was like magic. Yes, I have seen this magic happening so many times. Richard Bandler's first book itself after discovery of NLP was titled, 'The Structure of Magic'. It is in two volumes. What is magic? Magic is when you see something happening in front of your eyes which is unbelievable. The difference is that the magician is utilizing certain props and his or her skill to make it appear unnatural; whereas here we are utilizing certain skills that give us certain results. Many of you have been bold enough to utilize your newly learnt skills and thereby achieve results which seem to be unbelievable. I salute you all. (I cup right shoulder with my five fingers and complete the Milton Ericsson process)

Anwar comes up next.

Anwar: (looking at me) I can start, yes?

Keki: You can start.

Anwar: (looking at the group) so I went to my small flat in the evening yesterday, yes. I share the flat with a roommate, yes.

Keki: Hold on. (He was standing rather limp. So, I turned to him and with my right hand give a push on his left shoulder. He went flying Two Steps back backwards.) What is this? Come on. Stand firm. Open your feet little wider. (I kicked his feet from inside to spread them a little wider) imagine as if there are roots growing downwards in the ground from your feet and they are grounding you firmly. That is a little better. (Once again, I gave a push to his left shoulder. This time he went just a little bit backwards) Form fists in both your hands and open them out FULLY as if your roots are going deeper. (Once again, I gave a push on his left shoulder. This time he could take it.) Now continue.

Anwar: My roommate had not yet come home. He also works in the IT industry and generally comes home late, yes. Whoever comes home early yes, prepares dinner for both, yes. I was anxious yes, as to when to do my home play of rapport making yes and with whom, yes.

Keki: Stop. Do you know how many times you used the word 'yes' in the last few sentences?

Anwar: No, did I?

Keki: Six times. You are the one who had said 'But I have no idea how I can deal with my boss' while discussing the SMS yesterday morning, isn't it?

Anwar: He is a problem. Yes.

Keki: He may not be the problem. I wonder if he has any idea as to how he can deal with You. Let me tell you all, about the real case that we had while doing the Train the Trainer program. This gentleman had done the Practitioner's and the Master practitioner's program with another trainer of NFNLP. Some people use certain words as fillers. They are generally not even aware of it. This gentleman's filler was S O so. So, I asked him to repeat his sentence adding 'so' after each word of his sentence consciously. To assist you Anwar, I am going to write down your words on the board. (I wrote on the board from 'He also works..... ' up to '...and with whom, yes.' Anwar added a 'yes' after each and every word feeling foolish about it) Anwar, when you were using 'yes' as a filler your intonation was to make the 's' lighter than the 'y'. I want you to repeat the process but this time make the 's' much heavier than the 'y'. (Anwar does it) How do you feel now Anwar?

Anwar: Stupid, but something is different.

Keki: Good. I want you to repeat the same thing once again but when you are emphasizing the 'S' in 'yes' I want you to make a tight fist. (Anwar does it) how do you feel now?

Anwar: I feel confident (then pumping a fist and over emphasizing the 's' he says) YES.

Saira: Keki, was the person using 'so' as a filler looking for self-validation and does someone using 'Yes' for self-doubt or when not confident?

Keki: I don't know and let's not get into **paralysis by analysis**. We are already running late. Please continue Anwar. And speed it up.

Anwar: I was matching and mirroring him while having dinner as to what he is taking from the plate, how he is taking, his gestures, repetitive phrasing and continued it while clearing the table and cleaning up. Y . S (Became conscious, made a fist and corrected himself). Normally we hardly get a chance to interact for 15-20 minutes but last night it went on for over 45 minutes regarding his workplace and then, since we are both unmarried, further 45 minutes regarding our non-existent girlfriends. He confided several things with me which he had never done before. (Turning towards me) Did I make Rapport?

Keki: Of course. Why do you even ask? Say yeS, I made rapport.

Anwar: (Happily pumping his fist) yeS, I made Rapport.

Keki: Is there a second story?

Anwar: I wanted to do it in the morning but we slept so late there was no time in the morning, just rushing to get here.

Keki: That's fine (and I completed the Milton Ericson process)

Next to come up was Doctor Nirav.

Nirav: Yesterday evening after the program I went straight to the hospital. Day before yesterday I had performed an operation on a patient's chest to remove a portion of his lung. I was informed that he was having some breathing difficulty. The patient is 72-year-old. I went to his room and examined him. He was on Oxygen. I removed his oxygen mask just to see his actual condition. He was very happy to see me and took my hand in his hand. He pleaded with me and asked ' Doctor, tell me truthfully, am I going to survive? Will I be going home?' there was real anxiety in his voice. I put my other hand over his hand and matching his voice I said 'of course you are going home, why the anxiety?' 'Please promise that you will send me home at least for a few weeks, then I will be ready to die' he said.

Normally under such condition of a patient I would have prescribed some medicine and left for the nurse to take care of it. When he was talking about dying, I had felt slight increase in pressure of his hand. I pressed his hand slightly more and guessed correctly that he was having some unfinished agenda. I goaded him to talk more. Slowly he opened up and talked about his worries regarding some property matter that was becoming an issue between his children. I reassured him that he is certainly going home and will be in perfect health to take care of the pending issues. As we finished our talk for about 20 minutes, I noticed that he was now breathing more calmly and there was a shine in his eyes. I did not prescribe any further medicines. I made him promise that once the issue at hand is settled by him, he will take up something more purposeful and enjoyable for the family and keep me informed about the same. Then he did something which I will never forget. With tears in his eyes, taking my hand between his two hands and pulling it towards his forehead he said ' you are God to me, no doctor has spent so much time and shown any interest in my personal life, I want to touch your feet' saying so he started to get up from his sick bed but I prevented him from doing that.

As I was driving home, I was thinking about the flaws in our Healthcare system. We have been treating the symptoms rather than a human being (turning towards me) this has been troubling me for quite some time and that is when I started looking up on the net and came across NLP. And that is what has brought me to this program, Keki.

Keki: You know Doc., Years back we used to laugh and joke when somebody said 'Operation successful, Patient dead'. This is no longer a joke. In the past few years in my own close relations, I have actually had doctor saying that the operation was successful but unfortunately not for the patient. And there are so many legal safeguards for the doctor and very little for the patient. The fact is that somebody would have earned from your medicines but nobody has earned anything from you for the therapy which you gave. Therapy which was necessary and even the primary cause of his issue. Senior doctors have confided in me that so many unnecessary operations are taking place and unnecessary tests are being conducted so that the interest on the investments in all that equipment can be paid to the Bank. In fact, I believe, many hospitals have fixed a quota for their doctors to carry out certain minimum number of tests to make the whole thing financially viable.

Nirav: I have personally got into the bad books of my management for refusing to carry out some operations which were not going to give results. I also inform the family members that there is no cure for this.

Keki: That is one more thing. When a relative of ours in the USA was told by his doctors that there is no cure and he has to take a certain medicine for his lifetime. I explained to him that there is something called a **'surface structure' and a 'deep structure' to a sentence.** The surface structure is what he heard from his doctor; the deep structure of that sentence is that 'in the system that he follows, there is no permanent cure'. It does not mean that there is no permanent cure universally. It is simple common sense. If you are running a drug industry and your R&D comes up with two solutions, one which cures the disease permanently and the other which keeps it in suspension by taking certain medicine developed by you, which one are you going to promote? Obviously the second option is far more profitable.

Nirav: Our system is rotten. There should be a Holistic Health University with R&D under its control and producing Multi-Disciplinary Health Care doctors.

Keki: I have heard Bandler saying somewhere that **if placebos can cure 40% of the people, then there should be more research on placebos**. Anyway, it's a huge issue.

Nirav: It is, and therefore it should not be brushed under the carpet.

Keki: Do you have a second story doctor?

Nirav: I went home and there was this neighboring lady who sometimes comes to meet my wife. She is a big gossiper. I washed up myself, poured a drink and went to join her and my wife for a small hi hello. Normally I would have moved out to my study but today my head was filled with so many ideas and questions that I felt uneasy to go in the study. I sat there sipping my drink, half not listening to them. Suddenly I heard one of them say the word 'violin'; it was the Gossip Girl. Just for fun I matched her body posture and told her that while at the medical college I tried my hand playing a violin. My friends laughed at me and said 'Nirav it may be easier for you to get a donkey braying instead of the violin braying'. It turned out that she was herself a violin teacher at one time. She started telling me about those times. When I crossed my leg, I found her crossing her legs. To check further, I made the gesture of playing the bow and whether she is ready to teach me, she immediately matched my gesture and readily agreed to teach me. I thanked her and went to my study room.

Keki: (He looked at me to indicate that he was done) OK, close your eyes; you have had some major breakthroughs. Go through all you did and all you achieved and how simple it all is. (I completed the Ericsonian process).

Jaya was next to come

Jaya: (looking at me) I tried to do rapport with him.

Keki: Again him. Which 'him' is it this time?

Jaya: My husband of course.

Keki: Oh ok. Please continue.

Jaya: (facing the group) My husband as you know is a mama's boy. All evening till we finished dinner mama was around and I could not do anything. After dinner when he came to the bedroom and we were alone, I was sitting on the bed and he was changing into his night clothes. After he finished with that, I asked him to come and sit by my side because I wanted to talk to him. He asked me 'about what?' so I said about our relationship, about what I learnt today at the program. He refused to sit down saying that 'I don't want another lecture from you'. I even tried to maintain eye contact but he was not ready to co-operate.

Keki: Is anything about eye contact mentioned in the 10 points of rapport making?

Jaya: No, but it is important, isn't it?

Keki: This business of so-called **eye contact** is generally overrated and misunderstood. Some people start staring into the eyes of the other thereby not allowing the other person's natural eye movements. They get so involved with 'eye contact' that they miss out all the other movements of the body. Here we are looking not just into the person's eyes but the entire body so that even while looking at the eyes, if the other person's little toe moves you are aware of it and you are responding to it. **We call it looking with Soft Eyes.** Understood Jaya and everybody? Now tell me Jaya, what exactly did you match and mirror?

Jaya: I tried so many things but he was just not co-operating.

Keki: Tried what? Did you stand up and match his standing posture? Did you match his hand gestures even while he was standing and you are sitting? Did you even match his voice tone?

Jaya: No, how could I try anything when he was not ready to co-operate at all?

Keki: (to the group) There are some dirty words in the English language which are very harmful and damaging. No, they do not all start with an 'F...'. In fact, the 'F...' word may be slang but it is not a dirty word. Without that we all would not be present in this hall just now. Rape and murder are not considered as dirty words and are used freely by the media but 'F...' is considered a dirty word. Well Jaya used a far more damaging dirty word and it started with a 'T'. Can somebody tell me what it was? (Some responded 'TRY').

That's right. So, Jaya since you are using it so freely you must be knowing the true meaning of it and how it's done. (I pick the Marker Pen from the table, hold it in my open palm of the left hand and stand a step ahead of Jaya and looking forward turned my hand closer to Jaya. Addressing the group, I said) Now Jaya, try to take this pen; teach us how you try. (After sometime when the pen was still in my palm, I asked the group) what has she done? Did you all learn anything?

Manju: She was trying to take the pen.

Keki: I see. So, you think it is very difficult to pick up the pen from my palm. Jaya, try to take this pen. We want to learn how you try. (This time she picks up the pen. I asked the group what she has done and the group says she has taken the pen.) And the first time what did she do? (Most in the group say) She did not pick up the pen. So why she could not pick up the pen first time? What was she doing?

Manju: Because she was trying; she did not want to pick up the pen. She was moving her hand here and there trying to pick up the pen.

Keki: Yes Manju, like you may be knowing some people going here and there trying to meet their targets or doing, rather not doing, what they have to. Jaya, have you learnt anything?

Jaya: That I can either pick up the pen or I cannot?

Keki: Can? Is it so difficult? Was the pen stuck to my palm?

Manju: But in school they taught us to try, try and try until you succeed.

Keki: Of course. In school they taught us so many things. For example, I had learnt that the railway track rails have a gap at each joint so that in the hot season there is scope for expansion; this continued until the Japanese came up with welded rails Technology.

So, you still find people going cry, cry and cry until you succeed and they are still crying. So, Jaya, what have you learnt? if at all you have learnt anything.

Jaya: That I either do something or I don't. (The group claps) Do you want me to remove that word try from my dictionary? (With a smile on her face)

Keki: Certainly not. **You can use the word try when either result is acceptable**. Remember everybody. **Trying underwrites failure**. You are already preparing your subconscious for failure. Let me give you a concrete example. Who likes to hear a case-tory? (Some in the group say 'I'.) I didn't hear you. (Now the whole group including Jaya and Lily says loudly 'I'.) Great! Everybody seems to be awake now.

Many years back in our program was this lady. Her husband was a retired very senior army officer who was now into specialized corporate training. They used to get participants from around the world.

The lady must have discussed the day's proceedings with her husband. Because the next day evening her husband came over to talk to me. During the discussion he asked me as to how I can say not to use the word try, because so often one of the participants from his program would want to reach the Bombay airport for catching the flight and he would request for a rail ticket from Pune to Bombay urgently. (There was no net booking at that time. People had to stand in long queues, sometimes for hours together, to get a ticket. Either due to the actual load of the passengers or more likely, the collusion of the ticketing staffs with the black- marketers, the usual answer would be that all tickets are sold out.) I have to tell them that I will try to get the tickets.

I narrated the case of my wife, Aban, who had gone along with our 4 daughters to her parental house in Bangalore for the summer holidays. She got the same answer when she went to book rail tickets for returning to Pune. She never the less, bought the wait-listed tickets with number ridiculously over 140. She found out that at every major station there is a superintendent's office just outside, who has the emergency quota that he opens up 24 hours before the departure of the train. Aban went to this office a day before the departure of the train with an application stating that the Children's Schools were reopening and she had to be in Pune. She got confirmed berths for the 20-hour journey. **If your end goal is clear, you are bound to find alternatives.**

So, Jaya, close your eyes and go through whatever you learnt now and so far, (I completed the Milton Erickson process and asked her to go back to her seat; but she continued to stand there looking at my face.)

Jaya: Even Milton is saying it!

Keki: Saying what?

Jaya: To try.

Keki: My dear, Milton is saying emphatically 'you don't really learn something until you have practiced every piece of it thoroughly'. So, in your book 'practicing' is equal to 'trying', is it? Would you say that Doctor Nirav is practicing surgery or trying surgery? Would you go to a surgeon who will 'try' to operate on your appendix? Go now. Get lost.

Next to take the stand is Guneet Singh.

Guneet: Before I narrate my 2 success stories do I have your permission to say something? Keki.

Keki: What is it? Please make it snappy because we are already running beyond our time.

Guneet: Thank you, I will. Initially I wanted to come in the first half itself but everybody's sharing was so fascinating that I decided to listen first and then come. Suddenly I don't know why but I started remembering the F1 car racing that I had attended. There were all those finely tuned machines with the latest technology, designed and manufactured by experts. And then they were in the hands of the race drivers. I was observing the drivers as they accelerated, braked, took the turns, how they maneuvered to go ahead of others and how a few even crashed. I thought I saw the same similarities over here.

Now to begin with my first story; I went to my unit from here last evening. Like I am particular about people coming on time I am also particular on them leaving the factory on time to be with their family. Hence all the staff had already left and only the second shift people were working. I went to my cabin on the first floor and as requested, the Works Manager had left the first shift report on my table. After satisfying myself with everything and before leaving for home I thought I will have a chat with one of our older Employees with whom I had not interacted for quite some time. So, I called one such to my cabin. I asked him to sit down but he wanted to keep standing. I got up from my seat and told him if you are standing, I will also have to stand so why not we both sit down. He sat erect neither leaning forward nor resting on the backrest. I took the same position and started our conversation, matching and mirroring whatever I could. During the conversation whenever he was describing some past event, I noticed that he was looking upwards towards the right. Although the events were true the detailing and his interpretations were somewhat strange to me. I wondered if he was making up the stories. By now he was volunteering with much more information than I would ask. So purposely I asked him about certain things that I was sure of. Once again, his eyes would go upwards towards the right. I changed the conversation to his favorite song and asked him to recite the same in his mind. His eyes went horizontally towards the right. Now I knew that whatever he had said so far was not his creation but real as he knew them. There were quite a few revelations that I will have to work on.

Second story is what happened at home. It is a normal practice with my wife to sit separately with my daughter as well as my son and enquire about the happenings of the day. My daughter is 11 years of age and my son is of 8 years. Everything seemed fine in their lives. After dinner my son was playing in his room while three of us were watching the TV. I got up to go to my son's room, I also sat on the floor exactly the way he was sitting and started matching and mirroring him. To cut the long story short my son yesterday confided in me that he was having an issue of bullying in his school since almost a year and he was too ashamed to talk about it with anybody. I told him that we will be doing something about it and thanked him for sharing it with me. (Turning towards me) was that snappy enough?

Keki: Thanks, Guneet (and I completed the Ericson process)

Once the process was over and he wanted to go back to his seat I stopped him and said 'Guneet, I like your comparison of this session with the F1 racing'. Naturally in racing one wants to come first and the drivers would have to maneuver to go ahead of others. **In life however you will be happier and less stressed if you decide to compete with yourself instead of others. Your goal should be; Am I better today than I was yesterday? Did I add some growth either physically or mentally or emotionally or help someone else to achieve that; if so then I have lived today otherwise I have just seen time pass by.** Our education system with its marks and all the time hammering that 'this is the age of competition' has created a lot of problems. **People within a company or a team are trying to compete with each other instead of cooperating with each other, thus in fact pulling down the team or the company and engaging in internal politics.** What we need is to work in co-operation rather than competition. Each player in a football or hockey or cricket team, or even in a corporate team will make the team win only and only if he or she performs in cooperation with the other team members. So, compete with your own yesterday. You will grow, your team will grow, your Nation will grow and the world will grow. You will change your world. **This world needs cooperation more than competition.**

Guneet: Very well said, sir. I will always remember it.

Next to come was the final participant Manju.

Keki: Why are you the last to come, Manju? Or is it that you have the best thing to share.

Manju: Hun-hum. I went straight to the factory to find out what those people had done in my absence.

Keki: Those people! I see.

Manju: My workers.

Keki: And?

Manju: They had hardly done anything and were giving all the wrong excuses.

Keki: They should have given at-least the right excuses, isn't it?

Manju: No excuses. I got very angry and annoyed.

Keki: So, what did you do? Did you create rapport with anybody?

Manju: No rapport. I had no Time. I scolded them. I gave them a piece of my mind. I was angry.

Keki: No Time! Piece of your mind! At least you could have given them a piece of my mind or somebody else's. (I looked at Guneet. He had a smile of disbelief and dejection.) Manju, you look angry even now; so, you just stand here and relax, meanwhile I will talk to your friends over here.

No time! Perhaps the dirtiest word of the English language. We have heard our mother use it, our father uses it, our teachers use it, our bosses use it.

Who likes to hear a case-story, a real story? (The group responds loudly 'I'. I know they are also hungry by now.) I was once at an exhibition at the Engineering College grounds. A Young Man stopped me and said 'Hello, Mr. Darbary. Do you recognize me? I was at your two days program seven years back. You had a 2 hours session on Time Management. Since then, I have never used the term 'No Time' and my life has changed. I prospered, I married and I have a happy family now and a house of my own. I saw you and I particularly wanted to thank you for it'. We hugged each other and after a while we parted.

NASA has even produced as Zero Gravity equipment where they train the future astronauts in weightlessness. Has anybody ever produced a 'No Time' machine or a 'No Time' room?

Unless you are a Theoretical Physicist doing Thought Experiments at the Event Horizon of a Black Hole somewhere in the universe; for mortals like us on this heavenly planet Earth, for all practical purposes- **It is never, never, never a matter of 'No Time'. It is always, always, always a question of Higher Priority or Lower/No Priority. 'No time' is the stupidest, most idiotic statement that you can ever make.** It is wrong in Physics, it is wrong in Philosophy, it is wrong in History or in any other way. You should feel like vomiting and get the taste of vomit every time 'No Time' wants to come to your tongue. If you understand and follow it, your life will also change. You will realize the reason why, on the 4th day morning while we do Problem Solving. Manju, are you relaxed now?

Manju: Yes sir, very much.

Keki: So, what are you going to do now?

Manju: Even when I scold them, I become good to them the next day.

Keki: And?

Manju: I will have priorities.

Keki: And?

Manju: I said I will be good to them.

Keki: How? What will you do?

Manju: I don't know.

Keki: Have you heard of Rapport making?

Manju: Yes, yes. I will try that also.

Keki: When?

Manju: Today evening.

Keki: Go, take your seat. Show time; for some tea/coffee and snacks; but before that Lily has been giving me company since morning. Lily, you have spent four years learning Clinical Psychology, isn't it?

Lily: Yes.

Keki: You have also been working in a government hospital for quite some time now. (She nods) Have you come across anybody who might have generalized something based on a single experience?

Lily: Yes, I come across that very often.

Keki: What was your opening statement when you came here in the morning?

Lily: That I tried and it does not work.

Keki: What would be the factually correct statement to make?

Lily: That I tried once and it did not work.

Keki: Thank you Lily; that should be enough for today. Let us all go for tea/coffee snacks but while you are having it, I want each one of you to have at least 6 questions ready for discussion on rapport making and return in 15 minutes.

Keki: Ok, come on back, change places, change neighbors and jot down your six questions in your manual. (Once they are settled) Before we take up your 6 questions, I have certain questions. Tell me, yesterday morning when we were doing the sensory acuity exercise for Kinesthetic, when you were standing and touching with your fingers on the back of the palm of the third person sitting in the chair, your focus was on whom and what?

Shankar: My focus was on the hand of the subject sitting.

Ankur: Obviously on the subject sitting in the chair and his or her hand.

Keki: Really? Was it?

Nirav: No, my focus was on the partner standing next to me so that I could exactly match the way he was touching.

Keki: Exactly; the exercise was only possible if you stayed aware as to how your partner was touching, matching it and being consistent with it.

4 STAGES OF LEARNING

Let me ask you another question. Yesterday evening when you were doing the rapport making exercise of Monkey see, Monkey do, how many of you were at least a little uncomfortable? (Padma, Anwar and Manju raise hand with Anu raising just a bit.) So at least three and a half people are telling the truth. Saira, you drive a car, don't you?

Saira: Yes, I do.

Keki: Where did you learn driving? Open ground or the road? And who taught you driving? Was it somebody you knew or was it from a Driving School?

Saira: First couple of sessions were on the open ground, after that it was on the road and it was my uncle who taught me to drive on his car.

Keki: It must have happened somewhat like this. When she was small and had to go somewhere, one of her uncles said, 'come on, I will drop you there'. So, she sat in his car; uncle drove the car; Saira had no idea of what or how he drove the car. Total blissful ignorance. Whether it is Japanese language or Zumba; rock climbing or roller coasting; swimming or stamp collecting; cake making or cat walking; absolutely anything and you are not bothered about it; You are at

Stage-1: - Unconscious Incompetence, blissfully ignorant. When Saira turned 18, she wanted to learn car driving herself and her uncle offered to teach her driving. She might have collected some information about how to drive but she had never done it before. Her uncle offered to teach her driving. He took her to the open ground and made her sit in the driver's seat. He made her to start the engine by turning the key, got her to undo the handbrake, asked her to press the clutch, put the car into first gear and slowly release the clutch. She did exactly that, the car jerked and thach-thuch, it stopped. Panicked whether she damaged uncle's car she perspired. Uncle had expected this and put her through the same routine once again this time asking her to press the accelerator a little while starting. This time the car actually started moving and she perspired even more not knowing what to do next. She was now at

Stage-2: - Conscious Incompetence, This went on for some time and uncle moved her from the ground to the road. The more she practiced the more competence she gained. But one day suddenly when someone came in the way of the car, she jammed her foot on the floor. What do you think she pressed her foot on?

Padma: On the brake.

Ankur: (laughing) On the accelerator.

Saira: Yes, it actually happened once. Luckily Uncle saved the day.

Keki: This can happen. Under emergency you want to slam your foot down immediately on the brake, whoever will think of moving the leg in the opposite direction to remove it from the accelerator then take it to the side over the brake and then proceed down on the brake. Once Saira had learnt car driving her niece wanted to be taken for a drive. The monkey that she was, Saira asked her to sit in the back seat. While driving through the commercial area the niece saw something interesting little higher up on the opposite side from where Saira was steering and shouted out aunty, aunty look there, there, there, pointing upwards. Sarah had to bend down and peer through the windshield to look. And where do you think she found the car moving?

there, there, there, towards where the niece was pointing. Of course, she immediately corrected it. She was now at **Stage-3: - Conscious Competence.** As long as she remained conscious, she was competent. Nowadays she starts from home in a hurry sometimes with a sandwich in her one hand and a cell phone in the other rushing to her workplace and the phone rings; she continues eating the sandwich talking on the phone and driving almost automatically without worrying as to when she has to change gears or do anything else. She has reached

Stage- 4: - Unconscious Competence. Realize that when you are learning something new you are at stage 2 of Conscious Incompetence and that can and may make you feel uncomfortable. **But successful people are those who consciously give permission to their unconscious to become uncomfortable.**

RAPPORT FAQS

Ok it is time now to take up your questions on rapport making. Has anybody written down 6 or more questions? (Ankur raises his hand) Go ahead Ankur read them.

Ankur: Out of the 10 points of rapport making which ones are more important?

Keki: The ones which you observe and respond to. Next question.

Ankur: The next three questions are similar but with different contexts; shall I read them all?

Keki: Go ahead.

Ankur: How do you create Rapport when you are communicating on chat? How do you create Rapport when you are communicating on Email? How do you create Rapport when you are communicating on telephone?

Keki: Please continue

Ankur: When someone does not understand your spoken language?

Keki: Learn how to train a dog with Saira. Next question.

Ankur: How do you create rapport during road rage? (I signal him to continue.) Should we make rapport without reason? (I ask him to go ahead.) Can I ask you one more? Personal? (me-why not?) I am meeting my dream girl this evening what should I do? (laughter all around)

Keki: Send me instead. (more laughter). Ok, on a more serious note; create Rapport, be natural, ask fewer questions and share more. Somebody else with more questions.

Saira: When a person is very emotional how to get them to listen. And the other question is; How to respond to telemarketing nuisance calls-

Keki: Next person one by one.

Shankar: How to create rapport in a classroom?

Keki: Come for my Train the Trainer program. next.

Nirav: How do I match and mirror when a patient comes with acute pain?

Keki: Doctor, you did very well with your patient you had operated on the chest, continue doing the same. **There is a Meta Model language pattern (Appendix II) which helps you to clarify the other persons mind without you assuming anything; this will be useful during information gathering. Then there is a Milton Model of language pattern (Appendix III) where you are not giving any directions but getting things out of the other person's mind.** This should be useful for giving him confidence and speedy recovery.

Nirav: Are we going to do this during the program?

Keki: You will get the reading material because this is mainly information based. Next.

Padma: What about children? how do we do rapport with them?

Keki: Just the way you did yesterday evening. As for your children, please treat them as adults now. Next.

Anwar: When giving job interview in front of 5 or 6 people and secondly will rapport making make others give you more work?

Keki: As for your second question, welcome it because now somebody thinks that you are capable of doing it. Next.

Manju: Can we remove our negatives by rapport?

Keki: Yes; next.

Jaya: In team and family arguments. If someone is cutting down your Rapport how do you do it? Should we continue or step back?

MY QUESTIONS

Keki: What we are going to do now regarding rapport making is very important; much more than what we have done so far. What we have done so far is to give a very sharp razor in the hands of a child or a monkey. The child or the monkey is going to swing it here and there and is bound to get hurt or wound somebody else. When a corporate tells me that they can give me only one day for training I ask them to either break it up into two halves or I cannot teach them one of the most important part of NLP which is rapport making. So now I am going to ask you a few questions and you will answer them.

My Q. No. 1 is **"Is rapport making a manipulation?"** (some say yes, some say no) Rapport making is certainly a manipulation. The trouble is with the English language. The Webster's dictionary defines the word manipulate as 1. You treat or work with the hand or by mechanical means especially with skill. 2. To manage skillfully; sometimes, to manage artfully or fraudulently.

If somebody's shoulder is dislocated, he goes to the Bone setter or the Orthopedic and that doctor manipulates his arm back into the shoulder socket. If somebody is still using a needle and thread; she or he holds the needle in the left hand, wets the thread in the mouth to make it erect and skillfully passes it into the eye of the needle. The orthopedic, the needle and thread user, the rapport maker are all using their arms and body skillfully and artfully; yet we hang on to the last word in the dictionary and think of only fraudulent use.

My Q. No. 2 is **"Will Rapport making work always?"** (this time most people say yes but Manju and Jaya say no.)

The most emphatic answer to this question is (I make an x with index fingers of the 2 hands) N O, NO.

Rapport making cannot work every time. When will it not work? Any time the Rapport-maker has a negative idea or thought about the other person it cannot work. Oh, he is just an auto driver; these people are useless; she is a witch; he is a monster; any form of negative thoughts, beliefs, feelings will prevent rapport formation. And why is this? The answer is very simple. It is because **your body cannot lie.** Remember the breathing experiment that we did before the Rapport demo. Anwar could pick up breathing patterns of Ankur with his eyes closed. Whatever thoughts, beliefs, feelings that you may have about the other person; the other person's subconscious will pick it up and therefore you will not be able to create conditions of trust, harmony and cooperation.

My Q. No. 3 is **"Will making Rapport always get you what you want?"** (most in the group say 'No') That is right. You may not get the end result as you wished for, but with rapport you will get to know why he or she is not ready to give in to you and then maybe you can work around it.

My Q. No. 4 is **"Can anyone of you give me one instance or a condition or situation where rapport making is not useful?"**

Jaya: When you hate someone.

Keki: Is there somebody who disagrees with her? And if so, why?

Saira: I disagree. I disagree because I think the gap separating them from trust, harmony and cooperation can go on increasing with hate.

Keki: Very well said, Saira. I don't think I could have said any better. Life teaches us lots of lessons. All we need to do is, listen. I am proud of you, Saira. In my initial years of NLP, I was thinking that I had an answer. I said, 'war'. How can I be in rapport with my enemy! But I was wrong. I thought of the German General Rommel. Rommel was a highly professional soldier. He made his name in the African Campaign during World War 2. I have heard that he treated the Enemy's prisoners of War at the same level as his own soldiers. Same rations, same living conditions, but no weapons and no freedom of movement. I believe that at one time when the entire Regiment of the enemy was captured and he had no way of taking care of them he made them line up and put their weapons down on the ground and had a tank run over those weapons. He left them there and continued with whatever he had to do. Now compare this with you fighting along with your buddies at the border when the enemy picks up your best friend, takes him across the border, cuts him up into pieces and throws the pieces back at you. Which scenario is going to make your blood boil and make you fight even more fiercely? Naturally the second. So unknowingly Rommel's strategy was actually helping him.

My Q. No. 5 is **" Who is the most important person in your life that you should be in rapport with?"** When you had come home, I had asked you 'who is the most important person in your life?' and we had concluded that it is you yourself. **Therefore, you ought to be in total rapport with your own self. What does that mean? It means 'walk your talk and talk your walk'. Be the same inside and outside. Be sincere.**

Now look up your 6 questions and see if anything still remains to be answered.

Anwar: My question about facing interview panel of 6 to 8 people.

Keki: Who would like to answer it?

Gautam: I suppose you will create rapport with whoever is addressing you.

Keki: Absolutely. Any other questions?

Jaya: My Questions?

Keki: Yes Jaya, we will be dealing with difficult people and situations in the afternoon after lunch. Anybody else?

Saira: My question regarding somebody very emotional or very angry and telemarketing nuisance calls.

Keki: Regarding nuisance calls, you know how to break rapport and Ankur can tell you what to do with your gadget. Regarding a person being angry or highly emotional; remember the two water tanks which we discussed yesterday while dealing with the brain. So much is coming under pressure from the emotional tank that nothing can enter from the intelligence tank. So, it will be useless to appeal to the person's Logic or Reasoning. At such times keep your head and shoulders straight, not tilted as you have now, and tell the person 'Cool off and then we will discuss it' or something similar. Depending on the situation you may also raise your voice and then slowly lead the person to a slower and softer voice. Road rage will also fall anywhere between these and the exercise we are going to do after lunch.

Ankur: Can I have some more clarity on rapport during chat, email and telecon?

Keki: Who would like to take up this question? I suggest you first give the distinct requirements between the three.

Gautam: Chat is generally between friends or sometimes with an organization on the other side. Whenever we know the name of the person on the other side, we should use it as often as we can. I suppose the language, using representation system with V, A and K should be helpful. Email and Telecon can also be of either nature. Depending on the familiarity of the person on the other side our language can move from the unspecified words to the V, A, K and the use of the other person's name.

Keki: Very nice, Gautam. I hope you have some more clarity, Ankur. As all of you would have noticed **a lot depends upon our intentions. When you are in rapport with your own self, things will start happening more or less on its own.**

RAPPORT EXAMPLES

1. Discovery Channel once showed a program where 2 people were shown sitting in two different rooms. Both were told that they will get a visitor. One of them was asked to be friendly to the visitor and the other was asked to be non-committal. Each session was recorded. After a while they showed, under the table, that the person who was asked to be friendly, his visitor's legs were found to be in mirror image of the other; whereas the legs of the other pair were in total disarray. I said to myself 'yea, we know all about it'
2. If you have visited a restaurant, particularly during off peak period, you might have noticed, in some corner, a small table with two chairs and 2 people sitting, facing each other and in perfect rapport. Who are these two?

   Padma: Husband and wife.

   Saira: Before they were married. (laughter) Lovebirds is more like it.

   Keki: Absolutely. Just watch them. Both may be leaning forward towards each other, perhaps a bottle of cold drink in front of them and a plate of chips in the center with some sauce. The girl's hand goes forward to hold the bottle; she twirls it a little; soon the boy's hand also goes forward, he does the same. The girl picks up the bottle and sips the drink. The boy automatically follows the movement and takes a sip. The girl puts down the bottle and picks up a chip from the plate. The boy follows it up and the whole drama continues. You see, **when the conditions of trust, harmony and**

cooperation are already set in, then the body automatically gets into a rapport mode. If you are a regular at that restaurant then you may see this happening so often. But once in a way you may find that the girl is leaning against the backrest with eyes to the ground and the hands either on her lap or folded. The boy's body may be in a totally different way and you know, something is wrong. Maybe a lover's tiff.

3. The third example comes from our scriptures. You might have heard the name of Bhasmasur. Bhasmasur was a great devotee of Shiva. He was doing penance for Shiva and one day Shiva presented himself in front of him and said 'ask, whatever you want from me'. Bhasmasur said ' lord, give me a boon so that on whoever head I put my hand should burn into Ashes'. Shivji said Tathastu (so be it). Bhasmasur had a roving eye and Shiva's wife Parvati was very beautiful; he was also not sure if 'Tathastu' actually did everything or not. In order to check that out he extended his hand and went towards Shiva to put his hand on Shiva's head. Shiva got scared as to what he had done and ran to Vishnu. Vishnu asked ' Bholenath what happened, why are you huffing and puffing. When Shiva narrated the whole incident, Vishnu told him to relax, that he will take care of it. Vishnu took the form of Mohini the celestial dancer and came to Bhasmasur's ashram. I do not know what all she did out of the 10 points of rapport making but she started dancing. Bhasmasur was wonderstruck with her beauty and wanted to marry her. Mohini put a condition that if you dance along with me, only then I shall marry you. He immediately accepted and started dancing the way Mohini was. Now Mohini started slow and then increasing the tempo and the frenzy, finally put her hand on her head. That ended Bhasmasur in a pile of Ashes. Please take this only as a story and not an inspiration.

NLP AS PER BANDLER AND MY JOURNEY INTO NLP.

Now let us see how Richard Bandler himself wants us to understand NLP and if you are interested, then how I got into NLP. (the group says yes, yes).

Richard Bandler came to India just once in November of 1997. He took a weeklong program in Bangalore. I was in Bangalore at that time but

I was doing some advanced meditation program at one of the Ashrams and had no idea that he is in Bangalore or even in India. Later I have interacted with some participants who had attended that program. It appears that for the first two days the participants were so confused they did not know if it was an NLP program or a sex program. But from the third day there was a big rush to come and occupy the front seats. Bandler would do his magic on the participants and then his co-trainers would take up some exercises. People I met had undergone a transformation in themselves but they were not able to do it to others. I believe there was a lady who was wheelchair bound for a few years and was attending the program in her wheelchair but on the final day she went home walking. That is the power and magic of NLP.

If you want to know about my journey into NLP then I will have to start from the very beginning, and I do not know if all of you are ready for that.

Ankur: Sure, sure, we want to know everything.

Guneet: Whenever I have to make an investment in a consultant or in some costly equipment, I make it a point to take the person out for lunch or dinner, where I try to find out as much as possible about that person and that makes the transaction far more productive and meaningful.

Gautam: Sir, at most programs the speaker is introduced by somebody who preferably knows him personally and can share some personal details about the speaker. This puts the speaker's words into certain perspective and like Guneet says, more meaningful. So, I think we are all not just ready but waiting to get into the background that brought you into NLP.

Keki: Alright, you asked for it. So where shall I start? let me see. (Pause)

I can really see three individuals who really shaped my life and I am indebted to. I was eight years of age when I first started breathing the free air of Independent India, for this I am totally indebted to Mahatma Gandhi. Like Einstein said "generations to come will wonder that such a frail man walked this earth once".

The second person that I am indebted to is our first Prime Minister Pandit Jawaharlal Nehru. He talked about building the modern temples of India. These were the Hydroelectric projects, the Heavy industries, the Fundamental Research labs. He rightly picked up the exponential growth pattern that is suited to a large country of our size (even though the growth is slower in the beginning) as against the straight-line growth suitable for smaller countries and city States. When the newbie politicians ridicule the old guard and say 'what have they achieved in 60 years of Independence' they are not just ridiculing and insulting them but they are ridiculing and insulting our entire generation on whose shoulders they are gloating.

Muhammad Ali Jinnah is supposed to have said that 'I had just one typewriter and I got Pakistan; if I had a full office, I would have had the whole country'. Some even blame our founding fathers for the partition of India; maybe because they are not even aware that 45 years before independence the British, with their divide and rule policy, had partitioned Bengal into Muslim and Hindu areas, perhaps realizing that they will not last very long in this country.

I noticed that there is such a lot of misinformation going around and increasing by the day that it is impossible to believe something or somebody. Very often it is not just misinformation it is manipulative information, it is motivated information, it is malicious information, it is information for the convenience of some people. You think the media is giving you the facts whereas actually they are feeding you the information that someone wants to feed to you. This is not just restricted to media, even the history books are written and rewritten. This is not just restricted to India but it is a global phenomenon which is going on increasing and increasing. I have stopped believing in whatever is put in so called 'black and white'.

The third person I am indebted to is an Englishman Mr. Miller; works manager of a Tata Company. After completing my Mechanical and Electrical Engineering Diploma when I stood in the factory, I said to myself 'I do not know anything' because the syllabus that was set for us by the British, only taught the theory, enough so as to maintain the machineries being shipped to us. Mr. Miller was instrumental in bringing the Production Engineering program, on the UK pattern, for the first time to India just as I had completed my basic Engineering in 1961. After doing that 2year program when I stood in the factory, I said to myself 'there is nothing that I do not know'. It was also during this program that we were impressed with the idea that industry (or any other business) is 2% inspiration or Idea and 98% is human relations (whether it is design, planning, execution, procurement, marketing, finance, administration or anything else).

Armed with all this I quickly rose to the position of a General Manager looking after one factory at Bangalore and in few more years another at Tirupati. We were manufacturing the third hardest substance after diamond and the wear and tear on the equipment components was heavy. The breakdowns were time-consuming and costly. The repair and replacement had to be done on various other machines outside our factory. These mother machines that produce components for other machines come in various types. Fundamentally they have movements in x, y and z coordinates; with either the tool rotating or the job rotating. I designed a machine to incorporate all these features in one; a sort of one machine workshop. I was approaching 40. I said **this is one life, whatever I want to do I must do it now.** So, I resigned from my well-paying job in Dec.1981.

In the first 10 days I put down everything that was in my head on to the drawing board; then I took the drawings to the pattern maker for making wooden patterns; took the patterns to the foundry and got the castings poured; took the castings for machining along with other components for machining; brought them all into my garage to assemble my machine and by 4th of February 1982 I reached my machine from Bangalore to the All India Machine Tools Exhibition (IMTEX-82) at Mumbai.

The reviews were encouraging. I met the State Financial Corporation. They said oh, 'you are a first-generation entrepreneur, you are a qualified engineer, you will get this much from this scheme and that much from that scheme and if you go to the backward area c-zone of let's say Satara then you will get further financial benefit of this much. What they did not say is when I would get all those incentives and benefits. I prepared the detailed project report; put my request for finance as well as Land in the Industrial Area of Satara. Panchgani is a hill station close by to Satara where I had spent my childhood. By now I had four tiny daughters. We packed everything, put it in the truck and drove in my car down from Bangalore to Panchgani to reach there on our Independence Day 15th August 1982.

It took 4 years by the time all formalities were completed. I got the plot in the Industrial area, constructed the shed and started getting my machinery. By then not only all my savings had evaporated but even my Provident Fund had come down to zero.

During this intervening period, I had taken a table space at the prestigious Nariman Point, Mumbai, to start a recruitment agency and some consultation work. Managing from a distance was not new to me. One of my clients from Mumbai had an Industrial Valves manufacturing unit in Baroda. With just one visit per month, we had increased the production there by 6 times within 18 months with the same infrastructure.

When things got set at Satara, 3 of my own design machines were forming my capital equipment. I made them ready and they were also financed by the Financial Corporation. I was ready to take up actual production, so I went to my Bank asking for the working capital. They checked and said that my account was already 'sticky' so they can no longer provide any working capital. This was a slap on the face and remained a bone of contention. I had to immediately design a couple of new items which I could manage within the limits of finance. This sustained me for a few years on a hand to mouth basis. Things went from bad to worse. In 1993 ultimately the Finance Corporation exercised their right and took over the unit. Initially I would blame others or the system. But who was in charge of the project? Me. Who was in charge of smooth running of it? Me. Therefore in reality the fact is that I had totally messed it up. I was depressed. I was at my emotional lowest in my life. My total liabilities at that time were one and a half times my total gross salary that I had collected over my two decades of job career. Aban tried her best to take me to various people to come out of this mental condition. Nothing helped.

We moved from Satara to Pune to start a fresh life. Three of my daughters were in college and the youngest one in school. It was tough. Buying 1 liter of cooking oil at a time was a big issue.

At Pune I attended an HR conference hoping to meet some people where I could restart recruitment agency. The scenario was very different from Mumbai. But at that conference somebody in some context mentioned the name Neuro Linguistic Programming. It got stuck in my head as a Mantra. I had to make my own meaning out of it. There were no books in the market and no net. This is the period when I learnt about the Silva Method of mind control; Reiki; Yoga-meditation and such.

This was also the period when I attended a MITCON program to connect Small Scale Industry Entrepreneurs for their growth, with the help of consultants/ counselors. At this program six of the entrepreneurs became my clients. They have generally not been exposed to the big industry management concepts and neither can they afford to employ anybody of that caliber. So, I started taking one- or two-day programs to make them aware of relevant concepts.

In February of 1998 there was an advertisement in the newspaper regarding an NLP program in Mumbai. I immediately contacted them. The person at the other end recognized me. He was the same person who was organizing programs in Bangalore while I was in Bangalore. Many times, I had attended the program or sent some people from our factory to the programs. He immediately sent all the details. We were having a Silva Cottage meeting at my home, next afternoon when the courier arrived. I opened the envelope and straight away looked for the fees. It said ₹ 24,000/. I put it away saying this is not for me, I cannot afford it. Aban looked at the papers. She knew how keen I was regarding NLP. She said 'what is this Keki? We are in the middle of a Silva meeting; Silva is like design your destiny; why don't you at least program it'. I thought 'ok, programming it the Silva way is not going to cost me anything so why not I do it.' I did it and next day onwards I started talking about it to my clients and friends. Surprisingly they all said 'of course Keki you should go for it'. I said 'how? Who is going to sponsor me?' By the way, the relaxation exercise that we did last evening is from the Silva method.

Anyway, on the basis of actual collection or promise of payment of my pending bills or some advance payment and my promise of taking up a one- or two-day program if I go for this one, I felt a little hopeful. So, I called up the organizer and told him that I had collected only ₹ 11000. To my surprise he said 'come over'. I said 'what about the balance?'. His response was 'pay me as you can.' so there I was at the program beginning of May 1998.

Mumbai is at its hottest and sweatiest during this time of the year. On the second-last day of the program, at 1:45 in the night, I got up shivering. I had a thin cover around my waist. I wrapped it around myself to switch off the fan. My legs were shaking as I went to the washroom to relieve myself. I came back to the bed and said ' this can't be happening, tomorrow is the final day, if I miss it there is no certificate, my training will be incomplete and on top of it I still have to pay more than half the amount.' I somehow have an exercise that I had learnt 2 days earlier. To my great surprise in about 20 minutes, I could remove the cover from my feet, ankles, legs and the body and slept off. In the morning I got up as if nothing had happened. When I returned to Pune, I heard of somebody returning from Mumbai who was down with high fever; somebody else carrying the flu. So that was the proof of the pudding during the program itself.

My next experience of NLP happened within 10 days of returning. As I returned from outside one day, my wife, my daughter and her classmate who hails from up north, were sitting at the table. Soon as I entered Aban said ' let us get a man's opinion'. I was wondering as to what is coming next. So, I sat along with them. It appeared that this girl was being pursued by a guy from her hometown who was getting bolder by the day. As it is this girl was a little nervous and we had counseled her on couple of occasions during her examinations. My daughter said that she used to shiver at the very sight of this guy. I had a chat with this girl and made her to sit down for a 10-minute exercise that I had learnt. At the end of the exercise, I asked her not to think about it and just be normal, and see what happens. There was no news about her for a few days. One day suddenly my daughter came home exited and said ' daddy, daddy, do you know what happened?'. Then she narrated that it was their practical exams day and this guy had come to the lab, He called her out wanting to persuade her to travel to hometown for the summer holidays on the 40-hour train journey. When she refused, he tried to grab her hand but this girl caught him by the collar and said 'look here, I am no longer the same '******' so get lost and never show your face again. 'With this commotion the lab assistant came out and asked her if she needed some help. She replied 'no madam, I can handle him.' (I paused, concluding my story.)

Saira: Wow. Amazing. Did it really happen? Can it work like that?

Keki: Did what Really happen?

Saira: I mean the girl, your daughter's friend.

Keki: Tell me Saira; when you were sharing your rapport experience were you telling the truth or were you making it up?

Saira: No, no. I was telling everything as it actually happened.

Keki: Every word of what I said is truth. The whole truth, and nothing but the truth.

Saira; I am sorry. It is not that I was doubting you; but it is almost from a different realm.

Keki: It is. These two incidents one, during the NLP program and the other, soon after that, were the points of change. My life took a turn for the better and whoever has joined me in this journey of life, even if it is only for 5 days, have said that it has changed their life.

Guneet Singh: Actually, there are a lot more of WOW moments in your narration. It is only after the Gold goes through the severe heat of the Furnace that it gets Purified and Glitters forever. I for one am highly impressed.

Keki: Thanks, Guneet. (I see Ankur sitting with his eyes fixed to the ground) Ankur, you are very quiet today.

Ankur: You have left me speechless. I am even now trying - sorry not trying - digesting whatever I have heard so far. Can we have a small interval? -Please.

Gautam: I think we all need a small break.

Keki: Ok a break. Come back in 3 minutes; Sit at a new place, new neighbors.

Saira: Can I ask you one more question before we take a break?

Keki: Go ahead Saira.

Saira: Did this girl, your daughter's friend, remain aggressive from that point onwards?

Keki: Very good question, Saira. Did you notice that she did **not** become aggressive soon after the exercise? Everything is contextual. **From a lamb to a lion**; in what**?** 10 minutes. **Lamb-ness is also required in certain contexts and lion-ness is also required in certain other contexts. These are the individual's resources which they can bring out as and when necessary. So now her lamb-ness relaxes in**

the lap of the lion-ness knowing that she has both these resources and with that she can strive to reach any Pinnacle of Success that she wishes to achieve. Understood? Ok, a 3-minute interval.

(Once everybody returns and settles down.)

Keki: So now let us examine how Bandler wants us to understand NLP. (I distribute the Handout.)

The very first sentence is ***'NLP is an attitude.'*** What does that mean?

I can sit in this chair and (I sat erect with backbone, head and shoulders straight and with a firm voice) say 'I am very much interested in learning NLP'; or I can sit in this chair and (I make my body limp, slowly sliding down in the seat with each word and in a sing-song manner) say ' I am (pause) very much (pause) interested (pause and a casual wave of the hand) in learning NLP.'

Now these are 2 different attitudes. Which attitude do you think, is more likely to succeed? (the group says 'the first one')

It, further states ***'NLP is an attitude... Characterized by the sense of curiosity and adventure...'***

What is curiosity?

Saira: Wanting to know more.

Keki: Correct. If curiosity is wanting to know more, then what is adventure?

Ankur: Wanting to do more? Taking risks?

Keki: Wanting to do more. Taking risks. Are there no risks in curiosity? Why do we say that curiosity killed the cat?

Ankur: They also say that satisfaction brought it back.

Keki: In September of 2010 my youngest daughter jumped off from the 108th floor.

Padma: Aray Bhagwan! (Oh my God!) why? Where?

Keki: For fun. Stratosphere building in Las Vegas. She landed on the 2nd floor and exclaimed that those were the best 10 seconds of her life. (Padma took a deep sigh and said 'oh'.) so tell me, is life about curiosity or adventure? (Some said curiosity, some said adventure and a few said both.) All of you first heard something about NLP and maybe you got curious, maybe you wanted to find out more. Maybe you made some enquiries and found out how and where you can learn NLP. Then without knowing me personally or what was to happen during the five days; you enrolled and you are sitting here. First The curiosity then finding out more about it and a bit of adventure. Many others would have become curious but they did not take the next step. So, you are gaining something that those others are not.

Going further it says ***'NLP is an attitude characterized by the sense of curiosity and adventure and a desire to learn the skills to be able to find out what kinds of communication influences somebody and the kinds of things worth knowing... to look at life as a rare and unprecedented opportunity to learn.'***

Next it says ***'NLP is a methodology... Based on the overall operational presupposition that all behavior has a structure... and that structure can be modeled, learned, taught, and changed (reprogrammed). The way to know what will be useful and effective are the perceptual skills.'***

When you all said that the first attitude is more likely to succeed, what was it based upon? You were observing the structure of that behavior. If we would have video graphed both the attitudes, then slide by slide we could change one behavior pattern into the other.

The third thing it says is ***'NLP has evolved as an innovative technology enabling the practitioner to organize information and perceptions in ways that allow them to achieve results that were once inconceivable.'***

Most of you achieved a break-through result in your rapport making; but tell me, how many of you could have even anticipated or conceived that you could get the result that you got? None.

In Neuro Linguistic Programming the first word **neuro refers to** ***the Nervous system through which experience is received and processed through the five senses.***

Our brain contains 10 ^ 11 neurons, which means 1 followed by 11 zeros. Each neuron can connect to 1000 other neurons.

The second word ***Linguistic refers to language and nonverbal communication systems through which neural representations are coded, ordered and given meaning.***

Research shows that we are communicating only 7% by words, 38% is how we are saying those words, our tonality, and 55% is our body language.

Try saying these six-word sentence, six times emphasizing a different word each time. The sentence is 'I will goto (go to as one word) the NLP seminar' now say the same sentence for the seventh time in a very casual manner as if you are doing a favor to somebody. Did you notice how the meaning of the same six words changes in 7 different ways. Notice also that our emphasis is generally on the vowels.

3rd word ***Programming refers to, the ability to organize our communication and neurological systems to achieve specific desired goals and results.***

Programs are the neural Pathways and the circuits that we have created, and create in our brain. The very purpose of this program.

Now we come to one of the most important aspects of NLP. It is called

THE BASIC ASSUMPTIONS OF THE NLP MODEL.

Notice that we do not call these, the rules of NLP. One thing I like about NLP is that there are no dogmas.

What must have happened is in the early days of NLP trainings, the founders would have given the basic assumptions (or Presuppositions as they are sometimes referred to) along with explanations. People would have taken the notes as they could; and then some of them started writing books. So, there were various formats of presuppositions. Bandler ultimately appointed a committee to streamline all this and we have the final version with us. And it goes like this:

1) *The ability to change the process by which we experience reality is more often valuable than changing the content of our experience of reality.*

   Very simple, isn't it? Who would like to explain it? (all are looking at each other and confused). Ok, the key-words in the sentence are **'process'** and **'content'**. Content is the words. Process is the way those words are presented to you by way of tonality and your body language.

Imagine you have an important presentation next day afternoon. You have stayed back to dig out the missing information and made your lengthy report complete but it needs to be formatted. Next day morning within 10 minutes of reaching the office at 9 you take the report to the concerned person and tell him that you want this report completed and formatted by lunch time. He says 'yes, yes'. You hear it and come back satisfied. At 11:00 in the morning your boss calls you and asks you if everything is ready. You say yes sir, it will be ready by lunch time. The boss asks, are you sure? You respond ' yes sir, he promised, in fact he said yes, yes, twice.

2) *the meaning of the communication is the response you get.*

   You are always communicating. In English language there is a saying ' they also serve who stand and stare' So, at lunch time you go to the person, to collect the report. And what do you find? Those papers are lying on his table as it is, untouched by human hands. In fact, you had not paid attention as to how he communicated 'yes, yes' to you. Did he even lift up his eyes to look at you? What was his tonality? His body language? Do you know that he had already communicated to you that it is not going to happen? And you did not take any corrective action.

3) *All distinctions human beings are able to make concerning our environment and our behavior can be usefully represented through the visual, auditory, kinesthetic, olfactory and gustatory senses.*

   Those are the only five Windows that we have to the world.

4) *The resources an individual needs to effect a change are already within them.*

   Tell me, when you made successful rapport did you not change your behavior a little bit? Someone became little bolder, someone friendlier, most of you left your comfort zone even if it was only in some areas. These were your own resources. Did they come from a different planet? In fact, you always had all these resources but had not used it in this context. When we talk resources, we are not talking about material resources; we are talking about your internal resources. So, if somebody wants to be a super Industrialist, do not give me examples of Mukesh or Anil Ambani who inherited may be 200 billion worth Empires. Take the example of his father Dhirubhai who was a petrol pump attendant.

Now this makes my job, my task, as an NLP trainer/facilitator very, very simple. **I teach you nothing**. What do I do? **I just open some Gates and close some Gates**. I modify, add or delete some connections, some Neural Pathways in your brain. That is all, what I do.

For the next presupposition; (I pick up map of Pune and show it to everybody) tell me what this is? (The group says 'a map,' 'a map of Pune'.) My question is 'Is this Pune?' (The group says 'no, this is only a map of Pune'.) If I made this map as big as this room then will it be Pune? (the group again says 'no') and if I make this map as big as Pune itself and mark out each and everything about Pune, and then will it be Pune? (the group says no it will still be a map) (I put away the map and pick up my spectacles from the table. I show it to everybody and then hold it behind my back and say) I ask you to describe, what I just showed you, would you be describing what I am holding behind my back, or the impression it has left in your brain? (most in the group say 'the impression')

Manju: But both are same, isn't it?

Keki: Are they? Suppose I asked each one of you to write ten lines describing what I just showed you do you think everybody will write the same thing.

Manju: They will all write about your glasses.

Keki: Yes, on the topic of my glasses, my question is, will the description be the same?

Manju: May not be; but they will be writing about your glasses and there can be some differences.

Keki: Correct. The most important six words of NLP are:-

5) *The map is not the territory.*

Do you all want to find out how different our maps can be even for simple day to day things? (the group says 'yes')

I am going to say a few words; see what comes to your mind.

First word, glass; next cup; next pencil; next atom bomb; next dog; next Bill Clinton; next Boss; mother-in-law.

Ok, first word, glass, what came to your mind?

Manju: I saw your glasses which you had shown some time back.

Jaya: I saw the hotel glass from which I had water during the interval.

Anwar: I saw exactly the same thing as Jaya.

Keki: Oh, the same cylindrical glass. You are never seeing exactly the same thing as somebody else. So, describe it in your book, write down the height and diameter. (Anwar finished writing, Jaya could not) yes Anwar.

Anwar: 6 inches in height and two and half inches in diameter.

Jaya: I cannot tell inches or centimeters but I can show you with my hand. It was about this much in height and this much in diameter.

Keki: Is that how you saw it? Anwar.

Anwar: No, she is showing it much smaller.

Ankur: I think they are both out of mark. First of all, the glass is cylindrical only on the inside, outside it is 6 sided hexagonal and I think it is about 5 inches tall and 2 inches diameter inside.

Jaya: Is it really six sided?

Keki: OK what about the cup?

Padma; I saw the cup in which I have tea at home.

Anwar: I also saw the cup that I use at home.

Keki: Padma you must have seen the cup with the saucer, but I think Anwar might have seen it without a saucer. (both said yes almost simultaneously and Padma added 'how did you guess?). (I saw Vipul getting a little restless) so Vipul what came to your mind?

Vipul: A cup.

Keki: Describe it

Vipul: A Normal cup

Keki: And what would be a 'normal' cup for you? You must be having the most expensive Bone China cups for your rich clients.

Vipul: Oh no, I keep the most ordinary cheap ones.

Shankar: FIFA World Cup, concluded some time back and I saw the FIFA trophy.

Keki: What came to your mind when I said atom bomb.

Nirav: Death and destruction. (some said mushroom cloud, some others the Diwali cracker)

Saira: I saw my poor doggy getting scared of the big sound and hiding under the bed.

Keki: And what came to your mind when I said a dog? (I noticed Padma slightly recoiling) Padma?

Padma: I am too scared of dogs. I don't like them.

Anwar: I was picking up a stone to protect me. I was bitten by a dog when I was small and had to take 14 injections in my stomach.

Jaya: I love dogs. I was cuddling my Pom that I had lost, and was feeling sad.

Nirav: I was patting my neighbors' German Shepherd. He is quite well trained and does not jump all over you.

Keki: So, you see, when we are moving from inanimate objects to animate objects our feelings come into play. Even if I bring one dog for you all to see, somebody may feel fear, somebody anger, somebody love, somebody else sadness and so on. Let us move on to the next presupposition.

Shankar: Bill Clinton is still remaining!

Keki: I know what you have in mind.

Shankar: Monica (laughter all around).

Keki: Let us not worry about the boss and the mother-in-law. Somebody may hear us. (more laughter)

So, you see even for ordinary day to day items and words, our maps are so different. Forget about abstract words like courage, patriotism, love, hate, religion, spiritualism, meditation etc.

Nobody is talking of the reality; everybody is talking only about their own maps of reality. Sometimes I wonder how the hell do we communicate at all. I think we communicate based upon shared reality, or rather our maps of the same. If that is so then the question arises as to Who is right and Who is wrong. The simple answer is, nobody is right and nobody is wrong. If what you are saying from your map tally with what I have in my map, then I will say you are right. **The question of right and wrong just vanishes. In NLP our Emphasis is on what is useful or not useful. If it is useful continue using it. If it is not useful do something else.**

Sometimes you may be tempted to think that what the majority thinks must be right. Whenever such an idea comes to your mind think of Copernicus, think of Galileo. They were dragged through the streets because they said that the Earth is not in the center of the universe.

If you digest these 6 words "The Map, is Not, The Territory"; you can leave this hall right now and you will miss nothing. Your life will change.

The next presupposition says: -

6) The positive worth of the individual is held constant, while the value and appropriateness of internal and/ or external behavior is questioned.

Tell me, if we all get down on the ground on our fours and bark like a dog, in a crazy fashion, like we did yesterday, does that mean that we are all crazy people? (the group responds with an emphatic 'NO') That's right. If you behave stupidly for a little while your identity does not change to call you as stupid. Your positive worth remains the same, constant. Although your behavior at that point can be questioned. Is that clear?

Ankur: Clear. That means I can play my pranks at home and my mom still has to call me a good boy. (The group enjoys it.)

Keki*: #7) There is a positive intention motivating every behavior, and a context in which every behavior has value.*

If Ankur is playing pranks at home, his positive intention could be either to entertain his mom or to irritate her. It is only HIS positive intention, not a universal one and may not be his mother's. Obama's positive intention may be totally different from Osama's positive intention.

The next one says, #*8) successful communicators accept and utilize all communication/ behavior presented to them.*

In the first and second presupposition you saw what happened to your report that had to be formatted. Would you call such a person as a successful communicator? (the group agrees to a 'NO')

The final presupposition is

#9) Feedback vs failure - all results and behaviors are achievements, whether they are desired outcomes for a given task/ context or not.

You are achieving success or you are achieving failure, you are still achieving something, but in the latter case the outcome is not what you desired.

Now I know for certain that one person sitting over here failed in class 9. That person went home with a report card which showed the marks or the grades that she or he got in various subjects. At the end of it all was written, 'FAILED'. My question to you all is 'is that person a failure?'

Manju: That person failed in class 9 but that person is not a failure.

Keki: So, what is the report card saying?

Manju: It is saying in which subjects that person failed.

Shankar: It is giving a feedback to that person as to which subjects, she or he has to improve in.

Keki: Very good. There are no failures; only feedback. The so-called failures are actually opportunities for improvement; whether it is in the examination of a class, or examination of life. Understood? (the group says 'yes' but some in the group say it very softly)

And yet sometimes you find somebody hanging under a fan, in a mistaken notion that she or he is a failure, herself or himself.

The basic assumptions are like an onion. Every time you go through it you will find a newer deeper layer to it. Anytime I have found myself in a stuck situation or facing a tough issue, I have gone through the basic assumptions one more time and always found an appropriate and useful answer. Padma, do you use an onion at home?

Padma: Yes, I do. Almost daily.

Keki: Show me how you will get it ready for use. Imagine you have an onion in one hand and a knife in the other, what will you do?

Padma: It will depend upon how I want to cut the pieces after I peel it; weather I want long slices or diced or rings.

Keki: Go ahead and peel it. I will tell you how we want to use it after you get ready with it. Do the actions of peeling and cleaning. I think you are removing the bottom portion where the roots are. (Padma says yes and turns the imaginary onion over). Looks like we are removing the top portion of it now. (Padma nods and puts the knife down and uses her hands now). Now what are you doing?

Padma: I am removing the dry skin from the top.

Keki: Did you all notice what she has done before she can use the onion. She has **discarded all that appeared at the first sight and on**

the outside. This is the starting point for using an onion or using our basic assumptions. Thank you, Padma.

Now we are ready to use it whichever way we want. Initially it will have a raw smell. Then as we give it the energy of heat it starts giving out an Aroma, becomes sweeter, changes texture. The changes continue and if you are deep frying it, it will turn golden brown and crisp and will make many dishes very, very tasty.

Gautam: Superb.

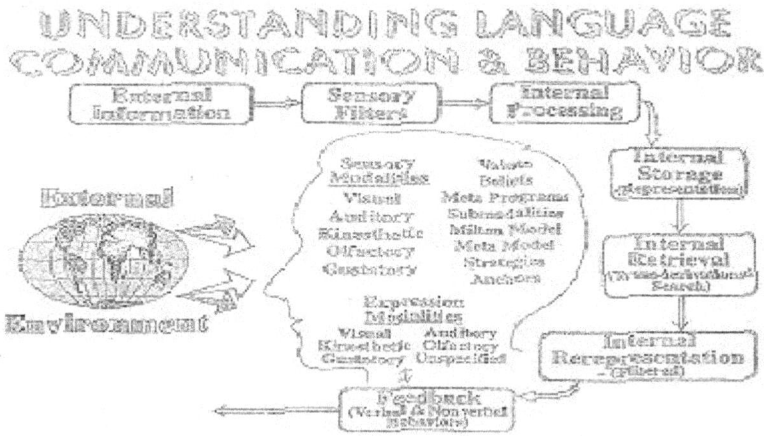

Figure 11

Keki: If you look at the accompanying figure you will notice that the external environment is constantly bombarding us with the external information. I believe that at any moment we are getting 400,000 bits of information. Our sense organs work within a limited range. For example, we can see from violet to red colors. We are not able to see ultraviolet, perhaps butterflies do; we are not able to see infrared, perhaps bats do. Likewise, we can hear from 20 cycles per second up to 20,000 cycles per second frequencies; dogs can hear higher and elephants can hear lower. All that reduces our capacity to 140 thousand bits of information at any moment. They say that we can process only 7 plus/ minus 2 bits of information at a time. Within the brain is your center called the **RAS or Reticular Activating System** that determines what is of importance to us and allows only those bits of information to get internally processed. Internal processing happens based on our values and beliefs. Here we may find some deletion, distortion and generalization taking place. Whatever passes through gets stored in our memory as a re-presentation of the original presentation. Whenever we are communicating with others it does a **trans-derivational search** to retrieve that information. Then it will filter out what we are not comfortable with sharing and we re-represent our internal representation as our verbal and nonverbal behavior.

EXTERNAL REALITY	SENSORY INPUTS	3 UNIVERSAL MODELING PROSSESES	OUR MODEL OF REALITY	OUR LANGUAGE & WORDS
(lila) (Maya)	V- Visual A - Auditory K- Kinesthetic O- Olfactory G- Gustatory	Deletion Distortion Generalization	Maps in the Mind	Words Tonality Body-Language Breathing Eye movements

Figure 12

As you will see in the table above the external reality is taken in by our sense organs, our internal processes undergo **three universal modelling processes- deletion, distortion and generalization**; which then results in 'our model of reality' and finally we are using words and language to communicate with others. Thus, our words and language are 5 steps removed from actual reality. It can never ever reach the reality. You may now want to think about our scriptures which talk about the Leela, or the dance of creation, and of Maya, our distorted view of reality; thank you.

It is already almost 2:30. The Diner will stop being served by 3 pm. I suggest let's all rush for the lunch and be back in an hour.

(After lunch)

Three Things to Practice

Keki: There are only three things that you will have to practice during and after the program.

#1 is rapport making. Consciously practice this for 21 days and it will become a part of you. Do not ever make a mistake, thinking that you now know it and you can use it whenever you need it. Initially when you are practicing it, you may lose out or miss out, on the words; but once you have practiced, then the words that are spoken and more importantly, what is not spoken, will all become far more meaningful.

#2 is getting into Alpha; the closing exercise that we did yesterday evening. If you all wish, I can give you a synopsis of that exercise and the switch by which you can get into Alpha instantaneously. But not now. Practice this also for 21 days.

At #3 is your sensory acuity. This is a lifelong process even for the Great Master whose story you heard yesterday morning.

All the rest of the things that we do during the program are 'fit and forget' type. And how does that work? At any moment your behavior and what you prefer to do, is determined by your past programming, your circuits in the brain, your Neural Pathways. Your RAS center determinants the 7 +/- 2 bits of information that are relevant and important to you at any moment. Hence you live out your life automatically as per what is important to you without putting any more special efforts.

After practicing these, it should and will, become a part of your attitude. There will come a day when you will suddenly wonder ' why is the world so good? why are everybody so nice to me?'. On that day you can say that rapport making has become a part of your unconscious competence.

YOUR GOAL SHEET FORMAT

So next we are going to make our own goal sheet. Today I will give you the format and show you how to fill it up at home. Tomorrow we will check what you have done. Then you will convert it into a wish list; and on the 4th day of the program, I will show you how to put it on autopilot. Fit and forget. Just see it happening.

Copy out the format on a plane sheet of paper in landscape orientation. You can also use Excel on your laptop when you go home.

AREAS OF IMP. IN LIFE		**TODAY (–) 5 YRS**		**TODAY**		**TODAY (+) 5 YRS**
	LoS	**COMMENTS**	**LoS**	**COMMENTS**	**LoS**	**COMMENTS**

Ok, so like that you will fill up about 8 to 10 areas which are important to you in your life. Leave about 6 to 8 blank, which you may use tomorrow.

Now come to the 'Today' column and fill up either today's date or tomorrow's date depending upon your preference of an auspicious day. There are two columns underneath this. The first one says LoS. Meaning your Level of Satisfaction. You will rate your present level of satisfaction in this area of life from 1 to 10. 1 being not at all satisfied and 10 being fully satisfied. Then you will fill up the LoS column for 5 years back on this day. You are rating may be higher or lower depending upon how you have progressed in this area of life. Now you will have to be sincere in finding the cause of the increase or decrease and write those comments in appropriate column. Just saying 'I was lazy', 'I was busy 'etc. will not be useful. All those excuses will not help you. You will find the reason why rating went up or down and put those as your comments. Do not at all touch the final column of five years from now. We will keep that for the final day. Any questions? Fine. I MUST have the sheet filled up, except the final column, by tomorrow morning when you come in.

The first column says areas of importance in life. 'Somebody please give me some area of importance in your life'. (Ankur - education; Professor - savings; Doctor - profession; Padma - children; Saira - love and nature; Jaya - relationship; Anwar - job; Manju - business; Guneet -life; Vipul - money; Gautam - community.

Ok, so, like that you will fill up about 8 to 10 areas which are important to you in your life. Leave about 6 to 8 blank, which you may use tomorrow.

MAKING RAPPORT WITH A 'DIFFICULT' PERSON

We have been saying that the first thing to do in any interaction is to create Rapport. However, there are times when you cannot even get an entry into somebody's cabin or somebody's heart, weather in professional setting or domestic setting. What do you do then? We will do this.

Over here we will form groups of 3 or four. One person will be a client who knows somebody that he or she finds difficulty with. The next person will act as a visitor. The third person will act as a counselor to the visitor and the fourth may assist the counsellor.

The process will be like this. The client, before taking his or her seat, will inform the group in one or two sentences as to who is the person with whom he or she is having difficulty and what does the client want from that person. You do not have to take any names, just the broad outline of that person. Then the client takes the seat and as long as he or she is in that seat the client will take on the role and behavior pattern of that difficult person. The visitor will take on the role of the client. The visitor will leave his or her place and go to meet the client with appropriate greeting. When that happens, the client, who is now in the role of the difficult person, will put up the same behavior pattern that he or she receives from that difficult person. The client will not except the greetings (may be an extended hand for a handshake) from the visitor. In this whole exercise the handshake is symbolic. A Handshake will mean a breakthrough. By now the visitor, who was in the role of the client, has experienced what the client experiences with that difficult person and has failed to create rapport. So. the visitor goes back. The visitor now calls the client by his or her name, and requests the client to come to him or her. As the client has vacated his or her chair the client is no longer in the role of the difficult person but acts as herself/himself. When the client has reached the visitor, the visitor says exactly these words; "Please give me a hint so that I can shake hands with you".

Realize that the client is the only person in this group who knows that difficult person. Therefore, she or he is the only person who can give any hint. After giving the hint the client returns to her chair resuming once again, the role of the difficult person. The visitor now confers with his counselor and co- counselor, as to what change of behavior he should put on. Armed with this changed behavior, he again approaches the client taking on her role.

If the client is satisfied that the new behavior pattern just might work, then there is a handshake otherwise the visitor goes back to his seat. He again repeats the process of calling the person to him and this time he says " please give me a better hint so that I can shake hands with you." this process continues until there is a handshake.

Anwar: I have a question.

Keki: I know. No questions right now. All questions will be taken up after you are finished with the exercise. Is this clear or you all want a demo? (the group says 'demo')

(I go to my chair and before sitting down I briefed the group,) This is a business setting; where there are two partners running an enterprise. One of them is the difficult person. I have been appointed as a consultant. I want to do my work which needs interaction with the top people and the first couple of meetings would go like this. I want one of you to come as a visitor. (Anwar comes. I stand up and clarify) Anwar, now you are taking over the role of me, as Keki. And as I sit down, I am becoming that difficult partner with his behavior pattern. (I sit down. Anwar comes up to me)

Anwar: Hello sir, how are you? (stretching out his hand for a handshake) there is something I have to discuss with you.

Keki (as the difficult partner): (I continue what I was doing. Writing something, working on the calculator, again writing, and generally ignoring him)

Anwar: Sir, I have some work with you. Can I have a minute just to tell you what it is?

Keki: (Again ignoring him. When he still persists) What? Why are you here? How did you come in? Can't you see I am busy? I have an important meeting at 4:00; it is already 3:45; it will take me at least half an hour to reach there; I am very punctual person. You can go to the shop floor. If I return, I will see you. (Obviously there is no handshake and I signal him to go back. He goes back and sits down not knowing what to do next.)

Gautam: (to Anwar) Call him here, by his name, to ask the question.

(Anwar looks at him quizzically as to what next. Gautam points at the whiteboard where I have put down the question statement.)

Anwar:(Calls me and I go to him.) Please give me a hint so that I can shake hands with you.

Keki: You heard that guy. He is a president of the Rotary Club. Big bloody ego. Look around in his office, see if you can find some new photograph, some new trophy, and butter his ego to the maximum and see what happens. Work it out with Gautam as your consultant. (I go back to my seat and resume the role of the difficult person.) (Anwar confers with Gautam and comes to me)

Anwar: (as he comes to me) Hello sir, how are you sir, good morning sir. There is something we have to discuss, sir.

(I continue writing in my book, using the calculator, writing again and basically ignoring him. From my peripheral vision, I make out that he is looking at Gautam for help and Gautam gives some signal.)

(Anwar continues) This is a new photograph, sir. Looks like somebody is giving you a Trophy or something.

Keki: (looking up at his face) This photograph? You know it came in the local newspapers also. You did not see it? It is my District Governor giving me the trophy for the best Rotary President of the district. Come, come. I think you came yesterday also. You know what? I could have seen you yesterday itself. It was that Rotary Club-Service meeting but nobody had come. Sit down. Sit down. (I get up from my seat and shake hands with him.)

(To the group.) Same old rigmarole, which has not worked so far. He would have had to go back but I think Gautam saved his day and he jumped to the hint. Cut out all that has not worked and jump straight to the hinted behavior pattern. Another mistake Anwar made was, not to extend his hand for a handshake as soon as he saw me melting. You have to take that initiative and not wait for or expect the 'difficult' person to do so. In fact, he or she is 'difficult' only because such persons are finding you in that category.

Form your groups and start the exercise. Follow the exercise to the dot; without a single shortcut or variation. Take real issues, hot issues, issues that are bothering you now. That person has to be in your life now and you have a need to deal with that person. Absolutely nothing hypothetical. Each person of the group will alternately take all the positions. I give you 20 minutes to complete the exercise. Start now.

(I now go down to my personal space near the swimming pool and return after 20 minutes.)

(Two groups have already finished the exercise; one is still working; in the 4th group the lady is stuck as to what hint to give regarding her mother-in-law. I tell her that 'amongst the worst of us there is some good'. Even if we are refusing to look at it; there is something that, that person likes for herself, some item, some event, anything. It most likely will not have anything to do with you. Find something and sincerely start praising her. That could possibly be the hint that you give. (' Colorful sarees', she said with a Eureka moment on her face. And I left them to complete the exercise. Once I saw the mother-in-law and daughter-in-law, hugging each other, I knew that the exercise was over.)

Keki: How many of you think that you had a breakthrough? How many of you think that the new behavior pattern as brought up by the visitor based on your hint may just about work? (most of them raise their hand)

Anwar: I have a question?

Keki: Please hold on. I will take your question once we are through with this. Everybody, please look up your basic assumptions of NLP model and tell me which assumption comes out very glaringly in this exercise. (Different people read different basic assumptions. I had to repeat the same sentence to all of them.) That too but something else comes out more glaringly. (until Gautam points out...)

Gautam: The resources an individual needs to effect a change are already within them.

Keki: You hammered the nail on the head. Very good. Now please explain how you say that this basic assumption comes out most glaringly.

Gautam: Because the client is finding some person 'x' as difficult but the client himself or herself is giving the hint as to how one could break through that person.

Keki: Absolutely. You see the client is so much stuck up in his or her existing behavior pattern that he or she is not able to come out of it. The visitor is calling the client to his chair. So, the client moves from his or her present position; in other words, dissociates himself and in that dissociated state, is capable of giving a hint. The visitor is doubly dissociated. He is totally uninvolved with 'x' and only has to act out the new behavior pattern coming out of the hint. Is that clear now?

Anwar: I am still confused.

Keki: Of course, you are. I am also confused as to how to look at your face. The way you are looking at me sideways through the hair falling over your eyes like a Poodle dog. Anybody will be confused. I want to see your bright forehead tomorrow morning. So, either cut out all that unnecessary fringe or wear a girl's hair pin. (many in the group laugh). Anwar, I am very serious, I do not want to see all that fringe in your eyes tomorrow morning. (Anwar meekly says 'yes')

Come on, let us all break for tea/coffee and come back in 15 minutes.

THE PACER TEST

(Once Everybody is in)

Keki: Now onwards you may have to make some statements about what you want. Whenever you make such statements, your statements will have to qualify a certain test. We call it a PACER test

'P' stands for being stated in the positive. Suppose somebody thinks that he is poor, somebody realizes that he gets angry very easily. And the person says 'I do not want to remain poor'; or the other one says 'I do not want to get angry'. Are these statements in a positive? No. The first one can be stated as 'I want to earn a lot of money'. The second one can be stated as 'I want to remain cool' or 'I want to be in control of my mind'

'A' stands for 'Achieve.' How will you know when you have Achieved it? For the person who says, I want to earn a lot of money, how much is 'a lot'? If he is earning 300 now, is 400 'a lot'? If she is earning 200 thousand, then is 300 thousand 'a lot'? Your statement has to be specific and measurable. If she says 'I will earn 300 thousand within one year, starting now', then it is specific and measurable both in value and in duration. The person who says 'I want to remain cool'; instead says 'today I will not lose my cool except maybe once and continue that for a week; then onwards maybe just once in a week; then onwards maybe once in a month; in six months' time, I am in total control of my mind'; then it is specific and measurable. The person will know at the end of the period, whether he has achieved it.

'C' refers to context. Suppose you say you want more confidence. In what context do you want that confidence. Is it to face your boss, your wife or your neighbor's wife?

'E' is for ecology check. When we say Ecology in NLP, we are not talking about plastic bags. Ecology check has two aspects: - i) how will what you want affect others?

Suppose you say 'I want promotion to the next level by 1st of Jan. next year'. Your salary may increase and that is fine but you may be sent to another city on promotion. How will that affect your family, your friends, your other activities, and the same thing about your wife and children? ii) the second aspect of ecology check is **'is what you want dependent on somebody or something?'** If that is so then the question immediately changes to **'what should I do so that so and so can do such and such?'** say for example, you want promotion to the next level by 1st of Jan. next year, then all you need to do is pick up your company letter-head, type out your promotion letter and sign it. Isn't it?

Anwar: How is that possible? I will be thrown out of the company if I do that.

Keki: Is that so? So how should it be done?

Anwar: The company management will have to write out that letter.

Keki: I see, and will you have to do anything so that they can do it?

Anwar: You mean I'll have to work still harder?

Keki: Oh no. Absolutely not. A headless chicken also runs around here and there and round and round and getting nowhere. I am not the one taken up by hard work**, I believe in smart work**. And that brings us to the final 'R' in the PACER test.

'R' stands for resources. These are not material resources. A fat bank balance is not considered a resource; **ability to create that fat bank balance is the resource.** These resources are your internal resources.

There is an exercise in your manual based upon what we have just done. You will pair up and do this exercise with each other. Let me read it out to you and explain. It says: -

INFORMATION GATHERING

The key to successful interactions

The meta model

From the works of Alfred Habdank Skarbek Korzybski

The key questions

1) *what do you want? (anything that you want to achieve in life, or a shorter period)*
   a) *stated in positive terms* (P of our PACER test)
   b) *initiated and controlled by client* (point ii of our ecology check)
   c) *specific sensory based, see - hear - feel.* (A of the PACER test)
   d) *small chunk size.* (if what you want is like a tall ladder you may have to break it down and take the first step and then the further steps)

1A) *What will that do for you?* (Just saying that it will make me happy or satisfied is not enough. Specify and enumerate concrete and preferably measurable benefits that it will give.)

2) *How will you know when you have it?* (again, 'A' of the PACER test; specific and measurable)

3) *Where, when, and with whom do you want it? Sensory based and ecological.*

4) *How will this affect other aspects (or people) in your life?* (point i of the PACER test)

5) *What stops you from having this already?* (Once again just saying I was lazy, I had no time, I was thinking about it, etc. will get you nowhere. Be sincere, address your fears if any. Only that will take you further.)

6) *What resources do you already have that will help you obtain your outcome?*

   Imagine, that our friend Anwar over here, is being considered by his company to be put in charge of a 20 million project. He has not done anything like this before. What he has done is, when he was 11 years of age, he and two of his friends had watched India win the Cricket World Cup. This inspired them and they wanted to play cricket. Three of them went to the market and found out that a cricket bat, a suitable ball and 3 wickets will cost them around 500. How to get the 500? One of them said that they have waste newspaper pile at home, he will ask his mom if he could go and sell it and keep 50% of that cash; another said he will make some sandwiches and sell them; the third said he has saved some pocket money and will save some more. Once that was done, they went and bought the equipment. They started playing. Neighboring boys wanted to join them. The group became seven or eight strong. They found that some of the boys were good at batting. some others at bowling, one was good at wicket keeping. They gave appropriate position to appropriate person. Soon more boys joined. Now they wanted to challenge the neighborhood and fixed up a match day. Cricket here is just an example.

   The very same resources which Anwar showed at age 11 are the resources which are required now for the 20 million project. They are all there, behind that shining forehead of his.

7) *This says 'what additional resources do you need to obtain it?'*. For the 20 million project Anwar may need a readymade computer engineer. He can then employ somebody like Ankur but he certainly has a resource, to learn something new.

8) *How are you going to get there?*

a) *First step, be specific and achievable.* (the first step could be that you will reach home and send out a mail; and set the ball rolling)

b) *Is there more than one way to get there?* (Always, there is.)

So now pick up your partner and start the exercise. You start asking questions to your partner. Bring him or her to a crisp and complete answer and ask him or her to write it in their own book in their own handwriting. I will give you 20 minutes to complete the exercise both ways.

(I return after 20 minutes from my favorite place near the swimming pool and check the first item and the last item to make sure that they have chosen the subject well and come to proper conclusions. I ask the group to pack up everything and get ready for the closing exercise. Once they are ready, I start the closing exercise.)

LOVE SCRIPT

Put your feet flat on the ground, sit up straight, backbone straight, push your tailbone into the chair, take a deep breath and while exhaling close your eyes and relax. One more time, take a deep breath and this time, hold your breath when you have filled your lungs with clean refreshing relaxing air. Hold it in. Keep your eyes closed. Now let your breath out slowly and feel yourself relaxing all over.

I want you to imagine now that all your tensions, all your tightness, and all your fears and worries are draining away from the top of your head. Let it drain down through your face, down through your neck, through your shoulders, through your chest, your waist, your hips, your thighs, down through your knees, your calves, your ankles, your feet, and out your toes. All your tension, all your tightness, all your worries and fears are draining away now from the very tips of your toes, and you are relaxing more and more.

Focus your attention on your toes now and allow your toes to relax completely. Each toe is loose and heavy. Now let this relaxation flow into your feet, into your ankles, your calves, your knees. Feel it flowing into your thighs, into your hips, into your waist, flowing up into your chest now. Feel your breathing easier and deeper, more regular and more relaxed. Now let the deep relaxed feeling go into your shoulders, down your arms, into your upper arms. your forearms, and into your hands and fingers, and flowing back into your forearms, your upper arms, your shoulders. Flowing into your neck, over your face, your chin, your cheeks, even your ears are relaxed, feel it flowing into your eyes and eyelids now. Your eyelids are so heavy and smooth. Flowing up into your eyebrows, over your forehead, over the top of your head, down the back of your head, and down the back of your neck.

A new heaviness is starting in your toes now. Twice as heavy as the first time. Imagine a heavy weight on each toe. Feel the heaviness deep and even more relaxed. And this heavy, deep feeling is going into your feet, your ankles, your calves, your knees, going into your thighs, your hips, into your waist. Flowing up into your chest now, relaxing your heart, relaxing your lungs, allowing your breathing to be more intense, more regular, more and more completely relaxed. Now, the deep heavy feeling is flowing into your shoulders, and down your arms, your upper arms, your forearms, into your hands and fingers. And now flowing back through your forearms, your upper arms, into your shoulders, and into your neck. Flowing over your face, into your eyes, over your eyebrows, over your forehead, over the top of your head, down the back of your head and down the back of your neck.

And a new heaviness is starting now at the top of your head. Twice as heavy as before. Twice as heavy. Imagine a heavy weight on the very top of your head, soft relaxed and heavy. Feel the heavy relaxation flowing down into your face and eyes now, down through your neck, your shoulders, flowing down through your chest, your waist, your hips, your thighs, your knees, into your calves, your ankles, your feet and toes. Deeply relaxed, loose and limp, and comfortable from the top of your head to the very tip of your toes.

Just go on relaxing more and more deeply. Feel yourself sink into the chair, mind and body drifting deeper and deeper into relaxation, deeper with each breath.

As you breathe in, imagine that you are breathing in a pure, clean, odorless anesthesia. The anesthesia is flowing, all throughout your body now. It is a warm, numb, tingling feeling, and the more you breathe in, the more you want to breathe in, and you allow your breathing to become even deeper now, bringing in more and more of this peaceful, relaxing, tranquil feeling. From now on until the end of this session, you will allow yourself to relax more and more completely with each breath you take.

I want you to imagine now that you are looking at a clear, blue summer sky. And in the sky, a sky-writing airplane is writing your first name in fluffy, white cloudlike letters. See your name floating fluffy, white, and cloudlike in a clear, blue sky. Now let your name just dissolve away. Let the winds just blow your name away into the blue. Forget about your name. Forget you even have a name. Names are not important. Just go on listening to my voice and allowing yourself to relax more deeply.

I want you to imagine now that you are standing on the top step of a heavy wooden staircase. Feel the carpet under your feet. The carpet can be any kind and color you wish . . . create it. Now extend your hand out and touch the railing. Feel the smooth polished wood of the railing under your hand. You are standing just ten steps up from the floor below. The stairs are curving very smoothly down to the floor below. In a moment we will walk down the stairs. With each step down you will allow yourself to relax even more deeply. By the time you reach the floor below you will be deeper than you have ever gone before. Take a step down now, down to the ninth step smoothly and easily. Feel yourself going deeper. Now down to eight, deeper still. Now down to seven . . . six . . . five . . . four . . . three ... two ... one. Now you are standing on the floor below. There is a door in front of you. Reach out and open the door. And from the room beyond the door a flood of light comes streaming out through the open doorway. Walk into the room, into the light through the open door. You are inside the room now, look around you. This is your room, and it can be anything you want it to be. Any size, any shape, any colors. You can have anything in this room that you want. You can add things, remove things, rearrange things. You can have any kind of furniture, fixtures, paintings, windows, carpets, or whatever you want because this is your place...your very own private inner place and you are free here. Free to create, free to be who you are. Free to do whatever you will, and the light that shines in this room is your light. Feel the light all around you, shining on the beautiful things in your room. Shining on you; feel the energy in the light. Let the light flow all through your body now. Going in through every pore in your skin. Filling you completely. Pushing away all doubt. Pushing out all fear and tension. You are filled with the light. You are clear and radiant, glowing with the shining light in your room.

While you are standing in the light in your room you will have the opportunity to express your love to many people and about many things. Now bring your **mother** into your room by mentally asking that she be present.

(Pause 5 Seconds.) Now mentally repeat the following to your mother as I say it: "Mother, I do not pass judgment on you. I do not have the wisdom to pass judgment on anyone. You gave me life, Mother, and you always did the best you could. I love you for that, Mother, and I bless you and release you to your higher self."

I will stop talking now for ten seconds while you express your love to your mother in your own way.

(Pause 10 Seconds.) Now bring your **father** into your room.

Now mentally repeat the following to your father as I say it: "Father, I do not pass judgment on you. I do not have the wisdom to pass judgment on anyone. You gave me life, Father, and you always did the best you could. I love you for that, Father, and I bless you and release you to your higher self." I will stop talking now for ten seconds while you express your love to your father in your own way.

(Pause 5 Seconds.) Now you will have the opportunity to bring other **people** of your choice into your room and express your love to them. They may be a spouse, brothers, sisters, friends, or even someone you have never met. You bring the people into your room by mentally calling out their names and greeting them with words such as "I love you and bless you and release you to your higher self" or use other words of your own choosing. I will stop talking for 30 seconds now while you do this. You may begin now.

(Pause 30 Seconds.) Now mentally repeat the following to yourself as I say it: "I send my love to all those people who I have not yet sent it to."

Pause 5 Seconds.) You may now express your love about many other things. Repeat the following statements to yourself as I say them. "I love life. I love all life, and I respect all life." "I love all the creatures on this earth even though I don't necessarily care to be around some of them." "I love all creatures because they are part of all creation just as I am, and they do their best to do what they must do to fill their role in life just as I do." "I love my country even though it has its faults." "I love myself in a quiet, self-appreciative way, and not in an egotistical, conceited way." "I love myself even though I have faults." "I love all the things I don't understand as well as all the things I do understand." "Love is the driving force in my life." Now take a deep breath and go deeper.

I will now stop talking for 20 seconds while you meditate on love and express your love about anything you wish. (Pause 20 Seconds.) Now take a deep breath and go deeper. You have created a powerful aura of love around yourself by your positive expression of love. This aura will attract love in many forms to you. Your life is greatly enriched as of this moment, and it will continue to be enriched the more you express love in your thoughts, words, deeds, and actions, and this is so. Love is the driving force in your life. Now take a deep breath and relax. Every time you think of this it makes you feel just wonderful. And each time you think of this you will relax completely. You will go even deeper than you are now, and the suggestions will go deeper and deeper into your mind. By using this faithfully, you will bring more and more love into your life at every level of your life.

The next time you hear this voice, you will allow yourself to relax ten times more deeply than you are now. And the suggestions I have given you will keep on going deeper and deeper and deeper into your mind.

In a few moments when you awaken yourself, you will feel very, very relaxed, and you will be completely refreshed, alive, alert, full of energy, full of confidence, and full of love. You will feel simply marvelous. All you have to do to awaken is to count with me from one up to five and at the count of five, open your eyes, feeling relaxed, refreshed, alert, in very high spirits. Feeling very good indeed. 1 . . . 2 . . . 3 . . . 4 . . . 5.

Eyes open, feeling fine, feeling happier than before, feeling healthier than before, more alert than before. Smile at the world and smile at your neighbors.

Good evening. Good night and see you all tomorrow with your Goal Sheet completed as required.

CHAPTER 4

CONVERSATION WITH ANUSUYA-ANUSUYA PLANTS THE SEED

Once the participant attends a program, our Association is lifelong. They pay again only when they are doing the higher-level program or the sitting fees while refreshing the old program.

Some participants become active again and contact us even after a decade. Some stay in touch and then disappear. Many contact us for having recommended our name to someone, and they can avail of a small discount when they are attending the next program.

Anu had sent us a mail giving her success story within six months of doing her first program. She refreshed the program a year after she had done the first one; and had sent a second mail few months after refreshing.

Based on these we had started sending her an invitation to join our NLP Master Practitioner program. Anu showed a desire to meet us and accordingly we met. The conversation went more or less as follows, after we welcomed her and had some small talk;

Keki: So Anu, I would like to hear your progress since your first program.

Anu: I had sent you a mail after my first program and in fact another mail after I had refreshed the program next year. Of course, that was also a year back.

Keki: Yes, Aban and I, both had read them but we would like to hear it from you in more detail.

Anu: Shall I tell you everything and frankly?

Keki: That is what we expect.

Anu: Frankly and although I did not mention this in my mail, at the end of the first program I was somewhat confused and also disappointed. Confused because I thought we were all here and there doing so many things and sometimes quite rapidly, but I was waiting as to when you were taking up my case, like you had taken up Padma's case during the rapport demo. Disappointed also because I was expecting that you would give me directions and actions to take.

Keki: I am glad you are sharing this with me now.

Aban: But Anu we both found your first mail quite positive.

Anu: It was truthful. I was quite thrilled with the unexpected results of my rapport making and for first few weeks at least, I continued with it. Then maybe because of my disappointment I left that also. In time I realized that people around me were changing. They were behaving differently towards me. My kid was playing more with me now and I was enjoying it. Even Suresh was taking me out more often. The maid became almost like a friend and even confided a few things in me. I had never expected this.

Keki: So, the people around you started behaving better with you; what about you? Did you notice any change in yourself?

Anu: Only after I wrote that mail to you. A few times I caught myself being more receptive and tolerant when things did not agree with me. So, I thought that perhaps unawares I was also changing and that's why I wanted to refresh the program.

Keki: And what happened after you refreshed the program.

Anu: That program was totally different from the first one. You did so many things which I felt we had not done during the first program. Am I making sense?

Keki: Oh, very much. Do you remember the Iceberg model of the mind which we do on the first day evening? Think of that model and many things will become clearer to you. And by the way does your husband Suresh have permission to enter your bedroom at night nowadays.

Anu: (Laughs) Now that my kid is almost 5 years of age, we have converted that room into a kid's room with lot of play things and I have shifted into Suresh's room. I am also thinking of opening a Boutique but Suresh thinks I should first have a talk with both of you. So, do you think I am ready for doing the Master Practitioners program and start my business?

Keki: I don't know, you tell me, do you feel ready?

Anu: Actually, I have to tell you much more. If you remember on the fourth day you had told that we should first do the program with you and then do it also with others. So actually, I did that. In fact, I did it with 3 others.

Keki: That's very good and, how were they?

Anu: They were expensive. One was talking more about his own religion every now and then and it was putting me off. The second was all based upon muscle testing, with hand out-stretched, which we do on the fifth day but he was relying so much upon it that he said that you do not need to develop even your sensory acuity. I thought developing sensory acuity is one of the main purposes of the program for our own growth. The third program I attended was at a beach resort. There were two guys from our city attending that program. One of them was attending the program but the other one was more interested in spending his time at the beach ogling the half-naked foreign tourist girls. As for Rapport making, they just showed a 10 minutes video. I think I wasted a lot of money.

Keki: I will not call it a waste of money. I am sure you would have found at least a few things useful.

Anu: Yes, but there were some other differences which were more or less common to them.

Keki: Such as?

Anu: Such as none of them had any pre-program meeting with the participants. None of them sat with the participants at lunch time. Nobody waited for any late participant to come in like you do.

Keki: Each one's style is different. Each trainer brings his or her background and personality into the program. And yes, somehow punctuality unfortunately is not a virtue that we find amongst us; but these are the people who need the program the most. It has always been a question with me as to how to do justice to those who are punctual. When a person comes late, he or she is not just missing out what happened during their absence but feels lost all through the day and cannot pick up everything that goes on. That is my belief. So, I give an opportunity for those present to catch up on their home play if anything is pending or we have a Nukkad, which is a chit-chat meeting without an agenda but regarding our subject.

Anu: I remember being late once and was surprised that you were waiting even after I came in, for somebody who was still awaited. But when you started after that person came in, I felt as if I have missed nothing. More importantly I remember your statement that **'successful people have a habit of calling up to inform if they are going to be late beyond 5 minutes'**; and on subsequent days I did not find anybody coming into the hall even a minute late.

Keki: Wow, you remember that? You see, Anu, you have not wasted any money anywhere. **There are two types of learning that you can have anywhere. One is that you are learning what to do. And the other; perhaps even more important is the learning of what not to do.** And you got both these learning from all the programs you have attended so far.

Anu: But there is something else also about those three programs. In almost all of them they were selling a lot of books and CDs. Even CDs comprising of some exercises or even a single exercise if it was little longer, and they were quite highly priced. I don't find you doing that.

Keki: I might make a few extra bucks doing that, but those turn out to be crutches and cripple the participant. **When any good idea or product gets commercialized it loses its focus from its essence to making a few extra bucks, or even a lot of extra bucks.** Take for example the first day closing exercise for relaxation, getting into Alpha. If I give you a CD of that you will want to put it on every time you want to do that exercise; you may become dependent on that, it may prevent you from making an effort to do the whole exercise on your own. I do not want to make anyone dependent on anything else except their own self.

Anu: You must write a book. (Almost jumping out of her seat)

Keki: What? Are you crazy? I am saying not even a CD and you are talking about a book?

Anu: But there are so many things you said over here in this meeting itself, which has not been said in the program even. Each program also seems to be like a new program. Why is that so?

Keki: I think it is mainly because of what people have shared in the pre-program meeting. The structure, the Skeleton, of the program is always the same but the meat that I put on to that skeleton changes.

Anu: That is precisely why you should write a book.

Keki: There are hundreds of books available in the market, maybe even in thousand and many of them are written by Masters much, much bigger than me. What is one more book going to do?

Anu: It will do what you have been doing at each and every program. I have come across some participants from your earlier batches and each one of them has said, it has transformed their life. During the program you are touching only a few lives. In the book you can consolidate from many programs and thereby touch many more lives.

Keki: Thanks a lot, Anu, but books can only inform, they cannot give the experience that you get at the program. Like you cannot learn cycling or swimming just by reading a book.

Anu: Whatever it is, after doing the Masters I also want to do the Trainers program and I think any good thing going should be recorded. You have to write the book. If not for others, will you write it for me?

Keki: So, you are coming for the Masters? There is a practitioner's workshop happening prior to the master's and to get the best out of the Master's I suggest you refresh the practitioner's since it is almost 2 years since you did it last.

Anu: OK. Bye. The book.

CHAPTER 5

DAY 3

(All the 13 participants are in their seats by the appointed time and I take my Central position.)

Keki: Once again, I welcome each and every one of you for this third day of our program. All Rise. (All 15 of us were standing now.) Good morning. (In a sing-song enjoyable voice and Dance like free movement of body and arms) Group: Good morning. (In similar manner of voice and body language.) Keki: Every morning is a good morning. Group: Every morning is a good morning. Keki: Because I make it a good morning. Group: Because I make it a good morning. Keki: Today is a good day. Group: Today is a good day. Keki: Because I am going to Make it a good day. Group: Because I am going to Make it a good day.

Keki: Thank you. Don't sit down.

Let us loosen out all the joints in our body with this exercise. Now lift up your right leg knee so that the Thigh is parallel to the ground like this. Good. Now rotate your ankle three times clock wise and three times anticlockwise; and while you are doing that, curl your toes during half the rotation and open them out during the other half. You can put your hands on your hips if you so desire. Very good. Now kick that leg out three times. Yes, that is the way. Now Straighten out that leg and swing it from your hip, left ward as you move it front and outward to right side on the way back. Do it three times. Now put the right leg down and repeat the whole process with your left leg. Good. Now stand on your two feet slightly apart and feel rooted. Just bend your knees a little and make circles, right knee clockwise and the left knee anticlockwise three times. Three time the other way. Now we will keep our upper torso straight without movement and rotate the hips, three times clockwise and three times anticlockwise. Yes, that's the way. Next, we will keep our hips and legs straight and rotate three times one way and three times the other way from the waist. Yes, normal breathing all through. Good. Now stretch out both your hands in front of you. We want to loosen the joints of the shoulders, elbows, wrists and five fingers of each hand. You will rotate your wrists in opposite directions and while doing that form a fist during half the rotation and open out the fingers during the other half. While doing that, you will also bring your hands closer to you by rotating your elbows. Do it your way so that you are giving maximum movements to your fingers, wrists, elbows and shoulders. Excellent. Now keeping your hands wherever you like, rotate both your shoulders three times one way and three times the other. We will have only one very slow rotation of your neck with your eyes open or shut as you like. So, drop your head forward so that your chin touches your neck and very slowly, start taking it to the right and back all the way and then to the left until your chin touches the neck. Now reverse it with the same slow motion. Full rotation and come to normal. This neck exercise, I believe, is also very good for your eyes. Yes, you can twist your backbone right and left like Saira is doing or even bend down and touch your toes. Ok everyone, you can take your seats now. (I go behind my table and sit down). How do you all feel? (Some say great, some Say fine, Saira says 'loosened up', Ankur says 'ready for the day', Gautam says 'Relaxed'.

QUESTIONS, ANSWERS & SHARING

Ok, so two days are over; any questions, any doubts, anything to ask, anything happened, anything to share? (Gautam shot up his finger immediately) Yes, Gautam.

Gautam: This morning I woke up 20 minutes later than the usual. I said, oh shit, I will be late for the program and rushed to the washroom to get ready. As I was brushing my teeth I suddenly stopped and looked at myself in the mirror. I could not believe myself that today I got up without any paralyzing pain in my stomach and lower back which has been troubling me since many years. Till today every morning, I had to struggle for at least 20 - 25 minutes to somehow get out of the bed.

Nirav: Didn't you take some medical help so far?

Gautam: I had been to many doctors and even specialists in Singapore. They took X rays, MRI scans and so many other tests. They gave painkillers, muscle relaxants, steroids; but instead of relieving I started developing the side effects of the drugs.

Saira: But when did all this start?

Keki: Excellent question Saira. I have increasingly found you to be asking the right questions at the right times. You should do your Masters and then perhaps even the Trainers. But Gautam, I am waiting to hear your answer to Saira's question.

Gautam: I can share a little background if you permit.

Keki: Go ahead.

Gautam: It was 12 years back when I left my father's house in Calcutta in a huff and we have had no contact with each other since then. This happened because he was constantly pestering me to become a doctor like himself. He was to retire from his government job in a few years' time and wanted me to take his job thinking that it will give me my life-time security. I had absolutely no interest in that and wanted to be my own Boss with my own independent business.

I stayed with my friend and was fortunate to get a scholarship for studying HR (Human Resource) in Singapore. After my MBA in HR, I was picked up by a large company at the campus interview for their Human Resource Development Department that also looked after the training needs of the employees. Five years back I fulfilled my dream of being my own Boss and started my own Training Institute. I was very happy and becoming successful. But in a few months' time I got into this health situation. (I knew that it was around this time that he lost his mother and could not attend her Funeral) This morning was the first time in so many years that I got off the bed without any issue.

Keki: (Gautam became quiet. All were quiet. As he was narrating the last few sentences, he was getting more emotional and his facial skin color was changing. I started talking slowly and softly.) Parents invariably want the best for their children. There is a Positive Intention Behind every Behavior. We need to identify and understand, what that positive intention could be. **When there is a clash of positive intentions of two people, there could be friction, mainly because each one has failed to realize the other person's positive intention.** Gautam, I am sure your father loves you.

Jaya: I could not sleep well last two nights. There is so much suffering in the world, even then while dealing with Manju during rapport sharing, you called it as ' Heavenly Planet Earth'. Where is the heaven? How can you say that?

Keki: Jaya, show me one more place, other than this earth, anywhere in this universe, where even a blade of grass grows.

Jaya: You mean there isn't any?

Keki: I like to believe that there has to be, but nobody has found it yet. When you find it, declare it to the world and you will be the most popular person on this earth.

Jaya: Then why God has put so much suffering on this ' Heavenly Planet' earth?

Keki: Now that is a different question and our Upanishad gives us the answer. It says ' **good and pleasant are two different things; what is good may not always be pleasant; and what is pleasant may not always be good'**. Please realize one thing always. **In nature, the lower cause gets sacrificed to achieve the higher cause. Sometimes the higher cause may be Apparent, but very often it May unravel much later in life.** When a tiger or a lioness hunts for its family, he or she targets the weaker deer in the herd, and thereby strengthens the gene pool of that herd.

Jaya: Do you mean there is no escape from suffering?

Keki: There is NLP. (some laughter)

Guneet Singh: After we all shared rapport experience, why were you putting your five fingers on our right shoulder during the Milton process?

Keki: If you do not get the answer by lunchtime today, do ask me again.

Ankur: Yesterday while you were sharing your life as to how you got into NLP, you said that because of so much misinformation and misleading information you have stopped believing something just because it is put into black and white. Then how do I proceed in life?

Keki: Do one thing. Put down 20th October 2020 in your book, but all in numerals. (Ankur writes down). Now read what you have written.

Ankur:20-10-2020.

Keki: What is that 10 doing over there?

Ankur: Why? You said October.

Keki: That's right, I said October. Did you go to school? Yes. Then you must have learnt that a square has four sides, pentagon 5, hexagon

6, heptagon (or septagon) 7, octagon 8, Nonagon 9 and decagon 10. Therefore, October should be the 8th month, November 9th and December the 10th.

Shankar: I have read about it in a book.

Keki: But my question is, have you or anybody else over here ever questioned on your own, as to why you are writing 10 when it actually reads 8? None. Surprising, isn't it?

Ankur: Oh God! No. But That should be Common sense; isn't it?

Keki: **Common Sense is the most uncommon thing in this world**. Common sense at one time told the world that the Earth is flat; it also told the world that the Earth is in the center of the universe. Maybe it told the world that the Apple falls down on the ground because when he falls, he also falls down instead of flying off!

Ankur: So how do we develop common sense?

Keki: I will give you some food for thought, Ankur. Work out why 1st of April is branded as 'All Fool's Day'? Why the wise king of ancient Persia, who gave the Solar colander considered 21st of March as the New Year's Day, which is celebrated as such even now by many? Why even today many follow the financial year from 1st of April to 31st of March? Why is a circle divided into 360 degrees? Why when we look down from what we consider as North, everything in nature on this earth is moving anti-clockwise except our clocks. And who do you give credit to for the profession in which you are today?

Ankur: To answer your last question, I will say to my college.

Keki: Exactly. Start looking beyond the immediate. The credit for computerization in our country goes to the reluctant pilot Rajiv Gandhi, who was thrown into the shoes of a Prime Minister at a moment's notice due to the Twist of Fate. Sometimes I wonder if he himself realized what a great Revolution he was bringing about. And while he was at it our so called other great leaders would sleep on the railway tracks to stop computerization in railways and banks. Whereas today, on each table of any bank there has to be a computer. Go beyond the immediate if you want to find the true answers.

All human Progress has been because just a few people. They did not just see something but observed something and questioned

it. Use your sensory acuity and look for the deeper layer that is hidden beneath. If you want to have an example of common sense then listen to Sadguru talk. He gets invited to the world conferences to give a talk. One of his statements which I am repeatedly reminding myself is **' Why do people believe in something? People believe something because they are not sincere enough to admit that they do not know.'** Very profound and very true, isn't it? Even when it is a belief regarding heaven or hell or even religious beliefs. Another Wise Man of our country has said that **every major religion has three aspects to it. Its rituals, its symbols and the deep- rooted philosophy. Differences and fights crop up mainly due to the first two whereas the Deeper philosophy and thinking of each major religion is almost the same.** As far as beliefs are concerned, **please realize that all beliefs are true. True for whom? True for the believer. Also, the beliefs have a way of proving themselves true.** What happens is that the RAS (Reticular Activating System) center in our brain picks up those signals which are important for our belief.

Jaya: Whatever we are doing in this seminar hall; whatever we are discussing, does that all fall under the purview of NLP?

Keki: What is the very first sentence of Bandler when he is explaining about NLP, Jaya? (Jaya seems lost and is looking at the faces of others)

Ankur: NLP is an attitude.

Keki: You can thank him, Jaya. But I want you to answer what the three letters in NLP stand for.

Jaya: N stands for neuro. The neurons in our brain, or the hardware. L stands for linguistics, the way we communicate. And P stands for programming, the programs in our hardware.

Keki: Very good. Everybody present in this hall has their hardware, right? (Jaya nods) Everybody is communicating, isn't it so? (nods again). And everybody is doing it from the programs that they carry in their hardware.

Ankur: Does that mean whatever we are doing at any time, is all NLP?

Keki: I leave the conclusions to each one of you.

Shankar: So, is NLP a science or art?

Keki: Professor Shankar. please tell me if two people have qualified themselves with the same syllabus from the same University and those two become professors and start teaching the students; do you think there will be a difference in the way they teach and the manner in which their students learn?

Shankar: Yes, I think there can be a lot of difference.

Keki: A lot of difference. And Doctor Nirav, between two doctors or 2 surgeons, can there be different results by the way one prescribes the medicines or does the surgery compared to the other?

Nirav: Major difference.

Keki: And Ankur, if two software writers are writing out the program for the same client and the same purpose, do you think one writer's program could be simpler, maybe faster and more user-friendly.

Ankur: Definitely.

Keki: Whether it is Engineering or Healthcare or computer science, education, finance, management, governance or any other field, **wherever applied science is used then it is the art of applying that science, which makes the difference.**

It reminds me of a case-story that I experienced during my initial year of NLP. A Prominent IT Industry was having their annual conference and they promised to give me 2 days to take up NLP. My programs are time specific. Certain things have to be finished by break time and lunch time. These people went on with their own business up to almost 12 noon. My Program got totally haywire. At lunchtime the CEO had asked me the same question that Shankar asked just now. That time I fumbled. That was perhaps the worst program of my life.

Nirav: I have two questions. The first is ' which exercise was it that gave Gautam the results that he got this morning?'

Keki: Frankly, I do not know. Let me illustrate this with a case-story that happened some years back. A Lady doctor who had done our program recommended it to a distant relative of hers from Gujarat. She called me up regarding her relative and warned me, 'Keki, she cannot tolerate smoke at all or even anybody smoking in her vicinity. She could not and did not attend even her own husband's funeral.' (She is a Zoroastrian and there is always fire and smoke during any religious ceremony.) Fortunately, or unfortunately when she came for the program there were four smokers. On the first day itself before the start of the program, when she came out from the seminar hall to the Ante room to collect a cup of tea; one of the participants entered that ante room from the lobby side with an unlit cigarette in his mouth. This lady yelled 'oh my God' and ran back into the seminar hall. Soon a participant from the seminar hall came to the lobby and told Aban that a lady has fallen off her chair and is on the ground convulsing. Aban rushed inside followed by me. Aban sprinkled some water on her and both of us gave her Reiki, revived her and relaxed her. Smoke was not the only issue with her as we came to know by and by. But on the third day after lunch and before the next session started, we found her sitting in the lobby outside the seminar hall with other participants and two of those participants were smoking. About a month later she returned to attend one of our regular monthly meetings just to convey that she had attended a full night prayer meeting for her departed husband. Till now I do not know as to which exercise did the job. **Our behavior patterns may not be a result of a single program but a multiplicity of programs in our mind.**

Nirav: Thank you. My second question is a bit of a sensitive type. Even if you prefer not to respond to it, it will be ok with me.

Keki: Doctor; I believe that everything that is happening in nature whether facts or imaginations, including ideas and thoughts. **Everything happening in nature is natural and therefore can be and should be discussed.** So, go ahead and shoot.

Nirav: I have been doing some Investigation on the net regarding NLP since I decided to do this program. I was a little taken aback reading about the court case between the founding fathers. I mean, when the basic assumptions of the NLP model are written so wisely and so comprehensively then how is this possible?

Keki: Very legitimate question. Let me answer that with another story. There was this old lady living outside a small town by the river bank. Across the river on the other side was a well-known Ashram and a renowned Swami used to hold regular discourses. This lady had been attending those programs regularly. One day after the discourse the lady persuaded the Swami saying that she may not last for very long and her earnest request is for the Swamiji to Grace her small hut, for a special meal that she has made for four of them. The Swamiji reluctantly agreed and asked her to go ahead and they would follow. Four of them reached the other bank of the river to her hut. One of them said 'I do not see any boat; maybe she has taken the long route downstream and then cross over the bridge and come.' When they saw smoke coming out of the hut from the wood stove, they entered the hut and were very surprised to find the old lady there. They asked her as to how did she come so quickly because they did not see any boat? The old lady replied 'Swamiji, it is you who has taught me that with faith you can even walk on water, and I have been doing it'

(After a little pause I continue) Professor Shankar will agree with me that in T A (Transaction Analysis) they talk about a person living out their own Life Script. Likewise families might have their own scripts, whole communities have their own scripts. Cultures and nations also have. So, if you happen to be from a Joshi family you may say we Joshi's are like this and that, or we Kennedys are like this and this.

Whenever a good product or an idea starts to become popular, we have a tendency to commercialize the same. Very often when that happens then the essence and the purpose of that product or idea can and does take a backseat and the profit motive and money may take the front seat.

Vipul: (who is a little offended) So you mean making money is bad. The whole world is working for money.

Keki: Making money or profit, is certainly not bad. If you are not making money then it is bad. Always your output has to be a little more than the input. If you continue putting in more money, then what you are getting out, then you are almost a parasite on the society because ultimately you will be using society's money. Tell me Vipul, do you mate with every beautiful woman that you see because it will give you pleasure.

Vipul: Certainly not. How can you even ask a question like that in front of everybody?

Keki: Just so. I see no difference between profiteering and womanizing, where 'my pleasure' is paramount. It is I, Me and Myself always, and God can take care of the others. Remember that **when one is thinking only about himself or herself then he or she is the only person on the face of this earth who is thinking about own welfare. When you**

start including others welfare in your thought and action then so many others are also thinking about you and your welfare.

Fine, are there any more questions from anybody. (I noticed Anu and couple of others shuffling a little)

Yes Anu, do you have something to ask or say?

Anu: I could not sleep last two nights and cried a lot.

Jaya: Even I could not sleep well last night after I tried to write down my goals.

Anwar: Same here. I was fearful of my job and whether to change the company and the boss.

Saira: He is looking so different with his front hair cut off.

Anwar: What?

Keki: She is saying that now we can see clearly because all the fringe is cut off. These first two days are very crucial. Some people may not get affected too much and that tells me that their existing programs or circuitry in the brain is fine. Some others may react and that is good because it is making some changes in the circuitry. Some may have extreme reaction and that is extremely good because a lot of programs existing in the mind are getting questioned and getting reprogrammed.

(I conclude the question - answer session and go behind my table and sit down in the chair. After a pause, as everybody is looking at me, I resume) Well, well, now that you all have finished this program with all your questions there is nothing more for me to do. So, what do you all want to do?

Saira: Whatever you say.

Gautam: You said, my question will get answered by lunchtime.

ANCHORS

Keki: Oh yes. The five fingers on the shoulder. But tell me, what do people do when they don't have anything to do? Particularly ladies?

Padma: They do house work.

Keki: But suppose a bus-load of ladies are going on a picnic and there is nothing to do.

Jaya: They gossip. or play some game, or sing songs.

Ankur: They play a game of Antakshari and sing songs.

Keki: Antakshari. What is that? How do you play that?

Ankur: The ladies in the bus could form two groups and somebody from one group will sing a song or a few lines of it. Somebody from the other group will have to start a new song from the ending syllable of the first song.

Keki: Really? How is that possible. You mean, from one syllable a whole new song will come up? Can it really happen? (I see a knowing smile from some in the group. I get up from my chair and go to Ankur who is wearing a Hawaiian shirt with Palm trees, beach and blue sky). Suppose I have a pair of scissors with me and I cut off 1-inch square piece of his shirt from under his left shoulder like this. Then I go to Padma who is wearing a red blouse and cut off a 1-inch square piece from under her left shoulder. Then I go to Saira and cut off a 1-inch square peace from her checkered top. Now I will have 3 pieces, one sky blue, one red and one checkered white. Out of the three I pick the checkered white piece and show it to you all, what or who will come to your mind? (the group says Saira) then I pull out the red peace and show it to you all; who or what will come to your mind? (the group says Padma)

So, we play Antakshari a little differently in NLP.

Tell me, did anybody here grow up with your grandparent and have very happy memories about it? (three people raise their hand) Jaya raised her hand first so I will take her up. Jaya, who was this grandparent of yours? How small were you? and how do you feel about those memories now?

Jaya: Very happy memories even now; She was my father's mother and she was there from my birth.

Keki: So, your earliest memories are from around what age?

Jaya: Maybe from around two to two and a half years of age.

Keki: Ok Jaya, just pull out your chair about 2 feet and sit down so that I can stand by your side and others can see us both. (She does it. I go and stand on her left, slightly behind). Tell me how would you call your grandma?

Jaya: Ammammi.

Keki: And how would Ammammi call you?

Jaya: Chimni.

Keki: Chimni? Why? What is that?

Jaya: Chimni means Sparrow in our language and they say I would talk too much and go chi, chi. chi. (smiles all around)

Keki: Oh Good. So, when Chimni was about two to two and half years of age her Ammammi would take her in her lap. Don't worry Jaya, I am not going to take you in my lap. Ammammi would put her hand on her head, pat and stroke it like this and say 'my Chimni is a good girl, my Chimni is a smart girl, my Chimni will grow up and earn name and fame'. (Jaya smiles, looks very happy and her face picks up color. I bend down and look into her face and she responds with a broad smile. I move back to my central position). You can take your chair back in position, Jaya. (she does it) how do you feel? Jaya.

Jaya: Very nice. Top of the world. (with a big smile).

Keki: Do you remember Ammammi's face? Jaya.

Jaya: Of course. But I was very sad when she passed away some six years back.

Keki: I think Ammammi also had a special way of calling your name; isn't it? Was it Chim-nee?

Jaya: Yes. How did you know?

Keki: I was there. I know all your pranks. So once when this sweet little Jaya was playing in her room, her mother called out from the kitchen 'Jaya'. No response. After a while mother calls out again 'Jaya come here'. Now she responds just a little with a 'huun'. Mom calls out' I want you here now' she responds '1-minute mom'. You know how long that one minute could be. Then from the other room Ammammi calls out 'Chim-nee' and immediately she runs to Ammammi. The question is, why does this happen?

Ankur: Because she likes her Ammammi more than her mom?

Keki: Mom has to take care of all aspects of Chimni including controlling her as and when necessary. Whereas the interactions with Ammammi were mostly of a pleasant nature. She would bring about a pleasant state in Chimni for most of the times. For Chimni her touch was always pleasant, her face was always pleasant, her voice, particularly when she called her name Chim-nee was very pleasant. These aspects brought about the pleasant state that Ammammi had installed into her and like Antakshari it brought out that whole state of body and mind. In NLP we call them as Anchors. Anchors are set when they first create that particular state and then they get fired back into that state again whenever some aspect of it props up. Ammammi's face is a Visual -V anchor; her saying Chim-nee is an Auditory -A anchor; her touch on Jaya's head was a Kinesthetic-K anchor.

Anchors bring back any state pleasant or unpleasant, good, bad or ugly. Did anyone notice how it suddenly changed from pleasant one to a sad one when she said 'I was very sad when she passed away some six years back'.

Nirav: I did.

Saira: Yes, even I did.

Keki: Her whole physiology changed. Her voice changed, her face dropped, her chin went in and the forehead came a little in front and even her shoulders pushed down a little. I had to bring her back to her happy state with my next statement.

Nirav: I wish I had learnt all this during the beginning of my medical career. It would have been so useful.

Keki: Everything happens at the right time doctor. Maybe you are taking in much more now than what you would have taken at that time. So now let us see how we can make use of this. (I bring two chairs and put one facing the group and the other at right angles on the left of that chair facing that chair. I sit on this other chair and ask) Who would like to warm up this chair? (pointing at the chair facing the group). Please come and occupy it. (Saira comes and occupies it).

Ok this is for the group. What were the two words that the Great Master would use in our story on the first day morning? (the group responds with 'watch me') Very good, but from now onwards it will be 'watch and listen, to both of us.'

Saira, take a deep breath and while exhaling, close your eyes and visualize Number 3, 3 times and relax, keeping your palms on your thighs. This exercise is:

ANCHORING AND ADD A RESOURCE EX.

Saira, think of something that you already do well, behavior or state that is already resourceful, but you would like to do even better.

Are you there? Yes. Good. Tell me what is it like to be doing that behavior?

(As she says 'I am feeling very good', I touch her left shoulder with my right hand. (Set the Event Anchor)

Now Saira, think of some other resource state or behavior that you could add so that you would be even more delighted with that resourceful behavior. The resource which you add could be anything like clarity, courage, compassion, humor or anything else that you feel will make the process even better. Have you decided? Yes. Good. (I remove my touch from her shoulder and with my left hand touch her left-hand elbow; thereby set the Resource Anchor)

Now take this resource (I again touch her left-hand elbow with my left hand; fire Resource Anchor) and relive that resourceful behavior (I touch her left shoulder with my right hand; fire the Event Anchor) with this additional resource available to you. Watch and listen to everything that happens as those two experiences combine to make you even more effective. Take the time you need and come on back, (I first remove my left hand from her elbow and then the right hand from her shoulder) you can open your eyes. (She opens her eyes and her smile broadens, her eyes grow even bigger.)

(I touch her left shoulder once again and ask her') how are you feeling now?

Saira: Fantastic.

Now that Saira has warmed up this seat, who wants to get into the hot seat next? (Saira goes back to her seat and Jaya comes to occupy the hot-seat)

Welcome Jaya; with Saira I used two kinesthetic anchors. I first set the event-state anchor by touching on her shoulder, then removed that hand. Then I set the resource-state anchor by touching on the elbow and removed that hand also. Thus, I established the event-state and the resource- state. Then I re-created (fired) that resource-state by keeping my hand on her elbow and simultaneously fired the event-state by touching her shoulder. I kept both the anchors fired for the resource to mix into the event. Then I first removed the resource anchor before finally removing the event anchor. This is how we used to do anchoring in the early days.

From now onwards we will be doing it differently. In what I did with Saira, the switch for setting and firing the anchors was a touch. In this case I am separating out my index and middle finger about an inch and a half and keeping it touched all through the exercise. The switch here is, pressure on the finger. If you recall the first day kinesthetic sensory acuity exercise, then you will realize that the placement of the fingers, area of contact, temperature and all other parameters remain the same. The switch that we will be using here is the pressure; which is also expected to be more or less the same every time you set or fire the anchor. Your communication with your subconscious is of a much higher order with this type of anchoring.

OK Jaya, take a deep breath and while exhaling, close your eyes and visualize Number 3, 3 times and relax, keeping your palms on your thighs. This exercise is:

CHANGING PERSONAL HISTORY EX.

(With my 2 fingers already on the back of her left-hand palm)

Jaya, think of a time when things did not happen the way you wanted them to, and you would like to feel differently about that memory. Or think of a memory, that you still think of from time to time, and it leaves you feeling in a way you would rather not. (pause) Are you there? Yes. Good. When you think of this now do you feel bad? (As she softly says yes, I simultaneously press my index finger to set an anchor for that problem state, and then remove the pressure.)

Jaya, what resource like courage, humor, helpfulness, would have made it possible for you to have had a much more useful experience in that situation? (pause) identified? Yes. Good.

Now think of a time in your life when you experienced a lot of this resource. Are you there? Good. Does it feel good to know that you have that resource? (As she nods, I simultaneously press my middle finger to set the resource-anchor, and once again remove the pressure).

Jaya, what color shoes are you wearing today? Red. They are looking good on you.

Ok. Now take this special resource (I press my middle finger to fire the resource anchor) back into that problem memory (I press my index finger to fire the event-anchor) and find out what happens with this resource available to you. Watch and listen and you relive that old memory in a new way. Take your time and then come on back. (I first remove the pressure from my middle finger then the index finger and finally pick up my hand. With My Head and Shoulders straight and an expressionless face I notice the look of satisfaction on Jaya). You can open your eyes now.

How do you feel now? Jaya.

Jaya: Very good. I think I can handle it now. I will.

Keki: Thank you Jaya. Who would like to take the hot seat next?

(Gautam comes up)

Gotham, take a deep breath and while exhaling, close your eyes and visualize Number 3, 3 times and relax, keeping your palms on your thighs. This exercise is regarding:

RE-PARENTING EX.

So, Gautam, think of a time when your parent(s) did not make the best choice in your life, something that has affected you ever since. (pause) Are you there? Yes. Very good.

When you think of this now do you feel bad? Yes. (While he is feeling bad, I press the index finger to set the event-anchor and then remove the pressure.)

Gautam, what resource like courage, humor, understanding, compassion; do you now have that you wish your parents had back then? (pause) identified? Good. Now you become your parent and use this new resource to achieve a better outcome. (I press my middle finger to set the resource-anchor and remove the pressure in a while.)

Did you have breakfast in the morning because I am beginning to get hungry? Oh, corn flakes and bread butter jam, good.

Ok, so, take this special resource (I fire the resource-anchor with pressure on my middle finger) back into another memory with the parent(s) (I fire the event-anchor by pressing my index finger and keep the pressures on) and find out what happens with this resource available to you. Watch and listen as you relive that old memory in a new way. Take your time and then come on back. (I first remove the pressure from the resource-anchor middle finger, then from the event-anchor the index finger and then lift up my hand from the back of his palm. Once again, with My Head and Shoulders straight and an expressionless face I notice a little smile slowly turning into a broad grin and a look of happiness on his face.

What difference do you notice? Gautam.

Gautam: Very promising.

Ankur: I get the Aroma of the 'Vade' and my hunger anchor is fired.

Keki: You people are learning fast. Ok, tea/coffee/snacks break and when you come back, you will pick up your partner and do all these three exercises.

(Once we assemble after the break)

Keki: Before you start with the three exercises let us clear out a few points. This time I told you to watch and listen to us. Firstly, what did you watch? How were we two sitting?

Shankar: You were sitting on the left of them.

Keki: That's right. The therapist sits on the left of the client.

Ankur: But why is that?

Keki: Because so far, we were doing FUN learning. Now as we get into deeper exercises of NLP, we are going to do FUNN learning. Which stands for Fundamental Understanding Not Necessary. You are riding a motorcycle, Ankur. For Riding the motorcycle, you may or may not know how it actually generates the power or transmits that power to the wheel. Somebody else may be using a computer but may or may not know the internal workings of it. So, learn the exercises and how to use them. But to answer your question, you may find the answer in the eye accessing cues.

Ankur: Ok.

ANCHORING & EMOTIONS

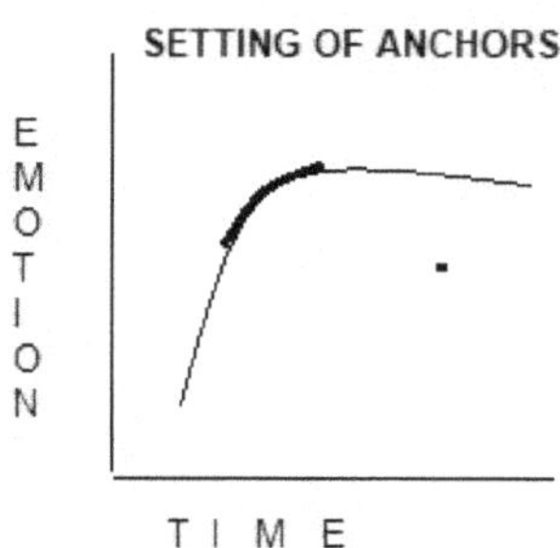

Figure 13

Keki: Figure 13 shows the Emotion on the y-axis and Time on the x-axis. With time, the emotion rises up and then starts dropping a little. We have to anchor it when it has sufficiently risen and is still rising; While it is on the way up, as shown by the thicker line.

Tell me if anybody remembers when Indira Gandhi was shot dead or when Rajiv Gandhi was blown up or 9/11 or 26/11.

Select any one of them that you remember the best. Now recall as to from whom or from what source you heard it for the first time. Where exactly were you when you first heard it. Around what time. Maybe you can recall that scene and the setting. What were the exact words that you heard? Recall all the minor details that you can.

(As I took up each and every participant, one by one, each one of them could recall in full detail as much as they remembered. Some were hardly 6 to 9 years of age. Some recalled even the dress they were wearing or the dress that the informer was wearing.)

Ok, Now go back exactly a week ago, at the same time and tell me what you were doing. (none could recall anything)

The question is why does this happen? **It happens because the event witch you recalled was so highly emotional that it has gone straight into your long- term memory; your subconscious part of the brain.** Whereas with the event one week prior to that, had no such emotional power.

Let me ask you another question. Lata Mangeshkar is right now singing a new song in her bathroom in Mumbai hundred miles away from here. The question is can you hear her? Obviously not. What will she have to do so that we all can hear that new song? That's right. She will have to go to the studio, sing it in front of a microphone, get it recorded. The audio wave generated by her singing is of much lower frequency and cannot penetrate through the walls. The studio will mix it up with a very high frequency carrier wave and then transmit it on radio frequencies. This is picked up by your radio set, the carrier wave is separated and thrown out and the audio wave is fed to your headphones or speaker.

Our emotions work almost in the similar manner and carry the event to our long- term memory, possibly in our right brain. **That is**

the reason we are asking the person to get in touch with their feelings/ emotions before setting an anchor.

Now pick up your partner and do all 3 exercises, either in one go, or finishing each exercise both ways, one by one. Before you start let me share with you a case-story. Who likes to hear a story? (The group shouts 'I'.) Years back I had a group of about 16 participants, most of them from a multi- level -marketing group, who were good in their work but rather poor in English language. The ladies requested me to explain these exercises in the Vernacular Marathi.

I had to think up something on my feet. So, in my sing song Satara style Marathi I explained. Take a cup of tea (=the event). Taste it (=test it, your feelings) what do you need to add (=resource to be added). In the first exercise we want to make a good thing even better. The resource to be added to the tea cup maybe sugar. We take it, we add it, we mix it, and we again taste it. (=test it).

In the second and third exercise why did I ask about the color of the shoes or whether somebody has had breakfast. In these two exercises somebody is taking up a negative case to be turned into positive. After identifying the resource and before adding it, we do not want the person to be in that negative state, so to break that state we are diverting the person's mind to something neutral or pleasant. It is as if you tasted the contents of the cup and identified the resource to be added, but it left a bad taste in your mouth and you want to correct it with something else before you bring the resource and add it to the cup and savor a good cup of tea. As for the cup of tea resource is concerned, the resource identified maybe, say Ginger. Now Ginger is not waiting next to the Tea and we are asking that person to go to the time and place where they used the Ginger, and bring it, and use it.

Are we clear? So now pick up your partner and start dancing. **Take up real issues, hot issues, issues that bother you; absolutely nothing hypothetical at all. And remember once again that you are here to train your partner. So even if you have done your exercise with me in the hot seat, you will do it on your partner and let the partner do it to you. Only this time you will pick up a different issue. Each exercise is a fit and forget type, however you can do the same exercise any number of times for different issues.** (and I move down to my personal space near the swimming pool)

(As I was sitting there, midway to the exercise I felt like going up the seminar hall to check the progress. As I approached the seminar hall, Aban came out from there)

Aban: Good you are here. I came out just to call you.

Keki: What is it?

Aban: The Re-parenting exercise. Padma says she can't find faults with her parents.

Keki: Can't or does not want to?

Aban: More like it.

Keki: And the second pair?

Aban: It's Lily. She is refusing to do the Re-parenting exercise. Says it is of no use.

Keki: What? Refusing? How can anybody refuse to do an exercise? Has she at least done it on her partner? Who is her partner?

Aban: No. I tried to convince her but she says it is useless. Anwar is her partner.

Keki: She is becoming a pain in the butt and harmful to the group. I think the group will be better off without her. We have not cashed her cheque yet, do you have it with you here? I feel like returning it and sending her back. We cannot tolerate anybody messing up the program.

Aban: No Keki; you are the one to say that these are the people who need the program the most. You will have to deal with this a little differently,

Keki: May be. Let's go in.

Aban: No wait. There is something else which you may find disturbing.

Keki; Now what?

Aban: During the break somebody saw Vipul giving a tip to the attendant and before we all entered the seminar hall, again the same person saw the attendant giving him a packet wrapped in a newspaper which he quickly put away in his bag. I think he liked the Vadeys very much.

(We both enter the seminar hall. I take stock of the proceedings and stand a little distance away from Padma.)

Keki: Please stop wherever you are. I have to tell you all something. You see, when I was in college, there were all different type of personalities there, with different behavior patterns. Naturally not everybody liked everybody else's behavior pattern or even thinking pattern. In our country it is mandatory to give a riding test even for riding a small 50cc moped but there is no test or license required to produce babies. Of course, there is the Institution of marriage and most of us go through it before producing babies. So, all these people with their various behavior patterns and thinking patterns, produced babies, like you and me. (I look at Padma and point at myself). Now, in our culture we are brought up to consider parents as the likeness of God and therefore god can do no wrong. But it is also said that 'to err is human' and at least I consider my mother as well as father as human beings. In our 3rd exercise of Re-parenting, the purpose is not to find faults, because we have seen that, behind every behavior there is a positive intention. The purpose is that if you had a choice to make, independent of anybody else, then your choice might have been different. Isn't it, Padma? (Padma nods). OK, that's all I wanted to convey. Now everybody, continue from where I interrupted you all.

(With that I go out into the lobby to await them finishing their exercises, soon Aban comes out with a smile on her face. I ask her to stay inside and let me know the result with both the pairs.)

(After some minutes, Aban comes out again to inform that everybody has finished including Padma. Added that when she asked Padma as to how she felt, she said 'I did not know that this event was so important'. But Lily and Anwar has still not done it. We both enter the hall and I take my Central position.)

Keki: So how do you all feel? (Good, fine, charged, happy; were some of the comments.) The exercises were so easy and simple, wasn't it? (most said 'yes') remember that **whenever we are doing such exercises, we do not think about it, we do not talk about it, we do not discuss it. We just leave it alone to take its course.** The reason for that is very simple to understand.

Imagine a plane sheet of Glass placed perfectly horizontally. Now take some container with water and pour some of it from a height on the glass. The water will make a certain pattern on the sheet of glass.

Dab it out to soak up the water. Once again take the same container and pour the same quantity of water, from the same height, at the same spot. You will notice that most of the water will follow the earlier pattern of distribution. This happens due to the surface tension of the Residual molecules of the previous pattern, particularly at the edges. We do not want that to happen with the circuitry in our brain. If you recall your earlier program in your brain by way of talking about it, thinking about it or discussing it, you are retracing the pattern and recreating that path. We do not want that.

Who wants to hear a story?

The group: I

Keki: I did not hear you. Who wants to hear a story?

The group: (much louder this time) 'I'

Keki: That's better. Looks like the Vades were not so good today.

Ankur and some others: They were yummy.

Keki: Ok. So, this happened when I finished my engineering and went to Mumbai for a job. Amongst the group of new friends there was one who was like a total loss. Nothing was going right for him, and I came to know that nothing had gone right for him from a long time. Somebody suggested to him that there is an expert palmist who sits under The Banyan Tree next to the hospital. He should consult that palmist and find out about his future. So, this guy goes and meets the palmist. The palmist takes his hand and twists it this way and that and says 'oh, ho, ho, how many cracks in your head line. Even in school. Did you fail sometime? The guy replies ' Panditji (=learned man) you know everything; you know how these teachers are. They take huge tuition fees and pass the students of rich families and we could not afford those fees, so he failed me.' Panditji said 'but in college also; what happened during college?' Guy replies 'Panditji you know everything; you know how college life is. There was this girl I used to meet; I would buy peanuts; we would sit somewhere, eat and chit chat. Then somebody came along and promised to take her for Buskin-Robin ice cream. She never came back to me'. Panditji said ' but there are other cracks also in your heart line.' This guy replies 'Panditji you know everything; you know how all the girls are. It kept repeating and I kept suffering'. Panditji said 'your health-line also has problems. Are you suffering from some disease also?' the guy replies 'Panditji you know everything; with all this suffering I started getting acidity which developed into ulcers and headaches. Please tell me when will all this get over'. Panditji asked his age. He said 26. Panditji again twisted and turned his hand and said ' up to the age of 33 and then....' before he could finish his sentence the guy said ' yes, yes, Panditji tell me what will happen after 33.

Panditji said 'after 33 you will get used to all this' (laughter all around).

There is absolutely no reason to get used to anything no matter how ugly it is. Like the Talk Show host Oprah Winfrey says **' Whatever you focus on expands. Focus on negativities and negativities will expand. Focus on positivity and positivity will expand. If you think your case is very unique then you should get familiar with Oprah's life story. A man once said ' I lamented that my shoes were torn, until I met a man who had no legs at all.'**

Gautam: I like all your stories. I wish I could take them down. All of them.

Keki: Thanks Gautam but let us now get on with the next exercise. This exercise is about someone getting stuck, or getting into a problem state, a resourceless state. In other words, whenever 'X' happens, he or she automatically gets into a 'Y' state, which is not a desirable state.

'X' could be the face of a person or an interaction with that person, a place, an event or anything like that. 'Y' is your automatic unhelpful response that you wish to change to a more useful response. Is there anyone here facing such a situation? (3 people raise their hands). Anwar raised his hand 1st. Would you like to get into the hot seat? Anwar.

Anwar: Ok.

Keki: Not ok, do you want to take the hot seat?

Anwar: Yes.

Keki: Then jump. (Anwar comes and takes the seat. I am sitting on the left of him). In this exercise there are 3 anchors so my first 3 fingers will be all the time (I turn his hand so that the left-hand palm is on his thigh) on the back of his hand sufficiently separated. The rest of you, please empty your laps and watch and listen carefully. This exercise is called,

CHAINING ANCHORS – GETTING UNSTUCK

Anwar, imagine that you are in a movie theatre and you are seeing yourself on the screen. Got it? (Anwar says 'yes') How far is the screen?

Anwar: I am in a multiplex.

Keki: Good. How big is the screen?

Anwar: It is 70 mm.

Keki: 70mm is about the width of your palm. It is the width of the film strip which is used. The screen will be several feet wide. How wide is it?

Anwar: About 20 feet.

Keki: Very good. Tell me, what do you see on the screen?

Anwar: Shahrukh Khan is singing a romantic song.

Keki: We will start again. (I rub out my three fingers from the back of his hand and place them once again) I am repeating; imagine you are in a movie theatre and you are seeing **yourself** on the screen. Did you get it this time? (Anwar says 'yes') where are you? (Anwar: - multiplex) how wide is the screen? (Anwar: - about 20 feet) how far are you from the screen? (Anwar: - I am in the second row, maybe about 20 feet away) what is happening on the screen? (Anwar - I see myself on the screen). Is that Anwar on the screen sitting, standing, sleeping or what?

Anwar: I am standing.

Keki: No, you are not. You are sitting here in front of me. I am talking about that Anwar on the screen. So, tell me what is that Anwar on the screen doing?

Anwar: That Anwar on the screen is standing facing towards right, no left, yes, his left.

Keki: Good. Ask him to please sit down on a chair facing you and relax.

Anwar: OK.

Keki: So, what are you seeing now and how does it look?

Anwar: I see him sitting and looking at me and relaxing.

Keki: Very good. Continue looking at him and relaxing more and more. (I press my index Finger to set the 1st anchor and point it out to the group with my other hand. After a while I remove the pressure and ask Anwar)

Did you like the Vades you had during the break? (he nods) How many did you have?

Anwar: 4.

Keki: (I fire the first anchor by pressing my index finger on his hand to make sure that the Anchor is set, and ask) what is happening now?

Anwar: You are pressing my hand.

Keki: (I know that the anchor is not yet set. So once again I rub it out with my fingers, replace the fingers and start all over again from the beginning. However, this time while setting the anchor I press it harder and rub it a little till it begins to hurt him.)

(I fire the anchor in the same way and ask the same question) what is happening now?

Anwar: I see myself on the screen sitting and relaxing.

Keki: Good. Now Anwar, I know for sure that from time to time under certain circumstances you are getting into a stuck condition which is not helping you and you want to come out of it, isn't it? Recreate that condition now, imagine it is happening right now. Are you there? (I could see his face changing and his forehead moving down a little. I anchor (#2) these feelings with the pressure of my middle finger and indicate it to the group. In a while I remove this pressure also.)

Now Anwar, take this stuck condition (I fire anchor #2 with the pressure of my middle finger) and give it to that Anwar on the screen (I fire anchor #1, with the pressure on my index finger). Done? Fine, do you notice some changes in that Anwar on the screen?

Anwar: He is looking a little scared and confused. He is not relaxed.

Keki: Good, let him be, because we are going to help him come out of such a situation and learn how to handle it.

Now Anwar, select some resource which you know you have and you might have used it even in your childhood; it could be anything like courage, confidence, humor, or a bundle of resources that you used in the past in any other context. Just identify it. (I could see his face changing with a little glow) Does it feel good to know that you have it? Yes. (I anchor (#3) this feeling by pressing my ring finger, and indicate it to the group).

Anwar, whenever you are put into this problem state (I fire anchor #2, the middle finger) you will immediately dissociate yourself (anchor #1 the index finger is pressed) and then like magic (I fire anchor #3, by pressing the ring finger) you will find yourself resourceful. (I watch for his positive response and remove the pressure from my middle finger #2, followed by the ring finger #3 and finally the index finger #1).

Would you like to do it one more time? Yes.

So, Anwar, whenever you find yourself into a situation which used to make you a little scared. confused, and tense (fired #2) you will automatically dissociate yourself from it (fired #1) and like magic you will be resourceful (fired #3).

Now Anwar, I want you to create a self-anchor, that you can use anytime you are in a similar situation, the anchor can be in V, A or K. Just think about what you can use when you get into such a situation.

Anwar: Can I use A and K?

Keki: Sure. Would you like to tell me what you have in mind?

Anwar: It is a tight fist with the words ' yes, I can'.

Keki: Sure, that sounds very good and Powerful. So, get ready and we will do it one more time. At the word 'magic' you'll fire your anchors.

Ready. Whenever you find yourself into a situation which used to make you a little scared. confused, and tense (fired #2) you will automatically dissociate yourself from it (fired #1) and like magic you will be resourceful (fired #3). You can open your eyes now and come back.

(Anwar opens his eyes, the grin on his face widens to a broad smile, with backbone and neck straight up looking an inch taller.)

I want you to think about the same situation again and fire your anchor and tell me what difference you find.

Anwar: Yes, I can and I did.

Keki: Good for you. Tell me, isn't this exercise also as simple and easy as the 3 which you did earlier?

Anwar: 3? But we did only 2; we didn't do re-parenting.

Keki: What? Didn't do. Let me make one thing very clear, Mister. I cannot and I will not recommend somebody's name to Dr. William Horton of NFNLP for certification if that person has not done even one of the exercises that we do. Is that clear Anwar. And that goes for everybody else also. (continuing to look at Anwar only) So before you come for lunch make sure you pick up somebody and do the exercise.

Each moment we are building upon what we have done so far. They say that the chain is only as strong as its weakest link. If you let a link snap, then you have lost it all.

Now move. Go back to your seat.

EVERYTHING IS TWICE BORN

I have a question for all of you. (I pick up a Marker Pen from the table in my palm and show it to everybody.) My question is, where was this born for the first time?

Jaya: Maybe in China. Is it?

Vipul: It will be written on the pen. Like 'Made in China' or something.

Keki: I will repeat my question. Where was this born for the first time?

Guneet Singh: I think for the very first time it has to be in somebody's mind.

Keki: Absolutely right. Where was the incandescent light bulb born for the first time?

Manju: In Edison's brain.

Keki: Excellent. Where was this table born for the first time? This room? This whole building? (This time quite a few people said 'in somebody's mind') That's right. Whether it is the pen, or the bulb, or this building, or whatever you decide to do; everything is first born in the person's mind. Then he or she works on it and makes it happen. When this building was completed, that was its second birth. Each and everything is twice-born. For the very first time when you came to know about NLP and you decided to find out something more about it; you were curious, that was the first birth, then you took action and found out more about it, that was the second birth. Maybe you liked what you found and you wanted to find out where and how you could do it, you are inquisitive, that was the first birth. Then you took action and maybe zeroed in on me; that was the second birth. Then maybe you called me with the idea of doing the program; that was the first birth; then you actually came to the program; that was the second birth. Each and everything is twice born.

It is something like the sperm of curiosity or inquisitiveness or idea interacts with the ova of action and there is conception; the first birth, even though it is still in the womb and you cannot see it. Then when you actually see the result, that is the second birth.

Saira: But isn't, curiosity for NLP, up to coming for the program a single continuous process?

Keki: It may appear so. Suppose Guneet here is manufacturing cars or a simpler mixer/grinder. Let us make it still simpler; suppose you came across a new recipe for making a cake. You may not have all the ingredients. Your first task will be to go and get them from the market. Your next task maybe to break up certain ingredients into certain size pieces. That ready. you may have to mix the dough. You may have used the oven for something else and the smell is still there, you have to remove it. And so on. Each program may have its own subsets or subprograms. Is that clear now. (Saira nods and I continue). You visualized the cake; 1st birth. On the way if you abort or have a miscarriage then there is no 2nd birth unless you resume your efforts.

REALITY Vs. IMAGINATION

Discovery Channel once showed a program where a person was sitting opposite the computer screen and with his head wired up to get the scan of his brain. They showed him several day-to-day items one by one and showed on the computer how his brain centers were making connections and lighting up. Then they placed a very different (complicated) item, which he had never seen in his life, in his hand and recorded the happenings in his brain. After that they diverted his mind to something else for a good amount of time and then asked him to just think of this unusual item which he had seen. They recorded the brain patterns for this unique item which he visualized. When they compared this pattern with the earlier Pattern when he actually had the item in his hand, they found that both were exactly the same. **The brain does not distinguish between reality and imagination**.

Jaya: Does that mean we will have to work on all these exercises that we did?

Anwar: For how long we will have to work? Till we get the result?

Keki: No and No. When you started the exercise and while you were doing it, or when your partner was taking you through it, you already had the intention of what result you wanted. You have already worked on it. It has already taken the first birth. Now you will not interfere with the process while it is developing in the womb, until you can see it take the second birth. That is why I say 'Fit and Forget.'

There is a very interesting story that actually happened at a wedding while I was living in the south. The guests sit down in rows with Banana Leaf in front of them for the meals. The second or third serving is generally of rice with sambar (=a thin vegetable curry). The serving boys carry this sambar in small plastic buckets and pour it over the rice with a ladle. One of the guests saw something very unusual and went to his family members who were having the meals. He warned them 'do not eat the Sambar because I saw the serving boy's snort fall from his nose into the bucket'. The ladies in their colorful sarees were devastated and immediately got up to gargle and wash their mouths. One or two of them actually vomited into the wash basin. When they were done the guest said 'look at them, the serving boy is still serving the sambar from that same red bucket'. At this one of the ladies said 'but we were served out from the blue bucket'. Just shows that **our mind does not distinguish between the so-called reality and imagination. Mind and body are one.**

LIMITING BELIEFS Ex.

Within our subconscious, there are the multitudes of programs which enable us to live a healthy, happy life. There are also a few programs that sabotage these and make us unhealthy and unhappy. Broadly these may be of the nature of; I can't do that, this is not for me, I am stressed, I can never get along with him/her, things will never change around here, I am perfectly Ok as I am.

More specifically it may include; I cannot have good relationships with x, y or z, those people are selfish and will never co-operate, I can talk easily in this language but not that, I can drive through an open road but not on the highway where other cars are speedily overtaking me or a road full of pedestrians, I can never have satisfying sex, I do not care about others as long as I am benefited, he/she is never going to improve (=what should I do so that his/her behavior is more acceptable to me? What prevents me? What limits me?), I am stuck in this situation and cannot get out of it, etc. etc.

This exercise is for getting rid of all such limiting beliefs so that we can change our life for a healthier, happier, more prosperous one.

This exercise is for changing our behavior. It is at behavioral level. In the Master Practitioner program, we do the exercise to change the belief about who we are, at our identity level.

I will take all of you through this exercise all together. So please empty all laps, put your feet flat on the ground, sit up straight, backbone straight, push your tailbone into the chair, take a deep breath and while exhaling visualize Number 3, 3 times, close your eyes and relax.

We will do this exercise making 4 frames. The first frame will be the frame of absurdity, next will be the frame of certainty. The third frame will be that of your limiting belief. The 4th frame will be the exact opposite of whatever you have taken up in frame number 3.

By now you may be having some idea of what you want to take up as your limiting belief for frame # 3. Your subconscious knows what is of utmost importance to you and while you are doing the exercise it may present you with that. Take that up for your exercise.

Frame #1, the frame of Absurdity. This morning when I went to my balcony, I saw in the clear blue sky a huge elephant flying with its big black bottom facing towards me and his tail twirling in-between. His legs were moving as if he was swimming in the air. His head held high with the S shaped trunk taken up between his two Ivory tusks and trumpeting away further and further from me.

Or, last night from my balcony, I looked up at the starry sky. You might have seen five kids playing four corners. Four kids are occupying four corners of an empty room and two of them want to exchange their positions. While they are doing it the 5th kid wants to run and occupy the vacant corner. I saw the five stars playing that game. Two stars were running to occupy each other's place and the 5th star from the middle was trying to occupy one of their places.

So, bring anything absurd like that on your mental screen now. The more absurd the better. Improve the submodalities. Increase the contrast, make it larger than life, more colorful. When you see something like this you get a feeling of, oh, how absurd is this, how can it ever happen. Get that feeling and double it. Now park this frame somewhere on your mental screen, maybe left-hand top corner. Remember where you have parked it, we will get back to it.

Now frame #2, the Frame of Certainty. Some event in the universe which you are sure of has to happen. Like tomorrow morning the Sun will rise is a certainty, that one day I will pop is a certainty. There are no two ways about it. So, take up any event like that and make a picture on your mental screen. Improve the submodalities. Make it brighter, bring it closer, larger than life. When you see something like that you get a feeling that, yes, it has to happen. Get into that feeling and multiply it. Park it somewhere on your mental screen may be left hand bottom corner. Remember where you have parked it, we will get back to it.

Now frame #3. The frame of your limiting belief. Take up whatever your subconscious gives you. Improve the submodalities of this also. Get in touch with your feelings. Listen to Your own voice, whether of fear, anxiety, stress, bravado, anger or whatever. These are all disempowering feelings. They are not allowing you to live fully. Whatever feeling you are getting, get into it and even double it. Now park this frame somewhere on your mental screen, may be right hand top corner. Remember where you have parked it, we will get back to it.

And now frame # 4. The exact opposite of whatever you took up in frame #3. If in the previous frame you took up that you cannot talk comfortably to a room full of people, see yourself talking to a full Auditorium of thousand people or why, 10,000 people, see yourself talking from the podium to 500,000 people from the podium. like Indira Gandhi. See all those people eating out of your palm, each and every word that you are speaking. If you thought you could not have good relationship with somebody. Hey, see yourself and that person as the best friend that you ever had, with the most intimate, desirable relationship that you can have. If you thought you cannot have good sexual relationship. See yourself having the most wonderful satisfying sex. Go ahead and have it now; nobody is looking at you. If it is a matter of talking in certain language; see yourself pitpiting in that language with ease and comfort. In our country if you do not know Japanese or Tamil, you think it is ok but if you do not speak English fluently then some people feel themselves inferior. Why? Language you speak maybe Richer, only you have not enforced it on others. Whatever limiting belief you took up in frame #3, see yourself doing exactly the opposite most competently and comfortably. Stretch the limits. Go beyond your wildest dreams. Remember that everything is twice born. The place, the place is here; the time, the time is now. And when your friends are seeing you doing it and they are praising you; how do you feel? Proud? Feel proud. Make that feeling 10 times stronger. Now park this frame somewhere on your mental screen, may be right hand bottom corner. Remember where you have parked it, we will get back to it.

Now take frame #3 and move it far, far away going all the way to infinity becoming just a dot; and bring it back towards you coming faster and faster as it comes closer and closer to you and when it comes to you, snap it on top of frame #1; The Frame of absurdity.

Now take frame #4 and move it far, far away going all the way to infinity becoming just the dot; and bring it back towards you coming faster and faster as it comes closer and closer to you and when it comes to you snap it on top of frame #2; The Frame of certainty.

Repeat this process by yourself 4 to 5 times making it faster and faster so that the last one is just a Zip- zap, Zip- zap.

Rub your hands together, rub it on your eyes and face, open your eyes and come on back.

EXTENDED BAD PATCH OF LIFE + PHOBIA

(After a pause for the group to recover)

Fears. They say we are born with just two fears. Fear of loud noises -like thunder and fear of falling -from a height. All the rest of the fears are gifted to us by our loving parents, peers and elders. The previous exercise was somehow about fears. Self-preservation is engrained into us. Fear is good and necessary. When threatened we get into a fight or flight response. Fear is only temporary. The next exercise now is about phobia. What is the difference between fear and phobia? In Phobia just a thought about something can create the physiology of fear inside someone. We had a person here who could not even look at a photograph or a picture of a snake (till after the exercise). These are irrational fears and lasts for a longer time.

Your mind is capable of multitasking. In this exercise we are going to do two exercises together simultaneously. In all my study of NLP with various trainers and various books and videos, I have not yet come across an exercise which deals with extended bad patch of life. I find this very important part of so many participants that come here. By extended bad patch of life I mean an unfortunate, unpleasant period lasting generally beyond 6 months. For some it might have started from birth- as in an unwanted child; and may have continued for many years. For some it could be school time or college or after falling in love; for some it could be after marriage or getting into a business deal or partnership; just about anything.

So once again get into the relaxed mode now, just the way we did in the last exercise.

Keep your eyes closed. I am asking you to raise your right-hand index finger for whoever may be having any phobia. (4 fingers go up. I go to each one of them and whisper 'what is it?' one says 'fear of flying', another 'dog', 'heights' forth says 'Cockroaches'. I come back to my Central position)

Ok. I have found that the extended bad patch of life affects a person far more than any phobia. So, everybody will take up that in this exercise and let the phobia run in the background.

Imagine you are entering an empty theatre, selecting a seat and sitting down. You are alone in this theatre and very, very safe. You are the director, the producer and the actor in this movie of yours which you are about to see. When I ask you to start you will start from the starting safe frame. The starting safe frame is a frame just prior to the beginning of that event; whether it is your birth, your new school, new teacher, your business partner, your heart partner (before these people started showing their true colors) or your business deal, anything.

As for phobia, you are on solid ground right now no chance of encountering a dog or a Cockroach and not yet entered the airplane.

You will end this movie of yours, with the ending safe frame. The ending safe frame is when the event ended but it has still left a bad taste in your mouth. The effect of that period Is still affecting. If the situation is still continuing then the ending safe frame is this present moment, now.

Start your movie now from the starting safe frame. See what all is going on, look at the characters. Do not fight the feelings, whatever they may be. Whatever feelings come up let them come, go through the important episodes and come to the ending safe frame now.

Now gently pull yourself out from your sitting self and stand behind your sitting self. You will run the same movie one more time. And your standing self, will be able to watch your sitting self, watching this movie. Pay attention to some episodes which you might have missed the last time. Are there any new characters in this drama? Maybe the first time that the phobia was installed in you may unfold right now. Start your movie once again now. You may notice that your feelings this time might be much diminished compared to the first time. Come to the ending safe frame now.

Up there behind you is the projection room. I want you to pull yourself out of your standing self and fly backwards to the projection room. In the projection room you have all the controls that you need. From the projection room you are able to see your standing self, standing behind your sitting self and all 3 of you are going to watch this movie once again. This time when you reach the ending safe frame, I want you to hold that frame on the screen. Start your movie now.

Come to the ending safe frame and hold it there. What we are going to do now is that you are going to do a rapid reverse rewind. You will can it up. Before you do that, I want you to put your right profile on the right edge of the screen looking outwards. When I ask you to do Rapid Reverse Rewind, your profile at the right edge of the screen is also going to walk backwards in a very funny way, Charlie Chaplin style so that in the front the screen is clean and white and the whole thing is getting canned up behind. Also, while you are doing it there will be some funny chinny chunky music also playing, but backwards. So, start your Rapid reverse rewind now with the funny chinny chunky music playing backwards and that Charlie Chaplin with your face, walking backwards in a hilarious manner,

Once again bring the ending safe frame back on the screen along with all the extras and do Rapid reverse rewind much faster this time. Repeat these 3 or 4 times so that the last one is just a zip.

Now leave all the controls in the projection room and fly back and merge along with your standing self. Let this standing self also now merge with the sitting self.

We are going to see your movie One More Time in a very different way.

Start your movie now. They say the world is a stage and each one of us is an actor and a character. In any play the villain is as important as the hero. In every good social movie or a novel, it is the villain who enhances the role of the hero or the heroin and makes it more meaningful. Knowingly or unknowingly, you have yourself been a villain to somebody sometime somewhere. Whether you believe it or not this has been a strengthening exercise. Any physical exercise breaks down the weaker cells to be replaced by stronger cells and then maybe in greater numbers. First and foremost, sincerely thank all the villains in your drama for having played their role so very well. Do it now.

Whether you believe it or not the universe is unfolding as it should. If you move the earth closer to the sun, the sun's gravitational force will increase, the earth will start rotating faster and the centrifugal force will throw it back into its original orbit. Likewise, if you move the earth away from the Sun the sun's gravitational force will decrease, it will start rotating slower and the centripetal force will bring it back into its original orbit. A leaf falling from the tree will fall exactly where it has to, depending upon its shape, size, weight, wind conditions. You cannot wish it to fall even half an inch this side or that. And so, with everything else in between. Everything happened the way it did because it had to. Remember what Upanishad has said that '**good and pleasant are two different things, what is good may not always be pleasant and what is pleasant may not always be good'.** So, while you are seeing your movie, whistle away and let your subconscious pick up all the wisdom and learning that is within it.

I once received a call from Mumbai from somebody who had to urgently fly to Bangaluru. He was shit-scared of flying and had not done it in many years. Once he had seen even the air-hostess doing the sign of the cross before the flight took off. He would enjoy driving big cars. So, I asked him to imagine driving his car on a runway, faster and faster. And as it moved faster, somehow wings started spreading out of the car. Soon he felt as if the car was getting lifted up leaving the ground. He has never felt the car moving so smoothly, leaving behind the lush green fields and small houses below him. I told him that he was in control and he should try out turning the car towards the left and then right and bank his body along with the turns like a bird flying in the air going wherever he wants to as per his heart's desire, just swaying with the turns and banks. And as he is going to go through the clouds, the varying moisture in the cloud will make the road quite bumpy, like he has gone over bumpy roads earlier. Just enjoy what your car has never done before because you are in control now. After he reached Bangaluru, he called me up to thank for the most enjoyable ride.

Whenever prawns or shrimp would come home my mom would separate out the heads, clean them up, add spices and fry them crisp. They used to taste so crunchy and yummy to all of us. And she would make some curry out of the body of the shrimp. My elder brother who was on ship used to say that the Chinese crew on his ship would butter up wide mouth bottles and leave them somewhere for the Cockroaches to collect inside. Then they would clean them up and crispy fry them. They would offer it to my brother saying they are as crunchy and yummy as your mother's prawn heads. But my brother never tried it. In large hotels he would sometimes have crunchy, crispy fried spinaches but he said that those would only be the second best compared to what mom used to make.

You must have seen small kids rolling and tumbling along with their pet dogs and having a Gala time. The dog allows all this because the dog is not afraid of the kid. Dogs are pack animals. They know who is the boss and act accordingly. They have very high sensory acuity. They know that when somebody is fearful of them, they can dominate them; and they do. I don't know where they learnt about the fight or flight response when one gets fear. Maybe they want to avoid a fight and wants you to take a flight. Those who grew up with pet puppies love dogs. Maybe I should start with a puppy.

When I went to the US there are so many buildings with over hundred floors. Many of them have galleries up above from where you can see the whole city. When you look down on the road you see the cars as if rows of ants are crawling. Some of them have a section with glass flooring. I was hesitant to step on that. I realized how stupid I was because already so many people were on it and so many others would have stepped on It every day since it was made. I took the first step and looked down. Emptiness for over a thousand feet. I felt dizzy.

Again, I felt so stupid because I was standing on solid ground, only that it was transparent. I started enjoying the moment. Even on the balcony at times I felt as if the outside was pulling me there. I felt as if I swayed outward also and realized that my mind was playing tricks on me and started enjoying the scenery, from down under me up to the horizon. It was beautiful. Anybody would enjoy it weather from top of the building or top of a mountain.

And now as you reach the ending safe frame of your movie, you are wiser than before, stronger than before, more confident than before, more ready to face the future than before. Come to the ending safe frame now. Rub your hands together, rub it on your eyes and face, open your eyes and come on back.

Like any other exercise that we do, we do not talk about it, we do not think about it, we do not discuss it, just let it be.

(I give the group some time to recover from this journey and when they are looking at each other's faces, I continue)

I do not know about you all but I am feeling hungry. Does anyone want to join me for lunch? (as the group responds to varying degrees of agreement) Before we move for lunch let me just look at your goal sheets which you have filled up. We will be working on it soon after lunch. (I examine the goal sheets just to check if they have filled up about 8 to 10 rows of 'areas of importance' in their life and scored their 'level of satisfaction' against each comment)

Jaya, you have not scored anything against your level of satisfaction and Manju you have covered only four areas of importance in life and that too mostly regarding your industry. I am sure there are many more important areas in your life. Please fill it up. Both of you will complete your goal sheet and only then come for lunch. Ok, lunch time.

(I leave the hall and from the washroom I proceed to my private place near the swimming pool, not really to await the two to finish the goal sheet, but to reminisce about the proceedings of the day. After some minutes I reach the Diner and find 5 seats vacant. I occupy one of them. Others were waiting for me so I ask the staff to start serving soup and salads.)

AT LUNCH

(Jaya and Manju walk in just as they start serving soup. Now 2 seats are still vacant.)

Keki; Where are the others?

Jaya: (With a smile on her face) Lily and Anwar are doing the Reparenting exercise.

Saira: Keki, you are a hard taskmaster.

Gautam: But only, when necessary, then he gets back to normal the next moment.

Guneet: You have to nip things in the bud. But Keki, do you lose your cool anytime?

Keki: Am I not human?

Saira: I wish I could be like you. But I work with the corporates. And these people are asked to evaluate the Trainer at the end of the training. I cannot afford to be tough or hard with them.

Gautam: There are limits while working with the corporates. First of all, they want standard packages which are well established, mainly in the US. You cannot innovate or add your own if the product is branded. That is why I prefer to have open programs also. The open programs give me my satisfaction because people have paid from their own pocket and they take back home much more. Of course, it gives me only my bread and butter. The Jam and Honey come from the corporate.

Ankur: Saira wants only Jam and Honey. (with a big smile) Just pulling your leg, Saira.

Vipul: I will bring something interesting for all of you next Saturday when we meet.

Shankar: What? some sweets?

Vipul: No. My Guruji's words on how to please God.

Saira: Please God or bribe God?

Vipul: God can never be bribed. My Guruji from the ashram is a very revered person. He has made a beautiful temple in the Ashram where many people come.

Keki: Vipul, please do not distribute anything without showing it to me and taking my OK.

Padma: I would like to bring some homemade sweets next Saturday. Can I?

Keki: (with a smile) Only if you let me taste it first.

Padma: I will bring a boxful just for you.

Keki: Shall we now focus on what's on the table and in our plates?

(Just then, Anwar and Lily walk in.)

Anwar: Sir, both of us have completed the re-parenting exercise both ways.

Keki: Good. That should be good for both of you.

(Anwar takes his seat and takes out a strip of medicine with two tablets in it. He reaches for a glass of water.)

Keki: What is that? Are you on some medication?

Anwar: No, no. This is for my headache.

Keki: Do you always carry it with you?

Anwar: No. I asked the hall attendant to get one for me but I do keep a strip in my drawer at the workplace and one at home.

Keki: Looks like you are getting it regularly. Do you want to get rid of it or you are taking two tablets together just now?

Anwar: No. Normally one tablet reduces the pain; Lily wanted the other one for herself.

Keki: So, Lily, you also have a headache?

Lily: I get cramp like pain in my seat quite often.

Keki: Oh good, because we want to give you all a pain control exercise which removes even years long Migraine problem in one sitting without recourse to any outside chemicals.

Nirav: I certainly want to see that.

Keki: Then we will do the exercise this afternoon itself and my request is not to take any medication right now, else you will not know what did the job.

Anwar: What if it increases?

Keki: Excellent, because you will have a better difference between before the exercise and after. This may be the last time you are going to have that pain.

(Anwar looks at Lily and puts away the medicine back into his shirt pocket. We resume lunch.)

(We reassemble post lunch)

Keki: Everybody please take out your goal sheets.

Anwar: What about my headache?

Keki: The way you say 'My Headache' reminds me of a story. You must have heard of society ladies getting together for their kitty parties. They may play cards and mostly do gossiping. At one such kitty party a middle-aged woman, wife of a rich businessman, was almost boasting, "My Headache, nobody can remove it. I have been to even specialist doctors; none could help. My husband took me to a neurosurgeon friend of his, and even he could not do anything about it".

Nirav: When it becomes unbearable, they go to a doctor, get temporary relief and then again get back to their original behavior pattern. Like you say, sickness is also a behavior pattern but doctors are largely taught to treat only the symptoms of the disease.

Keki: You hit the nail on the head, Doctor. So, whoever is having any pain please hold on to it for another half an hour and let us complete the goal sheet and then we will do the pain control exercise for those who want to get rid of it permanently.

GOAL SHEET – Contents

Now take a look at your goal sheets and one by one, read out the 'areas of importance in life'. I am writing all of them down on the whiteboard and those who feel they missed something can add it to their list. (I complete the list on the whiteboard and noticed some people adding certain areas in their list)

Let me illustrate the purpose of this by taking two real life examples.

Somebody has written out 1. Marriage/Relationship, 2. Career, 3. Health, 4. Money, & 5. Vehicle/bike.

As against that somebody else has written out, 1. Relationship with husband, 2. Relationship with sister, 3. Healthy body, 4. Healthy mind, 5. Recognition in career, 6. Money in career, 7. World travel, 8. Have a child adopted or own, 9. Give back to society, 10. Invest in a commercial shop 11. Expand my company, 12. Continuous learning/ knowledge, 13. PhD, 14. Music practice, 15. Write a Book.

Now the contents of what 'X' or 'Y' has written is what is important to them in their life, but just by looking at the sheer numbers and the variety; my question to all of you is, whose life do you think is richer and is going to be even richer? (almost all say 2nd).

Yes, please remember that and adapt it for yourself, if you also, want to enrich your life.

Now look at your goal sheets and tell me, in the 'today's column' whoever has scored the least.

Jaya: I have it as 1 for relationships.

Keki: Tell me how much was your level of satisfaction 5 years ago.

Jaya: I have scored it at 8.

Keki: Please read the comments you have put in both these columns.

Jaya: For 5 years back, I have put 'I had lot of friends, we used to meet and go out together, have parties and generally have a gala time'. (She looks at me)

Keki: And in today's column?

Jaya: I have written 'I got married, 2 years back.' (laughter all around)

Keki: No, this is not a laughing matter. Not for someone who's going through it. But Jaya, marriage is just an event which thousands of people went through in the last two years. Not everybody would rate it the same way as you have done. Therefore, your comments will not enlighten you or give you the directions. Furthermore Jaya, I do not understand why you have chosen to bring your relationship with all your friends with whom you had a Gala time to the Rock bottom.

Jaya: No, I have not; although our meetings and outings have become rarer.

Keki: Therefore, particularly in the area of relationships you have to group them separately like in workplace or family and within that if the boss and colleagues need different behavior patterns you separate them out and within family you may like to separate out your husband, your mother-in-law or anybody else which needs your special attention. Are we clear? Everybody? Good.

As far as the comments go, your initial note maybe just an excuse or a blame game. In any case when you point one finger at someone or something then three fingers are pointing towards you. **Keep questioning your comments as to what purpose is it serving for you, until you get to your own behavior pattern.** In general, we have to focus on what we did or did not do, that contributed in either increasing or decreasing our Level of Satisfaction score from 5 years back to now. This will give us the direction we should take to achieve whatever level we WISH to achieve in the next five years.

I will take just one more case before we proceed further. But before we do that, tell me, who amongst you has NOT scored even a single 10 on 10 on any area of life for today? (seven of them raise their hands). 7 out of 13. Isn't that a sorry state of affairs? These 7 are messaging to their subconscious that they are not satisfied in ANY area of life at the present time. My suggestion to them is to find at least one area of life where they feel they are feeling fully satisfied and add that into their list.

OK Anwar, what is the minimum score you have given for today?

Anwar: 2

Keki: Which area and what is your comment?

Anwar: Career. 'Lousy Boss'.

Keki: And what about 5 years before?

Anwar: 7. 'I graduated with good marks though it could have been better'.

Keki: I believe this is your 3rd job in less than 5 years, isn't it?

Anwar: Actually 4th. The first job was good, work wise, but the salary was not commensurate with my qualifications. I left it within a month and do not consider that as my job. I took up a better paying job but my boss was very rude and did not value my qualification. I was there for about 5 months.

Keki: What happened during the third job and the present one.

Anwar: The next job lasted for about 11 months and then they asked me to leave because the boss said I was not following his instructions.

Keki: And the present one?

Anwar: I want to leave it because this boss is also not giving me freedom to do things as I want, yes, although sometimes he agrees that my ideas are good.

Keki: Is that So? Tell me who is the common factor in all these jobs?

Anwar: The lousy bosses, yes.

Keki: Anwar, my question is, in these boss-subordinate relationships, who is the common factor?

Anwar: I told you. The boss.

Ankur: (Who could not stay quiet) You. Dude. You are the common factor, Man.

Anwar: Me? (surprised). So, what do you want me to do?

Saira: Apply whatever you have learnt so far; Anwar. Hasn't Keki already taught us that whenever, what you want is dependent upon somebody else the question automatically changes to, what should I do so that so and so can do such and such a thing?

Keki: I think I should now sit down and let these two take over the program. (Saira and Ankur look at me and mumble, 'sorry'. Now Anwar looks at me and I say). They are spoon-feeding you. Anwar.

Ok everybody, by now it should be clear to all of you as to how you have to fill up the first two columns for today and 5 years back, so that it gives you the direction in which you need to act. Make sure that along with the big picture areas you also include some minor achievements which you want, which could be a musical instrument or a vehicle or gardening or anything like that as well as at least one area where you are giving something back to the society. Like we said earlier, if you're thinking only about yourself then you are the only person on the face of this earth that is thinking about you. When you start thinking about others you get included and there are so many more people thinking about you. You are going to have 5 days to yourself till we meet again next Saturday and by Wednesday midnight I must have a mail from each one of you with columns for today and 5 years back filled in sensibly. I will go through it and send you my comments about filling up the third column. This 3rd column will be your wish list that you wish to achieve in the next 5 years. Next Saturday, on the 4th day I will show you how to put it on autopilot so that your wish-list starts working on you, rather than you working on your wish-list. This is just like how we are doing with each exercise that you do over here.

Your wish-list for 5 years from now HAS to be Specific and Measurable and as if it has already happened. e.g., For Health you may make a statement like " I am weighing xx Kg., yy inches around my waist and run z Kms with ease".

Do not pass any judgement on whether it is doable because your judgement will be based upon your present-day conditions; the very conditions that you wish to change. You should also put the Level of Satisfaction that you desire to achieve by that time.

You have to come ready with the final column filled in, when you come here next Saturday morning based on the comments you receive from me by Thursday.

PAIN CONTROL

(I place the hot seat facing the group and put a chair for myself on the left of it and sit down)

Keki: Whoever has some pain and wants to get rid of it permanently please come and occupy the hot seat. (Anwar jumps up and occupies the seat).

Ok Anwar, put your feet flat on the ground, sit up straight, backbone straight, push your tailbone into the chair, take a deep breath and as you exhale close your eyes and relax.

As for the others, I will be doing this exercise with Anwar at his speed and he will be talking to me about things relevant to him. Whoever else is having some pain can also do it along with us but quietly and as is relevant to you. The rest of you can watch carefully and learn the exercise because you will have plenty of occasions to use it. (three others from the group joined the exercise).

Anwar, are you having some pain or discomfort anywhere in your body?

Anwar: Yes.

Keki: Where?

Anwar: In my head.

Keki: Does it have your permission to go.

Anwar: Yes.

Keki: Does it have your permission to go forever?

Anwar: Yes.

Keki: Since how long are you having it?

Anwar: May be around four years.

Keki: Good. First of all, I want you to realize that pain is a friend. It comes on its own and it goes on its own. It always comes with a message. And the message is ' Hey Buddy, you did something which you should not have done or you did not do something which you should have done'. Pain is a friend. Do you realize what can happen if somebody's appendix is about to burst and he or she does not get the pain? What do you think can happen?

Anwar: The appendix can burst. A person can die.

Keki: Absolutely. So, you see, pain is a friend. The first thing I want you to do is to sincerely thank the pain for having come. Be sincere. You may or may not be aware of what is the message that this pain brings for you. Your subconscious knows it. Promise the pain that if and when you consciously get to know its message, you will work upon it and take appropriate action.

Now Anwar, give this pain or discomfort, some size, shape, color. The shape can be a regular shape like a ball or a cube or a disc or it may be shapeless like a cloud. What is its shape, size and color?

Anwar: It is round like a ball about the size of a basketball and dark grey in color, almost blackish.

Keki: Good. Now a basketball is much bigger than your head; so, tell me is it paining what is inside your head or even what is outside your head?

Anwar: Inside my head.

Keki: Good. You have already reduced it from the size of a basketball to the size of your head. Tell me roughly, what may be the diameter of it?

Anwar: About 8 inches.

Keki: Like I said before, it comes on its own and it goes on its own. Therefore, you have to do nothing. You are just an observer. You have already promised that if and when you get to know as to what message it has delivered; you will act upon it. And while you are thinking about it, it may have already started reducing either in its size, shape or even its color. So now tell me what changes do you notice.

Anwar: It is now in the upper part of my head, about 5 inches diameter and it has changed color to black.

Keki: Very good. It shows that you are both co-operating with each other very nicely. Now Anwar, from 8-inch diameter to 5-inch diameter, it has vacated a large area. I want you to focus on all those cells from where it has vacated, to be working rhythmically, healthily, in the pink of health. And while you are doing that, it may further reduce its size, shape, density, color, whatever. (Pause) Tell me what changes do you notice now, if any?

Anwar: Now it is like top 1/3rd of a sphere, like the opened coconut rather spongy and greenish grey in color. The diameter is about 2 to 3 inches.

Keki: You are doing fine Anwar. Once again it has vacated a big area. I want you to focus on all those cells from where it has vacated, to be working rhythmically, healthily, in the pink of health. We are in no hurry at all. We do not want even a speck to remain. (Pause) Now what is happening?

Anwar: It is like a coin, silvery but almost weightless.

Keki: Excellent. Like I said we do not want even a speck of it to remain. We are in no hurry. Once again it has vacated a big area. I want you once again, to focus on all those cells from where it has vacated, to be working rhythmically, healthily, in the pink of health. (Pause) How do you feel now?

Anwar: I do not find anything. It has gone.

Keki: Stay as you are and move your head from side to side, front and back and tell me if you find anything.

Anwar: Nothing. (with a smile on his face) can I open my eyes now?

Keki: Not yet Anwar. Do you know that your body is capable of producing whatever chemicals are required to keep this finely tuned machine of your body in perfect running condition? We only need bombardment of these chemicals from outside, when we are not taking care of ourselves. You can gently rub your hands together now, rub it on your eyes and face and open your eyes now.

Anwar: (looking all around then looking at me and saying) Amazing.

Keki: Many amazing things are about to happen to you Anwar. You have to just let it happen. (to the group) Isn't he glowing more and looking smarter?

Saira: I was also observing it and more so after he cut off his shaggy dog image.

(Anwar got up to go to his seat. Many in the group started clapping.)

Keki: There is no need to clap. NLP has done its job. Besides Lily, I saw Padma and Manju also doing the exercise. But first I have an important message for Anwar. Anwar, you have removed the discomfort concerning the message that it was bringing to you. If there is the different message in a different context you can and may get it again; understand?

Nirav: I was going to ask you exactly that. It is as if you read my mind.

Keki: Yes doctor. Normally I give this suggestion before getting the person out of this session; and that is how it has to be done. Well, so what happened with the other three?

Manju: (With his left hand on his right shoulder and rotating his right-arm round and round) I had pain in my right shoulder and was finding it difficult to even lift up my right arm, but now I do not find any problem.

Padma: I had twisted my left ankle while taking the steps out of the house this morning. I wanted to go back inside and apply the Ayurvedic oil which I have, but it would have made me late for the program. I was taking one step at a time even while climbing stairs to the lunch room. But now it is gone totally.

Keki: Just stand up and jump around and see that it is totally gone.

Padma: (Getting up and hopping up and down on the spot, higher and higher) totally gone.

Keki: How about you, Lily

Keki: I am comfortable, for now at least.

Nirav: Can we use it anywhere else besides pain?

Keki: Aban has used it successfully over a phone-call, for somebody having fever. But the best answer for your question is, just do it. There is only one exercise which has a caution and that, we will be doing on the fourth day. Besides that, whatever your subconscious decides to do, just do it, because you cannot harm anybody. And NLP is yet evolving. Just post us of anything new that you do and the results that you get. Let me add one thing over here. Whenever you have to do an exercise over the phone, please ensure that your client is not disturbed till the exercise is over and that she/he has a hands-free phone facility.

There is a very interesting case story that I must tell you all. One of our practitioners was regularly doing relaxation exercise with her six-year-old son. The son was hyperactive and couple of times she had done the pain control exercise with him. At one time he was alone with his grandmother, who had heart problems. Grandmother suddenly started having pain in her chest and became anxious as there was nobody in the house except her 6-year-old grandson. This kid asked her to lie down, did the relaxation exercise as he could and followed it up with the pain- control exercise the way he had learnt. Grandma and all the family members were so surprised with the positive and satisfactory result that they called us up at the first opportunity. At one of our monthly meetings that we used to have during those days, we called the kid and the mother to felicitate this youngest NLPer.

Let us break for some tea, coffee, cookies and come back in 15 minutes.

META MODEL - LANGUAGE PATTERNS.

I hope everybody has done their home play of reading up on meta model language patterns. Most of us have developed the habit of deleting, distorting and generalizing when we are communicating; leaving the listener to fill in the gaps from their own maps. This leads to miscommunication. Here we will be learning about how to recover the full information from the speaker's map regarding deletions, distortions and generalizations and the major sections in which it falls. One by one you will take up each section with the example given, and the response which you should give to recover the desired information. Let us start from the left over here. Shankar please start. Anyway, you are the professor of English language. Read from the top.

Shankar: *Meta model*. The first column gives the *Pattern*; second column the *Response* and the third column gives the Deletions, ***Prediction. - 1. Simple deletions a) simple deletion; example 'I am uncomfortable'.*** Keki: Stop. As a speaker of English language this sentence may be complete grammatically but is it complete in its meaning? Shankar: No. It does not say why I am uncomfortable.

Keki: That's right. While each person is reading the example given, I want all of you to relate it with your own life and see if you ever heard something similar to that and what was your response at that time and what should have been your response. Shankar, please read the suggested response.

Shankar: ***'About what; about whom.'***

Keki: And what is the purpose of this response?

Shankar: In the prediction column it says to *'recover deletion'*

Keki: Good. Thank you. Next person please.

Manju: ***Simple deletion b) Lack of Referential Index; example 'they don't listen to me'***

Keki: Stop. In the example which you just read; can you make out as to who that word 'they' refers to?

Manju: It does not say.

Keki: It does not say. That is why this type of statements are called 'Lack of Referential index'. I do not want all of you to bother so much about the nomenclature at this stage. We want to admire the entire flower and not dissect it into its parts and worry about their names. Go ahead Manju, read the other two columns.

Manju: The response column says ***'who specifically does not listen to you?*** *And the prediction column reads* ***'recover referential index'***

Keki: That's right. But Manju, even when you are asking 'who specifically does not listen to you' sometimes the person may respond saying 'all of them' or 'everybody'. They may generalize based on one or more observations and say that 'all bosses are like this' or 'all men are such' or ' all employees are like that'. We will see how to respond to that when we take up the generalizations, ok? Next person.

Padma: ***Simple deletions, c) Comparative deletions; example 'she is a better person'. In brackets (good, better, best, more, Less, most, worse, worst)***

Keki: These are examples of comparative words; isn't it? Now go ahead and read the response to that example.

Padma: ***'Better than whom?' 'Better at what?' 'Compared to whom or what?'***

Keki: And why are we asking such questions? What is the predicted expectation?

Padma: The third column of Prediction says ***'Recover comparative deletion'***

Keki: So, Padma, what do you think will happen if you get the correct answer to your response?

Padma: I do not really understand. Is it that I will narrow down from a larger area to a more focused area?

Keki: You are a clever girl, Padma. Next person.

Anwar: ***Pattern, Deletions, 'Unspecified Verbs' example, 'He rejected me'. Response, 'How specifically did he reject you?'. Prediction, 'Specify the verb'.***

Keki: And what do you understand by that?

Anwar: That I go to the root of the issue?

Keki: My, my. You are getting smarter and smarter by the hour. (Anwar smiles, and so does Saira and a couple of others). Next.

Vipul: ***Deletions. Nominalizations. Example 'Hari and I want to improve our communication'. Response, 'How would you like to communicate?', 'You are communicating what to whom?'. Prediction, 'Turn back into a process word and specify verb. Recover deletion and referential index'***

But Keki, for me, what I want to communicate is more important than how I communicate.

Keki; Vipul, maybe you already know what you want to communicate. If you say, you want to improve your communication, which means you want to improve the way you communicate or in other words, how you communicate; the process of your communication. Just think about it. Communication is a two- way process. Somebody may be making it one way and therefore there may be a breakdown.

Anyway, moving from the specific to the general, if you can imagine making a big enough basket then you can put even an elephant or a battleship into it but nouns which are derived from verb forms like communication cannot be put in a basket and are called nominalizations. Next person please.

Jaya: ***Generalizations. Universal Quantifiers; (All, every, never, everyone, no one, etc.) Example, 'She never listens to me.' Response, (find counter examples) 'Never?', 'What would happen if she did?'.***

Keki: Hold on. You are not reading a prose. While giving a Response to any of the Meta Model Patterns your Tonality is very important. The way you say. your words will make all the difference. So, say your response to that statement once again with appropriate tonality.

Jaya:(with proper emphasis) **'NEVER?'**, What would happen if **she DID?**

Keki: That's better. Next please.

Nirav***: Generalizations. Modal Operators of Necessity (required).***

(should, shouldn't, must, must not, have to, need to, it is necessary). Example, ' I have to take care of her'. Response, ' What would happen if you did? What wouldn't happen if you did not?' or also 'or?'

Keki: Doctor, please say that one word 'or' with better tonality.

Nirav: **'OR?'.** And the Prediction is to ***'Recover Effects/Outcome'***

Keki: Feel the difference? Good. Next.

Guneet Singh: ***Pattern. Generalizations. Modal Operators of Possibility (or impossibility.) (can/can't, will/won't, may/may not, possible/impossible) Example, ' I can't tell him the truth'. Response, 'What prevents you?' 'What would happen if you did?'. The prediction is to 'Recover Causes'***

Lily: ***Pattern. Distortions. Mind Reading (knowing someone's internal state). Example, 'you don't like me'. The Response should be ' how do you know I don't like you? And the prediction is to 'Recover source of information'***

Keki: But I like you Lily.

Lily: Vice versa (and a smile)

Saira: (Continuing the smile). The Pattern is ***'Distortions' called 'Lost Performative'. Lost performatives are (value judgements- person doing the judging is left out).*** The example given is ***'It's bad to be inconsistent'***. My response should be- to gather evidence- by asking ***'Who says it is bad?', 'According to whom?', 'How do you know***

it's bad'. And the prediction is that I will 'Recover the source of the Belief' or 'Recover Performative' or 'Recover the person's Belief Strategy'

Keki: Ho, ho, ho, slow down, Saira. Are you going to shoot all these questions all together? The person may run away from you.

In our country most of the value judgements may fall under the category of food habits, sex, religion or religious rituals and such other areas. To your question of 'who says it is bad', the person may reply 'my mother says it is bad' or more likely it would be the grandmother. You may be around 37 years of age and your maps might have formed while you were of age 7. At that time your grandmother might have been 67 years of age. So, the map of your statements that fall under these lost performatives today are at least reflecting what was happening 90 years ago and you are still propagating the same. There is an interesting theory about the 'Fourth Generation Change' that you can remind me sometime later, to narrate, if you are interested. For the present let us move on to the next.

Anu: ***Distortions; Cause - Effect (A> B) (where cause is wrongly put outside self). Example, 'you make me sad'. Response, 'How does what I am doing cause you to choose to feel sad'. (Counter example or How specifically?). Prediction, 'recover choice'.***

Keki: Did you understand anything, Anu?

Anu: No.

Keki: Because you are just reading what is written. Feel your response question and use your tonality correctly. Read it once again with correct tonality.

Anu: How does what I am doing cause you to choose to **feel sad**?

Keki: You are emphasizing 'feel sad' and maybe showing your empathy, but that is not the purpose and will not get you further. Try again.

Anu: How does what **I am doing** cause you to choose to feel sad?

Keki: Now you are emphasizing 'I am doing' and maybe taking the blame. Once again that is not the purpose. Which is the most important word in this question? Do You remember what we had done at home? (I hold out my left-hand palm, fingers spread out, facing upward and slap on it with my right hand and ask) when 5 people are looking at the same event what do you think happens?

Anu: They have five different perspectives.

Keki: Thank you, that's right. One may feel sad, another may feel mad, 3rd May feel glad and so on. Is the event telling them to feel the way they are feeling or is it by their own choosing?

Anu: They have no control over their feelings.

Keki: Right again. That's Good. Very good. (she smiles). Does it feel good when you smile? (she nods and says 'yes' in a soft voice). So, was it my choice to smile and feel good or was it yours? (softly 'mine') good, so read that sentence once again with the correct emphasis.

Anu: How does what I am doing cause you to **choose** to feel sad?

Keki: That's better, but not good enough. I want you to really emphasize the correct word. (I continue this process 3-4 times more, until I could see that she gets the sense of it truly). It is always our own choice of how we used to respond to somebody else or some situation. Isn't it? Anu. Like God says in our first day morning SMS that' uncertainty is inevitable but worrying is optional' and it also says 'pain is inevitable but suffering is optional'. Isn't it? (she smiles and I move on). Next.

Ankur***: Pattern; Distortions, Complex Equivalence (A=B). (two experiences are interpreted as being synonymous). Example, 'she's always yelling at me, she does not like me'. Response, 'how does her yelling mean that she ....' or ' have you ever yelled at someone you liked?'***

Keki: Yes. When I do something, it is ok but when you do the same thing it is not ok. Isn't it? Next.

Gautam: ***Pattern. Distortions; Presuppositions. Example, 'If my husband knew how much I suffered, he wouldn't do that'. The three presuppositions are i) I suffer ii) my husband acts in some way iii) my husband does not know I suffer. My response to each of these three i) how do you choose to suffer? ii) how is he reacting? iii) how do you know he doesn't know?***

The prediction is ***for i) specify choice and verb, for ii) specify what he does and for iii) recover internal representation and complex equivalence.***

Keki: (as Gautam looks at me with wide open eyes) Got it? (he nods)

Now close your books and help me rearrange the room. I want the floor totally cleared and put two chairs facing each other with enough leg room, at one end of the wall. This hall will not be sufficient for everybody so some of us will be working outside in the lobby, but with the same straight back chairs which are already brought over there.

META POSITION - EVENT BASED

Sometimes something happens and we cannot see Eye to Eye with somebody. The issue might have been boiling for some time and one day it boils over and leaves a bad taste for a very long time, which may still be existing. This exercise is to overcome that issue and those feelings.

You will perform the exercise in your own mind. One of those two chairs is your chair. You will sit in that chair and imagine that the other person is sitting in the other chair. If there has been a group instead of an individual then you will imagine the lead actor with whom you had the altercation. Sitting in your chair you will, very briefly, recall the event, which means, your thinking (your Left brain), regarding that event and then describe your feelings (your Right brain) about it to the other person. Having done that, you will get up from your chair and occupy the 2nd chair. Now you have become that other person and you are going to explain to yourself, sitting in the 1st chair, as to what that other person's thinking was, in this whole matter. Then spend maximum amount of time to get into the other person's feelings and convey that to you, sitting in the 1st chair. You should be able to discover some feelings of that person which, maybe, you were not aware of so far. How much you gain out of this exercise will all depend upon that. You perhaps, already know what was your positive intention behind your behavior. Get into what the other person's positive intention might have been behind that person's behavior.

Once you have done that, you will get up from the second chair and stand, say a foot away from both the chairs and watch them resolving the conflict. You will be an observer without passing judgements. You may be very uncomfortable, so take one step backward and continue the process. Still uncomfortable; take one more step backward and continue. Go backwards one step at a time till you reach a point where you feel, 'ok I can live with that.' That is when the exercise is not complete. Go and move away the position of those chairs. Do not sit in any of those chairs at all. Move away somewhere maybe in the lobby and sit quietly without any contact with anybody; not even an eye contact or a phone contact.

While leaving, make sure that you do not cross the space between the person doing the exercise and her/his chairs at any time. Once everybody has finished, I will call you all back into the hall and tell you what is the next step.

Remember, only real issues, hot issues, issues that bother you and most importantly that other person is still in your life as a relative or friend or from business. Take up live issues only. You can begin the exercise now.

(Once everybody has finished the exercise up to this stage and the hall is empty, I rearrange the chairs into its original parabolic formation. I go out into the lobby and find quite a few in a highly emotional state. In a soft voice I tell them) please come on back and occupy any chair that you like.

(I also occupy one of those chairs and tell them) OK, so what happened? Who would like to share first? One by one everybody is going to share their experiences. Sharing helps not only others but more so, to your own self. So please come and take the central position. (Gautam comes up first. He is in quite an emotional state and is quite speechless for a few seconds)

Gautam: (Once he composed himself a little). These last three days have been unbelievable. It is as if I have not come to India for this program but to make up my last 12 years with my father. Every day I am discovering something new. In the first chair I described my thinking and my feelings to him. But when I sat in the second chair, I felt as if I was the father and I was talking to my son. I had remorse. I had guilt feelings but I also discovered a lot of love. I only wanted the best for my son but why did he behave the way he did? (Gautam almost choked at this point and a tear was rolling down his cheek)

Keki: So, Gautam I think you got to know the positive intention of both, you and your father, isn't it? And you also got to know some emotion of his, which perhaps you were not aware of so far; is it?

Gautam: Yes. Love.

Keki: Very good. So, what are you taking back home? What are you going to do?

Gautam: Tomorrow is an important day for me. We are meeting tomorrow.

Keki: Very well. Thank you, you can take your seat and relax now. Next person please.

(I must say I was a little surprised to see Vipul coming up next)

Vipul and everybody else, just one- or two-line introduction of the event, to the extent that you are comfortable in sharing. You need not go into details of what happened in the first chair. But in the second chair, if you came across some feelings of that person which you were not aware of so far, followed by what you are taking back home and your action plan. Ok?

Vipul: Yes. It was about my son, about 10 months back. I want him to do textile engineering, where he can manufacture and I have a ready outlet for sales. Presently most of my profits are taken away by the suppliers. He does not understand this and we had a big argument. I hit him so hard that he had to be hospitalized. I should not have hit him so hard.

In the first chair, I told him all this and my disappointment at his disobedience. In the second chair he was telling me that I do not understand textile engineering and that he has some other plans. He felt that I was emotionally blackmailing him and using my authority as a father wrongly. He felt that I was doing injustice to him and that feeling of his was something new for me. What I am taking back home is that I will discuss this again with him. That's all.

Keki: That's good Vipul. They say 'Feelings are Facts' and you cannot argue about why or how they are getting it, but do you agree with his thinking?

Vipul: Some of it and I will remember them while discussing again with him.

Keki: Very good, Vipul. Please also remember that discussion is a two-way process. Talking is one part of it but Listening is a more important part of it. Ok? And keep your hands in your pocket this time. (he Laughs along with some others). Next.

Nirav: This is about me and my younger brother. He is 11 years younger to me and also a very successful and respected doctor. I was more like a father-figure for him and was instrumental in his education and career; but for over a decade now, he is keeping his distance from me and drifting apart. I am not happy with that and do not understand it. In the first chair I am just broaching the topic and expressing my unhappiness. In the second chair I realized that he was finding my brotherly love a little overpowering and often as interference. What I am taking back home is to lay all my cards on the table, maybe even apologize to him. Next month our birthdays are coming and one of those days I will invite him and his family to our place for dinner.

Keki: Did you realize all this now in your second chair?

Nirav: It must have been in my subconscious but I was not paying attention to it.

Keki: Thank you doctor. Please take your seat. Next.

Padma: I took up what happened three days back with my younger son that I shared with all of you while doing the rapport demonstration on the first day.

Keki: I thought you resolved all that with your rapport with him.

Padma: Yes, but I still feel bad that I doubted him and did not trust him.

Keki: Ok, so what happened?

Padma: In the first chair I told him everything and my feelings about it. In the second chair he repeated is explanations but behind his 'no issue' attitude I felt there was a hurt. So, I am going to sit down with him once again and tell him how a mother would feel and say sorry.

Keki: Good. Thanks. Please take your seat. Next.

Anwar: This is about a major argument I had with my boss a few months back. In the first chair I was letting him know why it could not be done the way he wanted and my feeling of confidence regarding the way I was suggesting. In the second chair I realized that both of us were actually wanting the same thing and that is, to complete the work to everybody's satisfaction. Which means that the positive intention of both of us was the same. He was feeling anxious about the result and irritated at my response. In the third position I still found both of them arguing. I was still confused. What I'm taking back home is that I should at least once follow all his instructions and prove him wrong.

Keki: So, you think proving him wrong will be the solution?

Anwar: What else can I do? Is there some magic formula?

Keki: There is. I am not sure if you are ready to use it.

Anwar: I am willing to try it out.

Keki: I can give you a Mantra. If you are going to use it, then please come here. (Anwar walks up to me). Next time instead of getting into an argument, listen to your boss completely and find out what is the end result that he wants. Then say exactly these words the way I am saying it; "Sir, leave it to me" and politely leave from there. (He takes a step backwards and starts moving to his chair) Not there, Anwar, take any other chair and sit down.

Anwar: (turning towards me) Sir, leave it to me.

Keki: You are definitely very intelligent. Next.

Jaya: The exercise started up with my husband but ended up somewhere else. Is that ok?

Keki: We will see. Please proceed.

Jaya: It began with my frustration in the bed with my husband. I told him I am married to you and I have some expectations. I was angry and I called him some names that he did not like to hear. In the second chair I realized that he was hurt; he was feeling helpless and confused but he said that he loved me otherwise. That is when the whole thing changed to my earlier relationship prior to this marriage, when bedroom used to be highly energetic and fun; and I went back to my first chair. I went back to the day of our breakup. And realized that I was egotistic and adamant. When I sat in the second chair, he was also using meaningless words and I realized that he was also egotistic and adamant. In the third position it dawned on me that like poles repel and opposite poles attract. So, I let go about my previous relationship and somehow saw me and my husband once again in the two chairs. Ours was a love marriage and except in the bed we actually love each other and that I should somehow help him. But I do not know how. Why can he not perform with me? Actually, I have caught him once, performing to completion when he was working solo

Keki: That is great. That shows some hope.

Jaya: Should I send him to you?

Keki: Absolutely not.

Jaya: (surprised) No? Why? How? Then what should I do?

Keki: You see, Jaya; the issue is not a simple one and several thoughts come to my mind simultaneously. I will present them one by one.

First is about love marriage vs arranged marriage. I believe this marriage of yours was initially arranged by your parents and then slowly you both fell in deeper and deeper love. Isn't it? (see nods a yes). So often, in love marriages we are putting the other person on a pedestal, and with time we find that the pedestal is hollow and the whole thing crumbles. As it happens so often in arranged marriages, a thought passes by, sometimes consciously or very often subconsciously that 'this is for keeps' and the mind works according to that.

I remember something from my school days where it was written that 'love drinks up faults, if you cannot drink up faults you cannot love'.

Something else that I had read during my college days, in the Times of India, 'Thought for Today' said 'one who is a friend loves; one who loves may not always be a friend; friendship profits always, love sometimes hurts'.

My wife Aban over here, has very often given free medicines to those deserving poor who needed them. These all landed up in the waste basket because their belief was that, only an injection in a proper clinic would cure them. Likewise, she has dragged some really deserving cases to these programs at a throw away cost to them and their take away has been rather poor.

Sometimes, listening to cases like yours, I do feel that test driving a car prior to bringing it to your garage is really a good idea. That apart, to answer your question as to what you should do; you can make yourself an example by utilizing whatever you have learnt, so that your husband as well as his mother are forced to ask you as to how you managed to make such a change, and then you can just mention about our programs and leave it to them.

This can be challenging. Are you ready for it? I know you love challenges and you are very capable.

Jaya: I will.

Keki: Next please.

Anu: This is about me and my husband. My keeping him away from the bedroom. In the 1st chair I was mainly talking about my feelings. In the second chair I realized that he has his own needs. He was feeling confused - not knowing my past history fully. Feeling hurt and rejected. In the third position I realized that I should talk to him completely and openly and change my map in this whole issue.

Keki: So, what are you going to do about it?

Anu: I will work on it and implement it.

Keki: When?

Anu: I don't know but soon.

Keki: Very good Anu. I know you have dealt with difficult situations in the past and I am sure you will be able to deal with this also. Next.

Saira: In the second chair was my teenage daughter. This is something that happened around 6 months back and it was about her boyfriend. In the first chair I was expressing my disapproval and apprehension. In the second chair she was defending her own position and was demanding her independence. I was aware of her hurt but I realized that my interference was irritating her much more. In the third position I realized that this was like a generation gap and I did not want her to suffer the way I have.

Keki: So, what are you taking back home?

Saira: That since this issue comes up every now and then, next time when it comes up again, I will share some of my own experiences in more details and ask her to keep her eyes and ears open so that her judgement it is not impaired. I will give her more freedom to learn a few things by herself without getting hurt too much.

Keki: Ok. Good. Next person.

Ankur: Over a year back I had a big issue with a good friend of mine over a small item like food and we have not been talking to each other since then. In the 1st chair even while talking about it, I felt so petty. In the 2nd chair he was also talking nonsense and I realized that he was perhaps getting even on some earlier hurt that I had caused him. In the 3rd position I realized that we were both going through the motions of some accumulated grudges and it was a senseless episode. There is no need to turn our faces to each other.

Keki: So, what are you taking back home and what are you going to do about it?

Ankur: Forget and forgive.

Keki: Yes Ankur; forgiving will protect the other person from further damage by you and forgetting will protect you from the same. You may feel better, but the whole episode could still be simmering within. So, are you going to take some action and if so, what?

Ankur: I suppose it takes moral courage to say sorry for such a silly thing, but I will call him up or rather, I will meet him and say sorry about the whole episode and hopefully we'll both have a laugh about it.

Keki: Good. Next.

Shankar: There is a court case going on between me and my brother regarding our ancestral property in our village. It is locked up for many years and is getting dilapidated. In the first chair I was explaining to my brother about my right in the property even though he was living in it and I was not. My feeling was that I was being cut off and that was unjust. In the second chair he was saying that he has no way of paying anything since he is not doing so well and he had looked after my parents. He was helpless. I realized his feeling of helplessness and inability to do anything. In the third position I realized the futility of the whole situation and the only person who was benefiting from this was the lawyer.

Keki: So, what have you decided to do about it?

Shankar: This is an unnecessary tussle between somebody's perceived rights and somebody's situation. I am going to withdraw the court case at the earliest and perhaps even get the whole property reconditioned at my expense so that my younger brother can move from his small place and tend to his family in a better way. (getting emotional and in a broken voice) I think that will please my Departed parents also.

Keki: I think that is excellent. Next person.

Guneet Singh: I really could not find any appropriate event but to understand and experience the exercise, I took up about a two decades old case which does not concern me now. Generally, when a case of disagreement arises, I make it a point to discuss the same with the other person without any emotions, to convince him or her or the other person convinces me or at least I understand that person better.

The case which I took up is about a girl who wanted to marry me and had said that if I also rejected her, she would end her life. In fact, it was that statement which was a red flag for me.

From my Chair I was explaining to her that I am only 22 now and I still have to establish myself in life, therefore I am not ready for any marriage at the moment. I also expressed my feelings that she is good looking, caring and ready to start a family. In the second chair I realized that her parents were keen to get her married and had arranged many proposals but somehow, they had not clicked. She had developed the feeling of being rejected and she thought that I was also finding only excuses. In the third position I still believed everything that I had said and somehow wanted to give her more confidence in herself.

Keki: In the second position did you come across some feelings of hers that you were not aware of so far?

Guneet: I felt as if she had come prepared in anticipation of a rejection.

Keki: So how had you concluded that meeting?

Guneet: I don't know if I did the right thing but I told her that she is going to be married very soon and if she calls me, I would like to attend her marriage; and in that case when I get married after five or six years, I would like her to come with her husband and children to my marriage.

Keki: You are natural NLPer. Thank you. Next please.

Manju: I put the machine operator who had purposely ruined my job by making it under-sized some two weeks back.

Keki: So, you had already made up your mind that it was done purposely?

Manju: Yes, it was. There was so much tolerance available on the size that nobody could make it undersized. So, I was really taking him to task and I was very angry.

Keki: What happened when you sat in the second chair?

Manju: I did not sit in the second chair because I did not want to give the same excuses as he was giving.

Keki: And in the third position?

Manju: I had decided to fire him and I had already fired him.

Keki: Manju, when I said that in the second chair you become that person it only means that for the period you are in that chair you will take on the thinking and feeling pattern of that person, you are not going to become that person permanently. It is important to follow each and every step exactly, just like how the others have done it so far. So, when you go home repeat this exercise once again following all the instructions correctly, only then you will get some wisdom out of it. Will you do it?

Manju: I will try.

Keki: Not try. I am asking you 'will you do it?'

Manju: I will do it. Keki: Thank you. Next person.

Lily: This is about my father and me. You know how my father is.

Keki: No, I don't. I have not interacted with him. I only know your perception of him from what you have told us so far.

Lily: Anyway, you know the ongoing problem I am having with him since many years.

Keki: For ongoing troublesome relationship we are going to have an exercise on the fourth day. This exercise, as I have already explained is event-based. Some event which has prevented you from seeing Eye to Eye with somebody. Any way you can tell me if you came across some feeling of his which you were not aware of so far, while sitting in the second chair and if you are taking back something new with you.

Lily: There has been no change so far and I am taking back home whatever I came with. Keki: Naturally. Because for taking back home something different you have to follow the instructions given, meticulously like how others are doing. Thank you, because you have been a learning process for many of us over here today .

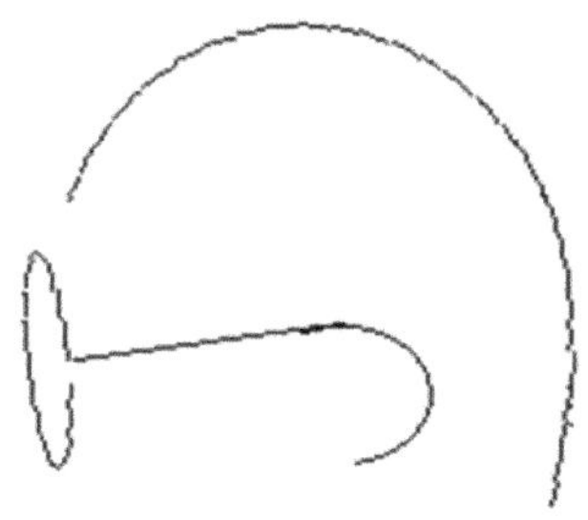

Figure 14

Do you remember these two lines that used to be drawn as given in the accompanying figure, by our national TV channel?

Saira: Mahatma Gandhi.

Keki: And what was the sentence that used to accompany these two lines? Saira: Hey Ram?

Keki: No. Nirav: Something about the greatness.

Keki: That's right. **'The greatness of this man was his simplicity'.**

Between now and Saturday next when you come back you will meet quite a few people and some of them may ask you as to what you do at the program. If you tell them that 'I sat in one chair, then I got up and sat in the other chair and then I stood in-between them. They may say 'are you gone mad? don't you have chairs at home that you want to go to an expensive hotel to stand between chairs?' (laughter) Do not get fooled by the simplicity of NLP exercises. They are very, very simple yet very, very powerful.

Now pack up everything and let us do the closing exercise for today.

Closing Exercise- THE AUTOBIOGRAPHY

Put your feet flat on the ground, sit up straight, backbone straight, push your tailbone into the chair, take a deep breath and while exhaling close your eyes and relax.

1. Become Completely Relaxed. Find a comfortable and quiet place in which to proceed with this exercise. Your favorite chair will do. It's a good idea to do this exercise sitting up rather than lying down, you want to feel very relaxed, and yet remain alert and attentive. It's time to relax, now. . . breathe . . . let your body relax. Breathe slowly . . . and deeply . . . and fully. it's all right to make noise when you breathe. Imagine that you have nostrils on the bottoms of your feet . . . and you can breathe air up your legs and into your lungs. Fill your body with good, fresh air. And while you're breathing comfortably and slowly and fully, think about what it's like to really appreciate yourself, as you are. As you feel your body relax, just let go of any bodily and emotional tensions you may have. Take a moment and check your body for any "holding feelings" you may be experiencing and let them go. Let them go, completely.

2. Think of Someone Who Loves You. Before beginning this process, think of someone who you know loves you. Think of someone who, you are certain, without a doubt, loves you: a friend, lover, husband, wife, parents, child, whoever; simply notice who it is for the process you are about to learn. If you can't think of anyone who you know loves you, then think of a person who you assisted in some way, and you know that person deeply appreciates you. Whether you think of someone who you know loves you or of someone who you know deeply appreciates you, in either case, simply notice who he or she is for now. You'll make good use of this personal resource later on.
3. Write Your Autobiography. Now, imagine that you are sitting at a desk writing your autobiography. You may be using a pen or a pencil, or perhaps a typewriter or a computer keyboard. In some way, you, find yourself writing your autobiography, telling the story of your life. You're quite comfortable as you write your autobiography. You can feel and see the desk and the chair you're using. You may notice, right away ... in a few seconds . . . or perhaps later on, how the words that describe your life begin to gently occur to you. And as you write, you become aware of the thought of someone who you know loves you ... or appreciates you. You begin to think even more clearly about that person who you know loves you.
4. See the Person Who You Know Loves You. Now, take your time to notice that, across the room from where you're writing your autobiography, you can see someone standing on the other side of a glass door, the person who you know loves you. And as you see this person who you know loves you or appreciates you, you become aware that he or she is looking at you, observing you. And you decide to describe this person in your autobiography, and the part he or she has played in your life. Take your time and describe this person, what you see and what you feel about this person. Even include what you hear yourself saying to your-self about the person who you know loves you. Write all of this down into your autobiography. Take all the time you need.
5. See Yourself from Another Perspective. Now that you have a full sense of what it's like to describe the person who you know loves you, gently allow yourself to leave your body at the desk and float

your awareness across the room through the glass door, and notice what it's like to stand next to the person who loves you. Take your time to look through the glass door and observe yourself writing your autobiography. Just stand there and notice what you look like from this perspective of being behind the glass door. And notice just how much you currently appreciate your-self. Notice your actual feelings about yourself as you look at yourself through the glass door. You may notice a great deal of self-appreciation, or you may only notice a little. Whatever you notice, simply accept this experience.

6. See Yourself Through the Eyes of Someone Who Loves You. Now, gently and tenderly, allow yourself to enter into the body of the person who you know loves you. Take all the time you need to do this in a comfortable and easy way. And when you are completely in the body of the person who you know loves or deeply appreciates you, look through that person's eyes at yourself as you write your autobiography. See yourself through the eyes of someone who loves you. Notice what you look like over there writing your autobiography. And notice how you move and breathe. Take enough time to fully appreciate the qualities and special aspects of yourself that you are aware of, perhaps for the first time, as you see yourself through the eyes of love. And since you're in the body of someone who loves you, notice the thoughts you hear being spoken about you and the feelings being felt about you. Notice the tone of voice of the positive, appreciative thoughts you hear as you see your-self over there, writing at your desk, from the perspective of someone who you know loves you.
7. Return to Your Own Perspective. When you are fully aware of the qualities and special aspects of yourself that make you who and what you are, gently, tenderly, allow your awareness to leave the body of the person who you know loves you, and float back, through the glass door, across the room, and back into your body at the desk writing your autobiography.
8. Write About Your Experience. You can take your time, now, to write into your autobiography what you just experienced by seeing yourself through the eyes of love or appreciation. As you write about what you experienced, be sure to describe several of the qualities

and special aspects you noticed in yourself when you saw yourself through the eyes of love.

9. Think of the Future. As you write this experience into your autobiography, begin to think of your future—both of future experiences you expect are coming, and also of those unexpected experiences that may surprise you. Think of all the places and times in your future . . . tomorrow, the next day, weeks and months and even years from now, when you'll want to be easily able to review, recall, and remember this precious experience of seeing yourself through the eyes of love, noticing your special-ness and deeply appreciating who and what you are in the world.
10. Return to the Present Moment. Now, begin to return to your full awareness, your full consciousness. At your own pace, gently become increasingly wide awake and alert. Come all the way back to this present time and place. feeling much better than before. Notice the sounds of the room. And you can notice the feelings in your body. And in a moment, you can open your eyes as you gently return to your full conscious awareness and stretch your arms and legs. Welcome back.
11. Notice the Changes. Now that you have had the chance to actually experience the self-appreciation that eludes so many people, please take your time and comfortably notice how this exercise has changed your inner representations of yourself in subtle and not-so-subtle ways. Notice the ways in which you can now actually see yourself from a new, more appreciative, and loving perspective. The experience you just went through has provided you with the kind of deep personal self-appreciation that is often a first step toward totally supporting and encouraging yourself.

CHAPTER 6

CONVERSATION WITH ANUSUYA-ANUSUYA NURTURES THE PLAN

By now Anusuya has completed the NLP Master Practitioner program. She now wants to do the 'Train the Trainer' program so that she can start taking the Practitioner's program herself. She called us up one day to say that she wanted to take things up further and would like to have a discussion with us. On the appointed day and time, she buzzed our door-bell exactly as the clock struck 4:00 p.m. Aban and I were very happy to see her sparkling and shining eyes and face. The moroseness and drooping eyes and lips from her first visit, were the thing of the past and totally forgotten. We should not have reminded her of that but just couldn't help commenting. It had no effect on her except that of a smile and saying that two of you were responsible for it. I once again corrected her that we only show the way and it is she who has walked the path. After some preliminaries about life in general and particularly with the family, she got down to the point.

Anusuya: The Book. Is my book getting ready?

Keki: There you go again. There is no book. There is not going to be any book. I think you are again looking for a crutch. Maybe because you want to do the TTT (Train The Trainer) program.

Anusuya: No. Absolutely not. If you want, I will collect the book after I have taken a couple of programs. I just wish that whatever you have been doing should see the light of the day.

Keki: We can talk about all that later. First you tell me how was the Master Practitioner's program for you. Tell me what you have found as the essence of it in 2-3 lines.

Anusuya: In the practitioner's program you just touched upon the Time-lines on the fourth day but here we went into the details of it and did so many exercises based upon it. But while doing those, one thing was very clear. I think the highlight of the program was when you asked us to go through each and every exercise that we had done in the Practitioner's and note down which ones were based on sub-modality changes. To our surprise, each one of us found that almost each and every exercise fall in that category. I am wondering if, each and every thought that we have or each and every sentence that we say has a spatial (=in space) connection with its own submodalities in V, A and K perhaps located somewhere outside our body. Is that so?

Keki: Anu, I am truly amazed at your Insight. We have had so many programs so far, and I might have asked this question to many but none has amazed me with their answer as you have done. Do you remember the research project which we had started? You were also a part of it. It was precisely for the purpose of getting answers to questions like this, but somehow it has gone into cold storage for the present. It is for people like you to revive it and go deeper into it. With original thinking like this, I am convinced that you are not looking for any crutch.

Aban: In my two decades with Keki, even I have never thought of it like that.

Anusuya: Can I say something more?

Keki: Some more fabulous insights?

Anusuya: I don't know but I am talking about one exercise where we give the resources from our 4 grandparents and our parents to ourselves. Ever since that exercise I have been curious to know more and more about my grandparents. I am able to get some information but not as much as I would like. I think you are also grandparents now. How many grandchildren do you have already?

Aban: We have five.

Anusuya: So, when their children or grandchildren ask them about Keki what will they answer? Will they say that, oh, he qualified as an engineer, then he worked as a brilliant engineer for 2 decades, then he struggled in life for another two decades and then, for more than two decades he cleaned everybody's brains? Will they be able to say anything more?

Aban: What are you leading to?

Anusuya: The Book. The Book of course. Do not write it for me. Do not even give it to me. Make five manuscripts and give it to your grandchildren. Please.

Keki: (with a smile) This cleaning everybody's brain reminds me of an actual story that happened to me. I was in the nursery school may be 4 or 5 years of age. God knows what happened to my teacher but she dragged me to the principal's office. The principal was a very old lady with scanty grey hair tied up in a tiny betel nut size ball at the back of her head. I can still picture her very well. She gave me a long lecture and admonished me, God knows for what, and asked me what I will do when I grow up. Will I be going to different people's homes to broom their rooms? Till date I do not know what it was all about but what I know is that nowadays people come to my room to get their brains broomed out. (all three of us have a laugh).

Anusuya: One copy of the manuscript for me to learn how you do the brooming. Yes? Done? I will collect it in my next visit. Thanks for the lovely tea and the cake; Aban.

Bye now, Keki; The Book.

(After she left, I told Aban, 'I can't stop admiring this girl'. To which Aban replied with a big grin. 'She makes a lot of sense, so better start writing')

CHAPTER 7

DAY 4

(All the 13 participants are in their seats by the appointed time and I take my Central position.)

Keki: How are we today?

Group: Great. Fantastic. Awesome. (are part of the loud responses from the group)

Keki: WOW. Everybody seems quite energetic today. Shall we take it further?

Group: (Loudly) YES.

Keki: Who wants to take it further?

Group: (Even louder) **... I**

Keki: OK. All Rise. (All 15 of us were standing now.) Good morning. (Standing erect and with hands pumping.) Group: Good morning. (In similar manner of voice and body language.) Keki: Every morning is a good morning. Group: Every morning is a good morning. Keki: Because I make it a good morning. Group: Because I make it a good morning. Keki: Today is a good day. Group: Today is a good day. Keki: Because I am going to Make it a good day. Group: Because I am going to Make it a good day.

Keki: Thank you. Don't sit down.

Let us do what I call as a circulation massage. With your right-hand thumb and one or two fingers start pressing the left-hand little finger from the tip all the way down up to the wrist, the way I am doing it. Now the ring finger. As you are pressing it you may find some point where it hurts. Press even harder at that point using a slight circular motion of the thumb. They say that each such point is connected to a certain organ in the body and it repairs that organ. The pain may not go immediately and you may have to get back to that point later on, several times. Do the same with other fingers and the thumb. Now with your left-hand thumb and one or two fingers repeat the process for your right hand. This is also known as the Sujok therapy.

Having done with your hands, once again with your right hand start from the left-hand wrist upwards towards the shoulder. While you are doing this in areas other than your palm you can have a slight movement of the pressure with your thumb and fingers. This movement has to be towards the heart. I am no expert in this but I find the whole process very invigorating. After the left arm do the same to your right arm. Then the neck. Your face. Then start from your ankle of each leg upwards to the hips and stomach. At the stomach, you can keep the stomach loose and knock it with the fingertips of your two hands with moderate pressure. Complete this process for the full body. Good. Please take your seats. How do you all feel?

Group: (most said 'lighter', some said 'refreshed', somebody said 'invigorated'.

Keki: Three days are over out of 5. By now all of you are at least 60% NLPers. Now you will want to start solving problems. But before we do that, any doubts, any clarifications, any questions, anything to share, anything happened?

(Gautam stood up. He was quiet. He was getting a little emotional)

Keki: You can sit down, Gautam. There is no need to stand up, for anybody. You can share whatever you are comfortable with and sitting down.

Gautam: I will make it short.

Keki: That is fine.

Gautam: I met my father on Monday as per the appointment. My aunt was also there. She had opened the door for me and stood aside. I and my dad just stood there looking at each other, speechless. My aunt must have briefed him about myself and everything that we had talked in the hospital canteen. Finally, he opened his arms and said 'my son, I am proud of you'. At this point we both moved towards each other. We hugged each other and I said 'I am sorry dad, I did not know about mom, otherwise I would have surely come'. At this point we both started crying. (While narrating this, Gautam took out a handkerchief from his pocket and started wiping his tears.) (There was silence in the seminar hall for quite some time.)

Keki: 12 years, Gautam.

Gautam: 11 years, 10 months and 12 days to the date when I had left the house.

Keki: Are you at peace now, Gautam? (I noticed at least 2 of the ladies in the hall wiping their tears.)

Gautam: (with a flush of happiness on his face) Very.

Keki: Did you meet him again?

Gautam: Almost every day. My aunt made it a point to call me either for lunch or dinner every day. I am glad that she is taking care of him. They wanted me to come and stay with them. Maybe I will do that after this program since they are living quite far away from this hotel.

Keki: Good, anything else you want to say?

Gautam: Yes. I told him about my shifting to Norway from Singapore and marrying the Norwegian girl. He said I could marry anyone I choose but I should not deprive him of the pleasure of getting me married by him in India. Now I am in a dilemma because my fiancé has made all the arrangements for our marriage in Norway and I will be shifting there in a few weeks.

Keki: Ok. Anybody else?

Anwar: I used your Mantra.

Keki: And?

Anwar: On Monday he ignored me, but on Tuesday he called me for a project which I estimate would take 6 days to complete. He wanted it ready by Friday evening. I just said 'Sir, leave it to me'.

Keki: And?

Anwar: He looked at me with some contempt and shrugged his Shoulders.

Keki: So, what happened?

Anwar: For a day I felt trapped but with anger within me I said I should show him his place. Thursday evening, I stayed back in office till 9 o'clock in the night, completed the project and double checked it. Friday morning itself I placed the project to him. He went through it once, then once again. I am sure he was trying to find some flaws, he couldn't. I asked him 'Sir, is it ok? He said, 'I will let you know if I need anything'.

Keki: I am impressed.

Anwar: I hope he is impressed too.

Jaya: Can I ask a question?

Keki: Go ahead, Jaya.

Jaya: Can we change the past?

Keki: What is the past?

Jaya: Something that has already happened.

Keki: Once again let me refresh your memory. (I take out my left-hand Palm facing upwards with fingers outstretched and slap my right hand onto it, onto the left-hand palm, and ask) if 5 people are looking at the same event, you all said there will be five different perspectives. Suppose they witness an accident. Somebody will blame the pedestrian for 'jay-walking', somebody else may blame the driver, a grown-up son sitting in the back seat may blame his mother for distracting his father from driving. So past is the way your memory presents you the event gone by. It does not necessarily mean it is so. The event will be there like for instance, the accident, but the way it presents to you and your perception of the whole thing can certainly change. Therefore, there can be a new beginning. Does that make sense to you?

Jaya: But what I have seen with my own eyes and heard with my own ears, or experienced, those are facts, aren't they? You said that facts are generally sensory based.

Keki: You are absolutely right. Tell me Jaya, whatever you saw, whether you saw it from the left side or from the right side; whatever you heard, whether you heard it from 5 feet of 15 feet away; whatever you experienced from which ever position; are they all not sensory based and therefore facts?

Jaya: That's what I am saying.

Keki: Therefore Jaya, the three people in the earlier car accident. The son from the back seat, the mother from the passenger seat, her husband who was driving as well as the onlookers, who either blamed the driver or the pedestrian; all of them had sensory experience of what they saw, what they heard and what they experienced, yet each one's conclusion was different. It is our conclusions that affect our emotions more than the mere facts. Conclusions can fall in the category of Opinions. Jaya, does that answer your question?

Jaya: Somewhat but it brings me to another question. Do I have to continue suffering my fate? Is it fate, first of all? Are we all prisoners of fate? What about Karma? Is life predetermined or in our hands?

Keki: My, my, Jaya. This is not just another question. This is a whole lot of philosophy you are asking me. Your questions are more or less answered in the 'SMS from God' that we went through at the beginning of the program on the first day. And if I remember right, even at that time you were asking 'who I am. Why am I here?' And God replied 'Seek not to find who you are, but to determine who you want to be. Stop looking for a purpose as to why you are here. Create it'. You seem to be having a philosophical side to you. Do you read a lot about philosophy?

Jaya: I have read Gita, and some Vedas and Upanishads. I feel good while reading it but again get back to my old questions. Why is that happening to me? Why do I find walls in front of me every now and then? What do I do?

Keki: Gita is like a manual for living your life. My own general reading actually started after I completed my college. After reading the books on cosmology, psychology and others, meant for general public, I came across a 10-rupee book called the Anthology of Upanishads. You cannot just read this type of book and feel good about it. I would read a sloka (=a stanza) and mull over it for a few days until I could digest it. After going through that book my reading stopped for the next 10 years. Whichever book, on whatever subject came my way, I read the title, the contents and about the author and said that I already knew everything about it. But let me answer your questions very briefly. Your first question, 'Do I have to continue suffering my fate?' the answer is 'suffering, absolutely not'; learning from it, absolutely yes.

Your next question; 'Is it fate, first of all? Are we all prisoners of fate?'. You already have the answer that all our present and future behavior and actions are based upon our past programming. So, are we prisoners of it? Absolutely not. We have NLP. NLP has not come from another planet but what people have been doing naturally, without knowing sometimes. I can point out at least more than a couple of people over here who have done it by themselves.

Your next question, 'What about Karma?'. The same answer as above.

Another question from you, 'Is life predetermined or in our hands?'. By now you should be able to answer it yourself.

Let me tell you something that will answer your further questions and maybe even what Anwar is having in his mind. **There are three types of foods.** Nutritious food, junk food and poison. Nothing happens even if you put any of these in your mouth, until your mouth salivates and starts masticating this item. Then it enters your body. The nutritious food will nurture you. The junk food will sap your energy and the poison will kill you or at least make you unwell. All this happens when you digest it.

Likewise, there are three types of information. Useful information, junk information and poisonous information. Nothing happens as it falls on your ears (=shravan) or even into your mind until you start digesting that information (=mannan). Once you digest it, the Useful information can make you wiser and more knowledgeable; the junk information will sap your time and energy; the poisonous information can hurt you, as well as the world. Therefore, you need to choose wisely. Nobody else will choose it for you. And to choose wisely, you only have that present moment. Remember that everything is twice born. The present moment is a 'present' to you from the universe. What you do in the present, will determine your future. Whatever you have done 'in your presented moment of the past' has determined your today. Whoever is facing the wall must realize that the wall was built sometime in the past by himself or herself at that presented moment. It is for that person to break it down and make it vanish in this present moment.

Anwar: How did you know what I had in my mind? I was actually thinking of getting some more clarification on what we talked the previous day.

Keki: It was written on your face. But are we going to keep on talking about philosophy or does anybody have some questions on some exercises or whatever we have done on the first 3 days?

Padma: …

Keki: Hold on a minute, please Padma. Sorry but I am reminded of a story. Who would like to hear a story?

Group: I (not loud enough because many were still digesting whatever was said so far)

Keki: I didn't hear you. Who wants to hear a story?

Group: (Louder this time) ... I

Keki: That's better.

There is this story of a very beautiful and sweet young girl, well educated, who was so happy to be married about 15 months back. Like it happens in so many marriages she was also going through the adjustment period. She was in a shock and devastated at the behavior of her husband and in-laws. One early morning she went to meet her grandmother, who used to live alone in a small Cottage all by herself. She knocked at the door and an old, frail, short lady (her grandma) opened the door. As soon as the girl saw her grandma she said 'Nana' and hugged her. She hugged her a little tighter and Nana felt a drop fall on her nape. Nana gave her time to empty out a little and then gently led her to a single two-seater sofa which she had, next to her kitchen area. Nana heard her entire story very patiently without interfering.

Then Nana gently asked if she could help her with the stove. She asked her to put about 3 cups of Water in the vessel and light the stove. As the water was about to boil, she asked her to slip an egg into the water gently without cracking it. Then she asked her to take a carrot from the vegetable tray and put one carrot into that vessel. After a couple of minutes, she asked the girl to remove the egg and the carrot into a plate and since she did not want to waste that hot water, she asked her to put a spoonful of coffee in it. When the coffee was ready, she asked her to put it into two cups and bring those two cups as well as the plate with the carrot and the egg in it to her.

When the girl brought all this to her, she made her sit by her side and said 'look my dear; this egg was so fragile before it went into the hot water, has turned out to be so hard; and this carrot which was so firm and straight went through the same process and has come out limp and listless; but look at this coffee. It also underwent the same environment but has changed the entire environment to make it exuberant and invigorating for all. All three went through the same circumstances. It is for you my child, to decide if you want to be like the carrot, like the egg, or like the coffee.

Yes Padma, you were about to ask something.

Padma: Can I do the relaxation exercise on others? Keki: Definitely. Not only the relaxation exercise but whatever you have learnt so far, you can and must use it at every opportunity you get. That is the only way to progress with NLP.

Padma: I was almost going off to sleep during that exercise. Can you give us the points of that exercise? Keki: Sure. Please remind me in the afternoon session.

Jaya: What should I do when somebody does not want to do the exercise. After all you can take the horse to water but you cannot make him drink. Keki: In my early days of NLP, I was asked this question little differently. The person asked 'if somebody does not want to change can you change him?' and my answer was 'no'. Then your horse statement came to my mind and I said I was making a mistake wanting the horse to drink. I should first make the horse thirsty and then take him close-by to water and perhaps he will drink it himself. This has been working ever since; although sometimes it might take a little longer and I might have to work a little harder and differently. You can also read up the Milton model of language patterns where you are not filling up anything from your map but allowing the other person to fill up details from her/his map.

Manju: What is Meta? That word came in so many different ways. Keki: Meta means going beyond or further. In the Meta-Position exercise that we did on the previous evening, you were yourself in the first position where you were explaining your thoughts and feelings to the second person in the second chair. In the 2nd chair you took the position of that 2nd person. Then when you took the third position facing the two chairs, you took the Meta Position as a nonjudgmental, uninvolved, observer. In the Meta Model Language Patterns, your response to the other person's statement was to go beyond what he or she has said and to get clarifications from his or her mind instead of you filling in from your map. If you open your dictionary, you will find quite a few words starting with meta and that should give you more clarification.

Ankur: Last time you promised that you will share some other case story about phenomenon.

Keki: There was this middle-aged widow living all by herself alone. She had become friendly with a middle-aged businessman from Mumbai.

This gentleman was half the time in business suit and the other half in Swami's clothes. It was this later part which attracted this widow to him. Whenever he would come down from Mumbai, he would spend time with her and very often stay at her residence. Things developed and he wanted to marry her. She did not want another marriage and they had a tiff. For almost one year they had not met each other. She felt bad about it and took up the case in the meta- position exercise which we did the previous evening. She wanted to contact him and apologize, but before she could do that, that person himself appeared and knocked on her door a few days later. He said he was already married and was having some issue with his wife. He wanted her to come with him to Mumbai and meet his wife to sort out some issues. His coming over after a year and within few days of the exercise can only be called a phenomenon.

Saira: So Ankur what is happening with your dream girl?

Ankur: Work in progress. Good. (Silencing her with a finger crossing his lips).

Saira: You had asked me Keki, to remind you about **the fourth-generation change.**

Keki: Have you seen a photograph or a painting of your great grandmother?

Saira: Yes, my fore-fathers were all in the military. There is one painting of my great grandfather with my great grandmother.

Keki: Recall that painting now and tell me what sort of a blouse is she wearing?

Saira: The blouse is covering almost up to her neck and the sleeves are up to her wrists.

Keki: That is what I expected. Have you seen your grandmother's painting or photograph?

Saira: We have a group photograph with my Grandma and Grandpa sitting in the middle with the entire family around and me as a toddler in my mother's lap.

Keki: Excellent. I wish you had that photograph with you right now, over here. Anyway, just recall it and now describe the blouse that your grandmother is wearing.

Saira: My grandmother's blouse neckline is a little lower than the neck and the sleeves are three quarters.

Keki: And your mother's?

Saira: In the photograph it is a little above the elbow but now-a-days it is mostly a little above half way between the shoulder and the elbow.

Keki: There is a fly sitting on your left shoulder, just shoo it off.

Saira: Where? here? (Brushing her left shoulder with her right hand; then with a big smile.) you mean now I am wearing sleeveless, is it?

Keki: Whether it is your neckline or your sleeve length; whether you can show your hair or how you wear it; whether it is about being an unwed mother or a live-in relationship and much of everything;

The 1st generation (plus a few before that) says 'no, never, nobody could'. The 2nd generation:' few do, we should never' The 3rd generation: 'some do, I will not'. The 4th generation: 'most do, why not me.'

Sociologically, the world is not moving at the same speed. Nations, cultures, segments, families and within the members of the families also, people can be at different levels. We get into clash of beliefs and may go at each other's throats also.

Saira: So how do we use this?

Keki: The director of Tata Management Training Center; One Dr. Francis Menezes, who taught us Dream Interpretation, used to say that "Awareness is Everything".

Now we have used up most of the morning session. There is still some time left. We will delay the tea/ coffee snacks. Please take a quick 3 minutes break. Run to the washroom if you have to. Come back and change places, change neighbors.

(once everybody is back)

PROBLEM SOLVING – OWN.

So, we said we will want to start solving problems. There are two things we can do. We can start solving our own problems or we can start solving other people's problems. We will do both. Question is, what do you all want to do first?

Group: Our own.

Keki: Everybody becomes an angel when they come here. There are two ways we can do both these. We will see the two ways of solving our own problems first. I am giving you a set of 6 questions. Force yourself to answer each and every one of them.

Q1. What is my problem? (I am not talking about Mr. Darbary's problem. I am talking about your own)

Q2. How long have I had it?

Q3. Where does the fault lie?

Q4. Who is to blame?

Q5. What is my worst experience of this?

Q6. Why haven't I solved it yet?

Once again please remember, real issues, hot issues, issues that bother you, absolutely nothing hypothetical. Start answering now.

(I leave the hall to go to my favorite place near the swimming pool and come back after giving them appropriate time)

Please make sure you have answered each and every one of the six questions first and then take up this next set of 6 questions and wait for me.

Q1. What do I want?

Q2. How will I know when I have got it? (which means what will you see, hear, touch, feel and when)

Q3. What else will improve when I get it? (there are always some byproduct benefits)

Q4. What resources do I have already that can help? (remember that all the resources an individual needs to effect the change are already within them)

Q5. What is something similar that I have succeeded in? (We had talked about the cricket team which you had started when you were 11.)

Q6. What is my next step? (like, you will go home this evening and send out a mail or anything like that)

Take as much time as you need to answer all these questions. My advice is that whatever you considered as your problem in the first set of 6 questions, convert that into what you want; just to show you the difference between the two sets of questions.

(once again, I leave them to write the answers and go down to my favorite place)

(I return after giving them sufficient time and find that some are still writing. I quietly ask others to show me their goal sheet, completed up to the final column. I just check that they have filled in the final column comments along with the ranking of level of satisfaction. I complete this process for all.)

Keki: A few of you have not filled in the final column of your goal sheet comments and/or the level of satisfaction ranking. Please make sure you complete this before coming for lunch. We are already running beyond time so let us complete the tea/coffee snacks and come back, when we will discuss the difference between the two methods of problem solving that we have seen.

(During the break after we had snacks, while I was having my cup of tea, Jaya singled me out, with a cup in her hand and said 'This is coffee. I normally prefer tea, but I am going to be Coffee. Do you really think that I am beautiful and sweet?' I replied 'Jaya, it is not important what I think, but it is very important what you think and what He thinks. And yes, anybody will say that you are very sweet and very beautiful. I would also add that at the same time you are also so very intelligent, very smart and very capable. I call out to the group 'come on back' and we all enter the hall).

Keki: Out of the two sets of questions regarding solving your own problems, which set do you think brings you closer to a solution?

(Everybody in the group says second except Manju, Vipul and Lily who said that it was the first. Anu does not answer.)

The Second, yes. In the first set of 6 questions, question #4 says 'who is to blame?' Who did you all blame?

(Everybody said 'myself', except Manju, who said 'my machine operator'; Vipul, 'my son' and Lily 'my father'.)

Sometimes we blame somebody or something for what is happening to us. Very often we blame stupidly. We go through four stages when we blame somebody or something stupidly:

Stage 1 - we believe it to be true.

Stage 2 - because we believe it to be true, we think that the responsibility lies somewhere else.

Stage 3 - because we believe that the responsibility lies somewhere else, we do not do anything about it, and

Stage 4 - because we do not do anything about it, nothing changes.

Sometimes parents blame their children; at workplace we may blame our juniors; teachers may blame their students. Perhaps these people have not learnt that **'if the student hasn't learnt, the teacher hasn't taught.'**

There is an interesting case-story of a participant from Gujarat. Somebody called me up once and said he wanted to do the NLP Practitioner's program. After we talked about why he wanted to do the program and what were his expectations, he asked about the investment. When I told him the amount, he said he had no money. Considering him as a deserving case I gave him certain facilities. The program was over two weekends as usual. He came over the first weekend and gave me a small cheque. For the second week-end he said he had no money even to travel. I told him it is dangerous to leave the program halfway and that he should manage it somehow. He did manage.

We deposited the cheque in the bank. We paid the bank for the bounced cheque. We informed him. He talked about the earthquake in Gujarat and how it has damaged his building. The tenants could not live there. He was not getting any rent. Nobody would buy the damaged building and he had no funds to repair it. He sent us another cheque. We again paid the bank, since this cheque also bounced.

He was enthusiastic. He experimented with firewalking. He burnt his feet. Finally mastered it. Started travelling across Gujarat and Maharashtra giving public talks and programs. Started claiming a lot of things at the public meetings and the Rationalist Association was after him. He was making money and wanted to do the Master Practitioner's program. He said he will pay up for the practitioner's and part payment for the master practitioner's. I think his one cheque went through but the other bounced. We paid the bank for that also. Every time it happened; he blamed the earthquake. Once while driving around in Mumbai, we got a call from him. He said he had gone beyond NLP and asked Aban to open any old newspaper, any page and look at the picture and he will tell us what we are looking at. Of course, it never happened but blaming earthquake continued. Perhaps I failed in my job.

Once a very high profile, world-renowned trainer was stopped by somebody, who told him 'Sir, you were wrong. 2 years back when I did your program you said that I will prosper. It is past two years now and I am still in the same mess. **'It was then that the trainer realized that the participants were putting the onus of change on him rather than taking action** (as originating from their subconscious) **by themselves.**

At a hardware store in Mumbai, there was this placard which read **'Thank God for giving you work but do not expect him to finish it also for you'.**

Yes, miracles do happen. **Expect miracles but do not Await them.**

Now let us move on to **solving other people's problems**. Once again there are two methods. We will start with the first. These are day to day type of problems. Examples could be that I cannot get up in the morning, I do not exercise, I am overweight, I do not know whether to do this or that, etc.

So, somebody please state your problem.

Vipul: My son does not obey me. Manju: My workers do not follow my instructions. Jaya: I do not know what to do about my husband. Saira: Should I do PhD or not.

Keki: These can be taken up but there are better exercises for them. Right now, I am looking for some mundane issues. Shankar: I cannot get up in the morning.

Keki: We can take up either Saira or Shankar. Ankur: Professor Shankar.

Keki: Ok so let us take up the professor's problem. We will use and practice the first method which is, **giving suggestions on the content**. Shankar, please state your problem.

Shankar: I cannot get up in the morning. Keki: Use an alarm. Shankar: I already do but I switch it off and go back to sleep. Keki: Keep it far away so that you have to get up and close it. Shankar: Done that also. I put a pillow over my ears and sleep off. Keki: Ask your wife to throw some water on your face. Shankar: I will get irritated and start fighting with my wife. Keki: Ask your milkman to keep buzzing the doorbell until you go and collect the milk and ask your wife not to respond to it. Shankar: No.

Keki: Everybody sit as you are and pair up with your neighbor. Take up any issue and let your partner give you 4 or 5 suggestions, advice, and then switch the roles. Do not get into any discussions. You have less than 2 minutes to complete the exercise both ways. Start now. (after 3 minutes) Stop now. Now let us take up the other method which is - **suggestions on the process**. We will continue with Shankar so that you understand the difference. Shankar, please define your problem again. Shankar: I cannot get up in the morning.

Keki: What do you mean? You are here just now so obviously you got up in the morning. Shankar: Yes, but it takes me 30 to 40 minutes before I could be out of the bed.

Keki: And what will happen if you have those 30 or 40 minutes every morning. Shankar: My day will go well. I can exercise.

Keki: Your day will go well because you got up 30 minutes earlier or because you will exercise?

Shankar: Because I will exercise.

Keki: We will see about the 30 to 40 minutes later but right now you tell me what makes you think that your day will go better if you exercise? Shankar: From my experience. 2 years back I used to exercise regularly and was feeling energetic all through the day.

Keki: And what difference does it make if you are feeling energetic all through the day? Shankar: Why, my interaction with students was much better. They would also be energetic and enthusiastic. I could make the classroom more fun and students would learn much more and much better.

Keki: And what would happen if you could make the classroom more fun and students would learn much more and much better? Shankar: Their results would be much better.

Keki: And what would happen to you, if that happens? Shankar: Why, obviously my progress will improve. I will rise higher and faster.

Keki: Good. Would that be good only for you or others are also involved. Shankar: Naturally my family, my wife, my students and even some others will also be benefited. Everybody will be happy.

Keki: Everybody will be happy, isn't it? All you have to do is exercise daily, right? Now tell me what can happen if you do not? Shankar: I am already finding my energy level is going down. I am not making it as much fun to learn as I used to. In fact, I feel like I am already stagnating.

Keki: And what do you think can happen if this continues? Shankar: Very bad. I don't want to think about it but it will make me unpopular, unwanted and not respected.

Keki: What else can happen? Shankar: My health. Physical and mental. Already some days I want to just go back to sleep and not go to work. My bank balance is not improving. Sometimes I find myself even arguing with my wife. So, our relationship.

Keki: So, what can be the worst-case scenario? Shankar: In one word, disaster.

Keki: So, Shankar, what do you prefer between making everybody happy including yourself, your wife, your students and others as against disaster. Shankar: Naturally the former.

Keki: And what are you going to do? Shankar: I will join the gym again.

Keki: Again? What happened the previous time? Shankar: Two years back I paid up the gym for a full year. That was wrong timing because the exams came and I got busy with that. I stopped going for 15-20 days and never resumed. Then I got an exercise machine home but used it only for a few days.

Keki: What is happening to that machine now? Shankar: (smiles) My wife is drying her inner clothes on it, what she does not want to put on the balcony clothesline. (laughter all around).

Keki: Was your grandfather healthy? Up to what age did he live? Shankar: Oh yes. Very healthy. He died at 96, a natural death.

Keki: Why don't you find out which gym did he go to? Shankar: What? No gym. There were no gyms at that time.

Keki: What? No gym? Then how could he live healthy up to 96? Shankar: They had a different Lifestyle. He was managing a 33-acre farm. Home grown food, fresh vegetables, fresh air, maybe free hand exercises.

Keki: Oh, so you already know the recipe for good health. Including free hand exercises. But you want to build muscles, isn't it? Shankar: Not really. I just want to be healthy and energetic.

Keki: You must be having a maid at home. What all does she do? Shankar: Sweeping, swabbing, cleaning utensils and helping my wife in the kitchen.

Keki: Can you squat on your two feet? (he nods questioningly). Then you squat on your two feet and do the sweeping - swabbing of the house, or give her 1 months paid leave and you do all that she is doing and see what happens to your body and energy level. When my children were small and in school, they used to have two periods per week for SUPW, Socially Useful and Productive Work, like raking the compound of dry leaves, gardening and so on. Just like your grandfather was doing SUPW. Shankar: (with a smile) I still need to get up 30-40 minutes earlier.

Keki: Oh yes. Tell me what time do you go to sleep and what time do you get up nowadays.

Shankar: I want to get up at 6 in the morning as the alarm rings and I sleep by about 11:30 and sometimes at 12:00.

Keki: I have read in Aban's medical books that the average sleep hours are 8. Tell me what time do you get up on Sundays and holidays? Shankar: I sleep for 3 to 5 hours more. But I do take Power Naps at times during the day.

Keki: The word sounds pretty great but personally I feel it is just a necessary Emergency Shutdown and nothing to be proud of, or feel great about it. If you are sleeping half an hour less for the first six days then you are creating, what is called a sleep- debt and on the seventh day you will sleep 3 hours longer to make up for it. This is not just happening in our country but is world over. So now tell me Shankar, what are you going to do so that you are energetic and you are making everybody happy including yourself, your wife, your students and others as against having a disaster. Shankar: I will have to reschedule my lifestyle so that I am sleeping latest by 11 and setting up my alarm to get up by 6:30. Then do free hand exercises that I already know, like Surya Namaskar, squats and other.

Keki: What you are telling me is what you will have to do. I want you to come here in the center, face the group and tell us what you are actually going to do. Shankar: (walking up next to me) I will become as energetic as before or even better. I am already feeling it. I will go home, discuss this with my wife, we will sleep off by 11:00 from tonight onwards. I will get up at 6:30 in the morning and do some free hand exercises. At least 10 repetitions leading up to 20 or more. We will also talk and improve our diet.

Keki: It can happen that on certain days for any reason you may not be able to do ten repetitions, in that case is 5, better than zero? (he says yes) and if you can't do even 5 then is even 1 better than zero? (says yes again). How is just one better than zero? Shankar: Because it will at least keep the rhythm of doing the exercises. It will help me mentally and emotionally.

Keki: Remember everybody. The best way to get up in the morning is without an alarm. Just before you sleep, picture your clock and see the time at which you want to get up. You will be amazed to find that you are getting up exactly at that time. Another thing to remember is that sexercise is the best exercise. It enhances your circulation system, your respiratory system, moves your lipids through the body, exercises your muscles and I have read that it even improves your immunity. Ok Shankar, you may take your seat now. (As Shankar walks to his seat some people start to clap). No clapping please. You may clap in 6 months' time when he shows the results.

Now pair up and do the exercise with each other. You may take the same partner and take up the same issue with this method. That will show you the difference. But even if you have a PhD in the matter which your partner has taken up; absolutely no advice and no suggestions. Everything has to come from your partner's mind itself. I took up the maid issue just to lighten the atmosphere. Hardly any Indian male will agree to do it. If the matter is so very apparent to you, but your partner is not getting it, then you may suggest as to 'have you considered this' or 'what would happen if you do such and such'. Take as much time as you need and learn this thoroughly. You will have many occasions to use it.

Vipul: How should we proceed? Are there some steps that we have to take?

Keki: Good question Vipul. Thank you. First of all, as it happens so often, people will talk about their symptoms rather than the real issue. Like Shankar's focus was on getting up from sleep rather than feeling energetic all through the day, which he believes he can be if he exercised.

Let me illustrate this with the actual case-story. One Monday morning a lady came to our house inquiring if we could improve the memory of her husband. After having some preliminary talk, I asked her to go home and tell her husband that she has got an appointment for him for Friday 6 o'clock evening and do not remind him again about it. He came on the appointed day and time. I will cut the long story short. During discussion it came out that he is the son of an influential politician in his district with many landed properties and businesses. He had taken a big contract with his father's influence but could not carry it out. Now he was being hounded. His memory was ok even for the amount spent in the market for household items. It was bigger payments and receipts that had disoriented him. Those were mainly in cash and often risky to even note down. He was insisting that his father should sell off a property and pull him out of this mess. But father had different plans.

The purpose of the story is that you first establish the real issue and not just go by the symptoms. The next step is to establish the best-case scenario and the worst-case scenario. Stretch the limits to the very best and the very worst. Which one you take up first can and may depend upon whether the other person is wanting to 'move away' from something or 'go towards' something. Having done this, ask the person to choose as to which scenario he/she would prefer. Do not assume anything.

Next you go into the modality of how that person will achieve it. What are the hurdles that he/she may face? How will the person overcome those hurdles? And what is that person's next immediate concrete step, reminding the person again about the scenario that she/he wishes to achieve.

Vipul: What if the person still selects the worst- case scenario?

Keki: Once again a good question Vipul. Remember that the therapist has to get all the answers from the client's mind. Therapist should not influence the client's mind from his own map. If you have done this then there is very little chance that the person will select the worst-case scenario. However, if he/she still does so, then check out what is the client's positive intention behind doing so. Obviously, what you think is the worst-case scenario is not what your client thinks. If you want to help the client then you are always working from that person's map.

Would you all like to hear the story of how Bandler dealt with it?

Group: (Rather loudly) Yes.

Keki: Who likes to hear a story?

Group: (lauder this time) ... I.

Keki: Bandler used to be called to mental health institutions. At one such Institute they brought an inmate to him who used to believe that he was Jesus Christ. He was becoming a big nuisance as he demanded a behavior appropriate for Christ from everybody else. Bandler went to his cell on Monday morning, requesting him to stand up and stretch out his arms. He pulled out a measuring tape from his pocket, took some measurements and left the cell. On Tuesday he went to this guy's cell with people carrying sleepers of heavy wood and asked them to leave those in his cell and left. On Wednesday he again went with some carpenters and left the carpenters with the inmate to prepare a huge and heavy cross. On Thursday he again went to the inmate's cell, asked him to stand up and removed some heavy black, long, nail spikes from his pocket, touched them to his palms and feet and said ' I think these spikes should take your weight, don't you think so? Of course, blood will flow but in one or two hours it will all drain out and you will be with your final destiny.'

This guy got highly agitated and blurted out 'what..., what..., what are you doing? Bandler replied 'Oh. tomorrow is your big day. You know Christ was crucified on a Friday. Tomorrow you will have a chance to carry your heavy burden of cross to that yonder hill (pointing out of the window to a hill far beyond) and you will be spiked on your cross.'

This guy almost started shivering and perspiring and screamed 'No, No. I am no Christ. I do not want to be crucified. Please, please save me, leave me.'

Keki: Who wants to hear another story of Bandler?

Group: (enthusiastically)...I.

Keki: This one is about how people hang on to their irrational beliefs. These things are not happening only in mental institutions. It is happening all around us in various forms and to various extent. So, at another institution a guy believed that he was dead. In the clinic the doctors tried to put some sense into him but it was no use. So Bandler held his index finger and poked it with a needle. Blood came out and he said 'see, you are even bleeding'. That guy answered 'Oh, you mean dead men also bleed.'

OK now, pick up your partner and complete the exercise. Do a good job for your partner.

(Once they all start, I leave the hall to go to my favorite place. I go back once Aban calls to say that all are done with the exercise.)

Keki: Did you all come to some conclusion? Group: (loudly) Yes. Keki: Did your partner do a good job? Group: (even louder) Yes. (some added) Very good. Keki: Who was your partner? Vipul. Vipul: Saira. Keki: Did you do a good job for him? Saira. Saira: (smiling) Ask him. He is still smiling. Keki: Did Saira do a good job for you Vipul? Vipul: Very good. I think she is an expert.

Keki: Once again we saw two methods. The first one was about directing your partner, giving him or her some advice. Something that we love so much to do normally. The second method was non- directive, where we pull out the answers from the subject's mind. My question to all of you is, 'which method brings you closer to a solution?' Group: (in one voice) The second.

Keki: And which method do we normally use; at home, at workplace, with our children, with our juniors and maybe others? Group: (in a low voice) The first.

Keki: Yes. And then we keep crying or complaining. 'Nobody listens to me.' 'Am I talking to the walls?' etc.' Why will anybody want to adopt your maps? But tell me which method is faster? Group: The first one. (some say it in a questioning manner)

Keki: Yes. Suppose there is a sudden fire in this room and I start asking our attendant Vishal as to which Fire extinguisher should I use? And he says,' I was listening to all that you people were doing, so tell me what type of Fire extinguisher is this? what type of Fire extinguisher is that? where would you use this type of fire extinguisher? where would you use that type of fire extinguisher? what type of fire is it? By that time, I will be half burnt. So there, I have to take his advice and do what he says. We generally do that when we meet an authority figure. As against that, imagine your assistant is coming to you with a paper and asks you as to which file, she should file it in. At that time, it is easier and quicker to say this file. Very likely she will not be able to retrieve it when you want it again. At such times it is better to ask her as to what type of a file is this? what type of a file is that? and what type of a letter is this? Which one would she file it in and why? With that type of investment in time, pretty soon she may not even have to come to you with such questions. So, it is quicker in the long run, saves time and promotes efficiency and happiness.

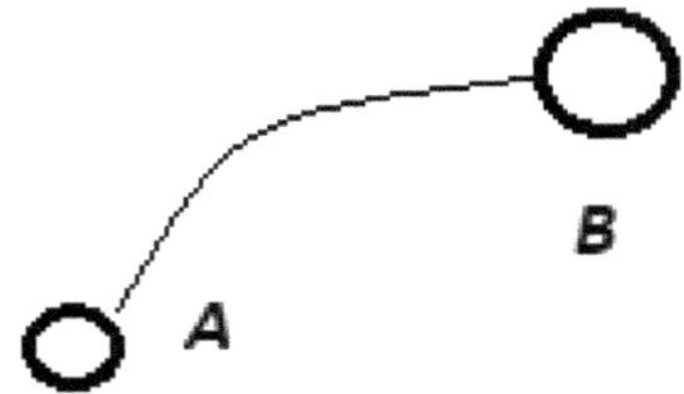

Figure: 15

Reframing:- Now let us look at problems a little differently. The word 'problem' comes from the Latin, Pro -ballein or thrown forward. In the accompanying figure - 15 you are at situation 'A' and you want to reach a situation 'B'. As long as you do not know how to reach from A to B you are in a problem state. Soon as you work out a way to reach situation B, you have created an opportunity to do something. Each and every problem is therefore an opportunity. Opportunity to achieve something, opportunity to get something, opportunity to improve relations, opportunity to have growth, opportunity to find different solutions.

Suppose your business is at A just now (figure - 16) and you want to take it to level B. On the left side you write down the problems you may face. Let us say that you started off your business from a small room some years back and you are doing good but your competitors have set up swanky offices and the new customers prefer to go to them.

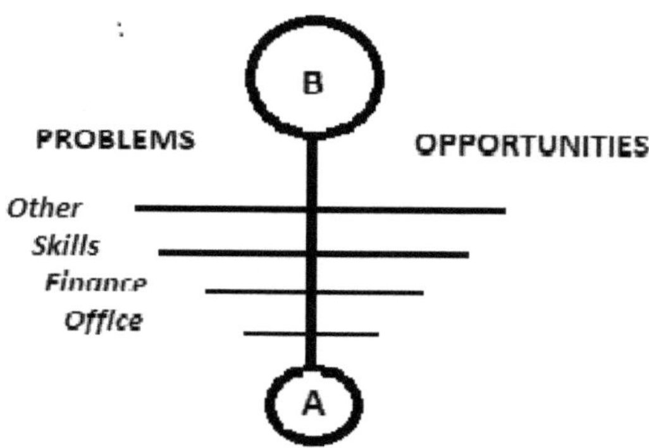

Figure: 16

This is an opportunity for you to do something. For starting your business, you might have taken loans from your friends and family members. They may be coming to you at any unplanned moment demanding some cash for son's higher education or daughter's marriage and create cash crunch for you. Now maybe is the time to approach a bank because the interest rates have come down and you can manage your cash flow in a more systematic manner; paying off the loans that you had taken. Take the case of skills in your organization. Employees work, not just for money but also for their own growth. If some of them are lacking certain skills, this is an opportunity to send them for training. It is also an opportunity to hire a specialist. And likewise, whatever problems you may think you are facing, each and every one of them is an opportunity to do something better. And then there is one more way of problem solving. Who likes to hear a story? Group: (loudly)... I.

Keki: Good. There was this young travelling salesman who happened to be at the market place of a small town, with the shopkeeper. A long procession was passing by and he asks the shopkeeper as to what is going on? Where are all these people going? Shopkeeper says it is a Funeral. So many people passing by; surely it must be some big and important person. The shopkeeper says 'no, a washerwoman's (=Dhobhan's) mother-in-law died.' Surprised, the salesman asks if she was a great social worker or what. To this the shopkeeper replies ' no, a big pain in the butt.' Even more surprised, the salesman asks if it was a very tragic death or what. When he gets the response, 'the washerman's donkey kicked her.'

Now the salesman is truly exasperated. Funeral of the washer-woman's mother-in-law! she is a pain in the butt! Died due to the kick of the family donkey and yet such a large procession with so many young men and women following! So, the salesman asks the final question, 'then why are so many young men and women following the funeral procession?' To this the shopkeeper replies 'they all want to buy the washer-woman's donkey. After all they all have their own mother-in-law also.'

(laughter in the group)

We may laugh at this story just now but so many times in life, we are ourselves looking for the washer-women's donkey as a problem solver. Let me give you all a real case-story.

Many years back there was a participant in our group who was himself a trainer. Not an ordinary trainer. He was a trainer in spirituality and used to lecture at many corporate places also. He had booked an apartment to buy and had made a big down payment. However due to recession in the construction industry he was neither receiving his apartment nor his money back. At the end of the program, I asked him what is he going to do. His answer was, 'I will hire somebody to go and crack his head'. End of his 'spirituality' and end of his NLP training. (nobody is laughing anymore).

Time to change Channels now. Let us do one exercise. Sometimes we may be in a dilemma. Shall I do this or shall I do that?

(Just then our hall attendant Vishal opens the door a little and waits for permission to come in. I nod for him to come in and he walks to me and says 'sir, your papers, 13 sets of Xeroxes.' I said I did not order anything and asked Aban if she had. When Aban also showed ignorance, I asked Vishal if somebody from here had ordered it. Vishal pointed at Vipul.)

Vipul: Remember I had asked you at lunch the previous day.

Keki: Oh yes and I also remember telling you to take my approval before you distribute anything. (turning to Vishal) Please leave it on the side table there. (Vishal leaves the bunch on the side table and again comes to me with a paper in his hand. I ask him) what is this now?

Vishal: Sir, the bill. The manager says that it cannot be added into your overall bill and he needs the cash for it.

Keki: (To Vishal) But who asked you to put it into the overall bill? (he again points at Vipul) Did you? Vipul.

Vipul: I thought since it is for the benefit of everybody.

Keki: I have yet to see the matter, isn't it? (To Vishal) Please give the bill to whoever has ordered it and collect the cash from that person.

(The hall attendance Vishal approaches Vipul with the bill. All eyes from the group are now on Vipul. I go to the side table to pick up a copy and browse through it. Out of the 10 pages, the last 4 pages are regarding his shop, and the earlier pages are about some prayers and some rituals of Pooja. I find it disconnected to our purpose. While I am doing this, I also notice that Vipul has grudgingly paid up the amount to Vishal and he has left the hall. My initial response would have been to eat Vipul raw, but his recent questioning gave me the impression that he was coming around and I decided to uplift him. As I look at Vipul)

Vipul: How can the hotel charge 6 times more than the market rate?

Keki: I am not at all surprised, Vipul. Xeroxing is not the hotel's prime business. It is a service they are providing to the inmates of the hotel so that they do not have to go to the market, but rather focus on their work and meetings. If, God forbid, your sales drop to half then as a businessman you know that the component of your fixed costs of salaries, rent and such will double as a percentage in your selling price. You know that, don't you? But I want to ask a question to Padma.

Padma, you had also promised to bring some homemade sweets for everybody today. You brought it and you distributed it during the tea/ coffee snacks break today. Did everybody enjoy it?

Group: Oh yes. (Ankur adds) It was yummy and she gave a box full to you. Lucky you.

Keki: Padma, you know that Karela (= bitter gourd) is very healthy and good for people to eat, isn't it? (she nods a yes) then why did you not bring Karela instead of sweets?

Padma: (smiling) How can I? Why do you ask? I would have had to take it back home. Would you have taken the box full of Karela from me?

Keki: So, you brought a box full of homemade sweets for me and also distributed it to your friends here. While doing so, were you expecting something in return from others?

Padma: Definitely not. I do not understand why you are asking all these questions to me. I just wanted to bring something that everybody would like.

Keki: And for that I am thankful to you, and I think, so is everybody else. Why I am asking you is because Vipul also wanted to give something to all of you for which I am thankful to him also. What I find is that out of the 10 pages, 6 are for performing prayers and Puja rituals and the other 4 are regarding his shop. Let us just check out how many over here do regular prayers or perform regular Puja rituals. (4 out of 13 raise their hands, and that included Padma as well as Vipul. I did not want to elaborate and left the results to each one's intelligence).

Ok now, let us proceed with the exercise but before we do that let us take a small bio break of 3 minutes and come back. When you come back do sit in a different place with different neighbors. Move now. But stop. Before we move away from this let us realize that any statement that a person makes can be Reframed to the advantage of the person who makes the statement. Suppose somebody says, 'my daughter is very stubborn'. It can mean that, once she decides on something then she will not be wavering. This is **Reframing on the content** or the meaning of the statement. It is very useful, maybe when she is deciding her profession. The same statement could be **Reframed on the context**. If she is stubborn, that can mean that she can protect her integrity if and when a man wants some undue favors from her. As you move out now for your 3 minutes break, maybe you can think about it, and see how you can apply it to your life.

(once everybody is back and has taken a different place)

(Once again, I sit on the left of the hot seat, facing it and patting that seat, I say) Who wants to warm up the hot seat? Anybody with any dilemma, please come. (Jaya comes and occupies the chair)

Keki: You know Jaya, my dilemma is that on the one hand (I wave one hand) I want to marry Pushpa, whereas on the other hand (and I wave the other hand) I want to marry Sushma.

Jaya: (with a big smile) but Aban is sitting there and listening to all this.

Keki: So, I will have these two hands, these two anchors, face each other like this (I hold my two hands as if I am holding an invisible basketball between them) and let them work out to find how Aban plopped up. This exercise is called:

'THE VISUAL SQUASH EXERCISE'.

But we are here to resolve your dilemma, so we will ask Sushma and Pushpa to get lost for the present and focus on your dilemma. You may like to share your dilemma with us or it is ok even if you do not.

Jaya: I would rather not but I know that you know it already.

Keki: So, put your feet flat on the ground, sit up straight, backbone straight, push your tailbone into the chair, hold your hands facing each other, elbows away from the body, take a deep breath and as you exhale close your eyes and relax. One more deep breath in and as you exhale let all the tension and stress of the day just sink down and out from your toes. That is good. Resolution will happen at the unconscious level. Allow your unconscious to take over.

You have already put one polarity in the hand that is appropriate. See what this part of you looks like, hear its tone of voice and so on. Do you realize how this part of you is valuable to you? (a very slight nod from Jaya and even with her eyes closed I could make out which hand she is referring to). Ask this part Jaya, what its positive function is? Now keep this part in that hand as you turn to look at your other hand.

Now do the same with the other polarity in the other hand. Which means, see what that part of you looks like, hear its tone of voice and so on. Do you realize Jaya, how that part is valuable to you? Ask that part what its positive function is.

Now look straight ahead, so you can see both the hands. Ask each if it understands and appreciates the value of the other part. Have each polarity express some appreciation for the positive outcome or valuable function of the other polarity.

You may be fascinated, Jaya, to observe some of the changes that occur in these two images as they start to come together only as fast as they can comfortably assimilate these changes. You may also be surprised by the image that is created when these two images finally join and become a single image, as they melt into each other and take on each other's capacity. And notice what that new image looks like, because this new part represents a combination of abilities you have never had before. . . as such, this new part will have additional skills and abilities that you would never have guessed at, that you can enjoy. . . new ways of accomplishing all of these important outcomes simultaneously.

(The hands are still struggling to get closer. Sometimes they come closer and retract. Sometimes one of the hands does it. I do not wait for things to happen but continue speaking to create an expectation in her mind. And continue.)

Now watch and listen to both these valuable parts of yourself, allowing two hands to come together, only as fast as those two parts can blend and integrate in ways most comfortable and useful to you. . . in such a way that neither part loses anything, retaining the usefulness and importance of both parts, each gaining from the other, the qualities and capacities that are lacking in themselves and present in the other.

(As I continue to watch the two hands getting closer and closer, I continue repeating appropriate sentences again and again until I see ultimately the two hands clasping each other. And when that happens, her taking a gasp of a deep breath, shoulders rising and her face totally changing. Then I continue)

When you are ready physically use your hands to bring this part into yourself, into your body somehow, maybe by holding both hands over your heart, so that it becomes a part of you and all your behaviors easily and readily available to you and as you are doing this you are feeling a Surge of energy in your body as this part reunites with you . . . Take your time to appreciate and enjoy the qualities of this unique new part. And think of the specific times and places where you want these integrated qualities and capacities to be fully at your disposal in the future.

Take your time and when you are ready rub your hands together, rub it on your eyes and face, open your eyes and come on back,

(As she looks at me with a stunned face but a glowing face, I keep my head and shoulders straight and my face emotionless. She looks around at the group then looks again at me and says 'Unbelievable. Wow'. We both stand up. She opens out her arms and asks 'can I hug you?' without waiting for a response we both hug each other.)

Ok everybody. Pick up your partner and start dancing. While giving instructions, you would have noticed me emphasizing certain words to make it seem like a command. Real issues, hot issues, issues that are bothering you. Speed up and finish before they stop serving lunch. Move. Jaya, you can relax a bit and then do the exercise on Aban so that you also learn it.

(I leave the hall and return when I get a call from Aban saying that accept two almost all have finished. I let everyone finish and then ask)

Keki: What is one word that comes to your mind at the end of this exercise?

Group: (some say resolution, some clarity, some awesome, some unbelievable, some joy, some wow)

Keki: (Vipul was under my scanner and I could perceive Joy on his face) you are looking happy Vipul. Who was your partner?

Vipul: Sir, I requested Saira again and she did a very good job this time also. Yes, I think I can move forward. Yeah, Karela and sweets and everybody else also. Can I distribute the papers now since I have paid for it so much?

Keki: Again Sir, is it? Sometimes Vipul, as a businessman you know, how and where to cut the losses. As far as the papers go it is between you and your friends, but in the evening after the program, not now. For now, let us all proceed to the Diner before they close the service. Before you all move, make sure that your goal sheet is complete in all respects with measurable comments and your level of satisfaction score for five years from now. The rest of us can rush to the Diner. Let's go.

(During lunch the group was in an animated, lively, enjoyable mood. I had to remind them that there is lot more for today to finish yet. As I entered the lobby outside our seminar hall, I found quite a few waiting for others to return from the washroom. As I reached Padma, she gave a smile and Jaya was with her back towards me talking to Aban in front. I put my two hands on Jaya's shoulders and started giving her neck a rub. She responded saying 'so good', turned her head, saw me and said 'you have magic in your hands, don't stop'. Others were returning from the washroom and I said 'Come on Back', leading Jaya with my left hand on her shoulder and thumb rubbing her neck while holding Padma's left hand with my right and trailing her behind me I reached my table and all three of us turned around to face the entry door. I called out to everybody saying:)

Keki: 'Shoulder Rub'. Everybody line up in front of me with back towards me facing the door. Somebody please stand behind Padma. (Shankar comes up). Rest of you also alternate Yin-Yang, Yin-Yang, male-female. We are six ladies and 9 gents in the group, so 2 gents will take up the two ends and not more than two gents together in between. One of our participants once named this exercise as a **'Train Massage'**. Each one of you will separate out your two fingers to sit by the side of the vertebra giving pressure in a circular manner clockwise and anticlockwise, starting from the top most at the neck you will go all the way down to the tailbone. If somebody needs more pressure then you will fold your fingers and use your knuckles. Start now. (I ask Jaya how she feels and she says 'fabulous'. Padma, at my back is giggling, and so is somebody at the front. To all I say.) Make sure you are massaging your partner and not tickling. (Once we have completed the round, I tell everybody.) now turn around 180 degrees and do it to your partner who was doing it to you. (I ask Padma as to how she is feeling and she says 'very, very nice') (once this round is also over, I ask the group to turn around 180 degrees and complete the train massage.)

Saira and Ankur: That's all?

Keki: I know some of you will want it to continue up to 6 o'clock evening but we have other things to do. So, thank your partners and take your seats. (After they settle in their seats) Physical touch is a very important thing for any human being or rather I would say any living thing. Do you all know that an infant can die even when they are provided all the life support things and nourishment but deprived of any human touch. Doctor Nirav, do you know what is the name for that?

Nirav: Marasmus is the name for infants dying of malnutrition but whether that malnutrition comes out of lack of touch, I am not too sure.

Keki: Even I thought it was marasmus. Within your family make sure that there is enough physical contact between all the members including the adults and the elderly. Unfortunately, in many conservative families in our country, the children are growing up without ever seeing their parents hugging or touching each other. This can create problems, later in their lives even when they get married.

Now take out your goal sheets. We are now going to convert **your goal-sheet into your wish-list** and put it on autopilot so that it is just like the other exercises. You are not to work on it but it will work on you.

Vipul: Does that mean we don't have to do anything at all?

Keki: Let me repeat. Just like so far you are listening to your subconscious all this time and doing things, you will continue to listen to your subconscious and do things accordingly. The messages you receive will be different. The actions that you take will be different. Your behavior will be different. The results that you get will be different. Your life will be different. Your world that you make for yourself will be different.

Ok, in the column for Level of Satisfaction what is the minimum points that you have given for five years from now?

Padma: I have given 7. Keki: In which area of importance in life and what are the exact words you have written?

Padma: The area of importance is 'children' and what I have written is 'My elder son's marriage'. Keki: Now that is only a statement, Padma. I have already told you last Sunday that Your wish-list for 5 years from now HAS to be Specific and Measurable and as if it has already happened.

Padma: Then what should I say? I cannot say that he is already married because it depends on him also. Keki: Precisely. It should only come in his goal sheet if he was making one. So, what is it that you could do?

Padma: You mean, I can talk to him and get him ready for marriage? Keki: I do not mean anything. It is for you to decide. And in the row for 'Children' is that the only thing that you wish?

Padma: Oh no. I have written that he has completed his engineering; he has a good well-paying job and now I will write that he is ready for marriage. Keki: And if all that happens then will you be fully satisfied? What will be your score?

Padma: Yes. Ten.

Keki: This reminds me of a story. Who wants to hear a story? Group: (loudly) ...I. (Ankur adds) Eveready.

Keki: At a Biology practical class, the professor had a bunch of butterfly cocoons that were ready to open out. They waited and the first one started cracking. When the crack became big enough the Pupa inside had already turned into a butterfly and a small head came out, then it struggled to come out and when it could come out completely it flew into the hall. One by one the cocoons started cracking and butterflies started flying out. While this was happening, the professor got a phone call and had to go out. He told the students to just watch the process. While he was out the remaining cocoons started cracking and butterflies kept coming out but one butterfly could not make it out of the cocoon. While it was struggling the remaining two or three cocoons did crack and the butterflies went flying. This one was still struggling badly. There was this sweet and kind girl who could not bear to see the struggle of this little insect, so she took a scalpel and opened the crack wider. This helped that butterfly to come out. It flew a little on the Bench, settled down and tried to fly again but could not. By that time the professor came back and saw that the butterfly had already folded its wings and was dead. The professor asked what had happened and the students told him. The professor said 'you silly girl, the struggle was necessary for the butterflies to strengthen its wings. Some could attain it sooner and some take longer. You did not help this butterfly you killed it'.

Ok, anybody else with a minimum score?

Jaya: 8. Vipul: Also 8. Keki: What is the message they are giving to the subconscious? Who would like to answer? Gautam? Saira?

Saira: That they are not sure? Keki: It is worse than that. The subconscious is possibly in the right brain. It does not use logic. It takes things literally. That is why we have affirmations. The message they are giving to the subconscious is that they do not want to be fully satisfied. May I ask Vipul and Jaya as to what are the sentences you have written against this score?

Jaya: I am happily married, Keki: Ok, it is written as if it has already happened but what is the measure of a happy marriage?

Jaya: How can you measure happiness? Keki: We are not measuring happiness as in 'I am happy'. You are talking about happiness in marriage. How many arguments, fights, in a day, in a week, in a month? The quality of sex and intimacy? And by the way, everybody, sex is a very important aspect of life. You cannot just brush It under the carpet. Whoever wants to improve the quality of their sex life and has not mentioned it should definitely do it and put it down in your wish-list.

Whether it is the plant Kingdom or all the way up to the mammals, including us human beings; **there are two things that are driving any living being. One is survival of the self and the other is survival of the species. These drives are hard-wired in our mind.** If you have seen programs on channels like Animal Planet, National Geographic etc. you would have seen the games being played by the little cubs and babies of these animals. Their frolicking is honing their hunting/ escape from hunting, skills or procreating skills. It could even be a little unwelcome or painful for some little ones. Same thing happens with human beings also. **But in nature, always, the lower cause is sacrificed for achieving a higher cause. The lioness targets the weaker member of a herd to provide food for her family but thereby improves the gene pool of the herd.**

What have you written against 8? Vipul.

Vipul: That my son has done Textile engineering and is manufacturing Textiles for me. But I wrote this a few days back, I am going to rewrite it.

Keki: You better, because your case is similar to Padma's. I hope the rest of you want to be fully satisfied and with the score of 10. I also hope that each one of you is giving back something to society and have at least one or two points regarding the same.

Manju: I do not have a 10 anywhere. I like to be more practical.

Keki: That is excellent. I have no doubt that you are a very practical man. That is how you have built up so much that you have. What I am not happy about is that you are not getting a full satisfaction out of it. Are you? (He moves his head a bit to his side) No, isn't it? But suppose you can achieve all that you want to, then, will that not make you happier? (he again shakes his head the same way) No? How come? I am actually inspired by whatever you had shared with me at home. Do I have your permission to share it with your friends over here about how you started and your struggle? (he gives a little shrug as if indicating he does not care, so I continue). My friend Manju over here is a totally self-made man. He had no knowledge of engineering and has no formal training in engineering yet he is ten times more knowledgeable than even graduate engineers that he has employed so far. He jumped into getting complicated and accurate parts; got it made from others and learnt his way upwards to finally set up his own facility. Today even government facilities are calling him when they want some complicated and accurate part developed. Sincerely I can say that I am very proud of him and I salute him for that. I really do not know any other person as knowledgeable as him in his field.

Manju: (a bit emotional and looking down) But I have enemy.

Keki: Enemy! Who? Where?

Manju: (still looking down) Wife.

Keki: Your wife? Why do you call her enemy? What has she done?

Manju: Puts me down every time. (slowly raising his head) Fault finding. No confidence in whatever I do. (All eyes are on him and he again starts looking down). Before her it was my father. Now her. (He takes a deep breath and straightens out).

Keki: (in a soft voice) Why did you not share this with me when you came home? The More you share the more chances you have to overcome it.
Manju: What can you do? She is over all this.

Keki: Not her, but you have certainly shown your father as to what you can do and you have done it. Isn't it? (He nods a little more this time). So first it was your father and now the pattern is repeating from your wife, is it?

Manju: (little firmly). Yes. Keki: I remember you saying that you wanted to buy a Farm. Right?

Manju: Yes, I am thinking of it. Keki: I am sure you want everything to go well over there at least.

Manju: Definitely. Keki: I imagine you may have to dig a borewell over there for water and you dug the borewell at some location based on somebody's advice. They went 50 feet and no water, 100 feet and no water, 200 feet and no water, even 400 feet and no water but they charged you for it. But you certainly need water. What would you do?

Manju: I will find some other way. May be get water by tankers. (pause) That will be ok only for the house. For growing something, I will dig another borewell and get some proven water-diviner to locate the place.
Keki: I know you are a problem solver and you would find a solution.

Lily you might have heard this story sometime about Psychologists in the US who wanted to find out more about how the twins grow up having undergone the same parents and the same exposure. They found one pair of brothers who were around 40 now but are exact opposite. They went to the first one who was living in a dark and dingy room with some old broken furniture, empty bottles here and there, fully drunk with a half-eaten sandwich lying on the table. They asked him who is responsible for this condition of yours and he replied 'it was my father. He was a drunkard. He would return late in the night fully drunk, beat up my mother and very often take out his belt and beat me and my brother, black and blue. What else could I be but what I am now.'

They went to the second brother, one who had a nice bungalow with flowers in the garden, married to a beautiful lady and having two very happy kids. They asked him what was the secret to his success and he replied 'it was my father. He was a drunkard. He would return late in the night fully drunk, beat up my mother and very often take out his belt and beat me and my brother. Black and blue. What else could I be but what I am now.' (Some Pause).

Everybody please do stand up. Raise your right hand and slap it on your left thigh and say loudly 'I am awake'; now raise your left hand, slap it on your right thigh and say 'I am alert'. Do it faster and faster. I am awake, I am alert. I am awake, I am alert. Continue for 2 minutes.

Ok, now everybody, change places, change neighbors and sit down.

Everybody imagine you are brushing your teeth this morning. Brushing it yesterday morning; day before yesterday; one week back. Come to the present. You are brushing your teeth tomorrow; the day after; one week after. Relax now.

Everybody has some vague Idea as to where, in which direction, their past lies and in which direction their future lies. So, in which direction did the frames of your brushing your teeth yesterday and earlier days go? In which direction did your frames of brushing your teeth tomorrow and later days go? Where did you see your today?

(Some said that the frames of the past went towards the left, for some it was behind. For some the frames of the future went towards the right for some it went forward. Some said today was in front of them where as a few said that it was within them.)

This is all about **TIME-LINES.**

In this program we will just get familiar with it. We do much more with time-lines in our Master Practitioner's program. When the timeline is passing from within you, we call it being **in-time**. And when the timeline is entirely outside of you, then we call it as in **through-time**. Now I will take up just a few cases to work with and then we will do something for everybody.

Guneet Singh, please stretch out your one hand to indicate the direction of your past timeline. (Guneet stretches out his left arm almost parallel to the ground and in line with his shoulders). Keep it there and tell me where is your present, now?

Guneet: I see it right in front of me.

Keki: Now stretch out your other arm to show me in which direction your future goes. (He stretches out his right hand little frontwards and a little more upwards.) So, all of you can see that his timeline is outside of him, not touching him and therefore he is in through-time. (I put my index finger under the wrist of his right hand and give a slight pressure outward and upward without finding any resistance from him. I stop when I find a little resistance and move it back very slightly towards the original position and ask him) How does it feel now? Is it better than before?

Guneet: I like it. Yes, better than before.

Keki: For a period of 6 months, it will stay there. If it is working for you better, it will continue to be there, otherwise it can go back where it belongs. You can relax now.

Manju, can you stretch out one of your arms to indicate the direction of your past timeline. (Manju stretches out his left arm to the left quite a bit downwards and somewhat frontwards) Manju do you sleep well?

Manju: That depends on what I have done before sleeping. If I have had four pegs or more then I sleep otherwise I keep tossing, turning for some time and also if I get up in-between. (I hold his left-hand wrist lightly and move it little to the back and ask him) can you still see that line? (He says, not now. So, I remove my hold from his wrist). Now Manju, show me the direction in which your future goes. (he stretches out his right hand straight in front of him very slightly upwards). And where is your present? (he says 'in my head'). So, all of you can see that Manju's timeline is in- time. (I hold his right-hand wrist very lightly and move it outwards towards the right. With my other hand as if chopping his right arm from shoulder outwards, ask) are you able to see the future frames little more clearly now? (he says 'yes' and now I lift up his wrist a little upwards till I find some resistance, go backwards a little and ask) Do you like this better than before? (he says 'yes') For a period of a year, all the changes that we made will stay there. If it is working for you better, it will continue to be there, otherwise it can go back where it belongs. You can relax now.

Saira, I would like to see the direction of your past timeline. (she stretches out her left arm quite a bit backward and downward) show me your future timeline. (She stretches out her right arm in front of her slightly towards the right and going upward at 60 degrees. I hold the wrist of her right hand and move it upwards. It moves straight up all the way without any resistance, so I ask her) How do you feel? Do you like it?

Saira: Great. I love it.

Keki: Very good. Have you read Jonathan Livingston Seagull?

Saira: No.

Keki: You should read it. For a period of a year, the changes that we made will stay there. If it is working for you better, it will continue to be there, otherwise it can go back where it belongs. You can relax now.

Jaya, you show me the direction of your past timeline. (She takes her left arm almost entirely backwards and pointing almost downwards.) Show me your future timeline. (She stretches out her right hand straight ahead almost parallel to the ground. I hold her right hand wrist lightly and move it outwards towards the right. With my other hand as if chopping her right arm from shoulder outwards-just like I did for Manju- ask) are you able to see the future frames little more clearly now? (she says 'yes' and now I lift up her wrist a little upwards till I find some resistance, go in reverse a little and ask) do you like this better than before? (she says 'yes') For a period of a year, all the changes that we made will stay there. If it is working for you better, it will continue to be there, otherwise it can go back where it belongs. You can relax now.

Ankur: Keki, we did not understand anything of what you did with them. At least I did not. I can't say about others.

Keki: Consider this as part of FUNN learning. Fundamental Understanding Not Necessary. Remember? When you are ready for the Masters you will learn more. Maybe what we do next will give you a little more understanding.

We are going to play around a little with our timelines. Ankur, you have seen a monkey with a long tail behind. He twists and turns his tail to maintain his balance as he leaps from one tree to the next tree. You will do something similar as you leap from here into your future. (Ankur and some others smile a little and Ankur pointing at himself says 'Me? Monkey?') Each one of you will first improve the submodalities of your past timeline. If you are finding any knots, any cracks, any breaks, any rough patches. Does it widen at some places and narrow down somewhere else? What color is it? do you like it? would you like to change the color? What happens when you change it to the color that you like? Remember that there are no failures but only feedback. Everything has happened in preparation of the future. There is a lot of learning in it. Express your gratitude to the universe for whatever it gave you. First be fully satisfied with your past timeline. Then take up your future timeline and change the submodalities to what you would love to have.

Ankur: What about the present? Keki.

Keki: The present is the present to you from the universe. Make that also as beautiful as you can so that you are looking forward to it. I will give you all, three minutes to finish this. You can keep your eyes open or closed as you wish. Start now.

(After they all finish and I see most faces are relaxed)

How was the leap for you Ankur?

Ankur: Very easy, relaxed and enjoyable.

Keki: How about others? How do you all feel?

Group: (great, confident, very good, something different, peace, all is well, are some of the comments they made)

Keki: We will now do one exercise based on timeline. The exercise is **regarding removing guilt**. Does everybody know how to do cartwheels? You spread out your hands and legs so as to look like the alphabet X or the multiplication sign and then turn yourself round and round on your hands and feet. Everybody can do it because you will be doing it only in your imagination.

Put your feet flat on the ground, sit up straight, backbone straight, push your tailbone into the chair, take a deep breath and while exhaling close your eyes and relax. Imagine your past time -line as we established it sometime back. Mark out on this time-line, event or events that maybe making you feel guilty even now. Something that you might have done which you think you should not have done or something which you should have done and you did not do.

Now pull yourself out of your sitting self and fly like a little birdy over your timeline to arrive just before the first such event from childhood and land there. Do the cartwheels over that event. As you come to the end of that event take off and fly forward towards the present and do the same over the next such event. Continue this till you complete all such events. Now merge back into your own sitting self, rub your hands together, rub it on your eyes and face and come on back.

I do not have to repeat; do not talk about it, do not think about it, do not discuss it. Just leave it.

Next, we will do an exercise regarding **grief**. Has anybody over here lost someone near and dear and you are feeling bad or sad about it even now. (Few raise their fingers including Gautam and Lily)

This same exercise can be used for **'mending a broken heart'**. A boyfriend ditched you or a girlfriend eloped with somebody; but just now we will be taking up the case of a Departed dear one.

Close your eyes once again, take a deep breath and relax. We will be doing this exercise making three different frames.

The first frame is the as-is frame, the way you recall the incident. Make it now, put a frame around it and leave it where it is.

For making the second frame, think of someone who was once very close to you but you have lost touch with that person now. It could be a school friend, a college friend, neighbor, somebody you met at a vacation, anybody. The important thing is that whenever you think of this person, happy, joyful memories come back to you. That person is somewhere in this world but you do not know where. Recall an event with that person and improve the submodalities of what you see. Make it more colorful, maybe brighten it, make it larger than life, bring it closer to you, so that you are feeling even better. Put a frame around this picture.

Now move this frame #2 closer and closer to frame #1 as much as you are comfortable with. It need not even touch frame #1.

Now we will make the third frame. Why do we grieve someone? If you are passing by the street and if you see a Funeral, you might make a small prayer and continue with your life. We grieve because we loved that person. We have some happy memories about that person. We had a good time with this person. And somehow if this person is also looking at you, how would that person like to see you? Happy or sad? Obviously when that person loved you also, that person will want to see you really happy.

If there is any unfinished agenda, like you want to say something to that person, like you want to do something for that person, do it right now. Bring it to completion.

Now think of the best time you had with this person. Some really happy moment. Make a picture of that. Improve the submodalities. Capture that happy moment. Even make the sounds more enjoyable. Put a very ornate, decorated frame around this beautiful, colorful, enjoyable, picture and make multiple postcard size images of it. Hold the pile of these pictures in your two hands and throw it up in the air so as to fall like in a Shish Mahal (=hall of small mirrors) so that wherever you see, whether on the ceiling, the floor, the walls, behind you, front of you, above you, below you, everywhere you are just seeing this happy memory of yours. Take your time and then rub your hands together, rub it on your eyes and face and come on back. (pause)

Once an angry old dog entered such a Shish Mahal snarling away. What do you think he saw? He saw thousands of other dogs, just like him, howling and showing their angry teeth to him. And that made him even more mad. But then at another time a little puppy, very happy, entered the same Shish Mahal wagging its little tail. What do you think he saw? He saw thousands of other puppies, just like him, happy and wanting to play with him and his Joy knew no bound.

Time to break for some tea, coffee, cookies. Let us go.

(Once we reassemble)

Padma: You had asked me to remind you about giving us the **steps for getting into Alpha relaxation**.

Keki: Thanks Padma. Here are the steps. Step 1. Close your eyes. Take a deep breath in and while exhaling visualize #3, 3 times. Another deep breath in and while exhaling visualize #2, 3 times. One more deep breath in and while exhaling visualize #1, 3 times.

Step 2. Counting downwards from 10 to 1 deepen your relaxation

Step 3. Progressive relaxation (or Yog Nindra). Starting from the top of your head, your crown, and going all the way down to your toes, become aware and relax each and every part including your skin, internal organs, muscles, tissues, tendons, bones, and each cell within them. (This is total physical relaxation. Become aware of this feeling and tell yourself that whenever you take a deep breath and while exhaling, visualize #3, 3 times you will automatically and at once reach this level of physical relaxation and more so every time you practice).

Step 4. Go to your favorite place of relaxation. Beautify it. Become aware that you are enjoying it. Then blank out your mind as much as possible (= savasana). Stay in that state for some time. This is total mental relaxation. Become aware of this feeling and tell yourself that whenever you take a deep breath and while exhaling visualize #2, 3 times you will automatically and at once reach this level of mental relaxation and more so every time you practice.

Step 5. Mentally state the affirmations that you might have made for yourself.

Step 6. Counting upwards from 1 to 5, at the count of 5 open your eyes and come on back fully refreshed and energized.

Fine. Let me tell you that I am truly satisfied with the progress that each one of you have made so far. The way to progress further with

NLP is to practice exercises as much as possible whenever you get a chance with anybody. Doing an exercise on somebody does help that person but I believe that it helps you equally.

Nirav: Is there any chance of harming somebody if we do not do it correctly?

Keki: None at all, Doctor. Firstly, the other person's subconscious knows how to protect that person. Secondly, as you go deeper, read more, see some videos, you will notice that different people sometimes do the same exercise little differently and still get the good results. Out of all the exercises that we have done so far, that we will be doing and that I have come across till now; there is only one exercise that calls for caution. And that is the Grief exercise that we just did. The caution is i) do not do it too soon after the event, ii) do not do it for a pregnant lady and iii) do not do it if you feel you may not be able to handle the extreme emotions of the person. Now what is too soon after the event? If an elderly person having led a full life, sleeps and does not wake up in the morning, that person's near and dear ones will feel the grief; but a month or two is ok for that. Whereas, if a young person suddenly dies due to some reason, then even a year maybe too soon for the parent. You need to use your judgement.

Ankur: When we come across a new exercise which we have never done nor experienced then how do we proceed?

Keki: Just like how we will be proceeding right now. I will be giving you not 1 but 3 exercises which you have neither done nor experienced anytime. Aban and I will be here but neither one of us is going to give you any help or clarify any doubts. Of course, you have your group. In most programs the participants form their group to support each other after the program. One of these 3 exercise is talking about a 'Cue Picture'. You can look up the dictionary to find the meaning of that word but I will explain it to you a little more to make it easier.

Before we do that let us understand a little bit about individual **Strategies.** People adopt different strategies and get different results even for similar situations. Like for example sometimes you buy something and you are very happy with the result. At some other time, you buy something and you feel as if you have wasted your money. Why does this happen? There are some trainers here. Does it happen that sometimes you have taken the training session and you are fully satisfied with it; whereas at other times even for the same training session you are disappointed?

Saira: It happens with me. Why?

Keki: Ok, Saira. The last training session that you took, was it good or not good?

Saira: Not good.

Keki: And which one was highly satisfying? when was that, even if the contents of the training were different?

Saira: About 2 months back, was a very satisfying session that I took.

Keki: Fine. Remember one of the presuppositions or the basic assumptions which says " All distinctions human beings are able to make concerning our environment and our behavior can be usefully represented through the V, A, K, O and G senses."

I'm looking at you Saira and I am aware of it, that is Visual-external-Ve.

I can close my eyes and still visualize you, that is Visual-internal-or Vi.

Likewise, I can hear what you are saying, and that is Auditory-external- Ae.

I can recall what you said, and that will be Auditory-internal-or Ai.

I admire your beauty and feel good about it, as Kinesthetic-external - or Ke.

While describing you to others, I may feel good admiring your beauty plus brains plus guts, that will be Kinesthetic-internal -or Ki.

By the way, Ke (Kinesthetic-external), Ki (Kinesthetic-internal) also happens to be my name.

Besides these six, Ve-Vi, Ae-Ai, Ke-Ki; there is also the Internal Dialogue -or Id when you are thinking something within your mind. Some people denote this as Ad. These are the only 7 building blocks to any strategy.

Now Saira, I want you to sit up straight, take a deep breath, relax and make as clear picture as you can, of the time when you started thinking as to how your last program would go, the one which you said you are not satisfied with; And answer my questions.

What is the first thing that happened with regard to that program?

Saira: I was walking to the hall wondering how this program would go.

Keki: (I noted down 'Id' and asked) And what were you thinking?

Saira: I was reminded of an earlier program with a new company where the participants were more or less pushed into the program and it was very difficult to hold their attention. (Me: you actually saw it on your mental screen?). Yes. (Me: I noted down 'Vi' and asked 'what happened immediately after that'). I felt a bit apprehensive. (I noted 'Ki' and said please continue, what next?). I entered the seminar hall and looked at that group. (I noted 'Ve', and asked 'what happened immediately after that?) I said to myself that these look-like tough cookies, but started with my program. (I noted Id, followed by 'K' for action).

Keki: Open your eyes Saira. Now close your eyes again and go back to your very good program which you had 2 months earlier. Once again tell me of the time when you started thinking as to how this program would go.

Saira: I am walking to the seminar hall thinking that I am going to enjoy this program. (I note down 'Id' and asked 'and what were you thinking?'). At the end of one program the participants had got up to clap. And I felt good about it even now. (I noted 'Vi' followed by 'Ki' and asked 'what happened immediately after that'). I entered the seminar hall and looked at that group. (I noted 'Ve', and asked 'what happened immediately after that?). I am pausing, giving a smile to the group and saying to myself that I should somehow Wow them and then I am starting the program. (I note down 'Ki' followed by 'Id' and then K for action.)

Keki: Ok Saira you can open your eyes now.

As I see it your No-Good strategy is; Id-Vi-Ki-Ve-K the action. As against that your strategy for a good program is; Id-Vi-Ki-Ve-Ki-Id-K the action. Your 'Ki' after the 'Ve' is making all the difference and even changing your internal dialogue. Of course, the quality of your internal dialogue and internal feelings is also making a big difference.

Your Cue picture is the 'Ki' that follows after you see the group (Ve). Cue is the stick that you use in billiards or snookers to hit the ball which sets all the other balls rolling.

Now pick up your partner and do the following three exercises on your own. Each one should not take you more than 2 minutes, so both-ways for all 3 will take you 12 minutes plus some consultation. I give you 15 minutes. Start now.

THE SWISH PATTERN

By Will Horton

This technique takes any unwanted behavior and transforms it into a desire to become more the person you want to be. It is useful any time you want to change unwanted behaviors or feelings.

1. Get a large dissociated picture of yourself at your very best. This image will be of the way you want to be (an image on a book cover, a film actor/actress, etc.) Make this picture as big and colorful as possible. If you wish you may attach sounds and smells to this picture to make it as real as possible. Store this as your "very best you picture".
2. Establish a picture of the problem or behavior you wish to remove (finger nail biting, cigarette smoking, etc.) This is an associated picture, through your eyes. Store this image as your cue picture.
3. Put the cue picture (the image of the unwanted behavior) in front of the "very best you picture". Place a dot in the center of the cue picture and have the dot open up, similar to a Camera shutter, so that all you see is a big colorful picture of you at your very best.

   Open your eyes.
4. Repeat this process 5-6 times.
5. Test.

Swish pattern exercises

1. Have your partner choose a compulsion you wish to remove. Ask them to visualize a large brightly colored image of the unwanted compulsion and set it aside for a moment.
2. Picture yourself as if you were already in control of your own destiny, having achieved all your desires in your life. Visualize this with a deep compelling intensity. To complete this picture, add a forceful voice that is confirming your need of this future.

3. Take the large bright unwanted compulsion image and put a small dark image of your desired state in the lower left-hand corner. Have the large bright picture suddenly get dark, as the small dark picture simultaneously springs up in size to replace it and gets very big and bright.
4. Repeat this process very quickly five times in a row, and make the sound 'Swish' each time. Open your eyes for moment after each time you complete the process.

OR

1. Place the image of the unwanted compulsion on a rubber band and push it all the way out to the horizon. When it is very small, have a tiny image of how you want to be, begin in the center of the compulsion and then release the rubber band so it 'snaps back' very quickly, into your face.
2. Try in vain to ever have the unwanted compulsion image effect you again in any but the most positive way.

Godiva Chocolate Pattern

1. Create an associated intense picture of something you are compelled to do, you love, etc. Get cues. Anchor (Anchor #1)
2. Break state
3. Create a picture of something you need to do but have trouble getting started - Bills, paperwork, taxes, etc. Dissociated (see yourself performing these actions). Anchor (Anchor #2)
4. Bring up the picture from Step 1. Fire and hold Anchor #1. As the person fades the image, bring up picture #2. Fire Anchor #2.
5. Hold both anchors simultaneously.
6. Test

(I return after about 15 minutes and find that two pairs are still working. Once they finish:)

Keki: Easy. Wasn't it? Aban, did anybody have any issues?

Aban: A few had questions on the second exercise, 'Swish pattern exercises,' but they sorted it out themselves. I think some did the exercise one-way and a few did it both ways. Overall, they did a pretty good job. They should continue to be in touch with each other, is what I have told them.

Keki: Excellent. **Ongoing troublesome relationship, or a relationship that you want to improve**. Who wants to warm up the hot seat?

(Jaya seemed to be getting ready for it. I moved my face away from her and started looking at Manju. Manju hesitated, got up and occupied the hot seat.)

Who was your partner for the 3 exercises? Manju.

Manju: Jaya was my partner.

Keki: You know Manju, Jaya is also very creative, just like you have been.

Manju: Yes.

Keki: (To the group) I will be taking Manju through the exercise but I want each one of you to do it within yourself as is relevant to you. If anybody has no issue with any relationship then they can take up any relationship they want to improve even further.

So, Manju, and all the others; please sit up straight, take a deep breath and while exhaling visualize #3, 3 times, close your eyes and relax.

Manju, when you think of this relationship, what animal comes to your mind that would represent the other person? When I say animal, it could be a reptile, or an insect, or mammal, or just about anything but other than a human being.

Manju: Cat.

Keki: In this relationship when the other person is represented by a cat, what animal comes to your mind that would represent you?

Manju: Dog.

Keki: What is the cat doing to the dog?

Manju: The cat is annoying me.

Keki: Not you Manju. We are talking about that dog which represents you now.

Manju: The cat is harassing, irritating and driving the dog mad.

Keki: For the sake of clarity, just how exactly is a cat harassing, irritating and driving the dog mad.

Manju: The cat is all the time mewing and sometimes purring.

Keki: And what is the dog's reaction when that cat is all the time mewing and sometimes purring? What does that dog do?

Manju: The dog cannot understand what the cat is saying. The dog goes away to his own corner with irritation.

Keki: Just for a moment let us reverse their roles. So, let that cat become that dog now and let that dog become that cat now. In the reversed roles that dog which has now become the cat is putting up the behavior pattern of that cat. How is that cat which has now become the dog responding?

Manju: It is not responding.

Keki: Now let the cat and the dog take back their original roles once again. You know, somewhere up above there is a third animal that does not represent anybody living on this earth, but it is an all- knowing animal. That third animal is watching all this drama going on down there. It wants to say something to this drama characters. What is it saying?

Manju: It says, be friends. Do not respond to words. Start acting as if you are great friends.

Keki: Are you ready Manju, to put up the new behavior pattern as suggested by the third animal for a trial period of just 30 minutes? (Manju says 'yes') go ahead Manju and tell me what is happening.

Manju: Something is happening. I do not know what but I am not getting so much irritated.

Keki: Extend it for a trial period of 2 hours Manju, and tell me what is happening.

Manju: She is mewing little less now. There is no purring. Sometimes she is behaving friendlier.

Keki: Extended it for a trial period of 7 days and tell me what is happening. (Manju says 'it is feeling good'). Would you like to continue with it? (Manju says 'yes'). Then continue with it and remember that the third animal is always there. Any time you have any difficulty or doubt you can always approach that third animal. Now rub your hands together rub it on your eyes and face, open your eyes and come on back. Everybody.

Manju: I want to say something. (I nod approval). Why was it that in the trial period I saw the big photograph, that my Orthopedic surgeon has in his cabin. It is showing his pet dog and the cat. The cat is curled up peacefully between the four legs of his sleeping dog, like as if, they are great friends.

Keki: This is the picture sent to you by the universe. Always keep it in front of your eyes.

Manju: Yes Sir.

Keki: Remember when I told you all, about the 20 questions that remain the same from bedroom to board-room and any repair that you do in one will reflect in the other. So how was it for the others?

Group: (very interesting, very powerful, very easy, were some of the comments. Guneet added 'I am awaiting your 20 questions').

Let us change channels now. **CRITICISM**. Did any one of you **ever felt criticized?**

(A few hands went up followed by many more.) What were the criticizer's exact words?

Saira: 'You are good but not as good'

Anwar: 'Very unprofessional, don't know how to manage time'.

Manju: 'You are good for nothing'.

Lily: 'You don't respect other's feelings'.

Keki: Ok enough. We will scrutinize these 4.

Normally when we hear such criticism we get into a fight or flight response. We either roll up our sleeves for a fight or an argument or we withdraw or sulk or imagine worst scenarios. But we can act differently.

In Saria's case I assume it is her client (she nods) who says 'not as good'. There is a comparison here. We can respond 'you would like it if my program was as good as someone that you have in mind'. If the client agrees she may perhaps ask 'who?' If client says Mr. X when she knows that Mr. X makes his program quite entertaining, then she may respond 'So you would like it if I make my programs also as entertaining as that'. I think the smile on Saira's face is reflecting the smile on her client's face.

Saira: (With a big smile). Very much possible.

Keki: In Anwar's case, possibly it is his Boss (he nods) who even gives him a hint and Anwar may respond, 'you would like it if I could prioritize my time better'.

Anwar: I think it will please him.

Keki: In Manju's case I suppose it is his wife (he also nods). If he responds 'I think you want me to buy you a new saree or do you want me to earn more money'. The same quizzical look that you are seeing on his face is what perhaps he would see on his wife's face. So, he may say 'you would like it if I changed somehow' (he thinks his wife is listening somewhat and adds) 'what would you like me to change first?' she may respond 'you are coming home late every night after drinking and not even having dinner over here'. He may respond 'I would like to have a smiling welcome and a good dinner when I come home early tomorrow night'.

Manju: Sir, that will be a bit difficult for me.

Keki: Who said it will be easy. Do you think it was easy for the dog and the cat to be friends? What is the end result you want? Can you still see the picture?

And Lily, was that criticism from your father or somebody else?

Lily: My father of course.

Keki: And what would happen if you responded saying, 'you would like it if I was not sensitive?'.

Lily: That may make him feel as if he was winning.

Keki: It will be foolish on our part to assume that the conversation will go exactly as we did now. But look at the common factors. **The criticizer always wants the opposite of what he or she is saying.** So instead of arguing or withdrawing, if you respond by softening up what the criticizer is saying, you are opening up the door for better understanding and better relationship. Once you open the door for better understanding then you can even put up your part of your difficulties. For example, Manju might tell his wife ' I have tried to make a change but every time, if I am getting only complaints and disagreements then that discourages me from spending more time at home.'

Now this is what we have done with our language patterns to improve our relationships and our life. Let us now look at an exercise for:

BUILDING SELF- CONFIDENCE - A Strategy for responding to criticism.

Sit up straight everybody, close your eyes and relax.

This technique allows you to stay resourceful when you are criticized, whether it is at home, at work, or with friends. This enables you to use criticism as feedback to improve your relationships. You may take up the same criticism that came to your mind earlier or any other real case.

1. See yourself in front of you. That Self in front of you is going to learn a new approach to criticism, while you watch from the outside. Do whatever you need to do to feel detached (dissociated) from the self. You can see that self, further away, in black and white, or behind a plexiglass (one way glass).
2. Watch and listen as that-self in front of you gets criticized and instantly dissociates. There are several ways that-self can dissociate. He/she can surround him/herself with a plexiglass shield when he/she is criticized. Or that-self can see the words of Criticism printed within a cartoon balloon (like in the comic strips). Or see 2 boards hanging above the criticizer one printed with that person's point of view and the other printed with your point of view. That self uses one of these methods to keep feeling neutral or resourceful.
3. Watch as that-self makes a slide or movie of what the criticizer is saying. What does that person mean? Does that-self have enough information to make a clear detailed picture? If the answer is 'no', gather information. If the answer is 'yes', proceed to the next step.
4. Have that-self decide on a response. For example, that-self can agree with any part of the criticism that you agree with. Or that-self could apologize, saying 'I will give it some serious thought', or, 'I see things differently now' and so forth.
5. Does that-self want to use the information you got from this criticism to act differently next time? If so, have that-self select a new behavior. That-self will then imagine using the new behavior in detail in the future. Next, that-self can step into this movie of using the new behavior, to feel what it will be like.

6. Having watched that-self go through this entire strategy, do you want this for yourself? If the answer is 'no', ask inside how you can modify this strategy so it fits for you. If the answer is 'yes', continue.
7. Thank that self for being a special resource to you in learning this strategy. Now pull that self into you, feeling her/him fill you, so that this knowledge becomes fully integrated into you.

   (After some pause)

Stay as you are, eyes closed, breath deep and deepen your relaxation for **THE CLOSING EXERCISE**.

We do not have human beings with inherent conflict which they must learn to live with; we have consistent human beings who have apparent self-conflict by acquired distress patterns which act contrary to their inherent rational nature.

We do not have bad people; we have good people acting bad when they are short-circuited by the emotional scar tissue which had been loaded on them by the environment.

We do not have people who purposely do wrong, because such behavior is enforced upon innocent humans by the unhealed residue of damages done to them.

We do not have mean, destructive, vicious humans; we have kind, constructive, loving humans compelled to mean, destructive, vicious behavior by unhealed distress of which they are the First victims.

We are not surrounded by un-understandable creatures; we are among people just as good as ourselves who can be understood easily where they are rational and whose distresses can be understood and gotten rid of where they are irrational.

We are not living among the people who are inherently bent on mutual destruction, we have a divinely gifted species who create art, music, science and beauty and make no negative moves except when 'turned-off' and acting as puppets whose strings are pulled by old scars of hurts, either of their own or ones that have become congealed in a rigid social structure our culture.

CHAPTER 8

ANUSUYA COLLECTS THE FRUIT

It was some 10 months back that Anusuya had visited our home. In the meantime, she had done our TTT, Train the Trainer program. She had started her boutique and was busy with the same. Her yoga classes which she had started 3 years ago were running well. She had called to inform that she was going to visit the US very soon for doing John Grinder's program and would like to meet us. As arranged, she came home exactly at 4 p.m.

I had kept a gift-wrapped packet ready for her. She was pretty much excited about her visit to the US and we also encouraged her for the same, citing examples of three other trainers of ours who had done the same program earlier. Once that was done, I got up, picked up her gift parcel, went to her and said, 'This is for you.'

Anusuya: What is this? Somebody's birthday?

Keki: Yes, it is the birthday. Would you like to open it?

Anusuya: (opening the parcel and almost jumping out of her seat) Yeh, Yippie. . .. The Book. The Book. You actually did it! WOW. Kekiee, I love you. (Gives me a tight hug). I can't believe it! (Looks at the book again). Even the cover and all! But what is all this collage on the cover? Animals and mountains? And is that a Yogini at the top left? Without her face? You seem to have put our NLP Society Logo instead of her face. No no. You have to explain all this to me.

AUTHOR: - **KEKI C DARBARY, DME, DEE, PGDPE**
Licensed Master Practitioner & Certified Master Trainer of NLP,
Neuro Linguistic Programming

Keki: It will need your patience. There is a whole lot of stories in it. Yes, the left-hand top corner shows a Yogini, as you rightly said. A feminine force. What is yoga? Yoga or Yuj means Union. You know much more about it than me. Union with the creation. Union with the creative force, which you may call as the Creator. It is the feminine force that gives birth to a new creation. Hence, the Yogini. She is not faceless. She has a face; only that it does not have to be a human face. So, you are right when you say that the face has our NLP Society Logo. There is a story regarding our logo.

Decades back, when I was a bachelor and staying in Mumbai, we used to go out trekking into the surrounding mountains. almost every third weekend. On one such trek, while walking on the ridge, returning back home, this piece of U-shaped wood was staring at me. Suddenly our eyes met and I just became curious at this oddly shaped piece of wood, perhaps shaped like this by termites. I did not bother and continued walking further, but something pulled me back. I went back to it, picked it up, brushed off the sand and mud from it, put it in my backpack and brought it home. At home, I went on looking at it and realized that it was actually in the shape of a questioning hand. Weeks passed, months passed and more and more I felt as if it was questioning as to 'what is all this?', later realizing that maybe it is my own question. Couple of years later, once again, at a similar trek I found this other piece in the shape of a zero. This was also perhaps shaped by the termites. I brought this piece also home. One fine day, with the help of a long hair, I hung up the zero between the thumb and the fingers of the first piece. It was the Eureka moment for me when I suddenly realized that the second piece, the zero, is the answer to the first piece asking 'what is all this?'. The more I gazed at it the more answers I started getting. I realized that the four almost invisible strands of the two loops of hair, hanging the zero are actually the four fundamental forces of nature that holds up all this; the universe or the multiverse. The thumb and fingers form the duality, which can form a powerful fist. I started wondering about each valley and furrow on the two pieces but haven't got all the answers yet.

Anusuya:(After a pause). I really do not know what to say, but continue.

Keki: That little lamb in the right-hand bottom corner looks timid and scared. This is how many people come to me for the Pre-program meetings. And that includes you. For many, the issue may not be as severe as the Angry charging lion, that the lamb in this picture thinks, is attacking it. In fact, the narration over here is of my first success story within the few days of learning NLP. I have described this case-story in Chapter 3 of Day 2 in 'my journey into NLP'. The scare of the girl was fortified with the courage of the lion. And it remained with her, as you can see in the center of the cover, the lamb is sitting in the lap of the lion. The change has enabled her, like most other people, to strive for Greater Heights till they rise to reach the peak of their goals or wishes; as shown on the right-hand top corner. Even goals such as the very top of Mount Everest; which, one of our participants has actually scaled when she was over 40.

Anusuya: Fantastic. I really don't know what to say. But there are two pictures of plants on the bottom left corner. I am sure that must be also having some significance.

Keki: I do not remember the botanical name of that plant but in ordinary language it is known as the Delicate Monster. This plant that looks so small has been with me one year longer than what Aban has been with me. It has travelled through four cities and seven residences. Its offshoots have grown taller and more Majestic with leaves 10 times bigger than these, where planted in the soil next to a big tree. The other photo is its shadow. It is just to remind of what the psychologists call as the Persona and the Shadow.

Anusuya: What is that?

Keki: I leave that for your research.

Anusuya: I can't wait to go home and start reading your book.

Keki: Do let me know when you are done. And enjoy Grinder's program as well as your US trip.

Anusuya: I will. I will also come and meet you after my US trip. But tell me, do I have your permission to share this 'The Book' with some others?

Keki: It's yours. Do what you like with it. But let me also have your friend's comments.

Anusuya: Certainly. You must be having a soft copy of it. Can I request you to mail it to me? That will make it easier to share.

Keki: I will.

Anusuya: Thanks. Bye Keki. You have made my day. Bye Aban and thanks.

Aban: Bye Anu. Have a safe and enjoyable trip.

Anusuya: I will. Both, The Book and the US. (And hurries home waving her hand.)

In seven days, Anusuya called me back. She was highly excited. She said 'I have read The Book. It is fantabulous. I was reminded of the programs I have attended but this one goes even beyond that.' Then she convinced me to add a page after the 'contents' page for introducing the characteristics of the Participants because it took her time to understand their behavior patterns in the beginning. She wanted me to send it to her so that she could add it into the manuscript before distributing. I agreed to do so. Then she was very vehement in saying that the book definitely cannot end with a chapter on her. The book is not about her. It is about me. I tried to convince her that the participants are my main focus and not me. But she insisted that The Final Chapter definitely has to end with the ending lines of each program and then leave it to the reader; just the way I leave it to the participants to lead their own new lives.

(This cover page has been replaced as explained in **Tributes / Acknowledgements** page at the beginning of the book.)

CHAPTER 9

DAY 5

I was waiting in the lobby awaiting the arrival of a few participants and talking to some others. Jaya came into the entrance lobby and as soon as she saw me her gait changed into a dancing gait and with her arms outstretched, she came up to me, gave me a big hug and said thank you, thank you. I love you, Keki.

Keki: What happened Jaya? You seem very bubbly and happy today.

Jaya: It happened. He actually started talking last night. Can I tell you everything just now?

Keki: (by now the last participant had also walked in so I said.) Not now Jaya. Let us start the program and maybe you can share it inside. Others may also benefit by it.

The Morning Invocation

Keki: Once again a hearty welcome, to each and every one of you, for this 5th and final day of Certified NLP Practitioner's Program. All Rise and Shine. (All 15 of us were standing now.) Good . . . (I stop and pause.) Group: Good . . . (the group also stops, awaiting me.) Keki: (I again say only the first word and then raise my hands to indicate to them to continue). Good . . . Group: Good morning. Keki: Every . . . Group: Every morning is a good morning. Keki: Because . . . Group: Because I make it a good morning. Keki: Today . . . Group: Today is a good day. Keki: Because . . . Group: Because I am going to Make it a good day. Keki: Thank you. Don't sit down.

Love yourself. Love your body. Press and rub every part of your body starting from the head going down to your waist and then starting from the toes coming up to the waist and as you are doing it appreciate and express gratitude for possessing such a fine equipment for yourself. Do it quietly in your own mind whichever way you can. Do the same whenever you are having a bath, preferably in front of a mirror, with no piece of clothing or anything interfering between you and your body.

(Once everybody is done). Now stand erect feet slightly parted and backbone straight. Take your left arm straight out to the left and horizontal. Move your right arm over your chest and in line with the left arm as straight as you possibly can make it. Turn your head to the right. Keep your mouth closed and make a Humming sound of a Bumblebee. Feel those vibrations in your head and skull. Do it three times as when you do it while chanting Aum. Repeat the same with your arms toward the right and your head turned to the left. Good. How do you all feel?

Group: (energized, calm, ready for the day, charged up, love, loving everybody and the world; were some of the comments.)

Keki: Ok. Final day. Final opportunity for the group to clarify any doubts, any questions any observations, any **sharing.**

Jaya: I want to share what happened last night.

Keki: Whatever happened to Jaya last night, I got a big hug from her as she walked into the lobby this morning. So, tell us what happened Jaya.

Jaya: I don't know what happened, how or why it happened but something happened between me and my husband that has not happened so far. He actually came and sat down next to me in the bed and started talking about the problem between us. For the first time I also listened to him patiently without defending or arguing. I will not share what were the contents but it was like a fresh beginning.

Saira: But you must have done something in the evening to make that happen.

Jaya: I do not think I did anything. I know what I did not do. I did not argue or defend myself even when his mother said 'you do not even understand my son, your own husband that you have married'. It came out from my mouth 'mom, you would like it if I understand him better, isn't it? even I want to, but I only want to have an opportunity for it.' I may have gulped down or preferred not to pay attention to some other insults from her.

Keki: You did that consciously or unconsciously?

Jaya: I don't know. Maybe both. Maybe I will try to be more conscious about it now onwards.

Keki: Recall the first day evening exercise just before you practiced rapport making. All of us were on the ground on all four barking like a dog at each other OAF, OAF, OAF. These three letters are the essence of our 5 Day programs. O stands for 'know your Outcome'. What is the end result you desire? A is for having the sensory Acuity to know where you are heading at any moment and F stands for Flexibility. The entire purpose of this program is OAF, OAF. Jaya has just exhibited it. Anything else? anybody else?

Gautam: We have decided that either my dad and my aunt will come to Norway to attend our wedding or, me and my wife will come down here for a second wedding in our style and custom.

Keki: Very good Gautam. We are all very happy for you.

Gautam: Thank you, but I certainly want to do the Master Practitioner's program before I leave and I will also persuade my wife to do your practitioners program if and when we come to India.

Keki: Most welcome. Anybody else?

Manju: I can't do it. I tried. She is still the same.

Keki: Did you wet your bed last night?

Manju: What is that? Wet how?

Keki: By urinating of course, maybe in your sleep. Up to what age were you urinating in the bed in your sleep?

Manju: That? Of course not. I am a big man now, how can I?

Keki: Yes, you are a big man now; No such habits. But you used to, isn't it? I asked you, up to what age were you doing it?

Manju: I remember my mother telling me some time earlier that up to the age of almost 7 I used to do bed-wetting.

Keki: Did you make a conscious effort to stop it at that age or it just happened naturally?

Manju: My mother used to scold me every time it happened but I think then it stopped naturally.

Keki: Even though you are consciously not aware of how you got rid of an unwanted habit, your subconscious always knows how to do it.

Tell me, would you like it if your Industry grows and prospers? You have put in so much of your time and energy and years of efforts and money into it. Would you like it if your employees understand you, get more loyal to you, get more disciplined towards the results they give you and to your satisfaction? Would you like it if the woman that you married, the woman that you once loved, the woman with whom sex was so romantic, so intimate, so enjoyable and that woman gave you 3 wonderful children. Just realize that I am not talking about the woman that you have now; I am talking about that woman whom you had married, the woman of that time. Would you like to have her back with even more caring, loving, more intimate and deeper relationship? (To each of my questions he nodded a Yes or even said yes softly. Then he was about to open his mouth and I knew that would be of a 'Yes but', nature where the "Yes' has no meaning to that person but the 'But' has. So, I quietened him down by saying) Let us do an exercise first for all those things that you cannot even imagine now and then see what to do.

So, please put your feet flat on the ground, sit up straight, backbone straight, push your tailbone into the chair, take a deep breath and while exhaling close your eyes and relax. Open out your left hand with Palm facing upwards. Like every other child you were also bed-wetting when you were very small but it continued till you were almost seven years of age. Then your mind learns how to stop this habit. Make a very clear picture of it and hold it in your left palm. Realize that you became absolutely free of that habit. How does it feel to realize that you got rid of that habit? Good. Very good.

Now open your right-hand Palm facing upwards. Know that others are throwing dirt at you in your factory as well as home. Imagine for this exercise that they are feeling as if you are urinating on them and in retaliation, they are urinating back at you. Make as clear a picture as you can of both they and you urinating on each other. Get into that lousy feeling. Double that feeling. It is bad. Somehow you want it to stop.

Now take that picture in your right-hand Palm and slap it hard on the picture in your left hand. Bring back your right-hand and once again slap it on the left-hand palm. Do these 3 more times on your own so that your right hand also learns what the left hand knows.

Your mother stopped scolding you once you stopped bedwetting. What are you doing now onwards when others are throwing dirt on you and what is the effect of that on others?

Manju: I have stopped reacting to them. I am doing what has to be done and they are also co-operating. Yes. (There was a visible change of satisfaction and confidence on his face.)

Keki: Take your time and when you are ready rub your hands together, rub it on your eyes and face, open your eyes and come on back. (He did that, opened his eyes, gazed at the wall in front, nodded as in 'yes' and stared into my face.)

Manju: Yes.

Keki: I want you to do one more thing, Manju. I want you to visit your Orthopedic surgeon and somehow get him to talk about how he got his cat and dog together so friendly as shown in that photograph.

Manju: I think I know the answer but I will visit him. I have wasted so much time, and so many years.

Keki: **SO, WHAT.** Everybody all together say **'so what'**.

Everybody: (all 15 of us) 'So what'.

Keki: Let each one of us take this opportunity to throw out what we might have considered too private or shameful and to be hidden from the world. Each one will make a statement of it and all 15 of us will say 'so what' in different tonalities. If it is something we are born with and cannot be changed, only then we will use the present tense but if it is some behavior pattern then we will not become a fortune teller and only talk about it in the past tense. Gandhiji says 'be the change you want to see' so I will start with myself.

See my left hand. (I raise my left hand) the middle finger is somewhat bent.

Everybody: So, what.

Aban: Keki and I were having arguments and fights sometimes. Everybody: So- what. Saira: I had goofed in couple of my programs. Everybody: So- what! Gautam: I ran away from home for 12 years. Everybody: so- What. Ankur: I found my dream girl in this program. Everybody: So- what? Anwar: I have hated all my Bosses so far. Everybody: so- what. Nirav: I would not comply with the authorities at times. Everybody: SO- what. Saira: I need a man in my life. Everybody: so- WHAT. Shankar: I am addicted to sex. Everybody: so- what. Lily: I hated all men. Everybody: So what. Vipul: I was getting attracted to my maid. Everybody: so- what. Manju: I have not touched my wife since last 3 years. Everybody: so- What? Jaya: My husband has not done it with me since marriage. Everybody: so- what. Anu: I did not share my bed with my husband as he wanted. Everybody: so- whaT. Padma: My younger son has p*** in his laptop. Everybody: So what. Guneet: My son was getting bullied. Everybody: So- what. Vipul: I did not give attention to my son's needs. Everybody: So- what. Aban: I am quite short. Everybody: SO- WHAT.

Keki: We have not started with the day's scheduled exercises as yet.

Ankur: (somewhat softly). So what? (laughter!)

Keki: So, let us start. But just a minute. Doctor Nirav.

Nirav: (suddenly jerking up) Yes.

Keki: You are looking very pensive. Is something troubling you?

Nirav: Sorry. Yes. Today is the final day and I do not have any resolution.

Keki: Resolution to what? Doctor.

Nirav: Like I told you before; medicine is supposed to be a noble pursuit. Sad to say but I have not found the people at the helm of things to be falling in that category. Whether it is individual hospital administration or even the medical education and as far as the Pharma Industry is concerned the less said the better. It is such a huge issue. I have been **wanting to do something and not doing it.** I think my ideas will get cremated when I am cremated. I cannot do anything about it.

Keki: Doctor, you are already doing something about it. What more would you like to do?

Nirav: No no. What I do hardly makes a dent. This is something which needs to be tackled at the highest authority of the government.

Keki: Tell me doctor, have you ever performed a very complicated operation for the first time in your life?

Nirav: I have.

Keki: Doctor. Please sit up straight with your backbone straight. Right now, I do not want you to think of that operation itself but rather as to how you prepared yourself for that operation which was totally new for you. Take your time and go through each and every stage of it.

Nirav: (after straightening up and taking control of himself) First I studied the malady thoroughly then I reconstructed what needs to be done. I checked and rechecked what problems I may face. I visualized doing that operation and facing expected as well as unexpected problems and I fine-tuned for it. I repeated that two or three times until I was confident and thorough with it. When I actually did that operation, I felt as if I had already done it before. It was a good success.

Keki: Excellent doctor. This is what I would expect from you. Tell me would you like other surgeons also to be able to perform this operation?

Nirav: Certainly, why not?

Keki: How will you teach them? They may be anywhere in the world.

Nirav: I will have to chronicle each and everything that I did for my preparation.

Keki: Very good. So now you have a far, far bigger operation in mind. How will you give it its first birth?

Nirav: (lighting up and with a smile on his face). Just the same way.

Keki: So Nirav, make a statement of what you are going to do.

Nirav: I will Chronicle each and every idea that is in my head and put it together as a comprehensive document.

Keki: And what will that achieve for you?

Nirav; (with a widening smile). I will spread it across grounds that I feel are fertile and maybe a womb will pick up that seed and get pregnant with it.

Keki: And what will that achieve for you?

Nirav: Increased chances of seeing my baby being born.

Keki: Very good. And what will that achieve for you?

Nirav: Why? Fulfillment of course. Purpose of my life fulfilled.

Keki: The ultimate?

Nirav: Yes. I can't ask for anything more.

Keki: Then what has stopped you from achieving it already?

Nirav: I think I wanted the whole thing at once without waiting for the first birth.

Keki: Did you ever jump into an unknown and complicated operation without prior preparation like you narrated earlier.

Nirav: Unfortunately, once. It was a mess but we managed to save the patient somehow.

Keki: There are no failures, only feedback, remember.

Now let us all start with what we wanted to.

Each one of you over here is in some leadership position. And remember that a housewife or a home- maker is responsible not just for herself but for all the members of her family. So, Mr. smart Ankur, what is the very first line of how Bandler wants us to understand NLP?

Ankur: NLP is an attitude.

Keki: Excellent. At least one person over here has learnt something. Let us now examine what is a **LEADER'S ATTITUDE** and what would be a follower's attitude.

Two housewives are cooking in their respective kitchens. (I stretch out my two hands in two opposite directions). One is cooking with the attitude of a leader and another is cooking with the attitude of a follower; what is the difference? Anybody? Everybody?

Manju: The leader will give instructions to her helper as to what to do.

Anwar: But if the helper is also a leader, then that person may do whatever is best for the purpose.

Keki: Very good. Remember that we are examining only the attitude and not the person. It so happens that both are alone in their kitchen and there is no one else in the house also. One is cooking with the attitude of a leader and the other is cooking with the attitude of a follower; and there is a huge difference. What is it?

Jaya: The leader attitude housewife is cooking whatever she wants to and the follower attitude housewife is cooking what she has been asked to cook.

Keki: Maybe, but today they are cooking exactly the same Dish. You must have seen the advertisements when they say 'come and learn 7 Punjabi dishes' 'come and learn 5 Chinese dishes' and so on, both these housewives had gone to one such program and just by chance today they are cooking exactly the same Dish; yet there is a big difference. What is it?

Padma: The leader attitude housewife will make her own changes to make the dish even better. The follower attitude housewife may be fearful of making some changes.

Keki: Maybe, but today both are following the recipes as learnt exactly to the dot and yet there is a big difference. (the group has run out of ideas and there is a pause). Somebody tell me why they are cooking?

Shankar: Obviously to feed their families.

Keki: Yes, Mr. foodie professor, but what is going on in their minds? Why is each one cooking?

Shankar: Because she wants to.

Keki: Who? Which one?

Shankar: Oh! The leader attitude one? (half questioningly)

Keki: Are you asking me or telling me?

Shankar: No. Now I am telling you. The leader attitude housewife is cooking because she wants to.

Keki: Absolutely. The Leader attitude house wife is cooking because she wants to. In that case Guneet, why is the follower attitude housewife cooking?

Guneet Singh: Because she has to.

Keki: Correct. The leader attitude house wife is cooking because she **WANTS** to, whereas the follower attitude house wife is cooking because she **HAS** to. Always, the leader attitude person is doing something because he or she WANTS to, whereas the follower attitude person is doing whatever he or she is doing because she HAS to. This is the first major difference.

In that case Shankar, who is enjoying the process of doing?

Shankar: The Leader attitude housewife.

Keki: Yes, but tell me Shankar when, if at all, will the follower attitude housewife enjoy or be satisfied? (I bring forward my right hand and twist my thumb and forefinger anticlockwise as if I am holding something. I repeat it and repeat one more time.)

Shankar: Oh! When the task is over. (in a questioning tone)

Keki: Once again Shankar, are you asking me or telling me?

Shankar: No. When she has finished cooking. I am telling you.

Keki: Yes, and maybe not even then. The follower attitude housewife is doing something because she thinks she has to. She may think, 'There, the cooking is over. They can have it whenever they want it and if they want it; but it is a never-ending chore. Now, washing the vessels, then cleaning the floor, then washing clothes. Can't do anything that I want to.' This is the second major difference.

Now tell me who do you think they are thinking about and what?

Manju: The leader will think about the appreciation she is going to get from the others.

Saira: I don't think so, but she may be thinking about how she is going to please the others in the family.

Keki: Nobody is saying anything about the follower attitude housewife.

Guneet: Since she is thinking that everything is a chore or a task, she is all the time thinking only about herself.

Keki: Very true. The follower attitude housewife is centered around herself and is thinking of her own self. The leader attitude housewife is thinking about those who she is going to feed, her family. The leader attitude person always has a larger picture. This is the third major difference.

But tell me, is the leader attitude housewife dependent upon the Shabash (=> pat on the back) from her family?

Gautam: No. It does not matter whether she receives any appreciation or not. Her attitude will not change even if she does not get it.

Manju: But some appreciation is always expected, isn't it?

Gautam: The leader attitude person is doing something because she/he wants to. As I understand it, it comes from within the person. Therefore, it does not need and will not depend upon any outside influence.

Keki: Very well put Gautam.

So, to sum it all up; the three major differences are:

i) **The leader attitude person is doing something because he or she WANTS to do it. (the follower attitude person is doing something because she or he HAS to do it)**

ii) The leader attitude person enjoys whatever she or he is doing. (the follower attitude person at the most will get some relief once the task is over) and

iii) The leader attitude person always has a larger picture. (whereas the follower attitude person is mostly thinking only about himself or herself).

No need to take the notes just now. I'll give you time to jot down your thoughts at the end of the exercise. This is only the beginning.

Two students are studying. After all, the exams are only two months away. One is studying with the attitude of a leader, the other is studying with the attitude of a follower. What is the difference?

Ankur: The leader attitude student is studying because he wants to and . . .

Keki: Stop. Why does he want to?

Ankur: Why? Because he wants to gain knowledge.

Keki: Very good. And the follower attitude student?

Ankur: Maybe just to pass the exams!

Keki: Maybe. But is there a difference in the way they are studying?

Ankur: I feel good when I am gaining some knowledge. If I get stuck or have a doubt then I have it clarified and when I want to know more, I search for it.

Keki: Very good. That is why you are what you are. What about the follower attitude student? How is he or she studying?

Shankar: Past question papers; likely questions for this year; guides; omit certain sections. Generally minimum efforts to get maximum marks and grades.

Keki: Yes. Sometimes when I am interviewing some candidates for my clients and I ask them a question which I might have learnt 50 years earlier; they scratch their head and say 'sir, I appeared for the exams 6 months back and I have forgotten the answer now.' Do you think I am going to employ such a person? But tell me professor, what will be such a person's nazariya (= the way of looking) at the examiner?

Shankar: In fact, such a student once actually came to me complaining about the examiner as a stumbling block in his career. He did not get admission for a professional program just because he had 2 marks less than the cut off. His grudge was, why was the examiner so miserly in giving him a few extra marks as if he had to give it out of his own pocket. He wanted me to do something about it. Unfortunately, some teachers, coaching classes and even institutions are encouraging this type of studying where Marks and grades are all they care for rather than imparting knowledge.

Keki: May your tribe increase, Shankar. But tell me Ankur, if you came across somebody, say even two years after you did the exams and found out that he was your examiner, then what are the two words you will say to him.

Ankur: I will say 'thank you' to him.

Keki: That is what I would expect. But Manju, why is Ankur thanking the examiner?

Manju: Because he gave him good marks?

Keki: Is that so, Ankur?

Ankur: No Manju. A leader attitude student is studying to gain knowledge. The examiner has given him feedback as to how he is doing. That is why the 'thank you'.

Keki: And thank you for your feedback to us. One last question to everybody. Is it necessary that the leader attitude student will always score more marks?

Shankar, Ankur and some more: No.

Keki: One more question Ankur. Who is the leader attitude student competing with?

Ankur: Nobody. Or rather with himself, because he wants to gather more and more knowledge.

Keki: I am truly very happy. But professor, what is our education system doing? Think about it because competing is actually a follower attitude, isn't it? And Ankur, do you ever share your knowledge with other students?

Ankur: Sure. This hones my knowledge also.

Keki: So, professor, if the education system would promote cooperation rather than competition, would we not be creating more leader attitude citizens rather than creating multitudes of follower attitude citizens? Just think about it?

Shankar: You are making age-old things stand on its head. But nowadays many Schools resort to group project works which I think should be satisfying you.

Keki**: Two employees** are working in their respective workplaces; one is working with the attitude of a leader and the other is working with the attitude of a follower. What is the difference? quick, quick, quick.

Manju: The leader attitude employee wants to be loyal . . .

Keki: Stop. We do not want to reinvent the wheel. What are the Three main differences that we have already seen, Manju?

Manju: But that was for the housewife.

Keki: Housewife and the student and for each and every person on the face of this earth including you. (loudly) What are the 3 main differences?

Manju: The follower has to follow the orders.

Keki: We are examining the attitudes of the people, not their designations or status in the organization or life. Give me the three main differences of a leader attitude person.

Manju: He wants to do what he is doing. He should be enjoying the work and should have a larger picture.

Keki: What is your larger picture?

Manju: That my industry should grow.

Keki: Ok, we will leave it at that for the present. Who would like to answer the original question? Anwar, you?

Anwar: The leader attitude employee is doing whatever he is doing because he wants to. (then looking towards Manju, adds) even if his boss is a bum. Secondly, he is enjoying whatever he is doing because he wants to do it. And thirdly he has a larger picture.

Keki: Very good Anwar. And what could be his larger picture?

Anwar: The larger picture could be the work, the environment, the company.

Keki: Very good, Anwar. Much better than what Manju gave.

Manju: But how do I get people with leader attitude? You do not get them nowadays. How can I convert their attitude? You said it comes from within.

Keki: Excellent question, Manju. I like it. Who would like to answer him?

Saira: I think people are the same all over the world, Manju. You are getting the people from the same job market in this city as perhaps Guneet Singh. Yet there is such a large difference between what you are thinking of your employees and what Guneet Singhji is thinking of. Not only that but it has shown in such different results. And I think the most important difference is in your thinking pattern and Guneet Singhji's thinking pattern. Is it possible that you may be running your industry because you have to and not because you want to? I think you should be thinking about that.

Keki: Saira, you surprise me every time you say something. I myself may not have been able to put it so clearly. I thank you. You are an asset to this country.

Before we move away from these two employees, somebody tell me what would be their Nazariya, or way of looking, at their Bosses?

Gautam: For the leader attitude employee, he may consider the boss as his FPG, friend, philosopher and guide. He knows that his goals are the same as his Boss's, only the boss's sphere of responsibility is much bigger. As for the follower attitude employee, he may be considering his boss as a stumbling block, a road-block, or a police man.

Keki: Yes. The follower attitude employee may say 'there he comes. Why does he have to come only when I am having tea. He never comes when I am working. He is a stumbling block even to my promotion.' Suppose you have 10 people working under you and you have trained them all so well that just about anyone could be promoted when the time comes. Now you want to take higher responsibilities and put one of them as in-charge of the others. What will you do?

Guneet: I actually faced such a situation once. I had six of them in the machine shop and any one of them could have been promoted as a charge-hand. I devised a questioner for them and put them through it. Most of them cleared it pretty well. So, I called them one by one and said, 'I know that you qualify to be a charge-hand and so do the other five. There will be a mess if I try to promote each one of you, so tell me besides you, out of the other five who do you think will be the best charge-hand.' When this exercise was over one name became more prominent than the rest. Which showed that person's popularity as well as acceptability. After some more tests I appointed him as a chargehand. And it went through very well.

Keki: Very well done indeed. But the rest of you tell me if you were one of those five, who were not promoted, will that affect your performance.

Anwar: It could.

Saira: If it does then it shows that the leader attitude in that person was very fragile and it was a correct decision not to promote that person. Isn't it?

Keki: I tend to agree with Saira. Take another scenario. Suppose that the company where you are working is sinking. Everybody knows that pretty soon it will close down and everybody will be out of job. People have started bad-mouthing the management. They have stopped putting in their best and one by one, leaving the company. If you happen to be in such a situation, what will you do? Vipul, Padma; if your own son happened to be in such a situation what will be your advice to them?

Vipul: I will immediately pull him out of the company and put him in my shop.

Padma: I will ask him to continue as long as he is getting his salary and at the same time look for another job.

Keki: Saira, what advice would you give, if it was your own daughter?

Saira: I will ask her to take greater responsibility and work on some project where she can make a positive difference to the company.

Keki: And why is that?

Saira: To me it is simple common sense. She will learn to take responsibility even under adverse conditions. She will learn to remain positive even under adverse conditions. But most importantly, she will be in the most positive and confident frame of mind when she goes for the next interview compared to all those who had given up hope and stopped performing.

Keki: Rest of you can take a lesson from her as to how in spite of so many adversities in life she has reached the position that she has.

Jaya: All this sounds quite utopian and far from living the practical life.

Keki: Maybe it is. All beliefs are true. True for whom? True for the believer.

Jaya: So, what do you want me to do?

Keki: Me? Nothing. Each one has to decide for themselves. I only show the possibilities. You can choose to dwell on the sound of the words, or you can choose, based on the results that some of you in this group have already achieved. Let us move on further. **Two citizens** are going to work in the morning. One is going with the attitude of a leader and other is going with the attitude of a follower, what is the difference? Jaya. Just tell me the three differences that we have already seen.

Jaya: The Leader attitude citizen is going because he wants to. The follower attitude citizen is going because he has to.

Keki: 'Has to'. To fill his 'paapi pate' (= sinful stomach) as some people call it. Call your own stomach sinful and then run to the doctor. What is the second difference?

Jaya: The leader attitude citizen is enjoying the process.

Keki: 'Enjoying the process'. Feeling good, may be whistling away or singing a song, generally eager to reach his work place. Whereas the follower attitude citizen may be irritated at the morning hour traffic or easily get angered by somebody and so on. What about the third difference?

Jaya: The leader attitude citizen has a larger picture.

Keki: 'A larger picture'. How large? Where is its limit?

Jaya: Maybe the company where she or he works?

Keki: So, you mean it stops at the compound wall of the company. Is it? For doctor Nirav it may be stopping at the hospital premises. For professor Shankar it may be stopping at the gate of the institution. For Padma it may be stopping at the four walls of her home. Is that what you are saying?

Jaya: No. I do not mean that. There may not be a limit. She or he will be definitely aware of her contribution to the company. Some may even feel that they are contributing to the community; or is it the nation?

Ankur: The whole world. The ripple effect, however small, can reach the whole world.

Keki: Very good. You have a motorcycle, Ankur. Consider two citizens riding on motorcycles or driving a car, are **stopping at the red signal**. One is stopping with the attitude of a leader and other with the attitude of a follower, what is the difference?

Ankur: They are following the rules. The leader attitude citizen wants to follow the rules, whereas the follower attitude citizen feels that he has to. There may be a cop ahead who may catch him.

Keki: Does the leader attitude citizen feel he is following somebody else's rules?

Ankur: No. He has adopted the rule as his own for greater safety.

Keki: Very good. For some people in our city the green signal means go, orange means go like hell and red means go like there is no tomorrow. And then unfortunately for some, there is no tomorrow. Once I was taking this exercise for the pre-graduate class and one of the students said 'Sir, the leader attitude person will just zip past the signal'. (laughter)

Finally**, Two Prime Ministers** or heads of state are working in their respective countries; one with the attitude of a leader and other with the attitude of a follower, what is their larger picture?

Guneet: The leader attitude head is thinking and acting for the progress of the whole world where as the follower attitude head is thinking about maintaining his chair, his power.

Keki: Well said, Guneet. There is a particular word in English language for the leaders with the world view. They are called the Elder Statesmen.

Let us now wrap it up. One type is always moving from one boundary to another boundary the other is moving from boundarylessness to boundarylessness. who?

Guneet: The follower attitude person is moving from boundary to boundary; like cooking is over now cleaning has to start.

Keki: One of them is mainly dealing with problems whereas the other is tackling opportunities. Who?

Guneet: The follower attitude person is faced with problems where as the leader attitude person is tackling opportunities.

Keki: Who is likely to create more leader attitude people?

Guneet: The leader attitude person.

Keki: Is it necessary that the leader attitude person should always have a few followers behind him?

Guneet: Certainly not. We are examining the attitudes.

Keki: I was at a factory in Canada once. And many hands-on engineers are reluctant to do the paperwork. I had to go to the washroom to do what I had to do. When I sat on the place where I had to sit for doing whatever I had gone to do; right opposite that seat was a board which read 'nothing is complete without paperwork'. (you see, they do not use water, they use toilet paper only). So even a leader attitude person may encounter some part where he or she will have to take the follower attitude. Do I make myself clear?

Group: (with a smile) Yes.

Keki: Good. Take a 3-minute bio break, come back fast, change seats, change neighbors and we will have a demo of an exercise before breaking for tea, coffee and hot snacks. Move now.

(Once everybody is back)

Keki: **REFRAMING OUTLINE. Getting rid of uncontrolled, unwanted behavior pattern.** You may have developed some behavior pattern which occurs automatically and you are not happy with the same. Let me illustrate this with two actual case-stories.

The first case-story is about a young girl. We were taking a two-day program on 'creativity and problem solving' at Nagpur for a telecom company. The participants had paired off to do each other's problem solving the way we did yesterday morning. Aban came out to inform me that one pair was having difficulties. Talking to that girl we found that she was a very efficient and a high performer. Recently she had acquired a 3-bedroom house, furnished it nicely and was ready to present it to her parents. However, she was feeling deeply depressed.

This was her pattern every time she would achieve something really good.

The hammer is a tool. But there is a goldsmith's hammer and a blacksmith's hammer and so many types in-between. We have to use the correct tool for the correct impact. Her issue was a too big an issue for the type of exercise she was doing.

We did what was necessary and found that when she was three years of age and had started going to the play school, she had won a prize and proudly brought it home to show it to her mother and father. At home was her cousin, who by mistake on mischief, dropped that prize and it shattered into pieces even before she could show it to her parents. This had broken her heart. Ever since then whenever she had achieved something great, she would get into depression.

This may sound very childish, because it is. But imagine a grown-up man doing very well in life, having built a beautiful house with twin garage, a fancy car in one and a utility car in the other. He has not yet taken the insurance policy and the entire thing goes up in flames. How do you think he will feel? It was exactly the same thing that happened to that 3-year-old girl.

We did the necessary repair work to bring her out of that uncontrolled, unwanted, behavior pattern.

The second case-story is about a young boy. He was doing very well professionally and was also a good football player. He has a very different issue which he resolved in the exercise. But as a byproduct benefit, he exclaimed at the end of it, ' Now I know why I do this.' When asked to explain what he meant he said, ' whenever I sleep at night, I have to make sure that all the windows and doors are closed properly.' When I said that would be quite natural and normal; he replied,' No, even if I get up in the middle of the night, every time I go back to sleep, I check all the windows and doors.' The reason turned out to be the same that he had realized while doing the exercise. And the reason was that as a child when he was living in Gujarat the houses would be on two sides of the road in ground plus two storied slices with most of the living on the first floor over the ground. Once while returning home after playing cricket, as he entered the house ground floor there were two robbers inside. He had an altercation with them but came out and called his father down and both of them beat the daylights out of the robbers. Ever since then he had developed this unwanted, uncontrolled, behavior pattern.

When I was in school, while walking up to the school a particular boy from the market side would sometimes catch up with me. Every few steps he would scratch his under arm with the same hand like a monkey does and make a sound somewhat sounding like a 'khunk'. I do not know whether he was even aware of it.

All of you are going to have just one and a half chance of getting rid of any such unwanted, uncontrolled pattern. One full chance is now and a 50% chance of having it after lunch. So, take your opportunity now. Anybody with any such unwanted, uncontrolled behavior pattern, please come and occupy the hot seat. (Manju comes up.)

Manju, put your feet flat on the ground, sit up straight, backbone straight, push your tailbone into the chair, take a deep breath, and while exhaling visualize Number 3, 3 times and close your eyes and relax. Keep your hands on your thighs facing downwards. One more deep breath and let all the tension and stress of the day just go down and out of your toes. Are you left-handed or right-handed? (Manju raises his right-hand index finger and puts it down again. I run my right-hand index finger over his right-hand index finger from the knuckle to the fingertip and say) whenever you want to say 'Yes' you will raise your right-hand index finger. (Then I do the same to his left-hand index finger and say) whenever you want to say 'No' you will raise the left-hand index finger. Do you understand? Are the signals established?

Manju: Yes.

Keki: No, the signals are not established. I will repeat what I did. (I repeat the process one more time and then ask) are the signals established now? (this time he raises his right-hand index finger). Good. Signals are now established. Talk to the subconscious part of your brain that is causing the behavior that you want to change. We will call it behavior "X". Now thank it for the good job it has done for you and let it know that you realize it has the positive intention in causing this behavior.

Ask that part 'are you willing to allow the conscious mind to know what it is of value that occurs when it does 'X'. Remember that you are asking only its willingness. When you get the answer, please let me know by raising the right-hand index finger for 'Yes' or the left-hand index finger for a 'No'. (he takes time to give a yes answer). Thank that part for showing its willingness and now ask it to go ahead and let you know what is its positive intention or the value, when it does 'X'. (Manju's both index fingers shake up and down alternately and finally gives an 'yes' signal. I address more to the group and say) even if it had chosen not to reveal the intention, we would proceed with the exercise.

Now ask if that part is willing to go into your creative resources and get three new ways to accomplish this positive function but with the behavior other than 'X'. Remember that the part is under no obligation to accept or use these choices but only to find them. Your creative part is a good friend of yours. It has so many alternative solutions for any issue. Ask it to give you 3 alternative behavior solutions in this case also and let me know each time you get one. (Manju raises his right-hand index finger) very good, thank it and ask it to give you another solution. (Manju gives a yes signal again) thank it once again and ask it to give you the third solution. (Manju gives a yes signal once again). Good. Thank it for being such a good friend.

Now Manju, ask that part to evaluate each new choice in terms of whether subconsciously it believes the choice is at least as immediate, effective and available as 'X'. Each time the part identifies one that it believes is, give me a yes signal. (Manju gives a yes signal) Very good, ask it to evaluate the second option.) Good once again. Thank it and ask it to evaluate the 3rd option. (more to the group) even if it says 'no' we can go back to the creative part and get one more alternative. (Manju gives a 3rd yes) Very good. Thank it once again.

Now ask the part to select the new way that it considered the most satisfying and available in achieving the same positive function and give you a yes signal when it has selected. (Manju gives a yes signal).

Ask the subconscious part if it would be willing to try the new alternative in appropriate situations and give me the answer when you get it. Once again remember that you are asking only its willingness. (Manju gives a yes signal). Thank it once again.

Ask the subconscious to go into a fantasy of trying out the new behavior in the appropriate context like trying on a new pair of shoes.

Walk around in appropriate situations to see how this new behavior feels. How does it affect others around you? Are there any harmful side effects? Ask all parts if they have any objection to using the new behavior. Make sure all parts agree. Have it notify to you either yes, it is working or no it isn't. If yes you have a new behavior. (Manju gives a yes signal) excellent. (To the group; incase the answer was no, we would go to the creative part once again to get one more alternate and follow the same procedure from there onward.)

Just like your creative part, your Immune Center is also a great friend of yours. Your body and mind are capable of producing whatever chemicals you need, whenever you need, in whatever dosage you need. Your immune center has protected you from harm since childhood, since the time you were born. Also, these Chemicals and your Emotions are interlinked. So, Manju, go to your immune center and ask it to do the needful in this case also.

Whenever you are ready rub your hands together, rub it on your eyes and face, open your eyes and come on back. (after he is done, looking around and then looking at me, I ask), how do you feel? (He lifts up his right-hand index finger, nods a yes and then after a pause nods again.

Thank you, Manju. We can all go for some tea, coffee and hot snacks now. You will pair up with each other and do the exercise along with your partner, when we come back.

(Once back from the break)

Keki: Ok. Pick up your partners and start dancing. Once again, real issues, hot issues, issues that bother you. Aban, can you pair up with Manju so that he also gets practice of doing the exercise on someone.

Aban: Sure. Come on Manju.

(Leaving the group to do the exercise, I went to my favorite place. While I was away this is what transpired between Manju and Aban.)

Aban: Is this exercise clear to you Manju, or do you want any clarifications?

Manju: Madamji, I am still thinking about what happened during the exercise. I am not ready for doing anything else.

Aban: That is perfectly alright. Do you want to talk about what happened?

Manju: Can I?

Aban: Of course, Manju. What happens to you is more important than you learning the exercise. So, what happened?

Manju: When Sirji talked about taking up the behavior pattern 'X' which I want to change, I could only think about what I am going through.

Aban: Can I request you one thing, Manju. From now onwards please stop calling us as madam or sir. What is it? You do not like our names or what? You will call me only as Aban and Keki as Keki. Can you do just that much? for me?

Manju: I will try but it is to give respect. I always called my father as papaji.

Aban: And papaji always called you as Manjuji, is it?

Manju: No. He never respected me. He would always find faults with me. And that is what was going on in my mind when Kekiji asked me to take up the behavior pattern.

Aban: When somebody has respect for somebody else it will show up. There is no need to make a show of it. You know that Keki respects you very highly and he has said it in front of everybody. Continue with whatever was going on in your mind during the exercise.

Manju: Even while at school, my father would continue finding faults with me; telling me that I was good for nothing. One day I picked up some money from home and disappeared. I took a bus to another town. I tried to do something or the other but nothing worked. I asked for some help but nobody helped, instead some body wanted to report me to the police. I ran away from there. All my money was over and I was hungry for two days. I had no money even to return home. I tried to request the bus conductor to take me back to my city but he refused. Finally, when the bus started, I hung on to the railing at the back which is there for taking the luggage on to the top of the bus. I travelled almost 100 kilometers in that fashion and finally returned back home. I slept for almost 10 hours. I got up when I felt somebody was stroking my hair and saying nice things to me. It was my father and I could not open my eyes. That is the best memory of my life. All this was going on in my head during the exercise when Keki asked what could be of value with behavior 'X'.

Aban: Actually, both the index fingers of your two hands were fluttering at that moment. What happened when you went to your creative part?

Manju: I was reminded of two dreams that I have had.

Aban: All this is very, very interesting. Why don't you share this with Keki and everybody when he comes?

Manju: No madam, I mean Aban, Keki may again find faults with me only.

Aban: Maybe but remember that he respects you a lot. Tell me about your dreams.

Manju: In the first dream I see a cobra that is biting everybody in the village. One day a Swami arrives and the villagers complain to him about the cobra. So, the Swami goes to the cobra and advises him not to bite the people.

In the second dream, the cobra is badly hurt by the stones that people are throwing at him because he is no longer biting. The cobra complaints to the Swami for his condition based upon the Swami's advice. The Swami responds by saying that he only asked him not to bite. He did not stop him from hissing to stop them from throwing stones at him.

Aban: This is highly profound. So, what is the behavior pattern that you picked up at the end?

Manju: The Swamiji's second advice.

Aban: Excellent. Remember that everybody loves you, respects you and admires you.

(I climbed up the steps to reach the seminar hall as Aban called to say that almost everybody is done with the exercise)

Keki: Did everybody have a new behavior to replace the old unwanted, uncontrolled pattern?

Group: Yes.

Keki: And how do you all feel?

Group: (most said) Happy.

Keki: Did anyone get a no signal after reaching all the way up to the end?

Gautam: My partner gave a no signal while trying out the new behavior pattern.

Keki: So, what did you do?

Gautam: I took him back to his creative center to get one more alternative, we evaluated it. Then we chose the one best suited and when he tried it out, he felt good.

Keki: Nice. Did anyone get a no signal any other time during the exercise? (4 others raised their hands. When inquired individually as to what they did; they all gave steps similar to what Gautam had already given.) Did anyone get a no signal after you got the willingness of that part to let the conscious mind know what it is of value that occurs when it does 'X'? (no hands went up) Our mind has a way of protecting us. Once in a while it may decide not to reveal the intention, in your own interest. And Aban, how did it go with Manju?

Aban: Very good. I will tell you all about it later. Right now, I would like to do one exercise if you give me 10 minutes.

Keki: Aban rarely makes such a request. But whenever she makes it, I know it is something important; so please go ahead.

Aban: (she came into the center of the hall and called Manju over to stand facing her. She puts her right hand upon his left shoulder. She calls out all the 13 others to surround Manju and put their one hand on either of his shoulders and asks Manju) Manju, please make a statement that you feel should be true for you.

Manju: Everybody loves me, respects me and admires me.

Aban: If you had to choose only two out of these three what would it be?

Manju: Love and respect.

Aban: I am so happy for you. You are passing each and every hurdle beautifully. Remember that the Leader Attitude Housewife or anybody else is not dependent upon the praises from others. Even though they may not verbalize it, you have told me how the most important person in your life did show his love, respect and admiration for you at the right time. You may be searching for it one more time but that does not change the things. Does it? (Manju says no, confidently) So please make a statement with the two most important things that you know you already have, even from the most difficult person in your life.

Manju: Everybody loves me and respects me.

Aban: Along with me, everybody will now loudly say:

All 14: Manju, everybody loves you and respects you.

Aban: Manju will repeat his sentence and all 14 of us will repeat what we just said with emphasis, loudly and clearly. We will do this 7 times.

Manju: Everybody loves me and respects me.

All 14: Manju, everybody loves you and respects you.

(We repeat these 6 more times. Aban and Manju exchange; Thank you, thank you)

Keki: Well, time to celebrate, isn't it? Time to sing and dance. Who feels like singing and dancing?

Group: (loudly) I.

Keki: All of us will sing, dance and celebrate before going for lunch. Right now, let us first do an exercise. This exercise is about **ROLE MODELLING.**

I want everybody to think about some quality or behavior pattern that you wish to enhance in yourself. (pause) Now, think of a person who you are 100% sure, has this quality already in ample measure and it shows up in his or her behavior pattern. This person could be a friend of yours or somebody you know or even personally unknown to you. However, you are absolutely certain that he or she has that quality.

Now sit up straight, close your eyes and relax. Imagine there is a stage in front of you and that person is on the stage, displaying that quality which you want to enhance in yourself and is putting up the behavior pattern appropriate to it. Watch that person minutely. Is that person sitting standing or what?

What type of clothes and attire is that person wearing? How is the fitment of those clothes? What are the color combinations? What effect does his or her attire have on that person's personality? Observe how that person is wearing her or his hair. How is that affecting his or her personality? Is that person wearing any ornaments? On her face, on her ears. His beard and moustache if any. Any other place on the body, wrist watch, bangles, anything at all. Observe everything minutely.

Let that person now put up the behavior pattern which displays this quality which you want to enhance in yourself. Observe his or her whole-body stance; half body stance; head and shoulder angle patterns. The movement of his or her legs, arms, hand and gestures as that person puts up the behavior pattern.

Observe that person's face. The eyes, the mouth. Listen to that person's words, the choice of words, the tonality, the variations in tonality, the emphasis, the gaps. Breathing. Watch carefully the interlinking of gestures, eye movements, the lips, head and shoulder angle patterns, the body movements with whatever is being said. The effect that all this has on whatever the person is communicating.

Now watch the tip of the nose of that person. This could be and is the tip of your nose. Imagine that face to be yours; that body to be yours; those gestures to be yours; those words and the tonality is yours.

Now imagine that you are leaving your seat and going up on the stage. At a certain point as you approach that person, you are breaking through and entering that person's sphere of influence and you are feeling some change in yourself. Go closer.

Now you imagine that you are leaving your body and entering that person's body. From inside there, you are able to listen to that person's thinking pattern. What is that person's thinking pattern while he or she is putting up this behavior so easily and so naturally? Adjust your Thinking pattern to that. What are that person's feelings while displaying this quality which is part and parcel of his or her personality? Feel that confidence which comes even without giving any thought to it. Feel that actually you are now putting up that behavior pattern and displaying that quality which you always wanted to enhance in yourself. Now that you have taken over, request that person to leave and see a big mirror come down where you were sitting earlier. Watch yourself in that mirror performing and putting up that behavior pattern and displaying that quality in yourself. Make any minor modifications that you may feel necessary. Realize that it is just you now, that is putting up this behavior pattern and displaying this quality so easily and so naturally. Let that mirror go back from where it came.

You want to check out this quality and behavior pattern under various circumstances, like while interacting with one person, with a few or even with a big crowd.

You are with one person. You are putting up the behavior pattern which comes out of this quality now enhanced in yourself. Make any minor modifications that you feel is necessary. Satisfy yourself and see the desired effect.

Now you are with a few more people. Once again you are putting up the behavior pattern which comes out of this quality now enhanced in yourself. Make any minor modifications that you feel is necessary. Satisfy yourself and see the desired effect.

You are in front of a big crowd. You are putting up the behavior pattern which comes out of this quality now enhanced in yourself. Make any minor modifications that you feel is necessary. Satisfy yourself and see the desired effect.

Take your time and when you are ready, rub your hands together, rub it on your eyes and face, open your eyes and come on back. (after a pause)

How do you all feel?

Group: (Charged up. More confident. A new me, were some of the comments that they made.)

Keki: So, is it time for song and dance now?

Group: (loudly) Yes.

Keki: Everybody come and stand forming a circle. Make the circle as big as possible. Move those chairs which may come in the way. That's good. Now close your eyes and relax. I will be talking to the person whose left shoulder I am touching. (I happen to be standing close to doctor Nirav. I stand a little to his left and put my hand on his left shoulder and ask) Doctor Nirav, imagine a circle on the ground in front of you. We are going to do something to that circle so that it becomes a **CIRCLE OF YOUR EXCELLENCE,** a circle of your confidence and that circle will always be around you wherever you are. So, tell me what is the size of that circle?

Nirav: Around 30 feet in diameter.

Keki: Please give it some color. What color is it?

Nirav: Grey.

Keki: Grey. Is that your favorite color?

Nirav: No.

Keki: Then give it the color that you would always like it to be. What color would that be?

Nirav: White.

Keki: Make it white and see if you like it.

Nirav: Yes, it is much better.

Keki: Does it have a border? If so, what color?

Nirav: It has a grey border but I would like to change that to silver.

Keki: Go ahead and make it. Tell me how do you like it now. Is there anything else in the circle?

Nirav: It is perfect now. I am inside that circle.

Keki: You stay outside of it for the present. We will be doing several things with it and then at the end you will be within it. (One by one I finish this process with the remaining 12. Somebody chose to have a circle as small as 10 feet, whereas somebody had it as big as the earth. All of them made it as best as they wanted it.)

We are going to invoke this circle now. First decide how you wish to invoke it. It could be either your favorite prayer, some Puja or a ritual or if you are of scientific bent of mind you can think of Einstein or Stephen Hawking also. Whatever force, whatever equation, whatever belief you have, that is making this fantastic universe unfold; seek its blessings for yourself and the circle that will be around you. Step into the circle now. Perform whatever you have to and then come on out of the circle. (I wait for the last person to come out and then.)

Life is about doing. It is about the actions you take. We want to make the circle vibrant with a lot of action. Each one of you is good at doing something. Somebody would have appreciated something which you do. Something with a lot of action. It could be anything from cooking to boxing, playing tennis, climbing mountains. Anything involving a lot of action and you are good at it. When I ask you to enter, you will enter your circle and perform that action with full energy. Bring it to its peak and while at its peak come on out of the circle. Enter now. (I wait for the last person to come out and then.) Now think as to what resource, your internal resource, you could add into this activity to make it even more effective. Go to the time and event when you might have used this resource in any other context also. Relive it. Know that you have that resource, Feel good about it. Take this resource with you now, enter the circle and perform that activity once again; move out when you bring it to its peak and come on out. (As the last person comes out)

Good. Now think of minimum four different resources which you feel you should always have. Identify them. One by one, go to the time and event when you exhibited that resource and was happy with the result. Then enter your circle and breathe it all into the circle and come on out for the next resource. (after they all completed minimum 4 resources)

Humor is an excellent resource to have at all times; good, bad or ugly times. When I was small and my mom thought I was up to some mischief, she would come behind me with a Cane in her hand. I would run around my dining table and she would be behind me with her hand raised with the cane to give me one. I would do something to make her laugh and the cane would become useless. How many of you took up humor as a resource which you always want to have? (only Ankur raised his hand). I want each and every one of you to think of a time when your situation was serious or could have turned serious but you defused it by using humor. Relive that event. Know that you have that resource. Feel good about it. Enter your circle and fill it all up with this. (I wait for the last person to come out and then.)

Another very important resource which each and every one of you should have at every moment is love. The Bible says 'love thy neighbor as thyself'. Unfortunately, we are all, already doing it. Unfortunately, because we love ourselves so little that, that is all we can give. How can we give something to anybody if we do not have it? Christ must have realized this. Because somewhere later on he says 'love as I have loved you'. Which means totally, as the person is, and without expecting anything in return. I have had this checked up with the Jesuit priest whose wife was attending our program. You can love anybody, everybody and everything without an exception. You may be walking past a stinking garbage dump. Nobody is preventing you from holding your nose. Realize that, that garbage dump is providing some poor boy his meals. One way or the other it is providing some poor girl her school exercise book. And by the way, who is responsible for that garbage dump? You and your home has also contributed to it. Responsibility means ability to respond. Each one of us has it, weather we choose to use it or not. As I have mentioned earlier, in any ordinary English language dictionary, there are more than 500 words with 18 or more different meanings. Love is one such word. Think of a time when you came across some situation with somebody or some event which was not to your liking but you accepted it as it was. Relive that episode. Know that acceptance as love. The moment of acceptance. Know that you have it. Make it Universal; enter your circle and breath it all into the circle. (after everyone is done).

Now imagine the surface of that circle as the skin of a big African Tom-Tom drum. We want to make that surface really vibrant. (I start some African Drum Dance music). Enter the circle now and stamp your feet hard on the ground as you dance to this music for about two minutes. Harder still and Shout oom-pah, oom-pah as you dance. Even harder and louder and come on out.

Now let us celebrate life in all its forms by dancing gracefully and with free-flowing movement without any hesitation anywhere. (I start the music and the song of 'Dholi Taro Dhol Baje'). Enter now and dance for the next three and a half minutes. Give yourself fully to it and enjoy as much as you can. Leave everything else and give yourself fully to the dance. Sing along. Come on out as the music and the song ends. (after they have enjoyed fully and come out of the circle).

I am writing down these 5 sentences on the board for you. I am (your name), and I am enough. I am (your name), and I love myself exactly as I am. I am (your name), and I love everybody exactly as they are. I am (your name), and I love everything exactly as it is. I am Free.

When I say enter, each one of you will enter your circle and say these lines in in 4 different ways matching your tonality and your dance to each word.

The first way will be with love. Then you will all come on out. Next when I say enter you will enter your circle and do the same with humor.

The third time will be in a very, very creative manner. And the Fourth will be truthfully believing each and every word.

Enter your circle now. Sing and dance each word and each sentence with love in your heart and mind. Then come on out.

Very good. Now make it even more effective and enjoy every word and sentence in a humorous way. Enter now. Good. You had your fun. Now enter once again and show me how creative you could be. Excellent. Creativity is one of the most important aspect of your life. Now for the last time, enter your circle, sing and dance to adopt, feel and imbibe each and every word that you are saying. Enter now. That was really good. How do you all feel now.

Group: Great.

Keki: Feel great and to stay great, when I say jump, all of you will jump into your circle with both your feet and let the whole things splash all over you enveloping you. Jump now. Very good. Feel the energy of your circle of excellence, your circle of confidence. Now onwards you will always be surrounded by this circle wherever you are and wherever you go.

Greet and hug each and every one present over here and tell them what you already like about that person. Start now. (After we have met everybody and expressed our appreciation the energy level in each one, has reached its peak.)

Before we break for lunch, let me tell you all that whenever you have an important meeting or and assignment or wanting to start something new, run the whole thing in your mind. See as to where you may need some additional resources. Go back to any other event in any other context where you used that resource; relive it, know that you have that resource, feel good about it. Add that resource where you want it, recheck till you feel you have full confidence and getting the results that you want.

Let us all move for lunch now.

(Once we are back from the lunch)

Keki: I want the strongest amongst you to come and stand next to me over here. (The men look at each other and finally Shankar comes up and stands to my left. I press his right-hand biceps and say) We will do some **Muscle Testing**. Shankar, I want you to extend your right hand straight out in front of you with Palm facing downwards and fingers pointing to that wall opposite. (I put my two fingers on the wrist of his extended arm and say) whenever anybody tries to pull your hand down you must resist. (I try to push his hand downwards but without any success). Wow, you are a strong man. Your hand is like a steel rod.

Now close your eyes and imagine that a beam of energy is originating from your shoulder and is passing through your hand to your fingertips and out to the wall opposite and it is pulling your hand, strengthening it even more; but I am going to cut off that beam now. (I slash my hand at his fingertips and immediately push his wrist down. His hand goes almost 30 degrees down and then springs back to its original location)

Open your eyes, Shankar. What happened? How did your hand go down so much?

Shankar: You cut off that beam of energy. Keki: Was there actually a beam of energy passing through? Shankar: You said so.

Keki: Now Shankar, close your eyes once again and stretch out both your hands. Aban, where is that big Helium balloon and the bucket for water?

Aban: He has kept it outside I will bring it to you. (she gets up, opens the door, goes out, comes back, closes the door, walks up to me and says) here.

(I take out my handkerchief and with one corner of it trace it on his left-hand wrist as if I am tying the Helium balloon, saying) you may not even feel anything just now but you can make a fist and keep your hand tight. Now I am hanging the empty bucket on your right-hand wrist. (I touch the Marker Pen in my hand on top of his right-hand wrist, and say) this bucket is empty now so you may not feel the weight but I am going to keep pouring water into it so you may as well make a tight fist of this hand also. (I already have two glasses, one full of water and one empty. I keep pouring from one glass to the other making the noise of pouring water and continue saying). As I keep filling up the bucket with more and more water, the more I pour into it the heavier it is getting and it is pulling your right hand downwards. As the bucket is getting heavier and heavier your right hand is getting pulled downward more and more. At the same time the Helium balloon is pulling your left arm upwards more and more. The right arm is getting pulled more and more downwards and the left arm is getting pulled upwards more and more. Resist your right hand going downwards and resist your left hand moving upward. But the more you resist the more they are moving. (By now the left arm has moved up at least three inches and the right arm has moved down almost 9 inches.

Stay as you are Shankar and just open your eyes slowly. (Shankar opens his eyes, has a perplexed look on his face, looks towards the ceiling, I Suppose to look for the Helium balloon, he looks downwards below his right arm, may be searching for the bucket, looks at the two glasses in my hands. He gets the point; bursts out laughing and looks at others laughing too. Lily's laugh is the loudest. He shakes off his two hands from the shoulder and we continue.)

Keki: Close your eyes once again. This time resist and do not let anybody pull your hand down at all. (I move closer to his ear and Whisper loud enough for others to hear also). Shankar, I know you are a good guy but I also know for sure, that you have done some bad, bad things. I want you to think of that and feel really bad. Keep telling yourself that you are a bad boy. (Lily is the shortest and most lightweight. I gesture her to come over and when she comes, I gesture her to wait and at my signal push his hand down all the way by her two fingers) You are a bad boy Shankar and you are feeling bad about it. Feel bad. (I signal Lily to pull his hand down all the way and she does it. This time he does not even bother to take his hand up again). Open your eyes again and see who pushed your hand all the way down. (Shankar looks at Lily in disbelief.) Does everybody realize how a negative thought can influence each and every cell of our body? It weakens us. Imagine what must be happening to a person who is most often in a negative frame of mind. Thankyou Lily and thank you Shankar. (I pat Shankar's back and tell him 'You are not at all a bad boy; you are a very good boy). Both of you can take your seats now.

No matter what the situation is, no matter what you are going through; it always helps to stay positive. Whenever you are positive you are not seeing things through the color of your glasses or the dirt on it. You are free of any unwanted baggage. When you are in that state, your mind will work more clearly and the probability of getting the true solution is much higher.

In the morning I told you that you will have only one and a half chance of getting rid of any unwanted, uncontrolled behavior pattern. You got your full chance in the morning. Now you are going to get probably only half a chance.

(While saying all this I observed that Lily was much more animated as well as a bit restless. I made it a point to have an eye contact with her as often as I could.) We may be stuck in that behavior pattern based on some issues, items or even personalities and personal relationships. Take your chance now. (I again make eye contact with Lily and say) the hot seat is waiting to be warmed up. (finally, Lily gets up and occupies the chair).

You are welcome, Lily. Please put your feet flat on the ground, sit up straight, backbone straight, push your tailbone into the chair, take a deep breath and while exhaling close your eyes and relax. While you are relaxing let me talk to your other friends.

Who likes to hear a story?

Group: (loudly) I.

Keki: (I got up to narrate the story.) This actually happened. In a housing township. There lived an elderly couple. Their Dining table was next to a big glass French window from which the neighboring house was clearly visible. Recently they had new neighbors. Every day when they were sitting for lunch, the new neighbor lady would come with a basket of washed clothes and put it for drying on the clothesline. On the first day itself this lady observed something odd but kept quiet. On the second day when she found the same thing again, she could not stay quiet. She told her husband 'Why is our new neighbor lady putting up dirty soiled clothes on the clothesline? Surely her detergent is not good. I should advise her on what we use. 'To this the husband replied 'stop poking your nose in other people's business. You put up your laundry on the clothesline so that she can see it and maybe one day, she will ask you herself. (Few days passed and suddenly this lady saw the neighbor's lady putting up very clean and bright clothes on the clothesline. She exclaimed to her husband 'look at that, her clothes are washed even better than mine! She must have changed the detergent'. To this the husband coolly replied 'I do not know about that, my dear, but I did clean up our window glass from the outside this morning.' (Pause)

Group: (they uttered something and from some voices I heard) Oh!

Keki: (I again took my seat on the left of Lily and said) You must be relaxed by now. (I lifted up her left-hand, by her wrist a few inches and let it drop. It should have dropped down heavy but it did not.) We will deepen this relaxation even more.

But before we do that let me ask you if you visit any Temple or Church or any religious place?

Lily: (in a soft voice) My mom used to take me to Temples when I was small.

Keki: Did you ever pray for something which you wanted?

Lily: Sometimes.

Keki: Did you ever get something that you prayed for?

Lily: Sometimes, yes.

Keki: Imagine you are entering that Temple now. This is the place where your prayers were answered the best. Believe that your prayers are going to be answered once again over here (and even with her eyes closed I point my finger at the chair where she is sitting.)

We are going deeper still in your relaxation.

DAVE ELMAN INDUCTION

Now take a long deep breath and hold it for a few seconds. As you exhale this breath, allow your eyes to remain closed and let go of the surface tension in your body. Just let your body relax as much as possible right now.

Now, place your awareness on your eye muscles and relax the muscles around your eyes to the point they just won't work. When you're sure they're so relaxed that as long as you hold on to this relaxation, they just won't work, hold on to that relaxation and test them to make sure THEY WON'T WORK.

Now, this relaxation you have in your eyes is the same quality of relaxation that I want you to have throughout your whole body. So, just let this quality of relaxation flow through your whole body from the top of your head, to the tips of your toes.

Now, we can deepen this relaxation much more. In a moment, I'm going to have you open and close your eyes. When you close your eyes, that's your signal to let this feeling of relaxation become 10 times deeper. All you have to do is want it to happen and you can make it happen very easily. Ok, now, open your eyes...now close your eyes and feel that relaxation flowing through your entire body, taking you much deeper. Use your wonderful imagination and imagine your whole body is covered and wrapped in a warm blanket of relaxation.

Now, we can deepen this relaxation much more. In a moment, I'm going to have you open and close your eyes one more time. Again, when you close your eyes, double the relaxation you now have. Make it become twice as deep. Ok, now once more, open your eyes...close your eyes and double your relaxation...good. Let every muscle in your body become so relaxed that as long as you hold on to this quality of relaxation, every muscle of your body will not work.

In a moment, I'm going to have you open and close your eyes one more time. Again, when you close your eyes, double the relaxation you now have. Make it become twice as deep. Ok, now, once more, open your eyes...close your eyes and double your relaxation...good. Let every muscle in your body become so relaxed that as long as you hold on to this quality of relaxation, every muscle of your body will not work.

In a moment I am going to lift your left hand by the wrist just a few inches and drop it. If you have followed my instructions up to this point, that hand will be so relaxed it will be just as loose and limp as a wet dish cloth and will simply plop down. Now don't try to help me, you have to remove relaxation. Let me do all the lifting so that when I release it; it just plops down and you will allow yourself to go much deeper.

(Lily was trying to put some of her own effort in lifting the hand, so I said) No, no, let me do all the lifting. You keep your hand loose and limp so that I get the whole weight of it. You will feel it when you have it. Do not help me. (I release her wrist and the hand falls on her lap. Once again, I lift her hand, move it slightly towards me and release it. It falls all the way down from her shoulder to her side.)

Now that's complete physical relaxation. I want you to know that there are two ways a person can relax. You can relax physically and you can relax mentally. You already proved that you can relax physically, now let me show you how to relax mentally. In a moment I will ask you to begin slowly counting backwards, out loud, from 100. Now, here is the secret to mental relaxation. With each number you say, double your mental relaxation. With number you say, let your mind become twice as relaxed. Now if you do this, by the time you reach the number 98, or may be even sooner, your mind will have become so relaxed, you will have actually relaxed all the rest of the numbers that would have come after 98, right out of your mind. There just won't be any more numbers. Now you have to do this. I can't do it for you. Those numbers will leave if you will them away. Now start with the idea that you will make that happen and you can easily dispel them from your mind.

Keki: Now say the first number 100 and double your mental relaxation.

Lily: (softly) 100.

Keki: Now double that mental relaxation. Let those numbers already start to fade.

Lily: (hardly audible) 99.

Keki: Double Your mental relaxation. Start to make those numbers leave. They will go if you will them away.

Lily: (no sound at all).

Keki: Now they'll be gone. Dispel them. Banish them. Make it happen. You can.

(REGRESSION)

Lily, you are standing in a long corridor. There are rooms on both sides of the corridor with the room numbers written on the doors. You are now standing between room numbers 27 and 28 and facing towards room number 1 and 2. Between them is a dark passage leading beyond. Each room contains the history of your life when you were of that age as given on the door number. Start walking slowly towards room number 1 and 2 and go back to the time from which your symptoms arise. Stop at whichever door attracts your attention. Read aloud the number written on that door. (pause)

Lily: 11. Keki: Would you like to enter that room?

Lily: Yes. Keki: Gently open the door, enter inside and tell me what you see.

Lily: (tears have started rolling down her eyes. Aban has already kept a pile of tissues on the table. I pick up one and put it in her hand. Between sobs she manages to say) - mom -sob -my. . . mom -sob - on the ground -sob - white -sob - cover -sob - people.

Keki: (obviously this was the last time she saw her mom at the funeral and I did not want her to linger more over here.) Do you see that 11-year-old Lily over there? (I take a fresh tissue, put it in her left hand and say) take this fresh tissue and throw away the old one which has become so wet. Tell me what is that 11-year-old Lily doing?

Lily: (she lets the wet tissue drop on her right. Takes the new tissue in her right hand. Wipes her face and says) grandma -sob - has taken her in her lap -sob - consoling -sob.

Keki: Do you wish to sit through all the ceremonies once again or you would rather give them strength to go through it and proceed further?

Lily: sob - proceed -sob.

Keki: Then say whatever you want to say to your mom, to your 11-year-old self, grandma and whoever else. Then say your prayers and come on out of that room blessing the room and everybody within it. (I observe the activity on her face and when I feel that she has finished what she wanted and her face is a bit relaxed. The other tissue is also dropped down on her right, and I replaced it.) Are you outside the room now? Did you bless the room and everybody and everything within?

Lily: Yes.

Keki: Face towards room number 1 and 2 and continue walking slowly till you come to another door that attracts your attention. (I observe her face and when I feel that she has stopped somewhere I asked) are you there? Please read the number on the door.

Lily: It is number 4.

Keki: Gently open the door and enter inside. Do you recognize this place?

Lily: Yes. It is where we used to live when I was small.

Keki: And tell me what you see.

Lily: I am there.

Keki: And how old are you?

Lily: 4 years (and her voice changes to babyish).

Keki: I want to talk to that sweet little four-year-old Lily. What is she doing over there?

Lily: In kitchen, playing.

Keki: Is somebody else also in the kitchen? My sweet little Lilly.

Lily: My mommy. (with distinct childish voice)

Keki: And what is she doing in the kitchen?

Lily: Cooking.

Keki: And what is happening now?

Lily: Daddah come. Want dinner. Mommy put plate with food. Daddah very angry. Throw plate down. He hit my mommy. -sob - I not goat. You grass eater. I want mutton. Mommy tell. You drink again. No money. No cooking mutton every day. Big fight. I cry. Go my room and hide under blanket.

Keki: Oh. Did my sweet little Lilly sleep off?

Lily: No. I wake up. Big sounds. Hitting. Screaming. I get up. Go to the door.

Keki: Where? To the kitchen?

Lily: No. They in their bed. Daddah sitting on mommy pushing and hitting. Mommy scream, stop, stop, you hurting me, paining.

Keki: Hitting with what? where? On her face?

Lily: No. Her face into the pillow. Sitting on her legs and slapping her back side. Hurting her.

Keki: Just point out where you are seeing them.

Lily: There. (she points out a few feet ahead and slightly to the right)

Keki: Remember where you are seeing them, we are going to come back and help them. Now gently open your eyes and stand up. (As she stands up with eyes open, I move her chair a little, go behind her to the other side, take the dustbin and start pushing her wet tissues into it. She turns towards me and says 'why are you doing this? let me do it.' I stop her and say 'relax, you have much more important things to do right now.' I return to my chair, sit down and ask her to sit down with her eyes closed and relaxed)

Lily, you are now 27 years of age and have far more resources then that sweet little Lily had at 4 years of age. Isn't it?

Lily: Yes.

Keki: One by one we are going to give resources to all the three. We will consider the entire episode from the kitchen to the bedroom as one. But tell me where do you see that sweet little 4-year-old at the door from where she is looking at her mom and dad on the bed?

Lily: The 4-year-old me is here. (points out a spot at about 45 degrees to the right and 2-3 feet ahead) and my parents are there. (She points out to the spot which she had showed earlier but a couple of feet ahead.)

Keki: Very good. Like I said, we are going to give resources, one by one to all three so that they have a much better experience out of this. Tell me who is the first person that you would like to give resources to?

Lily: My dad.

Keki: Lily, what resource do you now have that you wish your dad had at that point of time?

Lily: Love.

Keki: Now that you have given love as a resource to your dad, what change in behavior do you notice in him?

Lily: He has stopped hitting my mom. (pause) He is now moving backwards bending down and kissing her reddened back side. her bum. (pause) maybe he is feeling sorry now. Turning her over, he is wiping her tears and they are kissing.

Keki: Now that he has love as a resource, what other resource would you like to give him?

Lily: Understanding.

Keki: Along with love let him also have the resource of understanding. How is he now using the resource of understanding along with love? What change in behavior do you notice?

Lily: He realizes that mom is a vegetarian and he is not. He realizes that mom does not even like cooking non-vegetarian yet she is cooking it sometimes for his pleasure. He also realizes that there is constraint of money.

Keki: What other resource would you like to give him?

Lily: For the present this should do.

Keki: Temporarily we will withdraw both these resources from him and give some resource to your mom. What resource would you like to give to your mom?

Lily: I would like to give both these resources to mom also.

Keki: So, give both these resources to your mom and tell me what change in behavior do you notice.

Lily: She is saying 'I am sorry, I am sorry my dear. I knew even before marriage that you loved mutton so much. You used to have it every day. But I loved you and I still do. We will work out something in the morning but right now please get off me and make love to me properly.

Keki: Very good. Would you like to give any other resource?

Lily: Yes, patience.

Keki: Give patience as a resource along with the other two and tell me what change do you find in her behavior?

Lily: She accepts whatever is happening and waits for a proper time.

Keki: Good. Any other Resource that you would like to give now?

Lily: No.

Keki: Fine. We will temporarily withdraw all three resources from your mom also. Tell me what resource would you now like to give to that sweet little 4-year-old Lily?

Lily: Courage.

Keki: Give the resource of courage to that sweet 4-year-old Lily and tell me how she is utilizing it?

Lily: She decides to go back to her bed and sleep, if possible, but wants to talk to her mom and dad exactly what she thinks and feels.

Keki: Good. You have made her very Brave. Now give back all the resources to all three of them as you gave them and tell me what is happening.

Lily: All three are sleeping well but next day the 4-year-old is telling her mom and dad how scared she gets every time when they fight. Mom and dad are working out their differences. They also decide to do something to earn more money. They also feel that for the sake of their child they need to change their living pattern. Mom adds that she wants to overcome her resistance to cooking the non-veg. but who can help?

Keki: You have done a great job, Lily. I am very proud of you. Extend both your arms and pick up that 4-year-old sweet Lily into your lap. Hug her. Kiss her. Tell her how proud you are for her and say 'I release you to your higher self to grow up into a beautiful, courageous, useful human being full of love, understanding and compassion.' After you do that, rub your hands together, rub it on your eyes and face, and come on back.

(She looked a little dazed and lost, as she opened her eyes. She kept staring at me. Then she looked around at others. Got up. Waited. Opened her arms. Came closer to me and whispered 'can I hug you?' I said 'it will be my pleasure.' We hugged and she whispered again 'Sorry, I was nasty to you also'. I tightened my hug and said 'I understand and I am very proud of you. You are going to go places you have not imagined yet.' We parted and she went for her seat.)

Towards the end of this exercise Lily came up with a question of her mom as to 'who can help?' This is rather unusual and very rare; but in NLP you can expect anything to happen. I do not want Lily or anybody else to go back with this question unanswered. So, I tell her that Upanishad has a very interesting stanza which more or less defines life. It says that **'the eater of the food is the food for others'**. After death consciously or unconsciously we are offering this packet of proteins, either to the maggots or to birds and animals of prey in some communities. Only people who do not do this are those who cremate the bodies. The rest are all following this premise. You might have also heard the name of Sir Jagdish Chandra Bose. He with his precise scientific experiments, was the first to prove that **plants also do have emotions**. Remember this next time when you cut up an eggplant or a cabbage.

Ok, the rest of you pick up your partner and take them through the Dave Elman Induction. No need to take anybody through the corridor. Start now. Finish it and let us break for tea/coffee and cookies.

CHAPTER 10

ANUSUYA'S FEEDBACK; ANUSUYA'S DILEMMA.

This chapter appears over here because of the insistence by Anusuya that the final chapter has to be what I do after the evening tea/ coffee, cookies break on the final day.

Anusuya came to our house within 3 weeks of returning from the US. As she entered our house at the appointed time and I opened the door;

Keki: Hi Anu. What happened? You do not look your bubbly self today. Are you disappointed with the US program or what?

Anusuya: No, I am fine. The program itself was very good.

Aban: But something seems to be bothering you; but welcome in and sit down, Anu.

Anusuya: I do not wish to talk about my US visit. I came to talk to you about The Book. The review.

Keki: Must be pretty bad to put you in such a state.

Anusuya: Not at all. On the contrary it has been very encouraging.

Keki: You are hiding something from me. But anyway, continue whatever you have to say.

Anusuya: Soon as I received your mail introducing the book characters, I added it into the manuscript and distributed it to my various friends and also requested them to pass it on to two of their friends. I did that without taking your permission. I hope you do not mind.

Keki: Absolutely not. In fact, you did a very good job. Did you receive their feedback?

Anusuya: Thanks. The feedbacks are approaching almost a 100, and some are still awaited. The manuscript has reached some NLP trainers, including trainers from other streams of NLP; some of your practitioners, some practitioners from other streams and more than all that, from those who were new to NLP. So, I have divided it into these five groups. Which one would you like to hear first?

Keki: Very thorough as usual. This is what is going to make you a fantastic trainer/facilitator. The Book is meant for common people, to make them aware of something like NLP and to introduce them to the power of NLP. So, I suggest you start from them.

Anusuya: I too thought the same way and therefore I had put a suggestion that these people should preferably read the book along with somebody or in groups of four so that they may practice exercises rather than just read the book.

Many of them did that. Some read the book and then got one or more partners to do at least some of the exercises. Some started off reading and practicing the exercises with their partner/s. Those who did the exercises were highly thrilled. Some said it was like an awakening. The word 'awakening' has appeared in quite a few comments. Their take-home was the maximum. Those who just read the book, enjoyed the snippets that you give and the stories that you tell. The next c...

Keki: Can I interrupt you here. All this sounds good. I hope you are not saying all this to make me feel good. There must be some adverse remarks also.

Anusuya: Minuscule. In this category. One person said he does not read any book which is beyond 150 to 200 pages. Another said it was too high level for her. One gentleman said that all this sounds like pop psychology and he does not believe in it. I do not recall any other adverse comment. Does that make you happy?

Keki: Certainly not. But let us get on with the next category.

Anusuya: The next category is of course your practitioners. Each one felt as if they were reliving the program but much more intensely. Most of them said that you have packed in much more in the book than in the program they had attended. I have responded to each of them that this has to be expected because you have packed many more participants with similar characteristics into one and you are somehow dealing with them all. Was I right in saying so?

Keki: On the dot. I think I should leave my programs to trainers like you from now onwards.

Anusuya: (with a smile on her face) But many from the first category have expressed the desire to do the program with you and you alone. So, I have no chance.

Keki: That is why I want you to do it even better than mine. Go on. Continue.

Anusuya: The third category are the practitioners from other streams. This is a mixed bag. Most of them have said that this is very different from what they did. Some said they had spent more time on theory but appreciated the therapeutic value of this, particularly when they practiced one or more of the exercises either on themselves or on somebody else.

Keki: Did I, any time, mention the case-story of a participant in Bengaluru?

I was collecting and interviewing participants for the upcoming program. This is when somebody talked about a lady who had done NLP in the US. I took down her name and telephone number. I found out that she had done a month-long program in the US to learn NLP. I invited her to the program and told her that her fees would be only to give me a critical review of my program compared to what she had done in the US. Our programs were of four days at that time. At the end of the program, over a cup of coffee, she stated that she had learnt a lot more about NLP in 30 days but the amount of change that she found in herself during these 4 days, she had not experienced over there. I found that heartening. Now tell me about the fourth category.

Anusuya: In the 4th category are a few trainers from other streams. This again is a mixed bag. Most of them said that they have larger groups and they cannot sit down individually with each, for a preprogram meeting. One of them even said that he is not interested in each one's personal life. He even gave example where the number of participants run into thousands.

Keki: Trainers can also have different outcomes in mind. So, this does not move me one bit.

Anusuya: Relax. Some of them did say that they can and would implement some parts as needed. I am sure you want to hear regarding your own Trainers; The 5th category.

Keki: I am waiting.

Anusuya: They all said it was like a manual for them. Two of them were having their own programs but when they tried to implement it in toto, they could hardly cover 70 to 75% of what all you have covered for each day.

Keki: Thanks, Anusuya. This is to be expected since I have amalgamated several participants of similar nature into one and am dealing with more than one of the kinds on each day. Even I find it difficult to pack in everything every time, particularly when someone is knotted up and needs unknotting.

Seems to me that some unknotting is required right now.

Anusuya: What do you mean?

Keki: I know you are hiding something. Why now? You have not done it so far.

Anusuya: I do not want to take any programs.

Keki: You mean you are stopping your yoga classes?

Anusuya: Definitely not. I am talking about NLP programs.

Keki: How come? Did Grinder tell you something?

Anusuya: No, no. He was appreciative of my questions and even asked me about my trainer and my journey through NLP. It is what happened after the program.

Keki: What happened after the program? Do you want to share it?

Anusuya: I might have shared it with you earlier that a nephew of my dad wanted to marry me and had sent a marriage proposal saying that he would marry me and take me to the US; an offer that he thought I can never refuse. I had refused it stating that I wanted to stay in my country. He lives in the same city where I had been for the program and my parents wanted me to look them up. So, after the program I went to live with them for 2 days. I was unaware that his grandmother had drilled it into his head that I had refused the marriage proposal because my mother happened to be from a higher caste and that I considered him to be of a lower caste. It was such a silly thing to believe but somehow, he was still carrying that grudge. On the evening that I reached his house, Suresh- yes, his name is also Suresh and his wife, Sushma had also called their local friends John and his wife Shirley for dinner with us. All was fine till we finished the dinner and sat down for a chit-chat and the conversation went somewhat like this, to make it very brief.

John: Tell me Anu, how was your program and what is all this that you call NLP.

Anusuya: The program was excellent. I learnt a lot of new things. (then I explained to him about what is NLP).

John: Sounds interesting but I have never heard of it. So, are you going to go home and teach this to others?

Anusuya: Yes, that is why I came to America.

Shirley: And how do you find America?

Anusuya: It is nice, Shirley. Big Roads. Big cars. Big buildings. Sometimes big packets with a lot of gas also filled in it. People are friendly but I also find a lot of wastage. Once I went out with a friend from my program to the supermarket because she wanted a new mixer-grinder of exactly the type that she already had. She was buying new one because the molded plug had burnt out. I found it little funny because back home, I would have cut off the plug from the wire and screwed it on to an ordinary plug.

(John nodded somewhat in agreement but it was Suresh who flared up)

Suresh: They are all the same, John. They all act high and mighty. They all want to come to America but when they cannot then they start finding faults just to feel good, (etc. etc.)

(And he continued his tirade including his proposal to marry me and bring me to America and my rejection for being of a higher caste than him and so on. All this was totally new to me and I was shocked to hear all these lies but he would not even let me speak. He continued nonstop for at least half an hour)

John: Really? That's awful. You mean all this is still continuing? Seems like something from the dark ages.

Suresh: (pointing towards me) the sample is in front of you. (and continued saying)

'Now she will go back home and say that she is America returned and parrot some of the things that she has learnt here and those fools will just gulp it down. All this just because she does not have anything better to do'.

(I was annoyed. I was angry. I was on the verge of crying with all these lies when suddenly John asked)

John: What has your country given to the world anyway?

(I was preparing myself for a fight but this came as a sudden Jolt from a new direction. I got confused. I became tongue-tied. I just wanted to get up and go away from there, instead I froze.)

Keki: I would have answered 'Zero'.

Anusuya: Zero? Why Zero?

Keki: Because can you imagine a world without zero? Without zero there would be no numbering system, no mathematics, no computers. We would possibly be still in the dark ages. It was 1000-2000 years back that Aryabhata propounded the true meaning of zero, or what we call as Shunya. Not just Shunya but he went on dwelling on Shunyata which is the essence of Shunya or the property of Shunya.

Anusuya: I do not know and do not understand all this.

Keki: Frankly speaking, neither do I nor do most of the population. In our English medium schools, the primary school teacher asks the small children 'zero means . . .' and the children are taught to parrot '. . Nothing'.

Zero does not mean nothing. Zeroness or Shunyata goes much deeper. The closest that the English language may come to is 'Void' or 'Voidness' The way I try to understand it is by comparing it with something. An act of being kind or being inquisitive, which is at the conscious level, momentary and specific. This I considered similar to Shunya or zero. Whereas kindness or inquisitiveness is eternal, non-specific and whether you are aware of it or not. This is what I understand Shunyata as. The void versus the voidness. Something like what the quantum scientists talk about the dark matter and dark energy which they say constitutes 94% of the universe whereas what we can see is only 6%.

Anusuya: All this is beyond me. I could not have said anything like this.

Keki: Then you could have said that your country has given the world the Americas.

Anusuya: America? But Columbus discovered America.

Keki: That is true, but where was he headed for and why? In the Trainer's program you also saw that 15 out of the 26 alphabets of the English language are directly from our Devanagari script. The foreign rulers left our country more than 70 years back. When do you think, we are going to learn our own history?

Anusuya: Whatever, but like I said, I was tongue-tied and he stopped only when his wife Sushma said.

Sushma: Enough of it darling. Remember you are married to me now and I love you and we are happy. Let her do whatever she wants to do.

Anusuya: Next day I tried to explain things to Shusma but she was hardly listening. (after some pause). What should I do, Keki? Do you think I am a coward?

Keki: Coward, no. Cautious, may be. Suppose you have two friends. One is obese and the other one is very skinny. To the obese one you call out; 'Hi Jumbo' and the skinny one you say; 'Hello you matchstick'. What do you think will be their reaction?

Anusuya: They may not like it. They may get annoyed or offended.

Keki: And if you reverse it? You call the obese one as 'Hello, you matchstick' and the skinny one as 'Hi Jumbo'. Then what may happen?

Anusuya: They may look at me quizzically or they may think I am crazy.

Keki: I see.

Anusuya: You mean, I am believing what that guy is saying?

Keki: How should I know. But I know one thing. To me it looks like both of you were doing the same thing. Both of you were defending your own decisions. He regarding his decision of leaving the country and you regarding your decision of not leaving the country

Anusuya: Ok, but what about this caste business? People still believe in it in some pockets and some places.

Keki: Let them. Prophets and messiahs and wise men have observed and propounded remedies for that period and people. Some of it could be called as the eternal truth. But their followers and propagators over time could, should and would have modified the same either to suit the times or, more likely, to suit themselves. I have not read the Manusmruti but if Manu was born even in the US at this time, what will he notice and write? He will notice that a considerable population is involved in dealing with external threat and internal law and order situations, often by use of force. Them he named as Kshtriya in our country. They are almost totally looked after by the state or the kings of the yore. Next, he will observe a large population involved in educating, healing, learning. Them he called as Brahmins in our country. These are largely supported by the state and the general population. The third large category is involved in producing wealth. They also provide the state or the king their taxes. Them he called as Vaishya in our country. The remaining would render all sorts of services to all others. Them he called as Shudra in our country. He also observed that marriages and other major interactions largely happened within each group. Even their children often pursued the same profession and traditions

Tell me Anu, did you Congate today?

Anusuya: Did I what? You mean Colgate? I heard it as Congate.

Keki: Whatever.

Anusuya: No, I use Ayurvedic toothpaste.

Keki: Really? Even though these people advertise so many times in a day on almost every channel of the TV.

Anusuya: People are paying for those advertisements. You can sell a ₹ 5 product for ₹ 50 and even if you spend 20 rupees for advertisement you are making hundred percent profit.

Keki: Imagine you are holding your toothbrush in one hand, show me how you will put the paste on it from the tube in the other hand. (Anusuya goes through the motion). Oh, from one end to the another.

Anusuya: (with a smile) Only on the bristles.

Keki: Of course. You know, one tooth paste manufacturer wanted to increase their sales and was having a brainstorming meeting with the top employees. There were various suggestions. One engineer made some quick calculations and showed everybody that by increasing the aperture by just 1mm from 7 to 8 you can increase the usage by 30%. As an engineer it was a brilliant suggestion and quickly adopted. Why? Because people get easily hypnotized. No advertiser tells you to put the toothpaste from one end to the other. They just show you one visual and you ape it. Tomorrow you put just half of what you put normally on your brush. Day after tomorrow half of that. Find your own optimum. You will be surprised by the result.

Anu: But Keki, how much am I going to save even if I cut down my annual tube usage by half?

Keki: Not much at all But the attitude that you develop of optimal utilization of your resources; can and will save you hundreds, thousands, millions or even billions every year depending upon the amount of private and public funds that pass through your hands. Gandhiji says, there is enough in the world for everyone's need but not enough for anyone's greed. Imagine if only half the population follows this then most of this planet's problems will start to vanish.

In fact, independent research shows that only 14% of all advertisements give any useful information. The rest are making unsubstantiated claims or purposely misleading and stroking your greed. And the public just gulps it down.

Anusuya: Gulps it down. I totally agree. And that is what worries me. I do not feel ready for taking the programs. I may not do a good job of it.

Keki: Like I said, being cautious. Being cautious is a good thing. You can make each program better than the previous one. You know Anu; in the earlier days when I used to see the Vernacular school teacher teaching the children English, I was appalled because they could not themselves speak a sentence of English properly and I thought it should be stopped. Then I realized my mistake because they were bringing up the children from their level of English to at least her level. You must have heard me saying that NLP is like an ocean. When I see the videos of the great Masters doing NLP, I feel as if I know hardly 2% of NLP. But I feel good because I feel I can improve 50 times over.

You must have heard this story from the TV serial "Peshwa Bajirao"

Frogs decided to climb a tree. There was commotion. Many tried. Failed. All shouted "It can't be done!" "It has never been done" "Frogs do not climb trees" "We are all wasting our time & energy" They all gave up. One ordinary looking froggy attempted and attempted until finally she climbed the tree. She was DEAF.

Aban, did you notice that the Suresh that she married accepted her as she was, maybe because he saw the potential in her and has been encouraging her. Whereas the Suresh whose marriage proposal she had rejected and is discouraging her; she wants to follow his suggestions. How stupid can one get? Anyway, it is her choice and we can only respect it. Good luck. Bye- bye and a big thank you for all you have done. (Anusuya did not want to get up. So, I asked her) Do you even know the meaning of your name? Anusuya?

Anusuya: No. What is it?

Keki: Look it up yourself. You always had the intelligence to do the right thing.

Anusuya: I will be back.

(Aban said 'welcome' and I added 'always'.

CHAPTER 11

THE FINAL CHAPTER

Keki: NLP is not just about learning some skills or about doing some exercises. It goes much, much deeper.

NLP recognizes that we all are operating from six different logical levels or **SIX NEUROLOGICAL LEVELS.** This is a contribution to NLP by Robert Dilts. Robert was a student when Bandler and Grinder were studying the Great Masters. He would be present when the Great Masters were at work with their clients and take down minute notes as to how they were doing it. By the age of 26 he was the youngest trainer of NLP. On the net you may find 2 encyclopedias of NLP. The larger and more comprehensive is from Robert Dilts. I had the good fortune of attending one of his programs in Montreal.

Over here The Skeleton that I am using is from Robert Dilts but the meat that I put on it is mine.

At the first neurological level is our **Environment**. Our environment is our world that we have created for ourselves. Within the same geographical area there can be many worlds. For example, we are at this hotel right now. It is in hospitality industry. There is a certain class and type of people that come to stay here. The hotel staff and employees put up a behavior pattern appropriate to the hospitality industry while dealing with the clients. My youngest daughter has done hotel management and she has told me as to what happens when the same staff is behind the doors marked 'private' where no guests are allowed.

Walk out of the gate of this hotel and turn left. You will come to the Saint Mira's college. An environment of students, professors, libraries, learning and education. A totally different world from that of the hospitality industry over here.

Walk further and you come to the Don Bosco Sports Academy. An environment of physical fitness, physical skills, fine tuning for particular games and sports. The type of people who come here and the pursuits that they have is entirely different from that of hospitality or education.

Go further, turn left and turn left once again you will come to the Inlaks Budhrani hospital. If you have attended some patient for a few days in a hospital you will know what a totally different environment it is. An environment of Sickness. Healing. Blood and Gore, pain and pleasure, howling, death, crying, new life, babies, happiness. A totally different world.

Move out and walk further to the Osho International Ashram. A world of seekers. An international group of people involved in a very different pursuit far removed from whatever we have seen so far.

Walk further and we come to the North Main Road. A Commercial area. People from all these places might have to go there to conduct some transaction.

And surrounding this one block you may have some pickpockets who look at you and me and your back pocket, all the ladies' purses in a very different way. So, within the same geographical area you can have various Worlds.

Next neurological level is that of **Behavior**. How you portray yourself, interact and communicate with others in your world.

The next higher level is that of **Capabilities and Skills**. Skills and capabilities are learned behavior patterns. An Airline pilot is like a trained dog. You take out your hand and say 'paw' and the dog puts his paw into it. You take out a biscuit or something and hold it high and say 'jump' and the dog will jump. The Control Tower says 'dip left now' and immediately a trained pilot would dip the plane left, then and there. Whereas an amateur in a private plane may want to check with the Control Tower and thereby not only meet heaven himself but maybe take 200 more of a commercial flight with him. You and I cannot do something that a trained surgeon or a professional will do automatically.

At the fourth level come your **Values and Beliefs**.

These are the conclusions you have reached based upon your experiences so far in your life and your interpretations of the same. Once in a while you may find that a certain belief that you have does apply to someone or something other than yourself but you may not want to apply it to yourself. This can create issues for yourself and may not help. You may also have a **belief** that some terrorist or a tyrant needs to be eliminated and even if you are put in a 100% safe situation with a gun in your hand your **value** system may not permit you to pull the trigger to take another human life, or for that matter any life.

Higher than your Beliefs and Values comes your **Identity**. Who you think you are. Your perception regarding your own self.

You meet a person on the street and you ask him, 'sir, who are you? What do you do?' and he responds 'I am a surgeon. I operate at the Inlaks Budhrani hospital.'

(I take two steps to the left) I meet another person and ask the same question 'sir, who are you? What do you do?' and he responds 'I am a surgeon. My father spent 5 lakhs (500,000) to put me into the medical college. By the time I graduated that 5 L has become 10 L and by the time I became a surgeon that 10 L has become 20 L. So far, I have made only 12 L, let me cut up some more kidneys.'

(I come back to my original position and take two steps to the right) I asked the same question to a third person. 'sir, who are you? What do you do?' and he responds 'I am the healer of the human body and soul. I perform operations at the hospital to make my patients well. I am a surgeon.'

(I return to the central position) I meet another person and ask 'madam, who are you? What do you do?' and she responds 'I am a teacher. I teach history to the class 5 students' (I take two steps to the left) I meet another lady and ask 'madam, who are you? What do you do?' and she responds 'what to do, I need to feed my belly and even my family's belly, I have to teach history to those 40 brats'.

(I take the third position; two Steps right of the center). I ask the third lady 'madam, who are you? What do you do?' and she responds 'I am the molder of the future generation's mind. I teach history to class 5 students.

In the eyes of the world all three gentleman have the same designation, that of a surgeon. All three ladies also have the same designation, a school teacher. But what a great difference between the people in the third position and that in the second. A difference between Heaven and Hell.

I ask you all, who is the more useful citizen?

Group: (in one voice) number 3.

Keki: Who do you think has a larger picture? Group: (in one voice) number 3.

Keki: Who do you think is enjoying what they are doing?

Group: (in one voice) number 3.

Keki: That's right. Those in position 2 may also be motivated but they are a drag on the society. Those in position 1 are the vast majority of the mundane people. Let me ask you another question. If you had to be operated, which surgeon would you pick?

Group: (in one voice) number 3.

Keki: And if you had to send your child for education, what type of teacher would you pick? Group: (in one voice) number 3.

Keki: Number 3. These people in position 3 do not advertise their designation. They do not share their identity with anybody. It is their own private equation between themselves and their creator. Tell me, do these people in position 3 have to go for Goal-Setting seminars? Did Mother Teresa keep records of all those people whom she met every day? Group: (in one voice) No.

Keki: Tell me, do these people in position 3 have to go for Stress-management seminars?

Group: (in one voice) No.

Keki: No. Why? Because they are doing something that they want to do. They are enjoying the process. As against them, those in position 2 are doing something because they think they have to. Now tell me, do these people in position 3 have to go for Neuro Linguistic Programming seminars? (the group looks at me questioningly some with a broad smile on their faces.) The Definite answer is, No, there is no need. It is for you all to decide which position you want to take. If you are in position 1 where the vast majority of mundane people are, then you must, so that you can move into position 3. If honesty tells you that you are in position 2 then just be aware that you are a drag on the society and like somebody has already said 'Awareness is Everything'.

I am asking you now as to who amongst you want to realize your true identity. Remember that identity cannot be given, it has to be realized from within your own self. (majority of the group hands went up) ok, make sure that you participate fully in the exercise that we will be doing before leaving this hall today evening.

We said we operate from 6 neurological levels. So far, we have seen five. So, what could be the 6th level? The 6th neurological level is **Spirituality.** What is spirituality? Whether you are doing Pooja every morning, is that spirituality? Whether you are bowing down five times a day, is that spirituality? Whether you go or do not go to any place of worship is that spirituality?

There are two streams flowing on this beautiful planet that we call our Earth. This planet is so minuscule that it is akin to a single grain of sand on the beaches of the vast ocean of the cosmos.

On the one hand there is this power unknown, unknowable which is self-unfolding, self-propagating, self-repairing, which has made you and me in its own image. You have also been blessed with the same power within you, within the miniscule area of that tiny grain of sand.

On the other hand, we have created some powerful entities that we call as God. This we have made in our own image.

I am talking about that creative power, unknown, unknowable which is self-unfolding, self-propagating, self-repairing, which has made you and me in its own image.

Spirituality I say is how you link your identity with that creator and its creation. Your larger picture.

(I give a long pause to the group to mull over this and digest to the extent they could.)

These 6 logical levels or neurological levels can themselves form the basis of several different programs.

It can be used for therapeutic purposes at each level.

It can be used **for communication**. For example, suppose Jaya goes to her office tomorrow morning. She goes to her table and finds some dust on it. She runs her finger over it and shows it to the person who is supposed to have cleaned her table. She says 'Ramu, there is dust on my table'. What is she referring to?

Ankur: The environment.

Keki: That's correct. Now Ramu responds by saying 'madam, I cleaned it this morning. What is he referring to?

Saira: His behavior pattern.

Keki: Correct again. Now Jaya responds by saying 'but you did not do a good job of it'. What does that refer to?

Guneet: His capability and skill.

Keki: Good. Now Ramu responds by saying ' madam, why are you after me all the time?', where does that come from?

Gautam: His belief.

Keki: Very good. Jaya's response is 'you will remain an idiot always'. What is she attacking?

Saira: His identity.

Keki: Yes, but Ramu is also not such an idiot, so he responds 'what to do madam, whatever my God decided to make me'.

Shankar: (laughs) His spirituality!

Keki: In many large offices of the CEO of large companies there are two decorative pieces of furniture mounted on the wall. One says, The Vision Statement, the other says The Mission Statement. Very often even the top management team members may not be able to repeat what it says without looking at it. Working with these 6 logical levels you can breathe life into it not just for top officials but throughout the organization. In fact, you can create even more powerful Vision and Mission statements with the help of this and coming out of your employees.

Each one of you may have to do some project, either at workplace or even at home. Let us see how we can take help of this **for PROJECT MANAGEMENT**.

First of all, make six tablets on individual sheets of paper and with a Marker Pen in bold letters write it down,

1. Environment
2. Behavior

3. Skills and capabilities
4. Beliefs and values
5. Identity
6. Spirituality

Now lay down all these tablets on the ground in front of you from Number 1 to number 6 at an interval of about 20 inches or half a meter.

Stand in front the first tablet marked as 'Environment'.

We will take two extreme examples. One is that of a grandmother (=GM), 82 years of age, who wants to write a letter to her granddaughter who is in the US, giving her all our culture before it is too late. For the second case let us take up Mr. Ratan Tata (=RT) who wants to set up an automobile manufacturing plant from scratch - not the Nano plant but the original Indica car plant.

Imagine both of them standing in front of the first tablet. Naturally when you are doing the exercise you will have your own project in mind.

While standing in front of the first tablet of Environment, they will both think about their physical world and physical things needed.

So, GM (grandmother) is first thinking as to which stationary would she use. Will it be the Mickey Mouse stationery or the flowery stationery? She decides that since it is her culture, she wants to pass on it will be the flowery stationary. Next, she decides as to what color of ink will she use. Should it be Red or blue. Black is a definite no-no for GM. She decides on the red. But the red ink has not been used for so long and has almost dried up. She will have to find the red ink tablet and mix it with some water. How about the pen? Where will she sit to write? The netting on the chair opposite her letter-writer is broken and pokes. She will need her rubber ring from the cupboard. But the rubber ring needs to be inflated and has to be taken to the cycle repair shop. So on, and so forth.

For RT (Ratan Tata) environment is spelt out in waist high piles of print outs starting with how much land, where, what proximities, type and extent of buildings, machinery and equipment, storage areas, etc. etc. To the minutest detail.

Next, they will both take a step forward and stand opposite the second tablet of 'Behavior'.

In this position the GM is wondering as to when she can actually start writing. Even if she gets all the help to get things ready it will be at least 11:00 in the morning next day. She will need a minimum of 2 hours to write things. The post leaves by 3 p.m. She has to have her lunch by 12:30 otherwise it upsets her stomach. After lunch she needs to have a small Siesta of at least half an hour. So, the Letter cannot be posted by tomorrow. It will have to be finished by day after and posted.

For Ratan Tata it is not just his behavior pattern but of all the employees. Their housing, their children's schooling, their family's social life, medical needs, etc. etc.

Having gone through all aspects of the behavior required they will both move to the 3rd tablet of 'skills and capabilities'

Here the GM is wondering whether she should write in English language or Hindi. She knows she is not so good in expressing in English. She also knows that her granddaughter may not be able to read in good Hindi. She decides that she will do a good job writing in Hindi and the Granddaughter's mother which means her daughter, will help the girl understand.

For RT, he knows that his engineers have worked for many years with the Mercedes group and have done a good job in designing but he may need some assistance from Germany regarding testing of the suspension for local conditions and some testing equipment for the electronics in the car from Japan.

Next, they move to the tablet marked 'Identity'.

Grandma's identity is, 'why am I still alive?' only to pass on our culture to my granddaughter. He can lift me up after that.

Ratan Tata may think that it is high time for India to have its own car. He may think that Tatas pioneered cement; Tatas pioneered Steel; I am a Tata. I will Pioneer India's own car. Somebody else in his place who is also thinking of manufacturing a car for India may think that India has never made an Indian car therefore India cannot and must look out for some collaboration. That is the end of the Indian car dream for that person.

Now they both move to the 6th tablet of spirituality. Like we said earlier this is a private equation between the person and its creator. Nobody will flaunt it.

We already know the Grandma's spirituality. How she links her Identity with her creator and its creation.

Many CEOs of large corporations maybe having an Idea that prosperity travelled from Europe to America. From America it travelled to Japan. From Japan to the 5 Asian tigers and from there to China. Now it is India's turn.

Having done that, both will crossover to either one of the ends of the tablets and take a look as to where there could be some problem. Very often the problem may actually lie one step higher than what one feels. For example, if somebody feels that there may be an issue at the Skill and Capability level, the actual issue may be at the Belief level. You can deal with this either with your intelligence and logic or through an appropriate NLP exercise.

Here is a brief case-story. I was taking a two-day program on 'Creativity and Problem Solving' for a newspaper publisher who was putting up a second Press at Kolhapur. On the second day after the morning tea break, 18 of the 42 participants came to me and asked to be excused. I asked them what the matter was and were they fed up of me already. They said no they were the team that were going to Kolhapur to setup the new plant and would like to apply the six logical levels to that project. I said fine because an ounce of practice is worth a ton of theory. They returned 20 minutes late during lunch time and were all excited. They said they knew that they could complete the project within 70% of the time and the cost. I asked them 'where is my commission?'

We said you should **REALIZE YOUR TRUE IDENTITY** before we leave this hall this evening. Now is the time to do it and it can change your life forever. However, before we start on this, I would suggest that everybody take a 3-minute bio-break, comeback, change seats, change neighbors.

(once everybody is back)

This exercise can be done with anybody. Remember that a Housewife or a home maker is shaping the destiny of more than just herself. Here

I will take up somebody who is a salaried employee working in an organization so that we cover all aspects of the exercise.

Anwar: I want to come.

Keki: Please come and occupy the hot seat. (after he has taken his seat). Anwar, do you have a deity? do you pray?

Anwar: Not regularly but yes, when there is something important that I may want to happen.

Keki: Is this important and do you want the presence of your deity in front of you?

Anwar: Yes.

(I pick up a chair and put it in front of him, facing him)

Keki: You may invoke your deity for help in whichever way you do normally. (I wait for him to complete whatever he was doing and then) Anwar, I am going to ask you a question. It is not a philosophical question. It is a down to earth practical question regarding you and your profession. My question is 'Who are you? What do you do?'

Anwar: I am a Project Planning and Execution Officer. I plan out the projects that come to our office and get them executed.

Keki: Do you think what you are doing is something important?

Anwar: Of course.

Keki: How is it important?

Anwar: Why? Everybody gets their salary for the work.

Keki: Everybody. And you?

Anwar: Me included of course.

Keki: Of course. So, who is paying your salary?

Anwar: Who? The accounts department of course.

Keki: Of course. But who is actually paying your salary?

Anwar: Ms. Kulkarni in the accounts department.

Keki: Ms. Kulkarni pays you all from her own personal account?

Anwar: Of course not. She pays from the company account. (by now Anwar has already started getting a little irritated at my stupidity)

Keki: Your company account must be limitless; where does it get money from?

Anwar: Why? From the clients and customers that we serve.

Keki: Oh, I see. So, I will repeat my earlier question. Who is paying your salary? (Anwar's face now changes from irritation to a bit of realization)

Anwar: You mean our clients and customers?

Keki: I do not mean anything. I just want to get the facts from you.

Anwar: Ok, from that angle the clients and customers are paying our salaries.

Keki: Not from this angle or that angle. The question remains as to who is paying the salaries of the employees of any company?

Anwar: Yes, it has to be the clients and customers of that company. (Anwar's eyes actually open bigger and brighter)

Keki: (to the group) This was a bit of a digression. A digression necessitated by another case-story. I was doing this exercise for a bunch of very senior level executives of a premier government Bank. They were so convinced that the sole purpose of their institution was the government's social duty of providing jobs. They had no idea or had never thought about what could be the purpose and responsibility of that institution towards the general public. I had hell of a time getting them to realize the higher purpose of their institution. So, let us now get back on track.

Anwar, sometime back you said that what you are doing is something important? So, do you think you are contributing to the company?

Anwar: Certainly.

Keki: Do you think your company is contributing anything to the society?

Anwar: Yes, I think so.

Keki: How? what does it do?

Anwar: We provide solutions to the insurance companies.

Keki: And what happens when you provide solutions to the insurance companies?

Anwar: Their work smoothens out. They become more efficient.

Keki: And what happens when their work smoothens out and they become more efficient.

Anwar: They feel happier.

Keki: In which way are they feeling happier?

Anwar: Why, their customers may have taken life policies or property insurance or for goods. They will feel more secure, happier, more relaxed. Keki: Do you really believe it?

Anwar: I do.

Keki: So, have you taken any policies for yourself?

Anwar: (smiles) No, but I think I will, now. Never thought of it that way.

Keki: Now tell me Anwar, how is your company contributing to the society?

Anwar: By making it feel more secure, happier, more relaxed.

Keki: And where do you think it ends? Where is the boundary?

Anwar: I think, like Ankur talked about the ripple effect sometime back that there is no boundary. It is global. It may take time. That's all.

Keki: Now tell me what is a company? Is it the stone and brick building? Is it that board declaring the name? Is it that entry into the registrar's office? What is a company?

Anwar: No. I think it is the company of people. Likeminded people, preferably.

Keki: I think you also use a two-wheeler motorcycle, isn't it?

Anwar: Yes, I do.

Keki: There is a gearbox there. Do you know what it does?

Anwar: It transfers the power generated in the engine to the rear wheel.

Keki: Have you seen an actual gear wheel? It has teeth on the outer Periphery which mesh with the teeth of the other wheel to pass on the motion.

Anwar: I have seen it at the repair shop of my mechanic.

Keki: Can you tell me which tooth of which gear is the most important?

Anwar: No, I do not know. Which one?

Keki: Ok. Tell me if one of the teeth had to break while you are riding, what can happen?

Anwar: An accident? The Broken tooth may jam the gearbox and the bike? I may land up in a hospital?

Keki: That's right. You know your company also receives orders, you all process it and deliver the end result. Do you think that each person working from their own position and as per their responsibility is contributing towards the end result?

Anwar: They have to.

Keki: So, when you say that your company make people feel more secure, happier, more relaxed; who is actually doing it?

Anwar: All of us.

Keki: Also tell me whether the alphabets that denote your company are so very important or it could have any other name also?

Anwar: Any other name as long as they are giving similar service.

Keki: Now Anwar, your deity wants to pin a new designation on your shoulder and is asking you 'Anwar, who are you? What do you do?'. Based on what we have done so far and based on what you say your company does for the general society, what is your answer?

Anwar: I help my company to make people feel more secure, happier, more relaxed.

Keki: Your deity is concerned about you. Not who you are helping or how. Your deity also knows that whatever you are doing has a global effect. Just like our surgeon or the school teacher in the morning.

Anwar: (taking a deep breath) I make this world more secure, happier and more relaxed.

Keki: Your deity is not interested in any comparisons. That is why the surgeon or the school teacher had no such words of more, less, etc.

Anwar: I make this world secure, happy and relaxed. (as he is saying it, I run my thumb and index finger over his left shoulder as if I am pinning the designation on him.)

Keki: How do you feel?

Anwar: Whole. worthy, purposeful.

Keki: Say it one more time and tell me how you feel. Say it louder because your friends did not hear you last time.

Anwar: (pumping his hand and loudly) I make this world secure, happy and relaxed. (once again, I pin the designation on his shoulder) (He looks at me and then at the group)

Keki: Tell me Anwar, do you think this puts more responsibility on you or less.

Anwar: More.

Keki: Do you think it makes it easier for you to fulfill your responsibilities or more difficult?

Anwar: Much easier.

Keki: Please extend both your hands forward, palms facing upward to receive the appointment letter that your deity wants to give to you. (he does this and I put my left forearm into his two Palms, saying) Whenever you have any questions, all your questions are already answered in this appointment letter. Now Anwar thank your deity, take leave of your deity, go and enjoy your life.

Anwar: (getting up with a bit of a spring in his legs) Thank you, Keki. (He goes back to his seat)

Keki: The rest of you may now select your partner and request your partner to assist you in realizing your true identity. Complete the exercise.

Put your feet flat on the ground. Sit up straight. Backbone straight. Push your tailbone into the chair. Take a deep breath and as your exhale close your eyes and visualize Number 3, 3 Times. Take Another deep breath and as you Exhale visualize number two three times and relax yourself. One more deep breath in and as you exhale visualize number 1, 3 times and deepen your relaxation. Total relaxation. By now you have learnt how to stay relaxed even with your eyes open. Just keep listening to my voice.

You are about to take a fantastic journey. You are walking down a forest trail. All around you is a thick jungle. It is evening, cloudy and misty. You are comfortably clad. You can feel the cool air on the exposed parts of your body, your cheeks and your hands. The Aroma of the wet Earth is in your nostrils. The forest trail is carpeted by the fallen leaves, twigs and some bark of the trees. With each step your foot sinks half an inch down on that soft carpet of fallen leaves; mostly brown but some yellow, orange and even a few green along with the twigs. You see two squirrels spiraling around a big tree trunk chasing each other with their tails held high vertically and the three stripes over their backs.

There is a big Majestic tree in front of you. You are attracted towards it. As you walk towards it, a voice comes out of the tree and the voice says 'You are nature's unique creation. In the whole universe there is no one else exactly like you'. You are taken aback by these words coming out of the tree. The words ring in your ears 'You are nature's unique creation. In the whole universe there is no one else exactly like you'. You cannot but agree with those words. You are feeling grateful to that tree. With folded hands you are Bowing down to the tree doing your pranam, doing your obeisance. Respectfully straightening out and taking a couple of steps backwards you continue walking down deeper into that forest trail.

Now the clouds are clearing out and a beam of Sunlight is piercing through the forest trees at an oblique angle brightening up the surroundings.

You come to a tree which is marked number 9. As you approach that tree a voice comes out of the tree and the voice says 'Your creator has a purpose in putting you on this earth'. The voice says 'Your creator has a purpose in putting you on this earth'. You want to embrace this tree for giving you these words. With hands outstretched you are hugging this tree, with the cool dampness of the bark against your cheek and your palms. Slowly you undo your hug, take a step backwards and continue going deeper into the forest trail.

You are looking upwards through the gaps in the canopy of the forest at the clearing blue sky with some remaining orange and some white clouds. As you lower your eyes and continue walking further you see trees laden with fruits and their branches bowing down in humility with these riches.

You come to a tree marked number 8. As you approach that tree a voice comes out of the tree and the voice says 'All your needs are satisfied only to promote your creator's work'. The voice says 'All your needs are satisfied only to promote your creator's work'. You are looking back on your life mulling these words. You are shaping your own words to thank your creator as you walk further on that trail.

You are crossing an opening on one side with tiny tiny plants with tiny tiny flowers. Many bright yellows, some orange and red and a few blue.

You come to a tree marked number 7. As you approach that tree a voice comes out of the tree and the voice says 'Everything is ok, you are ok, I am ok.'

Thinking about it you wonder if these nine words could replace all the existing religions on the face of this earth.

As You Walk further thinking about this you come to a big, tall, straight tree. A tree marked number 6. As you approach that tree a voice comes out of the tree and the voice says 'Believe in yourself'. You go closer and look upwards to the very top of the tree and feel as if you have grown three inches taller. You bring your gaze gradually down the tapering trunk of this tree and reach your eye level. You still feel as if you have grown three inches taller. You thank that tree and continue walking your trail.

You turn and are looking upwards toward the top of that same tree and observe the clear blue sky with just one white cloud with a silver lining.

You turn forward once again and continue with your journey and come to a tree. A tree marked number 5. As you approach that tree a voice comes out of the tree and the voice says 'Qualify to deserve before you desire'. The voice says 'Qualify to deserve before you desire'. You are mulling as to how to digest this message and recounting your blessings. You bless this tree and move on.

The evening twilight is setting in. Suddenly the birds are crowding in the sky. They flock into two groups and fly crisscrossing into each other, chirping away and creating a cacophony, finding their mates to settle in their nests for the night. After a few minutes just as suddenly as it had started there is a sudden quietness and each bird has settled in their nest with their partner. There is total silence.

In that silence you arrive at a tree. A tree marked number 4. As you approach that tree a voice comes out of the tree and the voice says 'Everything you see around you was born as a thought. Everything man made you see around you was first born in a man's thought'. You are able to agree with the second part of the sentence easily. It is the first part of the sentence you are struggling to understand. What could be the message that has come through the voice of this tree?

You wonder. You do not wish to leave this tree as yet. But with a heavy heart and heavy feet you carry on further.

Now the woods are thinning out and you come to a young tree. A tree marked number 3. As you approach that tree a voice comes out of the tree and the voice says 'When the student is ready the master shall appear'. You are telling yourself, from your own experience, how true the statement is. Yes, 'When the student is ready the master does appear'. It has happened not just once but so many times.

As you wander through this forest further wondering at the words spoken by these trees you come to a bush barely coming up to your stomach. As you approach that bush a voice comes out of the bush and the voice says 'You can love everything and everybody'. With love in your heart, you are brushing your hand over the damp, cool, tiny, Green Leaves of that bush feeling as if you are brushing your hand over a sweet 4-year-old girl's hair on her head.

With love in your heart, you are moving towards the edge of the mountain where the last solitary tree is marked number 1. As you approach that tree a voice comes out of the tree and the voice says 'Realize that the best teacher you will ever find is your own self'. You are going to the other side of the tree, facing the tree with your back towards the edge of the Mountain, folding your hands, bowing down, doing your pranam, doing your obeisance to this entire magical journey. Slowly turning around, with your back to this journey and moving ahead to the very edge of the mountain from where the valley starts.

You stop short of where the sheer drop starts. The first thing that hits your eye is the huge Orange ball of the setting sun hanging about a foot above the opposite mountain range. It is dark Orange at the base and yellowish Orange on the top. Moving your eyes down to the valley you see a Hamlet of about 20 thatched roof huts. There is no movement. You can very easily make out one or two village stray dogs when you see some white or grey bugs like thing moving. What you can see is the column of smoke from the evening wood stove, rising about 6 feet straight up then curling and disappearing. It is a beautiful and pristine sight. Beyond this tiny village and bordering it, start the cultivated terraced fields. Mostly green, some yellowish and a few even barren.

But up ahead that big ball of the setting sun is now almost ready to touch the mountain range. And as you observe, it has now touched the mountain range so that it looks like an inverted pot with the mouth slightly open at the bottom where it has turned dark orange almost taking the hue of earthy brown with the top most portion still yellowish orange. Now as it has gone further down it looks like an inverted vessel red at the bottom and reddish Orange at the top. More than half has now disappeared and it looks like an inverted pan, earthy red Brown at bottom and reddish at the top. Still going down further it looks like a red saucer that is becoming smaller and smaller and smaller in diameter until even that disappears now.

The sunset.

Tomorrow is a new sunrise.

The Beginning

www.ingramcontent.com/pod-product-compliance
Lightning Source LLC
LaVergne TN
LVHW021146160826
845679LV00024B/2068

* 9 7 9 8 8 9 6 7 3 5 6 8 7 *